OWNING
the
RIGHT DOG

American Cocker Spaniel.

Golden Retriever.

OWNING
the
RIGHT DOG

First edition by
Joan Palmer

Revised by
Phil Maggitti

Consultant (Revised edition)
Richard Gebhardt

Tetra Press
No. 16001

All correspondence concerning the
content of this volume should be
addressed to Tetra Press.

Credits

Project Editor:
Christopher Westhorp
Designer: John Heritage
Colour reproduction: Scantrans
PTE Ltd., Singapore
Filmset: The Old Mill, London
Printed in Singapore

*Right: Two fine examples of a
smooth-coated Chow.*

Author (First edition)

Joan Palmer is a former honorary chairman, committee member and publicity officer of the National Dog Owners' Association of Great Britain. She has written a number of books on domestic animals and has contributed regularly over the years to the newspaper *Our Dogs*.

Editor (Revised edition)

Phil Maggitti is a former English teacher from Pennsylvania who took up full-time writing more than a decade ago. To date he has had hundreds of articles published in dozens of magazines and newspapers, the vast majority of them on animal-related subjects. He has bred and exhibited cats for 17 years, and currently breeds Pug dogs.

Consultant (Revised edition)

Richard Gebhardt has been a successful breeder and groomer of dogs for many years. His Japanese Chins won the 'Best of Breed' award at the prestigious Westminster Kennel Club show in New York for four years running. He has also co-authored several books on dogs and dog-related matters.

Contents

Part One
PROFILE SECTION

Detailed profiles of over 165 international breeds,
arranged in order of size.

Papillon

Part Two
PRACTICAL SECTION

Essential information for everyone who owns a dog
or is thinking of buying one.

Parts of a Dog
This annotated drawing shows the main anatomical parts of a dog and the accepted terms used to describe them. Further information on these and other technical terms used in the book can be obtained from the Glossary starting on page 184.

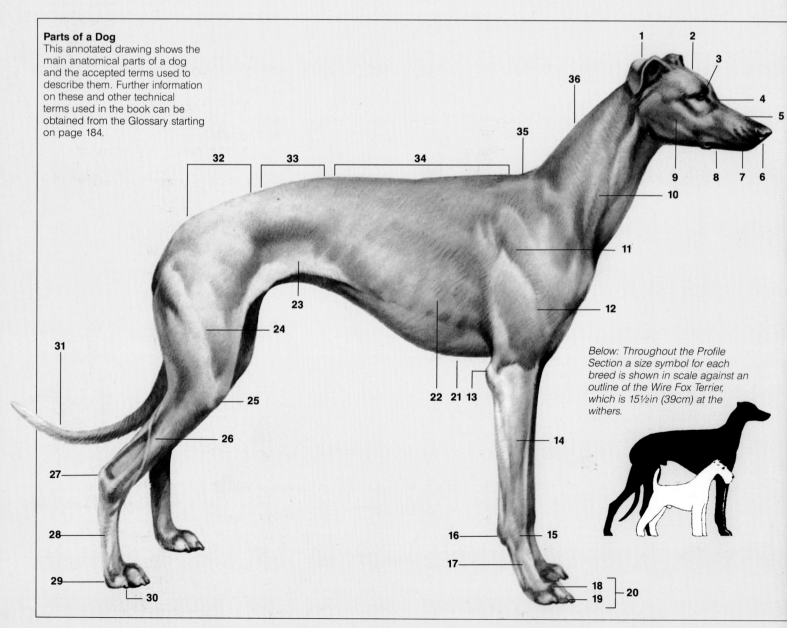

Below: Throughout the Profile Section a size symbol for each breed is shown in scale against an outline of the Wire Fox Terrier, which is 15½in (39cm) at the withers.

Part One

PROFILE SECTION

Detailed profiles of over 165 international breeds, arranged in order of size.

Parts of a Dog
 1 Ear
 2 Skull. The upper, back point of the skull is called the occiput or peak. The top of the skull is called the crown.
 3 Eye
 4 Stop
 5 Foreface. The foreface, nose and jaws make up the muzzle.
 6 Nose
 7 Jaws. The fleshy parts of the lips and jaws make up the jowls.
 8 Lips. Pendulous upper lips are called flews.
 9 Cheek
10 Neck
11 Shoulder
12 Upper arm
13 Elbow
14 Forearm
15 Wrist
16 Stopper pad
17 Pastern
18 Toes
19 Nails
20 Forefoot
21 Sternum (Breastbone)
22 Chest
23 Flank
24 Thigh (Upper thigh)
25 Stifle (Knee)
26 Second thigh (Lower thigh)
27 Hock (Heel)
28 Rear pastern
29 Hindfoot
30 Pads
31 Tail. In different types of dog the tail is known variously as the brush, flag, rudder or stern.
32 Croup
33 Loin
34 Back
35 Withers (Top of the shoulders)
36 Crest of neck

Most dog books present the breeds in groups based on the type of dog or on the role it was bred to perform, such as toys or gundogs. These groups vary in different parts of the world. Throughout most of Europe, for example, the ten groups recognized by the Fédération Cynologique Internationale (FCI) apply. These are:
 1 Herding breeds
 2 Guard dogs, police dogs and working breeds
 3 Terriers
 4 Dachshunds
 5 Hunting breeds (for large game)
 6 Hunting breeds (for small game)
 7 Pointing gundogs (excluding British breeds)
 8 Pointing gundogs (British breeds)
 9 Other British gundogs
10 Toy dogs

The Kennel Club in the United Kingdom (hereafter the Kennel Club) recognizes six groups. These are:
 1 Hounds
 2 Gundogs
 3 Terriers
 4 Utility breeds
 5 Working breeds
 6 Toys

The American Kennel Club recognizes seven groups. These are:
 1 Sporting breeds
 2 Hounds
 3 Working breeds
 4 Terriers
 5 Toys
 6 Non-sporting breeds
 7 Herding breeds

The Scandinavian countries recognize eight groups. These are:
 1 Spitz breeds
 2 Trailing and hunting breeds
 3 Gundogs
 4 Guard and working breeds
 5 Terriers
 6 Sighthounds
 7 Non-sporting and companion breeds
 8 Toys

In Australia seven groups are recognized:
 1 Toys
 2 Terriers
 3 Gundogs
 4 Hounds
 5 Working breeds
 6 Non-sporting breeds
 7 Utility breeds

Since this book is aimed at the widest possible audience, and particularly at those people buying a dog for the first time, the breeds are therefore presented solely in order of size. The Profile Section is divided into these parts:
 Small dogs (up to 28lb /12.7kg)
 Medium dogs (28-45lb/12.7-20.5kg)
 Large dogs (over 45lb/20.5kg)

But even this system has its problems: height standards alone exist for certain breeds; some dogs fall between two groups; and a few tall but relatively light breeds are by any standards large dogs.

The show standards quoted at the end of most entries are based on the official standards of the Kennel Club and are reproduced with their kind permission. A number of standards are also included from the FCI and the American Kennel Club.

A Selection of
SMALL DOGS

Why do you want a small dog? Because you have always loved them and their spirit? Because you are a town dweller living in a confined space? Because you think a bigger fellow might be more than you can handle? Because they cost less to feed?

Whatever your reason, if you purchase a small dog, you are unlikely to regret that decision. Little dogs are incredibly brave (often foolishly so), make good watchdogs (though they should not be allowed to yap) and are devoted to their owners. Even though they are often scornfully dismissed as lap dogs, tiny breeds will glady walk as far as you wish and ask for more.

There are many reasons for selecting a small breed. Transport is simpler, to begin with. Chihuahuas and Yorkshire Terriers rarely object to riding in a shopping basket. Small breeds are often more acceptable guests in hotels; and if not, boarding kennels often charge according to the dog's size. Small dogs are intelligent and easy to train, and there is less to groom, especially if you choose one of the short-coated varieties. Small dogs usually live longer than their heavier relations. On the debit side, however, they are not cheaper to buy and they do not have large litters.

If the man of the family says he won't be seen out with a toy dog, don't believe it — men often become willing slaves to the most delicate-looking animals. Perhaps this is a testimony to the sprite lurking inside most men and to the large spirit that inhabits most small dogs.

Very small breeds are not a good choice if there are young children in the family, however, as toddlers may think that they really are toys. A good choice for such a family is a dog of Cavalier or King Charles Spaniel size, or a sporty Miniature Schnauzer.

There is a wide range of small dogs from which to choose, in various colours and different types of coat. There are also scaled-down versions of larger breeds, such as the Miniature Poodle.

If you can't bear to leave a dog alone in the house, you can always find room for two small dogs. This is how a lot of us dog folk began . . . but that's another story.

Below: An alert-looking Papillon with its distinctive ears.

AFFENPINSCHER

Good points
- Affectionate
- Cute monkey-like appearance
- Good watchdog

Take heed
- No drawbacks known

The Affenpinscher is an enchanting little breed with an almost monkey-like appearance, whence the prefix 'Affen', which is the German word for monkey. In its country of origin it is often called the 'Zwergaffen-pinscher' ('Zwerg' means dwarf). The French have dubbed it the 'moustached devil'. In any event it is an appealing, comical little dog, the smallest of the Schnauzer and Pinscher breeds, alert, gentle and affectionate, but always ready to defend.

Size
Height: 9½-11in (24-28cm).
Weight: 6½-9lb (3-4.1kg).

Exercise
Like most toy dogs it will be content with a walk around the park, but it will gladly walk you off your feet if that is your pleasure.

Grooming
Regular brushing will keep the Affenpinscher in good condition.

Feeding
Recommended would be 5-7oz (142-198g) of a branded, meaty product with biscuit added in equal part by volume, or ¾ to 1¼ cupfuls of a dry food, complete diet, mixed in the proportion of 1 cup of feed to ½ cup of hot or cold water. When giving a dry feed, ensure that the dog has — as always — an ample supply of water.

Origin and history
Miniature Pinschers and Affenpinschers were, until 1896, classified as one breed. In that year, at the Berlin show, authorities decided that the long-coated variety should thereafter be known as the Affenpinscher.

The Affenpinscher is an ancient German breed that was depicted by Jan van Eyck (1395-1441) and Albrecht Dürer (1471-1528). There is, however, some controversy as to its origin, though its nationality has never been in doubt. Some believe it to be related to the Brussels Griffon; others attribute the Brussels Griffon to the Affenpinscher; a third school of thought is that the Affenpinscher is a toy version of the German coarse-haired terrier, the Zwergschnauzer. In any event, this delightful breed was recognized by the American Kennel Club (AKC) in 1936, and has also achieved recognition in the United Kingdom, being represented for the first time in the 1980 Crufts Dog Show.

SHOW STANDARD
General appearance. Wire-haired and stout, with an apish expression, the Affenpinscher is small but sturdy in build, is not delicate in any way, and carries itself with a comic seriousness.

Above: An adult Affenpinscher with the short, monkey-like face and winsome expression that are typical of this breed.

Above: This Affenpinscher pup, a tiny bundle of fur, has yet to grow into the comic expression that characterizes adults of the breed.

Colour. This should be black, although dark grey and black with grey, rich tan or brown markings are permissible.
Head and skull. The head is fairly small in proportion to the body; a domed forehead, broad brow and marked stop which, however, should not be intended. Muzzle blunt and short but not flattened as far as to cause wrinkling of the skin or difficulty in breathing. The chin should be prominent with a good turn-up. The distance between the dark eyes and black nose should form an equilateral triangle.
Body: The back should be straight and roughly equal to the distance from the shoulder to the ground. Chest reasonably deep, loins tucked up slightly.
Tail. The tail should be set high and carried high; it can be left a natural length or docked to the third joint.
Feet. These should be small, round and compact, and turn neither in nor out. The pads and nails should be dark.

Affenpinscher

The coat is a very important factor in the Affenpinscher. It should be short and dense in certain parts and shaggy and longer in others, especially around the eyes, nose and chin, giving the breed a monkey-like appearance.

CHIHUAHUA

Good points
- Handy, portable size
- Good traveller
- Ideal for town dwellers
- Intensely loyal and affectionate
- Keenly intelligent
- Wonderful guard dog in miniature
- Inexpensive to keep

Take heed
- Strong willed
- Brave to the point of stupidity—would fight a lion!
- Clannish—prefers the company of its own breed and owners
- Hates the cold—might grow rheumaticky

The Chihuahua is keenly intelligent, fiercely protective and inexpensive to keep. Also, being the world's tiniest dog, it is the least likely to fall foul of the landlord.

The adult Chihuahua usually takes a few weeks to reveal its true personality, keeping its new owner under careful surveillance, perhaps giving the impression that it is shy. Actually, it is weighing up which of them is to be master in the home!

Size
Weight between 2-6lb (0.9-2.7kg) (under 4lb/1.8kg preferred for show). There is no desired height in this breed's standard.

Exercise
The Chihuahua is ready, and able, to walk as far as most owners would wish, although it doesn't object to an occasional ride in a shopping basket. The fact that its exercise requirements are moderate makes this breed an ideal pet for the elderly.

Grooming
The Chihuahua should be groomed with a soft brush. A rub down with a velvet glove, or pad, will make the coat gleam. Nails must be clipped regularly, and the ears kept free of dirt.

Feeding
Eating habits vary: some Chihuahuas have voracious appetites, but others, particularly the smaller specimens, often go for a day without nourishment. The requirement of a very small Chihuahua should be 2-3oz (57-85g) of branded dog food with a handful of puppy biscuits. And, as they have small tummies, these dogs fare best on two or three small meals rather than one large daily feed. Bigger specimens can manage up to 7oz (198g) of branded dog food, or the equivalent, and a handful of dog biscuits. Uneaten food should be removed: dogs do not fancy stale food any more than we do.

Health care
Not as delicate as one might imagine, but they dislike the cold and appreciate a coat to keep them warm when out of doors in winter. These dogs are definitely not designed for kennel living. They prefer to snuggle beneath your eiderdown!

Watch out for the molera, a small opening on top of the skull. The Chihuahua's molera, unlike that of a human baby, may never fill in, so a blow on the head could prove fatal. This breed is prone to hiccups; a spasm can often be cured by lifting the pet purposefully up and down. They also have a tendency to shiver, a habit that evokes sympathy from onlookers and generally makes the owner seem the villain of the piece, folk wrongly imagining that the Chihuahua is terrified or frozen.

Origin and history
The known genealogy of the modern-day Chihuahua begins with the Techichi, a small, long-coated, heavy-boned dog much favoured by the Toltecs, who lived in what is now Mexico as early as the ninth century. The Techichi is thought to have been indigenous to Central America, and it is possible that the ancestors of this dog, which was somewhat larger than today's Chihuahua, may have existed in Central America as early as the fifth century.

Evidence linking the Techichi to the Toltec period can be found in pictures carved on stones that are part of the Monastery of Huejotzingo, constructed by Franciscan monks around 1530. On some of these stones, which were formerly part of the pyramids at Cholula built by the Toltecs, there are sketches that approximate the modern Chihuahua. In addition, the remains of pyramids and other historical clues found in Yucatan suggest that the Techichi may have existed also at Chichen Itza.

According to K. de Blinde, a Mexican breeder and authority on Chihuahuas, the Techichi were crossed with small, hairless dogs brought from Asia to Alaska over the land bridge that once existed where the Bering Strait now runs.

The earliest specimens of today's Chihuahua were found in the state of the same name about 1850 in old ruins close to Casas Grandes. These ruins are said to be the remains of a palace built by Emperor Montezuma I.

SHOW STANDARD
General appearance. An alert and swift-moving little dog with a saucy expression. Small, dainty and compact with a brisk, forceful action.
Colour. Any colour or mixture.
Head and skull. A well-rounded 'apple dome' skull, with or without molera; cheeks and jaws lean; nose moderately short, slightly pointed, definite stop.
Feet. Small with toes well split up, but not spread; pads cushioned. Fine pasterns (neither 'hare' nor 'cat' foot). A dainty foot with nails moderately long.
Tail. Medium length, carried up or over the back. Preferred furry, flattish in appearance, broadening slightly in the centre and tapering to a point.

There is a long-coated Chihuahua as well as the more usual smooth-coated variety. The only difference is in the coat, which should be long, of soft texture (never coarse or harsh to the touch), and either flat or slightly wavy (not tight and curly). There should be feathering on the feet and legs, and pants on the hind legs; a large ruff on the neck is preferred, and the tail should be long, full and plume-like.

YORKSHIRE TERRIER

Good points
- Affectionate
- Healthy and fearless
- Sociable with other pets
- Good watchdog
- Suits apartment living

Take heed
- Lengthy show preparation
- Needs frequent bath

The Yorkshire Terrier is one of the most popular dogs of the day. It rivals the Chihuahua for the title of the world's smallest dog. It is unlikely to be overawed by larger animals, however, and is not the ideal choice for the stand-offish because it wants to make friends with everybody. It has been described as a big dog inhabiting a small dog's body; in fact it thinks it is enormous.

Size
Weight up to 7lb (3.2kg).

Exercise
The Yorkie is well suited to town and apartment living, but will prove a tireless companion on a country walk.

Grooming
Many Yorkie owners are content for their pets to have a somewhat scruffy 'shaggy dog' look as long as they know that it is clean and healthy. The show aspirant, however, has a busy time ahead, for the Yorkshire Terrier is exhibited on a show box, which displays its immaculate coat to advantage, a condition that can be achieved only through endless grooming, shampooing and oiling. The show Yorkie spends much of its life, away from the ring, wearing curlers.

Feeding
Similar to that of other toy breeds, with four meals given in puppyhood, reducing to one meal at a year old, comprising ½ can of branded dog food (approximately 7-8oz/199-227g) supplemented by biscuits.

Health care
The Yorkshire has strong terrier-type teeth, but it is as well to have them scaled by a veterinarian at regular intervals. Toy breeds tend to lose their teeth at an early age (sometimes as early as three), but the avoidance of titbits will preserve them for as long as possible.

Origin and history
Despite the fashionableness to which it ascended during the late Victorian era, the Yorkshire Terrier was originally a working-class hero. Yorkies first appeared on the show bench — as broken-haired Scotch Terriers — in England in 1861. Nine years later they became known as Yorkshire Terriers after a reporter suggested that they ought to be called by that designation 'for having been so improved' by Yorkshire residents.

Four breeds contributed to the development of the Yorkshire Terrier: the Waterside Terrier from Yorkshire, the rough-coated, black and tan English Terrier from Manchester, and the Paisley and Clydesdale terriers, brought to Yorkshire by Scottish weavers who migrated from Scotland in the middle of the nineteenth century.

SHOW STANDARD
Consult an expert before rushing to buy the first pedigreed pup you see advertised. A roach or sway-backed Yorkie would be a non-starter in the show ring, as would too large a specimen. A breeder cannot guarantee the size to which a puppy will grow, but look at the sire and dam as a useful guide.

Selecting a potential show pup is never easy, but selecting a Yorkie will be less troublesome if you remember this: Puppies that will exhibit the correct adult colours when they mature are always born black with tan markings.
General appearance. Should be that of a long-coated toy terrier, the coat hanging quite straight and evenly down each side, a parting extending from the nose to the end of the tail. The animal should be compact and neat, the carriage being upright and conveying an 'important' air. The general outline should give the impression of a vigorous and well-proportioned body.
Colour. A dark, steel blue (not silver-blue), extending from the occiput (back of skull) to the root of the tail, and on no account mingled with fawn, bronze or dark hairs. The hair on the chest should be a rich, bright tan. All tan hair should be darker at the roots than in the middle, shading to a still lighter tan at the tips.
Head and skull. The head should be rather small and flat, not too prominent or round in the skull, nor too long in the muzzle, with a perfect black nose. The fall on the head to be long, of a rich golden tan, deeper in colour at the sides of the head above the ear roots and on the muzzle, where it should be very long. On no account must the tan on the head extend to the neck, nor must there be any sooty or dark hair intermingled with the tan.
Ears. Small, V-shaped and carried erect or semi-erect and not far apart, covered with short hair of a very deep, rich tan.
Feet. As round as possible; the toenails black. Forelegs straight. Hindlegs, viewed from the side, are slightly bent at the stifles.
Tail. Cut to medium length with plenty of hair, darker blue in colour than the rest of the body, especially at the end of the tail. Carry it a little higher than the level of the back.

*Long-coated
Chihuahua*

One of the most
popular dogs in the
world, the Chihuahua
has proved a well-
behaved and
consistently successful
competitor in the
show ring.

*Smooth-coated
Chihuahua*

The Yorkshire
Terrier has a
sharp and intelligent
expression. The
medium-sized, dark
and sparkling eyes
are placed so as to
look directly forward.

Yorkshire Terrier

PAPILLON
(And Phalene)

Good points
- Affectionate
- Dainty size
- Good house dog
- Usually strong and healthy

Take heed
- Not keen on visitors
- Possessive towards owners

The Papillon is a toy spaniel that takes its name from the French word for 'butterfly' because of the manner in which the ears are set on the head, fringed like a butterfly's wings. The Phalene is identical except that the ears are dropped, and this variety is known as the 'moth'.

The Papillon is an affectionate, lively little dog. It is resilient, whelps easily, is a good walker, and can adapt to extremes of climate. Its attractive appearance and friendly nature make it the ideal family pet. But, like some other toy breeds, it has a tendency to be possessive towards its owners and often resents visitors to the home.

Size
The ideal height at the withers is 8-11in (20-28cm). The dog will appear to be slightly longer than high when properly furnished with ruff and hind fringes.

Exercise
Like quite a number of toy breeds, the Papillon will happily walk its owner off his feet, or be content with a turn around the park. One thing is sure: you won't tire it.

Grooming
Frequent grooming is required to keep this breed in good condition.

Feeding
Recommended would be 7oz (198g) of a branded, meaty product, with biscuit added in equal part by volume, or 1 cup of a dry food, complete diet, mixed in the proportion of 1 cup to ½ cup of hot or cold water.

Origin and history
Believed to be a descendant of the Dwarf Spaniel of the sixteenth century and to have originated in Spain, the dainty little Papillon has been included in many paintings, including some by Rubens and Van Dyke. The Phalene, or Continental Toy Spaniel, is identical except for its drop ears. In the United States and the United Kingdom they are judged as one breed with almost identical standards except for colour variations, but specimens over 12in (30cm) cannot be shown in America.

The French Fédération Cynologique Internationale (FCI) separates the breeds by both type and weight variations, those over 5½lb (2.5kg) in weight entering a separate class. Papillons have done well in obedience classes.

SHOW STANDARD
General appearance. This dainty, balanced little toy dog should have an attractive head, an alert bearing and an intelligent and lively expression. Movement should be sound, light and free and not cramped or restricted in any way.
Colour. White with patches that may be any colour except liver (UK standard). A tricolour must be black and white with tan spots over the eyes and tan inside the ears, under the root of the tail and on the cheeks. The head marking should be symmetrical about a white, narrow, clearly defined blaze.
Head and skull. The skull should be slightly rounded between the ears, the muzzle finely pointed and abruptly thinner than the skull, accentuating the stop, which should be well defined. Length from the tip of the nose to the stop is approximately one-third of the length of the head. The nose should be black.
Tail. Long and well fringed, set on high, arched over the back with the fringes falling to the side to form a plume.
Feet. Fine and fairly long, as in the hare. The tufts of hair between the toes should extend far beyond them.

POMERANIAN

Good points
- Adaptable
- Devoted to owner
- Handy size
- Happy nature
- Ideal for apartment living

Take heed
- Will yap if unchecked
- Thinks it is a 'big' dog, so watch out that bigger dogs are not provoked

The Pomeranian is a happy, active little dog that will adapt cheerfully to life in a one-roomed apartment or a spacious dwelling, revelling in the role of lap dog or enjoying walks with its owner. Alternatively, it will amuse itself adequately in a garden or a fenced-in yard of modest dimensions. It makes a faithful and devoted companion.

Size
Dog 4-4½lb (1.8-2kg);
bitch 4½-5½lb (2-2.5kg).

Exercise
It is wrong to think that toy breeds are of use for little else except sitting decoratively on their owners' knees, and the Pomeranian is no exception. True, they adore being pampered and petted, but they are also lively little dogs, quite able to walk as far as their owner would wish — often further.

Grooming
This is not the breed for those who cannot spare the time for frequent grooming. Indeed, the Pomeranian has two coats to care for: a short, fluffy under-coat and a long, straight top-coat covering the whole of the body. Frequent brushing with a stiff brush is a must. The coat should be damped with cold water, and the moisture rubbed in with the fingertips; finally the dog is rubbed down with a towel.

Working from the head, part the coat and brush it forward from roots to tips. Make a further parting and repeat this procedure until the dog has been combed.

The Pomeranian requires regular trimming; obtain advice from a breeder or breed club as to how this should be carried out.

Feeding
As for Papillon.

Origin and history
The Pomeranian takes its name from Pomerania in Germany, and is generally thought to be of mid-European origin. However, it is a member of the Spitz family, which could mean that its history began in the Arctic Circle.

The known history of the breed dates from the mid-eighteenth century when it was introduced to several European countries. It became very popular until, following the raiding of the Summer Palace in Peking in 1860 and the appearance of the Imperial Pekingese, some of its popularity was usurped by that breed.

The Pomeranian in those early days was a very much larger dog, up to 30lb (13.6kg) in weight. It was bred down steadily, and by 1896 show classes for Pomeranians were divided into those exhibits over and under 8lb (3.6k). The Kennel Club in the United Kingdom withdrew challenge certificates for the over 8lb (3.6kg) variety in 1915.

Pomeranians were shown in miscellaneous classes in the United States as early as 1892 but did not gain championship status until 1900. Eleven years later the Pomeranian Club held its first specialty show.

SHOW STANDARD
General appearance. The Pomeranian should be a compact, short-coupled, well-knit dog. It should show great intelligence in expression, and activity and buoyancy in deportment.
Colour. All whole colours are admissible, but they should be free from black or white shadings (UK standard). At present the whole-coloured dogs are white, black, brown, light or dark blue (as pale as possible), orange (which should be as self-coloured and bright as possible), or beaver.
Head and skull. The head and nose should be foxy in outline or wedge-shaped, the skull being slightly flat and large in proportion to the muzzle, which should finish rather fine and be free from lippiness. The hair on the head and face should be smooth and short. The nose should be black in white, orange and shaded sable dogs; brown in chocolate-tipped sable dogs; in other colours it may be self-coloured; but it must never be parti-coloured or white.
Tail. The tail is one of the characteristics of the breed, and should be turned over the back and carried flat and straight, being profusely covered with long, harsh, spreading hair.

Feet. The feet should be small and compact in shape.

SMALL GERMAN SPITZ
(Kleinspitz)

Good points
- Adaptable to town or country
- Beautiful
- Excellent guard
- Loyal companion

Take heed
- Likes to bark
- Suspicious of strangers

The Small German Spitz is the small variety of the Great German Spitz (Gross-spitz). The only difference between the types is in size; characterisitcs and conformation are the same.

This is a happy, extremely intelligent little dog. It makes an excellent companion, does not need a great deal of exercise and adapts well to life in town or country. It usually loves its owners deeply, but does not care much for strangers. Perhaps its only drawback is that it rather likes the sound of its own voice.

Size
Height: 11in (28cm) maximum at withers; weight not more than 7½lb (3.4kg). (The Gross-spitz stands about 15¾in/40cm high.)

Exercise
Despite its ability to cover immense areas at speed, the Spitz does not require a great deal of exercise; members of this variety can live quite happily in a small town house.

Above: The Small German Spitz.

Grooming
Vigorous frequent brushing is necessary if you don't wish to be vacuuming your carpet all the time.

Feeding
As for Papillon.

Origin and history
It is difficult to pinpoint the origin of this variety of Spitz, for the pre-historic remains of such types have been found throughout Asia and the Pacific, and drawings of similar dogs were found among the remains of the ancient Pharaohs. There are a number of Spitz varieties, all of which are very similar in character and type.

Papillon

Phalene

The Papillon's ears should be large with rounded tips, heavily fringed, set towards the back of the head and far enough apart to show the slightly rounded shape of the skull. When the ears are erect, they should be carried obliquely like the spread wings of a butterfly.

Pomeranian

MALTESE TERRIER
(Maltese)

Good points
- Adaptable about exercise
- Extremely good with children
- Healthy
- Long-lived
- Sensitive
- Sweet-natured

Take heed
- Needs fastidious grooming

The Maltese Terrier is a good-tempered dog that makes the ideal family pet. It is reliable with children, adaptable about exercise and usually healthy, and it generally remains playful throughout its long life.

Size
Not over 10in (25cm) from ground to top of shoulder. Weight 7lb (3.2kg); 4-6lb (1.8-2.7kg) preferred.

Exercise
Can manage a long walk or be content with a stroll in the park.

Grooming
Use a bristle brush frequently from puppyhood and use baby powder on legs and underside to keep the animal clean between baths. Obtain advice from the breeder about show preparation; this breed may not be ideal for new show aspirants.

Feeding
Recommended would be 5-7oz (142-198g) of a branded, meaty product, with biscuit added in equal part by volume, or ¾ to 1 cup of a dry food, complete diet, mixed in the proportion of 1 cup of feed to ½ cup of hot or cold water. Such a diet is, of course, offered purely as a guide. The owner may occasionally substitute lightly cooked minced beef, mixed with biscuit. Water must be available to all breeds at all times.

Origin and history
The Maltese Terrier is described as the oldest of European toy breeds. However, there is some controversy as to whether it originated in Malta, although the breed has certainly existed there for centuries. The Maltese Terrier also found its way to China and the Philippines, probably due to enterprising Maltese traders.

Like the Papillon, the Maltese has been depicted by many artists, including Goya, Rubens, and the famous animal painter Sir Edwin Landseer, who in 1930 produced a portrait entitled 'The Lion Dog from Malta — the last of his race', which shows the breed's rarity on the island at that time. The breed first became established in the United Kingdom during the reign of Henry VIII and was a popular pet among elegant ladies. It had a class of its own for the first time in Birmingham, England, in 1864; since then it has gained immense popularity in both the United Kingdom and the United States.

SHOW STANDARD
General appearance. Should be

smart, lively and alert. The action must be free, without extended weaving.
Colour. Pure white, but slight lemon markings should not penalize.
Head and skull. From stop to centre of skull (centre between forepart of ears) and stop to tip of nose should be equally balanced. Stop should be defined. Nose should be pure black.
Tail. Should be well arched over the back, and feathered.
Feet. Should be round, and the pads of the feet should be black.

GRIFFON
(Griffon Bruxellois, Griffon Brabancon. The Griffon Bruxellois is known in the USA as the Brussels Griffon)

Good points
- Happy temperament
- Hardy
- Intelligent
- Long-lived
- Obedient
- Suitable for town or country living

Take heed
- No drawbacks known

The Griffon is an attractive, happy little dog that makes a first-class family pet. It has an almost monkey-like face with a knowing expression, and is hardy, intelligent and terrier-like in temperament. The breed, which is essentially Belgian, was originally used as a guard dog and catcher of vermin, particularly in stable yards. However, it took the fancy of royalty, thereby becoming a fashionable house-pet.

Above: A pair of delightful Maltese puppies enjoy the sunshine. This elegant and good-natured breed has been popular in Europe for centuries, and has been portrayed by several famous artists.

There are two varieties, the Griffon Bruxellois and the Griffon Brabancon. The only difference is in the coat: The Bruxellois has a rough coat, and the Brabancon a smooth coat. Rough-coats and smooth-coats can appear in a single litter. The only variation in the breed standard is in the coat; roughs are harsh, wiry and free from curl, preferably with an under-coat; smooths are short and tight.

Size
Weight: 5-11lb (2.3-5kg), most desirable 6-10lb (2.7-4.5kg).

Exercise
Adapts well to town life and does not need a great deal of exercise, but a romp in the countryside will be greatly appreciated. The adult Griffon is capable of holding its own in woods or in water.

Grooming
The rough-coat needs twice yearly stripping: best to seek advice, or have this done professionally. The smooth-coat should be brushed, towelled and gently rubbed down with a velvet glove or a piece of chamois leather. Watch with this and other small breeds that the nails do not grow too long. Purchase the proper nail clippers for the job from a pet store or pharmacy, and be particularly careful to cut down only to the 'quick' (the vein inside the nail).

Feeding
About 7oz (198g) of a branded, meaty product with biscuit added in equal volume, or 1-1½ cupfuls of a dry food, complete diet, mixed in the proportion of 1 cup of feed to ½ cup of hot or cold water.

Origin and history
The Griffon was first exhibited at the Brussels Exhibition in 1880 and is a truly Belgian breed. It seems likely that it derives from the Affenpinscher, to which it certainly bears a facial resemblance; the introduction of the Pug may be responsible for the Brabancon, or smooth-coat, which in the early days was not recognized.

An enthusiastic Griffon owner was the late Queen Astrid of the Belgians. Before World War I, the popularity of Griffons in their country of origin was immense, but the breeding programme was severely affected by the war.

Griffons have fortunately now found their way to most countries of the world, but showing differences exist. In its native land the Griffon is shown with cropped ears, a practice that is illegal in the United Kingdom, Scandinavia and Australia. In the United States the Brussels may be shown with its ears cropped or natural.

SHOW STANDARD
General appearance. A well-balanced square little dog, lively and alert, giving the appearance of measuring the same from withers to tail root as from withers to ground. Its action should be free, well-bent hocks giving the correct drive from behind and moving true coming and going. High-stepping front movement should be discouraged.
Colour. Clear red, black or black and rich tan. In the clear red, a darker shade on the mask and ears is desirable. Ideally each hair should be an even red from tip to root. Frosting on the muzzles of mature smooths should not be penalized.
Head and skull. The head should be large and rounded but in no way domed, and should be wide between the ears. In the rough variety, hair on the skull should be rather coarse. Nose always black, as short as possible, with large open nostrils, high set, sloping back to the skull with a deep stop between nose and skull. Wide muzzle, neat lips with good turn-up. Chin prominent and slightly undershot without showing the teeth, and (in the rough variety) furnished with a beard.
Body. The neck is of medium length and gracefully arched. The brisket should be broad and deep, the ribs well sprung and the back short and level. The forelegs are medium in length, straight, well muscled and set wide apart. The thighs are strong and well muscled, the stifles are bent and the hocks are well let down, turning neither in nor out.
Tail. Short docked, carried high, emerging at right angles from a level topline.
Feet. Small, thick, cat-like feet with black toenails.

The Maltese Terrier's beautiful white coat
should hang long, flat and silky over the sides of
the body almost, if not quite, to the ground. It
should be single, i.e., without an under-coat.

Maltese Terrier

Smooth Griffon (Brabancon)

Rough Griffon (Bruxellois)

Hardly the most attractive
of breeds, the Griffon
has won admirers throughout
the world by the sheer
force of its personality.

ITALIAN GREYHOUND

Good points
- *Affectionate*
- *Easy to train*
- *Graceful, diminutive appearance*
- *Intelligent*
- *Obedient*
- *Odourless*
- *Sensitive*
- *Rarely moults*

Take heed
- *Deeply wounded by harsh words*
- *Should not be kept in a kennel*

The Italian Greyhound is the perfect Greyhound in miniature, a graceful, dainty animal that makes an ideal house-pet. It does, however, need plenty of exercise.

Size
The most desirable weight is 6-8lb (2.7-3.6kg), and not exceeding 10lb (4.5kg). Height 13-15in (33-38cm) at the withers.

Exercise
Certainly not the dog to keep shut up indoors all day. It thrives on plenty of exercise, but adapts well to town living provided adequate walks and off-the-lead runs are possible.

Grooming
The Italian Greyhound needs little more than a rub down with a proverbial silk handkerchief. But remember that this breed feels the cold, hates the wind and rain, and needs a coat. Care must be taken of the teeth. Regular scaling by a veterinarian is recommended (this applies to all toy breeds), but cream of tartar — mixed into a paste on a saucer with a little water, and applied with cotton wool — will often remove unsightly stains.

Feeding
About 7oz (198g) of a branded, meaty product with biscuit added in equal part by volume, or 1 cupful of a dry food, complete diet, mixed in the proportion of 1 cup of feed to ½ cup of hot or cold water.

Origin and history
This obedient and easy-to-train little dog is thought to have originated from the Greyhounds depicted on the tombs of the Pharaohs. But it has existed in its present form for centuries and takes its name from its great popularity in sixteenth century Italy. It was favoured by Queen Victoria, who did much to popularize so many toy breeds during her long reign. Unfortunately for the breed, some English Toy Terrier blood was introduced in an effort to reduce the size further. This spoiled the breed character, and in an effort to restore it several dogs were imported from the United States. Alas, this did little to help matters and by the early 1950s only five registrations with the Kennel Club remained. However, fresh stock was imported from Italy and,

thanks to the determined efforts and dedication of breeders, the Italian Greyhound was once more firmly established by the early 1970s.

SHOW STANDARD
General appearance. A miniature Greyhound, slender in all proportions, and of ideal elegance and grace in shape, symmetry and action.
Colour. Recognized colours: all shades of fawn, white, cream, blue, black and fawn, and white pied.
Head and skull. Skull long, flat and narrow; muzzle very fine; nose dark in colour.
Tail. Rather long, fine with low carriage.
Feet. Long, hare feet.

NB: There are some variations in the US standard.

MINIATURE PINSCHER

Good points
- *Delightful hackney gait*
- *Easy to look after*
- *Fearless*
- *Good house dog*
- *Intelligent*
- *Rarely moults*
- *Suitable for town or country life*

Take heed
- *Do not overfeed*

The Miniature Pinscher (or Min Pin), sometimes called the 'King of the Toys', makes an ideal pet for the town dweller who, nonetheless, wants a lively sporting companion. It will follow a scent and give a good account of itself in obedience competitions. The breed's hackney gait is a delight to watch, as it trots along like a dainty little horse. It has the added advantages of rarely moulting and of requiring the minimum of attention to keep its coat in fine condition. It is not, as many people assume, a miniature version of the Dobermann.

Size
The height is 10-12in (25-30cm) at the withers. (There are some slight differences in the US standard as regards acceptable colour and size.)

Exercise
The Min Pin will exercise itself in a reasonable-sized garden or yard, or accompany its owner on a day-long trek. This adaptable dog will be happy living in a flat and being taken for walks around the park, or living a country life.

Grooming
An occasional brushing and a rub down with a chamois leather will keep the Min Pin in gleaming condition.

Feeding
About 7oz (198g) of a branded meaty product with biscuit added in equal part by volume, or 1 cupful of a dry food, complete diet, mixed in the proportion of 1 cup of feed to ½ cup of hot or cold water.

Origin and history
The Miniature Pinscher is not a smaller version of the Dobermann Pinscher, but a much older breed descended from the German Smooth-haired Pinscher. It is suggested that the Italian Greyhound and the Dachshund contributed to its make-up. In any event, it was given pedigree status by the German Pinscher-Schnauzer Klub, founded in 1895.

SHOW STANDARD
General appearance. The Miniature Pinscher is structurally a well-balanced, sturdy, compact, elegant, short-coupled, smooth-coated toy dog. It is naturally well-groomed, proud, vigorous and alert. The natural characteristic traits that identify it from other toy dogs are the precise hackney gait, fearless animation, complete self-possession and spirited presence.
Colour. Black, blue or chocolate with sharply defined tan markings on cheeks, lips, lower jaw, throat; twin spots above eyes, chest, lower half of forelegs, inside of hindlegs and vent region, lower portion of hocks and feet.
Head and skull. Rather more elongated than short and round. Narrow and without conspicuous cheek formation. In correct proportion to the body. The skull should appear flat when viewed from the front. The muzzle must be rather strong and proportionate to the skull. The nose well formed, black only, with the exception of chocolates and blues, which may have a self-coloured nose.
Tail. A continuation of the top line, carried a little high and docked short.
Feet. Legs straight, medium bone. Feet cat-like; elbows close to body; nails dark.

ENGLISH TOY TERRIER
(Toy Manchester Terrier)

Good points
- *Affectionate*
- *Easy to care for*
- *Good with children*
- *Intelligent*
- *Lively*
- *Good at expelling vermin if need be*

Take heed
- *Tends to be a one-person dog that resents outsiders*

The English Toy Terrier is a most attractive, affectionate and game little dog, marvellously intuitive and loyal, but tending to attach itself to one person to the exclusion of others. It is usually healthy, easy to keep clean, odourless and an easy whelper if you wish to breed. In the United States it is called the Toy Manchester Terrier, being considered a variety of the Manchester Terrier.

Size
The ideal weight is 6-8lb (2.7-3.6kg), and a height of 10-12in (25-30cm) at the shoulders is most desirable.

Exercise
Adapts well to town living provided adequate walks and off-the-lead runs are possible.

Grooming
Occasional brushing will suffice. One of the advantages of this short-coated breed is that it does not shed. The coat can be massaged to effect a sheen; or equally beneficial is a weekly teaspoonful of cod liver oil in the food. Dry the coat with a towel after excursions on rainy days. Although the breed is robust it will, in common with most toy breeds, appreciate a warm coat in bitter weather.

Feeding
Recommended would be 5-7oz (142-198g) of a branded, meaty product, with biscuit added in equal part by volume, or 1 cup of a dry food, complete diet, mixed in the proportion of 1 cup of feed to ½ cup of hot or cold water. The owner may occasionally substitute lightly cooked minced beef, mixed with biscuit. Water must be available to all breeds at all times.

Origin and history
(See also Manchester Terrier)
The English Toy is a smaller version of the Manchester Terrier, once a prodigious ratter and descended from the old Black and Tan Rough-haired Terrier. The English Toy Terrier's fitness owes something to the Italian Greyhound and the Whippet. The breed began in England under the name Toy Manchester Terrier, and was later known variously as Toy Black and Tan and Miniature Black and Tan. It was recognized as the English Toy Terrier (Black and Tan) by the Kennel Club in 1962.

SHOW STANDARD
General appearance. A well-balanced, elegant and compact toy with terrier temperament and characteristics.
Colour. Black and tan: the black should be ebony and the tan can be likened to a new chestnut, deeply rich. These colours should not run or blend into each other, but should meet abruptly, forming clear and well-defined lines of colour division.
Head and skull. The head should be long and narrow with a flat skull, wedge-shaped without emphasis of cheek muscles and well filled up under the eyes.
Body. Moderately short with robust loins and well-sprung ribs. The back, which is slightly arched at the loins, falls again towards the tail. The height at the tail is the same as the height at the shoulder. Forelegs straight and well under the body. Hindlegs carried back.
Tail. The tail should be thick at the root, tapering to a point, set low and not reaching below the hock. A gay tail carriage is undesirable if displayed to excess.
Feet. Dainty, compact, split up between the toes and well arched, with jet black nails; the two middle toes of the front feet are rather longer than the others, and the hind feet are cat-like.

In the late 1880s, the English Toy Terrier was popular as a vermin killer and frequently appeared in the rat pit, a favourite sport among working- and upper-classes alike. Present-day specimens should be sleek and cleanly built, giving an appearance of alertness combined with speed of movement.

English Toy Terrier

Miniature Pinscher

The Min Pin's tail is docked, and its cropped ears can be pricked or dropped. Indeed, were it not for these characteristics and colour variations, one might be forgiven for mistaking it at first glance for an English Toy Terrier. The broad skull and bulging eyes once prevalent in the breed have been replaced by the wedge-shaped head preferred in the Dobermann.

Italian Greyhound

The Italian Greyhound looks more fragile than it really is. It will happily chase small game, and in Scandinavia slightly larger specimens are used for coursing.

BICHON FRISE
(And Bichon Bolognese)

Good points
- *Good pet*
- *Happy temperament*
- *Attractive, lamb-like appearance*

Take heed
- *Requires meticulous grooming*

The Bichon Frise has been recognized by the British and American kennel clubs only over the past 20 years. It is a most appealing and happy little dog, which will surely become more popular when the public becomes acquainted with the breed.

Size
Height: less than 12in (30cm), smallness being highly desirable.

Exercise
Will enjoy a romp but fits well into town living and regular walks. Will also enjoy the occasional off-the-lead country run and a game in the garden.

Grooming
This is not the breed for novice exhibitors, or for those who are not prepared to spend time in meticulous grooming, bathing, trimming and scissoring. The effect, when complete, should be of an elegant white 'powder puff', the head and body trimmed to give a rounded effect, but showing the eyes. Hair around the feet should also be trimmed. Ask the breeder for a showing and grooming chart, and for a demonstration.

Feeding
Recommended would be 5-7oz (142-198g) of a branded, meaty product with biscuit added in equal part by volume, or 1 cupful of a dry food, complete diet, mixed in the proportion of 1 cup of feed to ½ cup of hot or cold water. Always ensure that the dog has ample water.

Origin and history
The Bichon, like its cousin Caniche, is a descendant of the Barbet (water spaniel), from which the name Barbichon originates; later it was abbreviated to Bichon.

The little dogs are said to have originated in the Mediterranean area and were certainly introduced by sailors to the Canary Islands prior to the fourteenth century. There were then four varieties: the Bichon Ténériffe, the Bichon Maltaise, the Bichon Bolognese and the Bichon Havanais. The breed later found favour with the French and Spanish nobility and was included in paintings by Francisco Goya (1746-1828).

A period of obscurity followed until, after World War I, soldiers took a few when they left France. A breed standard was written up in France in 1933, when the name 'Bichon à poil frise' (curly-coated Bichon) was adopted, and the word Ténériffe omitted from its title. Crufts Dog Show in London included a class for the Bichon Frise for the first time in 1980.

The Bolognese is very similar to the Bichon Frise and is registered with the Fédération Cynologique Internationale as an Italian breed.

SHOW STANDARD
General appearance. This gay, happy little dog has a coat falling in soft, corkscrew curls. The head carriage is proud and high; the eyes are alert and expressive.
Colour. Pure white. Under the white coat, dark pigment is preferred; black, blue or beige markings often found on the skin.
Head and skull. The skull is longer than the muzzle, but the whole head in is in balance with the body. The muzzle should not be thick or heavy; nor should it be snipy; the cheeks flat and not very strongly muscled; the stop should be slight and the hollow between the eyebrows just visible. The skull must be flat when touched, although the hair tends to make it look round. The nose should be round, black, soft and shiny.
Tail. Normally carried raised and curled gracefully over the back but never tightly curled. It should not be docked and should not touch the backbone, but the hair should always fall onto the back. Slightly low set.
Feet. Small, rounded and well knuckled up. Nails preferably black.

TOY POODLE

Good points
- *Affectionate*
- *Dainty and appealing*
- *Excellent retriever*
- *Intelligent*
- *Long-lived*
- *Good sense of fun*
- *Useful in obedience competitions*

Take heed
- *Noisy if unchecked*
- *Perhaps not the best choice of child's pet*
- *Sensitive*

The Toy Poodle has a character full of fun. It is intelligent and obedient. In the United Kingdom, it has proved a useful competitor in obedience competitions. It has a fondness for water, if the owner permits, but is much favoured for the show ring where, exhibited in the traditional lion clip, it is a beauty to behold. It is also, debatably, the most difficult breed to prepare for the ring, involving the handler in a day's canine beauty treatment.

Size
Height at shoulder should be under 11in (28cm). (There is a slight reduction in the height requirement in the United States where Toy Poodles may not exceed 10in/26cm at the withers.)

Exercise
The Toy Poodle will enjoy a ball game in the garden, practising obedience exercises or trotting beside you in the park. The toy variety is obviously a good choice for the apartment dweller.

Grooming
Use a wire-pin pneumatic brush and a wire-toothed metal comb for daily grooming. The lion clip is an essential for the show ring, but pet owners generally resort to the more natural lamb clip with the hair a short, uniform length. It is possible to clip your own dog with a pair of hairdressers' scissors. However, if, despite the help which is usually available from the breeder, you find the task tedious, there are numerous pet and poodle parlours to which you should take your dog every six weeks. Regular bathing is also essential.

Feeding
Five-7oz (142-198g) of a branded, meaty product, with biscuit added in equal part by volume, or 1 cupful of a dry complete food, mixed in the proportion of 1 cup of feed to ½ cup of hot or cold water.

Health care
Fanciers will confirm that the Standard Poodle is the soundest of the varieties. It is possible to acquire healthy Toy and Miniature stock, but care should be taken to purchase from a breeder who puts quality ahead of daintiness. Watch out for signs of ear trouble, nervousness and especially joint malformations. Teeth need regular scaling. Nonetheless, a 16-year-old Poodle is not a rarity.

Origin and history
The Poodle was originally a shaggy guard, a retriever and protector of sheep, with origins similar to the Irish Water Spaniel and, no doubt, a common ancestor in the French Barbet and Hungarian Water Hound.

The Poodle may not be, as many suppose, solely of French origin. It originated in Germany as a water retriever; even the word poodle comes from the German 'pudelnass' or puddle, and from this fairly large sturdy dog, the Standard Poodle, the Miniature and the Toy have evolved.

The breed has been known in England since Prince Rupert of the Rhine, in company with his Poodle, came to the aid of Charles I in battle. The breed was favoured also by Marie Antoinette who, rumour has it, invented the lion clip by devising a style that would match the uniform of her courtiers. It is also popular in the United States.

SHOW STANDARD
General appearance. A very active, intelligent, well-balanced and elegant-looking dog with good temperament, carrying itself very proudly.
Colour. All solid colours. White and cream Poodles to have black nose, lips and eye-rims; black toenails desirable. Brown Poodles to have dark amber eyes, dark liver nose, lips, eye-rims and toenails. Apricot Poodles to have dark eyes with black points or deep amber eyes with liver points. Black, silver and blue Poodles to have black nose, lips, eye-rims and toenails. Cream apricot, brown, silver and blue Poodles may show varying shades of the same colour up to 18 months. Clear colours preferred.
Head and skull. Long and fine with slight peak at the back. The skull not broad and with a moderate stop. Foreface strong and well chiselled, not falling away under the eyes; bones and muscle flat. Lips tight fitting. Chin well defined, but not protruding. The whole head must be in proportion to the size of the dog.
Body. The distance from the breast bone to the rump should approximate the distance from the highest point of the shoulders to the ground. The chest is deep and moderately wide with well-sprung ribs. The topline is level but for a slight hollow just behind the shoulder.
Tail. Set on rather high, well carried at a slight angle away from the body; never curled or carried over the back; thick at the root.
Feet. Pasterns strong; tight feet proportionately small, oval in shape, turning neither in nor out; toes arched; pads thick; hard and well cushioned.

Below: An alert and appealing Bichon Frise pup. An older dog's coat falls into corkscrew curls.

The Bichon Frise was given its official standard in France in 1933, after virtually disappearing during World War I. It was introduced into America in 1956 and officially registered in 1972. A breed class was included at Crufts for the first time in 1980.

Bichon Frise

*Toy Poodle
(English saddle or lion clip)*

AUSTRALIAN SILKY TERRIER

(Silky Terrier/Sydney Silky Terrier; see also Australian Terrier)

Good points
- Alert
- Affectionate
- Dainty nature
- Hardy
- Makes a good pet

Take heed
- No drawbacks known

The Australian Silky Terrier is a dainty little dog, similar to the Yorkshire Terrier in appearance. The Silky is alert and hardy and has a merry and affectionate nature.

Size
The most desirable weights are 8-10lb (3.6-4.5kg). Height approximately 9in (23cm) at the withers.

Exercise
Despite its small stature the Silky has well-developed terrier instincts and is a first-class ratter. It will adapt well to apartment living and town walks but is in its element chasing across the fields, getting that straight, silky coat into magnificent disarray.

Grooming
Ideally the Silky should have a well-groomed appearance, which calls for a coat length of 5-6in (12.5-15cm) from behind the ears to the set-on of the tail. Legs from knees and hocks to feet should be free from long hair.

Feeding
Recommended: 5-7oz (142-198g) of a branded, meaty product with biscuit added in equal part by volume; or 1 cupful of a dry food, complete diet, mixed in the proportion of 1 cup of feed to ½ cup of hot or cold water.

Origin and history
The Australian (or Sydney) Silky Terrier was derived from crossing Yorkshire Terriers with the Australian Terrier, which has Norwich and

Below: The Australian Silky Terrier is an alert and dainty dog. It is also a keen rat catcher and enjoys a good chase over the fields.

Cairn terrier and probably also Dandie Dinmont in its make-up.

The breed, which in America is shown in toy classes under the name of Silky Terrier, has been recognized in the United States since 1959 but is a relative newcomer to the United Kingdom, where separate standards now exist for the Australian Terrier and the Australian Silky Terrier.

SHOW STANDARD
General appearance. The dog is compact, moderately low set, of medium length with a refined structure but of sufficient substance to suggest the ability to hunt and kill domestic rodents. It should display terrier characteristics, embodying keen alertness, activity and soundness; the parted, straight silky hair should look well groomed.
Colour. Blue and tan, or grey-bue and tan — the richer the better. Blue on tail should be very dark. The distribution of the blue and tan as follows: silver-blue or fawn topknot desirable; tan around the base of the ears, the muzzle and on side of cheeks: blue from base of skull to tip of tail, running down the forelegs to near the knees and down the thighs to the hocks; tan line showing down the stifles; and tan from the knees and hocks to the toes and around the vent.
Head and skull. Of moderate length, slightly shorter in length from the tip of the nose to between the eyes than from the same position to the top rear of the occiput. The head must be strong and of terrier character, being moderately broad between the ears; the skull flat, without fullness between the eyes. Long fall of hair on foreface and cheeks is very obectionable. Fine silky topknot, not falling over the eyes. Nose should be black.
Tail. Should be docked and carried erect, but not over-gay.
Feet. Small, well padded, cat-like; closely knit toes with black nails.

TIBETAN SPANIEL

Good points
- Confident
- Easy to train
- Happy nature
- Intelligent
- Good household pet
- Suitable for town or country

Take heed
- No drawbacks known

The Tibetan Spaniel is an attractive small dog with a happy, if independent, nature. It is easily trained and makes an ideal family pet, being reliable with children. In appearance it resembles a rather large Pekingese. It is also an enjoyable dog to show.

Size
Weight: 9-15lb (4-6.8kg) is ideal. Height about 10in (25cm).

Exercise
This dog requires average walks and off-the-lead runs.

Grooming
Needs frequent brushing.

Feeding
Six-13oz (170-369g) of a branded, meaty product with biscuit added in equal part by volume, or 1¾ cupfuls of a dry complete food, mixed in the proportion of 1 cup of feed to ½ cup of hot or cold water.

Origin and history
The Tibetan Spaniel was first discovered in the Tibetan monasteries where, to quote a reference in *Champion Dogs of the World* (G. Harrap, 1967), 'Reports indicate that it still turns the prayer-wheel of Tibetans who seek to reap the rewards of a devout life without the inconvenience of physical exertion'. However, this charming practice may have ceased since the Chinese takeover and outlawing of dogs. It is a close relative of the Tibetan Terrier and Lhasa Apso, both of which also originate from Tibet. The Tibetan Spaniel was first seen in England in the late nineteenth century. It did not appear in the United States until the 1960s.

SHOW STANDARD
General appearance. Should be small, active and alert. The outline should give a well-balanced appearance, slightly longer in body than high at withers.
Colour. All colours and mixture of colours allowed.
Head and skull. Small in proportion to body and proudly carried giving an impression of quality. Masculine in dogs but free from coarseness. Skull slightly domed, moderate width and length. Stop slight, but defined. Medium length of muzzle, blunt with

Above: First discovered in the monasteries of Tibet, the Tibetan Spaniel makes the perfect pet.

cushioning, free from wrinkle. The chin should show some depth and width. A black nose is preferred.
Body. The neck, which is moderately short, strong and well set on, is covered with a mane or 'shawl' of longer hair. The distance from the point of shoulder to the root of the tail is slightly longer than the distance from the withers to the ground.
Tail. Set high, richly plumed and carried in a gay curl over the back when the dog is moving. Should not be penalized for dropping tail when standing.
Feet. Hare footed, small and neat with feathering between toes often extending beyond the feet. White markings allowed.

Below: Two delightful Tibetan Spaniel puppies, only a few weeks old. These dogs are easy to train and adapt happily to town life.

The Australian Silky Terrier's attractive coat should be fine and glossy and of a silky texture. It is usually parted on the head and down over the back to the root of the tail. On the top of the head the hair is so profuse as to form a topknot. Groomed carefully for the show ring, the Australian Silky Terrier looks truly magnificent.

Australian Silky Terrier

Short-nosed specimens of the Tibetan Spaniel were once likened to the Pekingese, but careful breeding has produced an unmistakable and very popular breed.

Tibetan Spaniel

BEAGLE

Good points
● *Adores children*
● *Good with other pets*
● *Intelligent*
● *Merry and affectionate*

Take heed
● *No drawbacks known*

The Beagle is a merry, affectionate little fellow, loving humans and other pets alike. The Beagle adores children and is a wonderful companion, equally ready for a romp or to lie by your feet on the hearthrug. This breed is at home in a small house or a mansion and will guard its home and owner faithfully. It is not a barker, being mostly heard at the chase in full cry. But, like most other hounds, it has the wanderlust, so care must be taken never to leave the garden gate, or the gate to the backyard fence, ajar.

Size
It is desirable that height from ground to withers should neither exceed 16in (40.5cm) nor fall below 13in (33cm). In the United States the height limit is 15in (38cm) at the shoulder.

Exercise
Exercise is no problem because Beagles keep themselves fit as easily in a small garden as on a farm. But, like most dogs, they should be taken for a walk every day. They are notoriously healthy and robust, so you rarely need the services of a veterinarian.

Grooming
The short coat of the Beagle is tough and weatherproof, and needs little grooming. It is recommended that after a muddy walk the Beagle is left in its box to clean itself up.

Feeding
One meal a day is sufficient for a full-grown Beagle, with no titbits afterwards, as this is a breed that is inclined to put on weight. Thirteen-20oz (369-567g) of a complete meaty diet to which biscuit should be added in equal part by volume, is adequate; or 2-3 cupfuls of a

Below: The Beagle enjoys daily walks and a chance to wander.

dry food, complete diet, mixed in the proportion of 1 cup of feed to ½ cup of hot or cold water.

Origin and history
The Beagle is one of the smallest of the hounds, embodying all their virtues in the least compass. An ancient breed, it has proved a joy to sportsmen for hundreds of years; Beagles were first mentioned by name in writings published in 1475. Followed on foot and on horseback, they have been hunted in packs after hare from time immemorial and were first imported into the United States for this purpose.

Beagles are esteemed all over the world and have hunted many different quarries in varying climates, including jackal in the Sudan and Palestine, wild pig in Ceylon and deer in Scandinavia. In the USA and Canada today they are used as gundogs to seek out and retrieve game and to hunt by scent in competitive field trials.

The earliest Beagles in the United States looked more like straight-legged Bassets or Dachshunds than today's Beagles. Dogs imported from the 1860s on — and the establishment of the National Beagle Club in 1888 — helped to refine and standardize breed type.

SHOW STANDARD
General appearance. A sturdy and compactly built Beagle should convey the impression of quality without coarseness.
Colour. Any recognized hound colour other than liver. Tip of stern should be white.
Head and skull. Head fair length, powerful in the dog without being coarse, but finer in the bitch; free from frown and excessive wrinkle. Skull slightly domed, moderately wide, with indication of peak. Stop well defined and dividing length between occiput and tip of nose as equally as possible. Muzzle not snipy, lips reasonably well flewed. Nose broad and nostrils well expanded; preferably black, but less pigmentation is permissible in the lighter-coloured hounds.
Tail. Sturdy and of moderate length. Set on high and carried gaily but not curled over the back or inclined forward from the root. Well covered with hair, especially on the underside.
Feet. Tight and firm. Well knuckled up and strongly padded. Not hare-footed. Nails short.

CHINESE CRESTED

Good points
● *Handy size*
● *No hairs on the carpets!*
● *Intelligent*
● *Devoted companion*
● *Novelty—always the centre of attraction*
● *Good with children, the bitch being particularly gentle*

Take heed
● *Apt to be greedy*
● *Some folk find the reptilian skin on the hairless variety unpleasant*

The Chinese Crested has much to recommend it, as both pet and show dog. It is a handy size, clean and odourless and does not shed. It is dainty, alert, intelligent, courageous and gentle. It seldom requires veterinary aid and is a free whelper. It adjusts to cold or warm climates as its body temperature is 2.2 deg C (4 deg F) higher than that of humans; in fact, it has its own central heating system, the body feeling hotter to the touch after the animal has eaten. It has the ability to grip with its paws in a charming, almost human fashion.

A strange fact about the breed is that in almost every litter there are one or two haired pups, known as 'powder puffs'. Although these haired specimens have been excluded from selective breeding over a period of years, they are still apparent. Many people believe that the powder puffs are nature's way of keeping the hairless pups warm. And some think that breeding a hairless dog with a powder puff results in healthier stock, the powder puff being allegedly the stronger. If you intend to breed this species, remember that although a reasonable price may be obtained for a powder puff bitch, because she is quite likely to produce hairless pups, the powder puff dog will command only a very moderate price as a household pet.

Size
Varies a lot, maximum 12lb (5.4kg).

Exercise
The Chinese Crested is a lively little dog and enjoys a brisk walk. However, it happily works off a lot of surplus energy running after, and playing with, the chews and other toys that it so likes.

Grooming
The Chinese Crested needs frequent bathing, and the skin should be regularly rubbed with baby oil to prevent cracking and to keep it smooth to the touch. Care must be taken to prevent sunburn and to maintain the skin free of blackheads — to which they are prone in adolescence — and other blemishes. Facial hair and whiskers are usually removed.

Above: Chinese Crested powder puffs such as this one can occur in the same litter as the virtually hairless variety of this breeed.

Feeding
Usually a rather greedy dog, this breed should nonetheless be content with 5-7oz (142-198g) of branded dog food or the fresh meat equivalent, and a cupful of small dog biscuits. It is a good idea to keep a bowl of biscuits accessible, so that the animal may help itself when peckish, but remove them if your pet shows signs of becoming overweight.

Health care
These dogs lack premolar teeth, and thus it is inadvisable to give them bones. They are also allergic to wool.

Origin and history
Up until 1966, an elderly lady in the United States owned the only examples of the Chinese Crested in the world. Mrs Ruth Harris introduced four of these to the United Kingdom. Today the Chinese Crested is thriving, and classes for the breed are being included in an increasing number of dog shows. It is recognized by the Kennel Club and is also shown now in championship classes in the United States.

SHOW STANDARD
General appearance. A small, active and graceful dog; medium to fine bones; smooth hairless body, with hair on feet, head and tail.
Crest. Flat, high or long-flowing; sparse crest acceptable, but full crest preferred.
Colour. Any colour, plain or spotted. Skin should be smooth and soft, and warm to the touch.
Head and skull. Long skull, slightly rounded; slight stop; moderately long muzzle; lean cheeks.
Tail. Up and over the back or looped, never curled. Plume on the lower two-thirds of the tail. Sparse plume acceptable but full plume preferred.
Feet. Hare foot, nails moderately long. Hair should not come above the first joint from the floor.

Beagle

The Beagle is renowned for its hunting qualities throughout the world. In America, where Beagles are used for hunting hares, two size varieties are recognized:
those not exceeding 13in (33cm) at the shoulder, and those over 13in (33cm) but not exceeding 15in (38cm).

The lively and terrier-like Chinese Crested tends to stay puppyish for a longer period than other breeds. Curiously, the skin lightens in the summer and darkens in the winter.

Chinese Crested

KING CHARLES SPANIEL

Good points
- Hardy, despite small stature
- Clean
- Loves children
- Usually gets on with other pets

Take heed
- Needs monthly bath (except in cold weather)
- Needs frequent grooming

The King Charles Spaniel is known in the USA as the English Toy Spaniel, the varieties of which are Prince Charles (tricolour), Blenheim (red and white), Ruby (chestnut red) and King Charles (black and tan).

In 1903 an attempt was made in the United Kingdom to change the breed name to Toy Spaniel. However, the change was opposed by King Edward VII, a devotee of the breed, and it has retained the name, probably attributed to it because of Van Dyck's seventeenth-century paintings, which frequently showed King Charles with these pets. Although toy spaniels had been known in England for more than 100 years before the reign of Charles II, many people mistakenly believe that the breed was introduced to England during Charles' reign.

The King Charles is an ideal choice. It is a good mixer, marvellous with children and — despite its small stature — very hardy. It does, however, require frequent grooming, regular bathing and, like the Pekingese, to have its eyes wiped every day; care must also be taken lest canker should develop in those well-concealed ears.

Size
The most desirable weight is 8-14lb (3.6-6.4kg).

Exercise
The King Charles will look forward to its daily outings, whether accompanying its owner on a shopping trip or going for a scamper in the park. It will be quick to learn how to carry its lead or a newspaper. Don't forget to rub it down with a towel after it has been out in the rain.

Grooming
Regular brushing with a bristle brush is essential. Examine paws for any trace of interdigital cysts, and ears for canker, often detectable by an unpleasant smell. Wipe eyes with cotton wool dipped in a weak saline solution to keep them clear of unsightly tear streaks.

Feeding
About 5-7oz (142-198g) of a branded, meaty diet with biscuit added in equal parts by volume; or, if a dry food, complete diet is used, 1 cupful of feed mixed in the proportion of 1 cup of dry feed to ½ cupful of hot or cold water.

Origin and history
The King Charles is generally thought of as a British breed, but it can be traced back to Japan in 2000 BC. The original breed was much in evidence at the English sixteenth-century court, when it closely resembled the present-day, longer-nosed Cavalier King Charles. As short-nosed dogs became fashionable, the King Charles Spaniel evolved.

The breed has many royal associations; one was found hidden in the folded gown of Mary, Queen of Scots, after her execution, and Macaulay, in his History of England, recalls how King Charles II endeared himself to his people by playing with these spaniels in St James's Park, London, 'before the dew was off the grass'.

SHOW STANDARD
General appearance. Compact

Above: A King Charles pup with black, white and tan markings.

and cobby, on refined lines, chest wide and deep, legs short and straight, back short and level. Movement free, active and elegant.
Colour. The only recognized colours are: (1) Black and tan — a rich, glossy black with bright, mahogany tan markings on muzzle, legs, chest and linings of ears. (2) Tricolour — ground pearly white with well-distributed black patches, brilliant tan markings on cheeks and linings of ears, under tail and over the eyes; a wide white blaze between the eyes and up the forehead. (3) Blenheim — a ground of pearly white with well-distributed chestnut red patches; a wide clear blaze with the 'spot', a clear chestnut red mark, in the centre of skull. (4) Ruby — whole coloured, a rich, chestnut red.

In the United States this breed is known as the English Toy Spaniel and is classified according to colour.
Head and skull. Skull massive in comparison to size, well domed, and full over the eyes. Nose black with large wide open nostrils, very short and turned up to meet the skull. The stop between skull and nose should be well defined. Muzzle square, wide and deep, and well turned up; lower jaw wide; lips exactly meeting, giving a nice finish. The cheeks should not fall away under the eyes but be well cushioned-up. A protruding tongue is objectionable but does not disqualify.
Tail. Well flagged and not carried over the level of the back.

CAVALIER KING CHARLES SPANIEL

Good points
- Hardy, despite small stature
- Clean
- Loves children
- Usually gets on with other pets

Take heed
- Needs monthly bath (except in cold weather)
- Needs frequent grooming

Many people find it hard to distinguish between the King Charles and the Cavalier King Charles Spaniel; the Cavalier is larger, and there are marked differences in the head formation — the skull is almost flat between the ears and its stop is much shallower than that of the King Charles. However, it has the same characteristics of courage, hardiness and good nature, which make it a suitable pet for any age group.

Size
Weight: 12-18lb (5.4-8.2kg). A small, well-balanced dog within these weights is desirable.

Exercise
Normal exercise requirements. Will adapt easily to town or country living. It should not, however, be kennelled out of doors.

Grooming
As for King Charles Spaniel.

Feeding
As for King Charles Spaniel.

Origin and history
Reports by Pepys and other British diarists tell us that King Charles II spent more time playing with his 'toy spaniels' during Council meetings than he did dealing with matters of state. He even took his dogs into his bedchamber.

The Cavalier and the King Charles originate from common stock. When it became fashionable to produce a King Charles Spaniel with a short nose, the original type almost disappeared; but in the late 1920s a group of breeders combined to bring back the old type of King Charles, prefixing its name with the word 'cavalier' to distinguish it from the newer, quite separate variety.

Today the Cavalier is popular with a number of well-known people in the United States — Ronald Reagan among them — but it does not enjoy championship status.

SHOW STANDARD
General appearance. An active, graceful and well-balanced dog. Absolutely fearless and sporting in character and very gay and free in action.
Colour. The only recognized colours are: (1) Black and tan — raven black with tan markings above the eyes, on cheeks, inside ears, on chest and legs and on underside of tail. The tan should be bright. (2) Tricolour — black and white well spaced and broken up with tan markings over the eyes, on cheeks, inside ears, inside legs and on underside of tail. (3) Blenheim — rich chestnut marking well broken up on a pearly white ground; the markings should be evenly divided on the head, leaving room between the ears for the much-valued lozenge mark or spot (a unique characteristic of the breed). (4) Ruby — whole coloured rich red. Any other colour or combination of colours is undesirable.
Head and skull. Head almost flat between the ears, without dome. Stop shallow. Length from base of stop to tip about 1½in (4cm). Nostrils should be well developed and black in colour. Muzzle tapered. Lips well covering but not hound-like. Face should be well filled out underneath the eyes. Any tendency to appear snipy is undesirable.
Tail. The docking of tails is optional. No more than one-third to be removed. The length of the tail should be in balance with the body.
Feet. Compact, cushioned and well feathered.

Below: Cavalier pups with Blenheim (left) and tricolour or Prince Charles (right) markings. They also come in solid chestnut or black and tan.

King Charles Spaniel (Ruby)

King Charles Spaniel (Tricolour)

The Cavalier King
Charles Spaniel is larger
than the King Charles
and it has a longer nose, but
confusion still arises between the two breeds.
In the United States, the King Charles Spaniel is
known as the English Toy Spaniel.

Cavalier King Charles Spaniel (Blenheim)

JAPANESE CHIN
(Japanese Spaniel)

Good points
- Affectionate
- Loyal family dog
- Hardy
- Good with children

Take heed
- Silky coat tends to shed
- Guard against vigorous exertion and overheating in warm weather

The Japanese Chin is a handsome, bicoloured dog, lively in temperament and dainty in appearance with a smart, compact carriage and a plentiful coat. First registered by the American Kennel Club in 1888, the Chin was known as the Japanese Spaniel until 1977 when its name was changed officially to Japanese Chin. The spaniel designation was, indeed, misleading since this breed exhibits more of the perkier confidence of the smaller breeds than it does the characterisitcs of the spaniel.

Size
Weight: 4-7lb (1.8-3.2kg). (The daintier the better, if type, quality and soundness are not sacrificed.)

Exercise
This is a happy little dog that will delight in going for walks and playing games with all the family. It will walk as far as its owners wish, or be happy with a run in the park. The Japanese Chin is quite tough, despite its delicate structure, and will enjoy careful handling by youngsters. But it does like to climb so be careful it does not fall and injure itself. And don't forget that young pups should not be taken for long walks during the first months of life, when muscles can be strained or overdeveloped.

Grooming
Frequent grooming with a pure bristle brush will maintain the Chin's luxurious, silky coat in good condition. Always give this breed a bath before a show.

Feeding
Depending on the size of the dog,

Below: Black and white is the most common Japanese Chin pattern.

approximately one 6oz (170g) can of tinned food daily or ⅓ of a cup of dry food plus one 3.5oz (99g) can of tinned food.

Origin and history
Because images of dogs closely resembling Japanese Chins have been found on ancient Chinese pottery, embroidery and temples, most observers believe that the Chin originated in China. Thence the Chin was exported to Japan, most probably as a gift from a Chinese to a Japanese emperor.

For more than 1,000 years Chins were the much-coddled favourites of Japanese emperors, one of whom decreed that all Japanese Chin should be worshipped. Some tiny specimens were even kept in hanging cages in the manner of small oriental birds.

The breed is reputed to have found its way to Europe with returning seamen in medieval times. However, the Japanese Chin did not make its appearance in the British show ring until 1862, and is not recorded as being shown in the United States until 20 years later.

When Commodore Perry left Japan in 1853 — after establishing trade relations between Japan and the rest of the world — he was presented with several Japanese Chins. Upon returning to England, the commodore gave a pair of these dogs to Queen Victoria. The association with the Queen served to establish and promote the Chin in the United Kingdom.

Before long, Chins were taken to America, but there is no record of the date of their arrival in that country or of the persons responsible for introducing Chins there. Some people believe that the first Chins to arrive in America had been removed from Japanese kennels without their owners' consent. Whatever the case, when Perry opened Japanese ports to the world at large, he also opened Japanese kennels, and for a time virtually every ship leaving the Orient debarked with a number of Chins on board that were sold to eager buyers around the world.

This bustling trade in Chins was interrupted by World War I, which cut off the supply of dogs leaving Japan. Breeders in the United Kingdom and America were obliged to make do with the stock they had previously imported, and the Chin's progress in those countries was impeded severely. In addition, Japanese breeders have taken up other breeds, and the supply of Chins from Japan is not as abundant as it was once. Yet Chins are widely distributed throughout the world, particularly in the United Kingdom, France, Switzerland, Austria and Germany.

SHOW STANDARD
General appearance. The Japanese Chin is a lively dog, essentially stylish in movement, lifting the feet high when in motion, and carrying the tail, which is heavily feathered, closely curved or plumed over the back.
Colour. Black and white or red and white. Red includes all shades,

sable, brindle, lemon or orange. The brighter and clearer the red the better. Colour evenly distributed on the cheeks and ears and as patches on the body. Should be not too heavily marked. White should be clear, not flecked.
Head and skull. Large, but in proportion to the size of the dog; broad skull rounded in front, rounded between the ears, but in no way domed.
Tail. Set high on a straight back profusely feathered, closely curved or plumed over the back.
Feet. Should be slender and hare-shaped, feathered at tips.

PEKINGESE

Good points
- Beautiful appearance
- Calm and good-tempered
- Brave guard dog
- Healthy and intelligent

Take heed
- Aloof, independent nature
- Subject to eye trouble
- Needs daily grooming
- Best for adults only
- Guard against vigorous exertion and overheating in warm weather

The Pekingese likes to remind its owners of its regal background, and expects to be petted and pampered. It is not, however, a delicate creature; in fact, it is fearless and fun, and loves having toys to play with.

It is good with children, but comes into its own as an adult's sole companion, being the centre of attention and, preferably, having the run of the house.

Size
Not to exceed 14lb (6.4kg). There is not, as is often supposed, a miniature Pekingese, but within a litter may be found 'sleeve' specimens weighing no more than 6lb (2.7kg). Sleeve Pekes are so called because they could be concealed in the flowing sleeves of the garments worn by Chinese mandarins.

Exercise
The Peke will happily trudge across fields with its owner, or be content with a sedate walk in the park.

Grooming
The Pekingese needs daily brushing with a brush of soft bristles. The grooming of the underside is usually

Above: A 'sleeve' Peke, a specimen that is smaller than usual.

carried out with the Peke lying on its back, the rest of the job being tackled with the pet standing on a table, or on one's lap. Grooming a dog on a table is good preparation for a possible show career!

Feeding
A Peke will thrive on 10-15oz (283-425g) of tinned food per day or ¾-1 cup of dry food, and 4-6oz (113-170g) of tinned food.

Origin and history
This regal, little Lion Dog — which had been popular for more than ten centuries in its native China — was brought to the United Kingdom in 1860 after British forces had looted the Summer Palace in Peking, liberating four Imperial Pekingese dogs from the women's apartments. Previously it had been forbidden for anyone other than the Chinese royal family to own a Peke, and their theft was punishable by death.

One of the Pekes taken by the British was presented to Queen Victoria; it was appropriately named 'Looty', lived until 1872, and was the subject of a painting by Landseer.

The Pekingese was first exhibited in the United Kingdom in 1893. The dog who had the greatest influence on the breed in the early 1900s was a large, black and tan male named Boxer, who was never exhibited because he had a docked tail. Boxer had been obtained by the British Major Gwynne during the Boxer Rebellion in 1900.

SHOW STANDARD
General appearance. A small, well-balanced, thick-set dog of much dignity and quality. It should carry itself fearlessly in the ring with an alert, intelligent expression.
Colour. All colours and markings are permissible and equally good, except albino or liver. Parti-colours should be evenly broken.
Head and skull. Head massive; skull broad, wide and flat between the ears, not domed; wide between the eyes. Nose very short and broad, nostrils large, open, and black; muzzle wide, well wrinkled, with firm under-jaw. Profile should look quite flat with nose well up between the eyes. Deep stop.
Feet. Large and flat, not round. The dog should stand well up on its feet, not on its pasterns. The front feet should be turned slightly out. Absolute soundness is essential.

The eyes are a distinctive feature of the Japanese Chin. They should be large, dark and set far apart. The white should show in the inner corners, giving the breed a characteristic look of astonishment or even making it look cross-eyed.

Japanese Chin

The Pekingese, for many centuries a royal dog in China, was first exhibited in Europe in the late 1800s; the Pekingese Club of America was formed in 1909.

Pekingese

MINIATURE DACHSHUND

Good points
- *Affectionate nature*
- *Courageous*
- *Easy to look after*
- *Loyal family pet*
- *Great sense of fun*
- *Good watchdog*

Take heed
- *Prone to disc trouble—don't let it jump, or get overweight*
- *Self-willed*
- *Slightly aggressive with strangers if unchecked*

The Dachshund (or Teckel) was bred as a badger hound in its native Germany. Badger hunting required a short-legged hound with a keen sense of smell, coupled with courage and gameness; a dog that could burrow — an ability which, if unchecked, today's pet Dachshund will demonstrate in your garden.

Some dachshunds are still bred as hunting dogs and will bravely tackle an opponent larger than themselves, such as the badger. They would also defend their own until death. However, their role nowadays is mainly as a companion. They like children, but can be a little aggressive with strangers if unchecked. They are affectionate, full of fun and, despite their short legs, can cope with as much exercise as you can give them. They have a large bark for their size and are good watchdogs.

Size
Long-haired, Smooth-haired and Wire-haired: ideal weight 10lb (4.5kg). It is most important that judges should not award a prize to any dog exceeding 11lb (5kg) in weight. It is also important that owners do not allow dachshunds to become overweight.

Below: These Smooth-haired Miniature Dachshund pups are full of fun and will make excellent pets.

Exercise
Regular exercise is important as the tendency to put on weight must be discouraged. This doesn't mean you should take your Dachsie on 10 mile (16km) treks every day, but short, frequent walks are a must with plenty of runs in a fenced garden or yard.

Grooming
The Dachshund's coat is easy to keep in condition. The Smooth-haired needs only a few minutes' attention every few days with a hound glove and soft cloth. A stiff-bristled brush and comb should be used on the Long-haired and Wire-haired varieties.

Feeding
About 5-7oz (142-198g) of a branded, meaty product with biscuit added in equal part by volume, or 1 cupful of a dry complete food, mixed in the proportion of 1 cup of feed to ½ cup of hot or cold water.

Origin and history
The Dachshund was bred as a badger hound, or hunting dog, and is known to have existed prior to the sixteenth-century and to have been derived from the oldest breeds of German hunting dog, such as the Bibarhund.

In 1840 the first volume of the *Deutscher Hunde-Stammbuch*, an all-breed stud book, was published. It contained the names of 54 types of Dachshund, but it did not always provide complete pedigrees or coat-length notations for the Dachshund. Thirty-nine years later a standard for the Dachshund was established, and in 1888 the German Dachshund Club or Deutscher Teckelklub was founded.

Today there are three varieties, with miniatures of each type: the Smooth-haired, Wire-haired and Long-haired. The Wire-haired Dachshund arose through crossing with the Scottish Dandie Dinmont and other terriers, the Long-haired by crossing the Smooth-haired with the spaniel and an old German gundog, the Stöberhund.

Both bandiness, due to a

Above: Long-haired Miniature Dachshunds are well mannered, friendly and good with children.

weakness in the tendons, and exaggerated length have now been eradicated.

In his book *The Dachshund* (*Popular Dogs*), the late Eric Fitch Dalglish refers to the severe blow dealt to dog breeding in the United Kingdom and elsewhere, during World War I. 'All breeds were affected,' he writes, 'but none, perhaps, so tragically as the Dachshund'. Ever since its appearance among us the little Teckel had been recognized as the national dog of the Teutonic Empire, and with the outbreak of hostilities it came in for a share of the scorn heaped on everything made in Germany. This sad state of affairs continued in the United Kingdom and other parts of Europe during World War II, when dachshunds were unfairly discarded, shouted at and even stoned in the streets because of their German ancestry. Happily this behaviour is now long past and the sporty, lovable Dachshund has come again to the fore in popularity polls.

The miniatures, like the standards, were also introduced for a purpose. Towards the end of the nineteenth century, German sportsmen required a hound to go to ground after rabbits. Some were produced by chance, the smaller, weaker members of a litter, but there also appears to have been a miniature type, known as the Kaninchenteckel, which was intentionally produced by mating lightweight dachshunds to toy terriers or pinschers. The early miniatures aparently had little of the quality of the show Dachshund about them, but selective breeding produced a far better type — for many years known as the dwarf Teckel — but with the shallow chest, short head and full eye that had characterized its predecessor.

SHOW STANDARD
(all three varieties)
General appearance. In conformation the Miniature Dachshund should be in all respects similar to the Dachshund of standard size: compact, short-legged and long in body, well muscled and strong with a bold and intelligent expression. The body should be neither so plump as to give an impression of cobbiness nor so slender as to

impart a weasel-like appearance. Height at shoulder should be half the length of the body measured from the breast bone to the base of the tail, and the girth of the chest double the height at the shoulder. The length from the tip of the nose to the eyes should equal the length from eyes to base of skull.

Colour. Any colour. No white is permissible except for a small spot on the breast and even this is undesirable. The nose should be black except in dapples and chocolates, in which it may be flesh-coloured or brown. In all cases the coat colour should be bright and clearly defined. In black and tans, the tan should be rich and sharp. Dapples should be free from large unbroken patches, the dappling being evenly distributed over the whole body.

Head and skull. Long and conical when seen from above, sharp in profile and finely modelled. Skull neither too broad nor too narrow, only slightly arched and without prominent stop. Foreface long and narrow, finely modelled. The lips should be tightly drawn but well covering the lower jaw, neither heavy nor too sharply cut away. The corners of the mouth slightly marked.

Tail. Set on fairly high, not too long, tapering and without too marked a curve. It should not be carried too high and never curled over the back.

Feet. Broad and large in proportion to the size of the dog, straight or

Above: The Wire-haired Dachshund, most recent of the varieties, has a strong coat for hunting through undergrowth.

turned only slightly outwards. The hindfeet smaller than the fore. Toes close together and with each toe well arched. Nails strong. The dog must stand equally on all parts of the foot. The whole should be poised equally on the ball of the foot, not merely on the toes.

The Smooth-haired Miniature Dachshund has achieved consistently high ratings in the show ring because of its self-confidence and gay, lively manner. It is also very popular around the world as a pet dog, especially for people living in small apartments.

Smooth-haired Miniature Dachshund

Long-haired Miniature Dachshund

The coat of the Wire-haired Miniature Dachsund is evenly short and harsh with a dense, soft under-coat to keep out the cold and rain.

Wire-haired Miniature Dachshund

NORFOLK TERRIER

Good points
- *Adaptable to most life-styles*
- *Equable temperament*
- *Fearless*
- *Good with children*
- *Hardy*
- *Lovable*

Take heed
- *No drawbacks known*

The Norfolk Terrier co-existed with the Norwich Terrier for more than a century until, in 1932, it gained recognition by the Kennel Club. There were two distinct types, those with drop ears and those with erect or prick ears. However, in 1964 the British Kennel Club agreed to separate the types, the breed with the drop ears becoming the Norfolk Terrier, the prick-eared variety henceforth being known as the Norwich Terrier. The appearance and size of the breed is otherwise the same. They are gay, hardy little dogs with an equable temperament, adapt well to almost any life-style, and are fearless and sporty. (In the United States the Norfolk Terrier was known as the Norwich Terrier (Drop Ear) until 1 January 1979, when it was officially recognized as a separate breed.)

Size
Ideal height 10in (25cm) at the withers.

Exercise
The Norfolk Terrier will settle for regular walks in a town but is in its element enjoying off-the-lead runs in the countryside. It is adept at ratting and rabbiting.

Grooming
Little grooming or trimming is required.

Feeding
Recommended would be 6-13oz (170-369g) of a branded, meaty product with biscuit added in equal part by volume, or 1½ cups of a dry, complete food, mixed in the proportion of 1 cup of feed to ½ cup of hot or cold water. Increase rations if the terrier is in hard exercise.

Origin and history
These sporty little terriers from the eastern counties of England were once popular with Cambridge students; the dogs were red in colour, rarely weighed more than 10lb (4.5kg) and included both prick-eared and drop-eared varieties. They were shown at dog shows from 1870.

SHOW STANDARD
General appearance. A small, low, keen dog, compact and strong, with a short back, good substance and bone.
Colour. All shades of red, red wheaten, black and tan or grizzle. White marks or patches are undesirable but do not disqualify.

Head and skull. Skull wide and slightly rounded with good width between the ears. Muzzle wedge-shaped and strong; length of muzzle slightly less than half the length of the skull. Stop should be well defined.
Tail. Medium docked, not excessively gay.
Feet. Round, with thick pads.

NORWICH TERRIER

Good points
- *Adaptable to most life-styles*
- *Equable temperament*
- *Fearless*
- *Good with children*
- *Hardy*
- *Lovable*

Take heed
- *No drawbacks known*

Prior to 1964 the Norwich Terrier and the Norfolk Terrier were recognized as just one breed by the Kennel Club. In 1964 the Norwich gained independent status as the prick-eared variety of the two. Its appearance and characteristics are otherwise identical with its Norfolk kin. In the USA both prick-eared and drop-eared varieties were known as the Norwich Terrier until 1 January 1979, when separate breeds were recognized.

Size
Ideal height 10in (25cm) at the withers; this ideal height must not be attained by excessive length of leg.

Exercise
The Norwich Terrier will settle for regular walks in a town but is in its element enjoying off-the-lead runs in the countryside. It is adept at ratting and rabbiting.

Below: Norfolk Terriers enjoying a good scamper by the river.

Grooming
Little grooming or trimming is required.

Feeding
Recommended would be 6-13oz (170-369g) of a branded, meaty product with biscuit added in equal part by volume, or 1½ cups of a dry, complete food, mixed in the proportion of 1 cup of feed to ½ cup of hot or cold water. Increase rations if the terrier is in hard exercise.

Origin and history
There is some controversy as to whether Colonel Vaughan of Ballybrick, Ireland, or Mr Jodrell Hopkins, a horse dealer from Trumpington, England, deserves credit for founding the Norwich Terrier breed.

Colonel Vaughan hunted in the 1860s with a pack of small red terriers that had evolved from the Irish Terrier. As there were many outcrosses, terriers with drop and prick ears came about, and breeders tended to crop the ears of the drop-eared animals until the practice became illegal. When it did, the Norwich Terrier Club protested loudly about the admittance of the drop-eared variety; when the breed was recognized by the Kennel Club, the Norwich Terrier Club requested that the standard should call for only those with prick ears.

Mr Jodrell Hopkins owned a bitch, a number of whose pups came into the hands of his employee, Frank Jones. Mr Jones crossed them with other terriers, including the Irish and the Glen of Imaal terriers, using only small examples of these breeds; the progeny were known as 'Jones' or 'Trumpington' terriers. There is a breeder today who claims a direct line from Mr Jones' dogs.

The Norwich is a breed that has not been spoilt; for, perhaps surprisingly, it has — in common with the Norfolk — never gained immense popularity.

SHOW STANDARD
General appearance. A small, low, keen dog, compact and strong, with good substance and bone. Excessive trimming is not desirable. Honourable scars from fair wear and tear should not be penalized unduly.
Colour. All shades of red, wheaten, black and tan and grizzle. White marks or patches are undesirable.

Above: The Norwich Terrier can prick up its ears when aroused.

Head and skull. Muzzle 'foxy' and strong, length about one-third less than the measurement from the occiput to the bottom of the stop, which should be well defined. Skull wide (good width between the ears) and slightly rounded.
Body. Moderately short, compact and deep with a level topline. The ribs should be well sprung, and the loins should be short. The distance from the top of the withers to the ground should be equal to the distance from the withers to the base of the tail.
Tail. Medium docked, set on high to complete a perfectly level back, and carried erect.
Feet. Round, with thick pads.

The Norfolk and Norwich terriers, among the smallest of the terriers, are remarkably strong and sturdy for their size. They are fearless working dogs, being originally bred to hunt rats, rabbits, foxes and even badgers. They are, nevertheless, not quarrelsome and have a lovable disposition.

Norfolk Terrier

The hard, wiry coat of the Norfolk and Norwich terriers lies close to the body and has a thick protective under-coat.

Norwich Terrier

SHIH TZU
(Chrysanthemum Dog)

Good points
● *Adores human company*
● *Affectionate*
● *Hardy*
● *Intelligent*
● *Loves children and other animals*
● *Suitable for town or country*

Take heed
● *Best to tie back the topknot with a bow, or your pet could develop eye trouble*

The Shih Tzu is a happy and attractive little house-pet which adores human company and hates to be neglected. It is extremely intelligent, arrogant, and looks forward to the long, daily grooming sessions for which time must be allocated if you decide to buy this delightful breed.

Size
Weight 10-18lb (4.5-8.2kg); ideally 10-16lb (4.5-7.3kg). Height at the withers not more than 10½in (26.5cm).

Exercise
Short, regular walks and off-the-lead runs.

Grooming
Daily brushing with a pure bristle brush. Do not neglect this task or combing out tangles will be painful. Keep the topknot from getting into the eyes and take care that the ears are free of matted hair or other objects.

Feeding
Six-13oz (170-369g) of a branded, meaty product with biscuit added in equal part by volume, or 1½ cupfuls of a dry, complete food mixed in the proportion of 1 cup of feed to ½ cup of hot or cold water.

Origin and history
The Lhasa Apso was highly prized by the Dalai Lama of Tibet, who would habitually give prized specimens to emperors of China. It is likely that the Chinese may have crossed the Apso with the Pekingese to develop the Shih Tzu. As with the Imperial Pekingese, export of the Shih Tzu from China was forbidden, and it was not until the death of Empress Tzu-hsi in 1908 that the little shaggy dogs were smuggled out to Europe.

SHOW STANDARD
General appearance. Very active, lively and alert with a distinctly arrogant carriage. The Shih Tzu is neither a terrier nor a toy dog.
Colour. All colours permissible, but a white blaze on the forehead and a white tip to the tail are highly prized. Dogs with liver markings may have dark liver noses and slightly lighter eyes. Pigmentation on muzzle as unbroken as possible.
Head and skull. Head broad and round, wide between the eyes. Shock-headed with hair falling well over the eyes. Good beard and whiskers; the hair growing upwards

Above: Two beautiful looking Shih Tzus. These popular show dogs revel in looking good; their owners must revel in grooming.

on the nose gives a distinctly chrysanthemum-like effect. Muzzle square and short, but not wrinkled like a Pekingese; flat and hairy. Nose black for preference and about 1in (2.5cm) from tip to stop.
Tail. Heavily plumed and curled well over back; carried gaily.
Feet. Firm and well padded. They should look big on account of the wealth of hair.

LHASA APSO

Good points
● *Affectionate*
● *Confident*
● *Good with children*
● *Hardy*
● *Suitable for town or country*

Take heed
● *Needs lots of grooming*
● *Not keen on strangers*

The Lhasa Apso, like the Tibetan Terrier and Tibetan Spaniel, comes from the mountains of Tibet. It is a shaggy little dog, rather like an Old English Sheepdog in miniature, and makes an excellent pet. The only possible drawback is its natural suspicion of strangers.

Size
Ideal height: 10in (25cm) at the shoulder for dogs; bitches should be slightly smaller.

Exercise
This lively breed needs plenty of walks and off-the-lead runs.

Grooming
Brushing and combing daily — and not for a few minutes only.

Feeding
Six-13oz (170-369g) of a branded, meaty product with biscuit added in

equal part by volume, or 1½ cupfuls of a dry, complete food, mixed in the proportion of 1 cup of feed to ½ cup of hot or cold water.

Origin and history
This is the dog that the Dalai Lama of Tibet offered to the Chinese emperors. It existed for centuries in the Tibetan mountains until brought to Europe and elsewhere by early explorers and missionaries. The words 'lhasa apso' mean 'goat-like' and it was perhaps as guard and protector of the wild goats of Tibet that this glamorous breed of today first found favour.

SHOW STANDARD
General appearance. The Apso should give the appearance of a well-balanced, solid dog: gay and assertive but chary of strangers. Free and jaunty in movement.
Colour. Golden, sandy, honey, dark grizzle, slate, smoke, parti-colour, black, white or brown.
Head and skull. Heavy head

furnishings with good fall over the eyes, good whiskers and beard. Skull moderately narrow, falling away behind the eyes in a marked degree; not quite flat but not domed or apple-shaped. Straight foreface with medium stop. Nose black. Muzzle about 1½in (4cm) long, not square; the length from tip of nose to be roughly one-third the total length from nose to back of skull.
Body. Distance from point of shoulders to point of buttocks should be longer than distance from height of withers to the ground.
Tail. High set, carried well over back and not like a pot-hook. There is often a kink at the end. Well feathered.
Feet. Round and cat-like with good pads. Well feathered.

Below: A Lhasa Apso with pup. A glamorous show exhibit, this breed also makes an excellent pet — albeit one that is not keen on strangers.

The Shih Tzu was first seen in the United Kingdom in 1931 but it was not until 1940 that the breed was registered separately from the Lhasa Apso. The breed arrived in America in 1938 and was given show classification in the Toy Group on 1 September 1969.

Shih Tzu

Lhasa Apso

The Lhasa Apso is the most recent of the Tibetan dogs to become known in the Western world: it was first exhibited in London in 1929.

BEDLINGTON TERRIER

Good points
- Adores children
- Always keeps its figure
- Good family pet
- Well behaved

Take heed
- Formidable fighter if provoked

The Bedlington Terrier is an attractive, hardy little dog that resembles a shorn lamb. It is a dog whose dainty appearance and love of children belies its first-rate watchdog qualities. It is also a breed that trains easily, and a number have been used successfully in obedience competitions.

Size
Height should be about 16in (40.5cm) at the shoulder, allowing slight variation below in the case of a bitch and above in the case of a dog. Weight should be 18-23lb (8.2-10.4kg).

Exercise
The Bedlington, like most terriers, is a lively, inquisitive breed and will enjoy an off-the-lead run or energetic ball game. It will, however, adapt very happily to apartment life as long as it is given regular, adequate walks.

Grooming
This breed's coat does not shed, which makes it a boon for the house proud. The dead hairs stay in the coat until they are combed out.

The Bedlington should be trimmed regularly (otherwise the coat will become tangly) and given a good brushing frequently with a fairly stiff brush. Do not bath the animal too often or this may weaken its coat. Hair should be removed from inside the dog's ears fairly regularly, which can be done quite simply by pulling the hair with finger and thumb or a pair of tweezers.

Feeding
Recommended would be 9-13oz (255-369g) of a branded, meaty product with biscuit added in equal part by volume, or 1½ cupfuls of a dry food, complete diet, mixed in the proportion of 1 cup of feed to ½ cup of hot or cold water.

Origin and history
It is possible that the Greyhound or Whippet played some part in the origin of the Bedlington Terrier, and the soft topknot gives strength to the suggestion that it may share common ancestry with the Dandie Dinmont Terrier. Certainly a strain of similar terriers existed with tinkers in Rothbury Forest, Northumberland, in the eighteenth century; and in 1820 a Mr J. Howe came to Bedlington, Northumberland, with a bitch named 'Phoebe'. This bitch was given to a man called Joseph Ainsley, who mated 'Phoebe' to a dog named 'Old Piper', producing 'Young Piper', the first dog with the new name 'Bedlington' Terrier. From

that time, 1825, a systematic breeding of the Bedlington began. The breed was shown in the ring during the 1860s and the first Bedlington Terrier Club was formed in 1875.

SHOW STANDARD
General appearance. A graceful, lithe, muscular dog, with no sign of either weakness or coarseness.
Colour. Blue, blue and tan, liver or sandy. Darker pigment to be encouraged.
Head and skull. Skull narrow, but deep and rounded; covered with a profuse silky topknot that should be nearly white. Jaw long and tapering. There must be no stop.
Tail. Of moderate length, thick at the root, tapering to a point and gracefully curved. Should be set on low, and must never be carried over the back.
Feet. Long hare feet with thick and well-closed-up pads.

MINIATURE POODLE

Good points
- Affectionate
- Dainty and appealing
- Excellent retriever
- Good sense of fun
- Intelligent
- Long-lived
- Useful in obedience competitions

Take heed
- Noisy if unchecked
- Perhaps not the best choice of child's pet
- Sensitive

The Poodle has a character full of fun. It is intelligent, obedient and has even proved a useful competitor in obedience competitions. It has a fondness for water, if the owner permits, but is much favoured for the show ring where, exhibited in the traditional lion clip, it is a beauty to behold.

Size
Height at shoulder should be under 15in (38cm) but not under 11in (28cm), (United States 10in).

Exercise
The Poodle will enjoy a ball game in the garden, practising obedience exercises or trotting beside you in the park. The miniature variety is a good choice for the apartment dweller.

Grooming
Use a wire-pin pneumatic brush and a wire-toothed metal comb for regular grooming. The lion clip is an essential for the show ring, but pet owners generally resort to the more natural lamb clip with the hair a short, uniform length. It is possible to clip your own dog with a pair of hairdresser's scissors. However, if despite the help which usually is available from the breeder you find the task tedious, there are numerous pet and poodle parlours to which you should take your dog every six weeks. Bath regularly.

Feeding
As for Bedlington Terrier.

Health care
Fanciers will confirm that the Standard Poodle is the soundest of the varieties. It is possible to acquire healthy Toy and Miniature stock, but care should be taken to purchase from a breeder who puts quality ahead of daintiness. Watch out for signs of ear trouble, nervousness or joint malformations. Teeth need regular scaling. Nonetheless, a 16-year-old Poodle is not a rarity.

Origin and history
The Poodle was originally a shaggy guard, a retriever and protector of sheep. Its origins are similar to the Irish Water Spaniel and, no doubt, they have a common ancestor in the French Barbet and Hungarian Water Hound.

The Poodle may not be, as many suppose, solely of French origin. It originated in Germany as a water retriever; even the word poodle comes from the German 'pudelnass' or 'puddle', and from this fairly large sturdy dog, the Standard Poodle, the Miniature and the Toy have evolved.

The breed has been known in England since Prince Rupert of the Rhine, in company with his Poodle, came to the aid of Charles I in battle. The breed was favoured also by Marie Antoinette who, rumour has it, invented the lion clip by devising a style that would match the uniform of her courtiers.

SHOW STANDARD
As for Toy Poodle.

PUG

Good points
- Manageable size
- Happy disposition
- Good with children
- Affectionate
- Intelligent

Take heed
- Overfeeding will result in a gross, short-lived dog rather than an elegant, healthy companion
- The Pug's breathing apparatus isn't all it might be, so owners must guard against vigorous exertion and overheating in warm weather

The Pug is a gay little dog that looks extremely elegant if not allowed to indulge its inherent passion for food. It makes a charming family pet and an amusing, devoted, impish companion.

Size
The weight should be 14-18lb (6.4-8.2kg), but if allowed to over-indulge the Pug will eat itself out of the toy dog category.

Exercise
An energetic dog, the Pug will relish more exercise than many breeds of similar size. But remember that gluttony and a tendency to over-weight go hand in hand, as will

fatness and lethargy if the animal's greed is indulged.

Grooming
A frequent brushing should be sufficient.

Feeding
About 6-9oz (170-255g) of a branded dog food with biscuit added in equal part by volume; or 1 cupful of a dry food, complete diet, mixed in the proportion of 1 cup of feed to ½ cup of warm water.

Origin and history
Pugs originated at least 2,500 years ago in the Orient, where these rascally looking dogs were favourites in the Buddhist monasteries in Tibet, the earliest known source of the breed. From China, Pugs matriculated to Japan and then to Europe. They were fawned over by members of the royal court wherever they went.

After a Pug had saved the life of William, Prince of Orange by warning of the approach of the Spaniards at Hermingny in 1572, Pugs became the official dogs of the House of Orange. Thus, several Pugs were included in William II's retinue when he landed at Torbay to be crowned King of England.

Soon afterwards the breed became particularly fashionable in England and then in France, where Josephine's Pug Fortune is said to have bitten the future emperor Napoleon when he entered the bedchamber on his wedding night.

An irresistible and stalwart little dog that meets life head on, the Pug sports its own motto — 'Multum in Parvo' — which means 'a lot of dog in a small space'.

SHOW STANDARD
General appearance. A decidedly square and cobby dog that is characterized by compactness of form, well-knit proportions and hardness of developed muscle.

A lean, leggy Pug or one that has short legs and a long body are equally objectionable.
Colour. Silver, apricot, or fawn with an intensely coloured black mask and a somewhat less intensely coloured black trace down the spine. There should be a distinct and obvious contrast between the body colour and the facial mask and trace. Pugs also come in black, which should be a deep, even black all over.
Head and skull. Head large, massive, round — not apple-headed — with no indentation of the skull. Muzzle short, blunt, square but not upfaced. Wrinkles large and deep.
Body. Short and cobby. The chest should be wide, the ribs well sprung, and the legs well under. Proper lay back of shoulder is critical to the proper alignment of the front legs.
Tail (Twist). Curled as tightly as possible over the hip. The double curl is perfection.
Feet. Neither so long as the foot of a hare, nor so round as that of a cat; well-split-up toes; the nails should be black.

The Bedlington Terrier is a more robust and lively dog than its elegance suggests. When roused, the eyes should sparkle and the dog look full of temper and courage. Bedlingtons are capable of galloping at great speed and should have the appearance of being able to do so. This action is very distinctive; rather mincing, light and springy in the slower paces, and could have a slight roll when in full stride. When galloping, the animal should use the whole of its body.

Bedlington Terrier

Miniature Poodle
(Lamb clip)

The Pug shares the foolhardiness of the Chihuahua, and certain other Toy breeds, in believing that attack is the best form of defence. Like the Bulldog, the Pug also has a tendency to snore and to pant heavily in warm weather or during vigorous exercise.

Pug

BORDER TERRIER

Good points
- Good natured
- Handy size
- Hardy
- Reliable
- Sporty working dog
- Unspoilt breed

Take heed
- Needs space for exercise

The Border Terrier is the smallest of the working terriers. It is a natural breed that evolved in the Border counties of England and Scotland, where its task was to worry foxes from their lair. It is a hardy, unspoilt dog with an equable temperament, and it usually gets on well with other animals.

Size
Weight: dog 13-15½lb (5.9-7kg); bitch 11½-14lb (5.2-6.4kg).

Exercise
The Border Terrier has immense vitality and is able to keep pace with a horse. It is unfair to keep one unless you can give it adequate exercise.

Grooming
The coat needs a little trimming to tidy up for the show ring but otherwise requires the minimum of grooming.

Feeding
Recommended would be 6-13oz (170-369g) of a branded, meaty product with biscuit added in equal part by volume, or 1½ cups of a dry food, complete diet, mixed in the proportion of 1 cup of feed to ½ cup of hot or cold water. Increase rations if the terrier is in hard exercise.

Origin and history
The Border Terrier was derived in the Border counties of England and Scotland in the middle of the nineteenth century, when it was the practice to produce a terrier tailor-made for the task it would perform. Sportsmen wanted a hardy dog able to run with hounds and bolt the fox from its lair.

The Border Terrier with its otter-like head still works with hounds and has been less changed to meet the dictates of the show ring than almost any other breed. It was first recognized by the Kennel Club in 1920.

SHOW STANDARD
Colour. Red, wheaten, grizzle and tan or blue and tan.
Head and skull. Head like that of an otter, moderately broad skull, with a short, strong muzzle. A black nose is preferable but a liver or flesh-coloured one is not a serious fault.
Tail. Moderately short and fairly thick at the base, then tapering; set high and carried gaily but not curled over the back.
Feet. Small with thick pads. The feet should be compact.

AUSTRALIAN TERRIER

Good points
- Courageous
- Devoted to children
- Hardy
- Keen, alert watchdog

Take heed
- No drawbacks known

The Australian Terrier is a loyal and devoted dog, game, hardy and utterly reliable with toddlers. It is an exceptionally alert watchdog but, having given the alarm, is more likely to kill intruders with kindness. It makes an excellent companion, and its alertness and speed combine to make it an excellent ratter. The Aussie's coat is weather resistant.

Size
Average weight about 10-11lb (4.5-5kg) — in Australia, approximately 14lb (6.4kg). In both the United Kingdom and Australia, the desired height is approximately 10in (25cm) at the withers. (The desired UK weight seems to be changing in line with that of the Australian Kennel Club.)

Exercise
This is an active and keen scenting dog with the skill and courage to hunt and attack food for itself. Nowadays it is rarely asked to use these abilities, but it should have the opportunity to unleash its energy with regular walks and off-the-lead scampers. Nonetheless, it will adapt to apartment living.

Grooming
Regular grooming with a bristle brush will stimulate the skin and encourage a good coat growth.

If you are planning to show your Aussie, bath it at least a fortnight before the show; but during spring and summer, when show dates may be close together, don't bath on each occasion, as frequent washing will soften the coat.

Feeding
About 6-10oz (170-283g) of a branded, meaty product with biscuit added in equal part by volume, or 1 cupful of a complete, dry food, mixed in the proportion of 1 cup of feed to ½ cup of hot or cold water.

Origin and history
First exhibited in Australia between 1868 and 1876, the Australian Terrier was also known as the Broken-haired Terrier, the Rough-haired Terrier and the Australian Rough. As its sundry names suggest, the Australian Terrier is a melting pup of different breeds. The old Scotch Terrier, the Dandie Dinmont, the Irish Terrier, the Black and Tan (known today as the Manchester Terrier) and the prick-eared Skye Terrier are thought by various observers to have made their contributions to the Australian Terrier's development.

The first Australian Terrier club was formed in Melbourne in 1889.

The Aussie was granted breed status in the United Kingdom in 1933 and was admitted to the American Kennel Club's registry in the United States in 1960.

SHOW STANDARD
General appearance. A rather low-set dog, compact and active.
Colour. First choice, blue- or silver-grey body, tan colour on legs and face (the richer the tan the better), with a topknot of blue or silver. Second choice, clear sandy or red with a soft topknot.
Head and skull. Head should be long, skull flat and full between the eyes with a soft topknot; long powerful jaw, nose black.
Tail. Docked.
Feet. Clean, small and well padded with no tendency to spread. Black toenails.

CAIRN TERRIER

Good points
- Intelligent
- Adaptable
- Hardy
- Gay disposition
- Family companion

Take heed
- A bundle of energy; needs the opportunity to release it occasionally

The game little Cairn Terrier comes from Inverness in Scotland. Although a popular show dog elsewhere, it is still in Scotland that the Cairn really comes into its own as a family pet. Indeed, when I lived in a Scottish village during World War II, it seemed as if every villager was the proud possessor of a perky Cairn Terrier.

The Gaelic word 'cairn' means 'a heap of stones' and is therefore a most suitable name for a terrier that goes to ground. The Cairn is an affectionate, sporty little dog with an almost rain-resistant coat. Very active and rarely stubborn, it makes an ideal family companion.

Size
Weight: 14lb (6.4kg).

Exercise
The Cairn is an energetic dog and an expert killer of rodents. It is in its element trotting with its owner across the fields or playing a lively ballgame with children. It will adapt to controlled walks on the lead and sedate town living, as long as it has a good-sized garden in which to romp.

Grooming
The Cairn is an easy dog to groom or, indeed, to prepare for the show ring, as it is presented in a 'natural' condition. It should be brushed and combed and have any excess feathering removed from behind the front legs and the tail. Any long hairs about the ears and on the underside should also be removed for tidiness.

Feeding
Small terriers do well on 10oz (283g) of branded dog food supplemented with a handful of dog biscuits.

The Cairn is not a greedy dog and may prefer to have two small meals each day, rather than receiving its rations all in one go. It also enjoys the occasional large dog biscuit to chew — as many another breed does, too.

Origin and history
It is a matter of historical record that James VI of Scotland (James I of England) ordered from Edinburgh half-a-dozen 'earth dogs or terriers' to be sent as a present to France. These, it is believed, were forerunners of the present-day Cairn, suggesting that more than 300 years ago a working terrier of this type was used for killing vermin in Scotland. Indeed, Mr J.W.H. Beynon in his work The Popular Cairn Terrier, says that every Highland chieftain in ancient days had his pack of hounds and terriers, the latter being used to bolt the foxes, badgers and smaller fur-bearing vermin. He also writes that as far as he could learn, the oldest known strain of Cairns is that founded by the late Captain MacLeod of Drynoch, Isle of Skye, which goes back well over 150 years.

Mr John MacDonald, who for over 40 years was gamekeeper to the Macleod of Macleod, Denvegan Castle, kept this strain alive for many years. At that time the Cairn was known as a Short-haired Skye Terrier. Incidentally, interbreeding of the Cairn with the West Highland, or 'Westie', was permitted until 1924.

The Cairn Terrier became very popular during the 1930s when it was much favoured by members of the British royal family.

SHOW STANDARD
General appearance. Active, game, hardy and 'shaggy' in appearance; strong, and compactly built. Should stand well forward on its forepaws. Strong quarters, deep in ribs. Very free in movement. Coat hard enough to resist rain. Head small but in proportion to body. A foxy appearance is the chief characteristic of this working terrier.
Colour. Red, sandy, grey, brindled or nearly black. Dark points such as ears and muzzle are very typical.
Head and skull. Skull broad in proportion; strong but not too long or heavy a jaw. A decided indentation between the eyes; hair should be full on the forehead. Muzzle powerful but not heavy. Very strong jaw, which should be neither undershot nor overshot.
Body. That of a strong, well-muscled, active dog. The ribs, in addition to being well sprung, should be coupled to strong hindquarters. The medium-length back should be level and should give the impression of strength and activity without giving the appearance of being heavy.
Tail. Short, well furnished with hair but not feathery; carried gaily but should not turn down towards back.
Feet. Forefeet, larger than hind, may be slightly turned out. Pads should be thick and strong. Thin, ferrety feet are objectionable.

The Border Terrier is essentially a working terrier. It should be able to follow a horse and should combine activity with gameness. The coat is harsh and dense with a close under-coat that will keep out the cold and wet when the dog is running down a fox in thick undergrowth. The breed also makes a fine pet, being particularly good with children.

Border Terrier

The Australian Terrier is supposed to have a hard-bitten appearance; exhibitors should not brush the hair on the muzzle forwards as this gives the dog a Yorkshire Terrier appearance, quite wrong for this breed.

Australian Terrier

Cairn Terrier

The Cairn Terrier is traditionally a hardy and game working dog. Cairn Terrier clubs throughout the world have made it their aim to preserve the essential nature of the breed and to resist passing fashions in the show ring that may begin to erode its unique qualities as a sporting terrier.

IRISH TERRIER

Good points
- Alert and loyal protector
- Courageous
- Good with children
- Not as snappy as most terriers

Take heed
- Can be a prodigious fighter

To describe the Irish Terrier as a dog that looks like a small Airedale with a self-coloured yellow coat would far from satisfy the many lovers of this ancient and most attractive breed. We have today in the Irish a fine watchdog, a loyal protector and a most excellent family pet. Its only drawback is its somewhat exaggerated reputation for fighting other dogs. True to its terrier blood it is tremendously courageous, and stories of faithfulness to its master are legion.

Size
The most desirable weight in show condition is: dog 27lb (12.3kg); bitch 25lb (11.3kg). Height at the shoulders should be approximately 18in (46cm).

Exercise
The Irish Terrier is a sporty little dog that has been trained successfully to the gun and is first-class at destroying vermin. It has also been a creditable performer in obedience competitions. It will, however, adapt happily to life as a household pet provided it has a garden to romp in and is taken for regular walks and given plentiful off-the-lead runs.

Grooming
Like the Airedale, the Irish Terrier will need hand stripping several times a year, and it is best to have this done professionally — at least until you have learned the knack. An inexperienced attempt at stripping could prove a painful experience for the dog and even do some harm to its temperament. Some owners resort to clipping, and this is excusable with an elderly animal but causes loss of colour and condition. Normally, a frequent brushing will suffice to keep this healthy, hardy dog in smart condition.

Feeding
Recommended would be 13-20oz (369-587g) of a branded, meaty product with biscuit added in equal part by volume, or 1¾-3 cupfuls of·a dry, complete food, mixed in the proportion of 1 cup of feed to ½ cup of hot or cold water. This breed will appreciate a big bonemeal type biscuit as an additional treat.

Origin and history
Irish sources say that the Irish Terrier was established in the country even before the arrival of their patron saint, St Patrick. Some go so far as to say that the Irish Terrier is a smaller version of another of their national dogs, the Irish Wolfhound; but the relationship seems somewhat remote. It is more likely that the Irish Terrier is a

descendant of the Black and Tan Wire-haired Terrier whose purpose was to hunt fox and destroy vermin in the United Kingdom 200 years ago. Study of the Welsh and Lakeland terriers shows the similarity between the breeds, and it would certainly seem that all have the old Black and Tan Terrier as a common ancestor. It is said that in the area around County Cork in Ireland a large Wheaten Terrier existed that could have been the forerunner of the Irish Terrier and also have contributed to the evolution of the Welsh and Lakeland terriers.

The standard breeding of the Irish Terrier did not take place until 1879, before which there was considerable variation of type, size and colour; it is said that the Irish Terrier in Antrim was black, brown and white, whereas those in Whitley were of a reddish colour and those in Kerry were black or black/brown. In 1879 a specialist breed club was formed, and in the following years the Irish Terrier in its present form and colour became tremendously popular.

It is perhaps worth mentioning that many enthusiasts insist that a terrier similar to the Irish was included in Noah's famous ark.

These dogs were used as messengers in World War I. There is a tale about Ordinary Seaman Foc's'le, a nautical terrier on a Canadian destroyer in the Atlantic during World War II, who raised the alarm when an enemy submarine was not picked up by the ship's instruments and kept the crew going during the engagement with barks of encouragement.

The Irish Terrier Club was the first body in the British Isles to bring about the banishment of the practice of cropping dogs' ears. Unfortunately, this practice has yet to be outlawed in the United States, which generally lags behind the United Kingdom in matters pertaining to animal rights and welfare.

In addition to his exploits in the twin sports of war and hunting, the Irish Terrier exhibits the flair of a born showman. As intrepid looking in the ring as in the field, the Irish Terrier has been called 'the D'Artagnan of the show ring'.

SHOW STANDARD
General appearance. The dog must present an active, lively, lithe and wiry appearance with lots of susbtance, but at the same time it should be free of clumsiness, as speed and endurance, as well as power, are esential. They must be neither cloddy nor cobby, but should be framed on the lines of speed, showing a graceful racing outline.
Colour. Should be self-coloured, the most preferable colours being a bright red, red wheaten or yellow red. White sometimes apears on the chest and feet and is more objectionable on the latter than on the former, as a speck of white on the chest is frequently to be seen in all self-coloured breeds.
Head and skull. Head long; skull flat and rather narrow·between the ears, getting slightly narrower

towards the eye; free from wrinkles; stop hardly visible except in profile. The jaw must be strong and muscular, but not too full in the cheek, and of a good punishing length. The nose must be black.
Tail. Generally docked to about three-quarters; should be free of fringe or feather but well covered with rough hair, set on pretty high, carried gaily but not over the back or curled.
Feet. Should be strong, tolerably round and moderately small, toes arched and turned neither out nor in; black toenails are desirable. Pads must be sound and free from cracks or horny excrescences.

SHETLAND SHEEPDOG

Good points
- Beautiful
- Intelligent
- Faithful
- Ideal for competitive obedience
- Intuitive

Take heed
- May be wary of strangers

The Shetland Sheepdog is the perfect Rough Collie in miniature, a handy size for the owner who feels, perhaps, that the Rough Collie is too large for his home.

The Sheltie is a good family dog. A little wary of strangers, it does not take kindly to being petted by those it does not know. It is faithful, supremely intelligent and generally gives a good account of itself at training classes and in obedience competitions. It is good with horses, and a few are still used as sheepdogs.

Size
Ideal height measured at the withers 14in (35.5cm) for a bitch, 14½in (37cm) for a dog; anything more than 1in (2.5cm) above these heights is considered a serious fault.

Exercise
Provided the Sheltie has a largish garden in which to expend its energy and receives regular daily walks, it will be happy.

Grooming
Not so difficult to keep spick and span as might be believed. Brush regularly with a stiff-bristled brush and use a comb to avoid tangles, particularly behind the ears. Frequent bathing is unnecessary but is advisable when the bitch loses her winter coat. The Sheltie is meticulous about its appearance and you will often find this breed cleaning itself.

Feeding
Thirteen-20oz (369-587g) of a branded, meaty product with biscuit added in equal part by volume, or 1¾-3 cupfuls of a dry food, complete diet, mixed in the proportion of 1 cup of feed to ½ cup of hot or cold water.

Origin and history
The Sheltie originated in the

Shetland Islands off the north coast of Scotland, an area also famous for its tiny Shetland ponies, which, like the Shetland Sheepdog, have been bred with thick coats to protect them against the harsh climate.

The breed has bred true for some 125 years, but controversy at one time existed as to the aims and requirements for which the breed was intended. The ideals of the club formed at Lerwick in 1908 conflicted with the desires of the Shetland Collie Club, whose desire was simply to produce a collie in miniature. Both groups were similarly named. Luckily, agreement was reached in 1914 when the English Shetland Sheepdog Club was formed, and the Sheltie received separate classification by the Kennel Club. Today the breed's popularity is universal.

The first challenge certificate was awarded to the breed in the United Kingdom in 1915. The first specialty for Shelties in the United States was held in 1933.

SHOW STANDARD
General appearance. The Shetland Sheepdog should instantly appeal as a dog of great beauty, intelligence and alertness. Action is lithe and graceful with speed and jumping power great for its size. The outline should be symmetrical so that no part appears out of proportion to the whole. An abundance of coat, mane and frill, with shapliness of head and sweetness of expression, all combine to present the ideal Shetland Sheepdog.
Colour. Tricolours should be an intense black on the body with no signs of ticking, rich tan markings on a tricolour to be preferred. Sables may be clear or shaded, any colour from gold to deep mahogany but in its shade the colour should be rich in tones. Wolf, sable and grey colours are undesirable. In blue merles, a clear silvery blue is desired, splashed and marbled with black. Rich tan markings are preferred, but their absence is not to be counted as a fault. Heavy black markings and a slate-coloured or rusty tinge in either top-coat or under-coat are highly undesirable. The general effect should be blue. White markings may be shown in the blaze, collar, chest frill, legs, stifle and tip of tail. All or some tan markings may be shown on eyebrows, cheeks, legs, stifles and under tail. The nose must be black whatever the colour of the dog might be.
Head and skull. The head should be refined, and its shape when viewed from the top or side is a long blunt wedge tapering from ear to nose. The width of skull necessarily depends upon the combined length of skull and muzzle, and the whole must be considered in connection with the size of the dog.
Tail. Set on low, tapering bone must reach at least to the hock joint, with abundant hair and slight upward sweep.
Feet. Oval; soles well padded; toes arched and close together.

Irish Terrier

The Irish Terrier is a remarkably good tempered breed, notably so with humans. They develop an extra-ordinary devotion for their masters, and have been known to track them almost incredible distances.

The Shetland Sheepdog's eyes are a very important feature, giving expression to the dog. They should be of medium size, obliquely set and of almond shape. The colour is dark brown, except in the case of merles, where blue is permissible.

Shetland Sheepdog

GERMAN HUNT TERRIER
(Deutscher Jagdterrier)

Good points
- *First-class hunter, retriever and gundog*
- *Good traveller*
- *Robust*

Take heed
- *Needs a lot of exercise*
- *Somewhat aggressive*

The German Hunt Terrier is a popular breed in its country of origin. It is also well established in Austria and other German-speaking regions. It has yet, however, to be recognized by the British or American Kennel Clubs. It can be kept as a household pet but is essentially a worker. It needs plenty of exercise and has a somewhat aggressive temperament.

Size
Weight: dog 19½-22lb (8.8-10kg); bitch 16-18lb (7.3-8.2kg). Height at the withers not more than 16in (40cm).

Exercise
Needs plenty of exercise.

Grooming
Frequent brushing is required.

Feeding
Six-13oz (170-369g) of a branded, meaty product with biscuit added in equal part by volume, or ¾-1½ cupfuls of a dry, complete food, mixed in the proportion of 1 cup of feed to ½ cup of hot or cold water.

Origin and history
This is an essentially German breed derived from crossing the English Fox Terrier with the Lakeland and others with a view to creating a hardy, dark-coated terrier. The first results were not encouraging although good working terriers were produced. However, by 1925, a satisfactory German Hunt Terrier had evolved that was able to go to earth and retrieve small game from land or water. It is a courageous dog willing to take on fox and boar as well as rats and small rodents, but it has a somewhat aggressive terrier temperament.

The Association of the German Hunt Terrier has a list of work tests designed specifically for the breed. It accepts for breeding only Hunt Terriers that have achieved high pass marks.

LAKELAND TERRIER

Good points
- *Excellent with children*
- *Fine guard with strong warning bark*
- *Good family dog*
- *Handy medium size*
- *Sporty, but adapts well to home life*

Take heed
- *Might be too lively for the elderly*

The Lakeland Terrier is similar in appearance to the Welsh and Airedale terriers. It makes a first-class family pet, being of sound temperament and convenient size, and is also a fine guard. It has been used in the past for both fox and badger hunting but nowadays is kept mainly as a pet and has, in recent years, been a very successful contender in the show ring.

Size
The average weight of a dog is 17lb (7.7kg), bitch 15lb (6.8kg). The height should not exceed 14½in (37cm) at the shoulder.

Exercise
Unless they choose a toy breed, like the Yorkshire Terrier, people should not choose a terrier unless they want a pet with plenty of zip. The Lakeland Terrier, true to its breed, is gay and fearless, always ready for a walk or a game. It is suitable for apartment living as long as its owner can provide regular exercise and, hopefully, those much loved days out in the country for the off-the-lead runs.

Grooming
Trimming the Lakeland for the show ring requires some skill. Frequent brushing will help keep the coat tidy but, even for a pet, professional stripping in spring, summer and autumn is recommended.

Feeding
Recommended would be 6-13oz (170-369g) of a branded, meaty product with biscuit added in equal part by volume, or ¾-1½ cupfuls of a dry, complete food, mixed in the proportion of 1 cup of feed to ½ cup of hot or cold water.

Below: The compact and sturdy Lakeland Terrier makes a lively pet, for it needs plenty of vigorous exercise to stay in top condition. Originally bred for hunting, the Lakeland Terrier has become a firm favourite in the show ring over the course of many years.

Origin and history
The Lakeland Terrier is among the most ancient of working terrier breeds, having been established long before kennel clubs or official stud books. The Lakeland originated in the Lake District of England, hence its name, but was originally known as the Patterdale Terrier in places where it went to ground working with the local hunts. Although known as a working dog long before, the Lakeland did not make an appearance in the show ring until a breed club was formed in 1932.

SHOW STANDARD
General appearance. Smart and workman-like with gay fearless demeanour.
Colour. Black and tan, blue and tan, red, wheaten, red grizzle, liver, blue or black. Small tips of white on feet and chest do not debar. Mahogany or deep tan is not typical.
Head and skull. Well-balanced. Skull flat and refined. The jaws are powerful and the muzzle should be broad but not too long. The length of the head from the stop to the nose should not exceed that from the occiput to the stop. Nose should be black.
Tail. Well set on, carried gaily but not to curl over the back.
Feet. Small, compact, round and well padded.

WELSH TERRIER

Good points
- *Affectionate*
- *Bold*
- *Good temperament*
- *Great fun*
- *Handy size*
- *Obedient*

Take heed
- *No drawbacks known*

The Welsh Terrier has much in common with the Airedale, Irish and Lakeland terriers and resembles a small Airedale in appearance. It

makes a good household pet, generally has a good temperament, and is affectionate, obedient and great fun.

Size
The height at shoulder should not exceed 15½in (39.5cm). In working condition, 20-21lb (9-9.5kg) is a fair average weight.

Exercise
Regular daily walks and a romp in the garden will suffice, but like most terriers it will appreciate a run in wide open spaces. It was, after all, originally bred to run with a pack of hounds.

Grooming
The Welsh Terrier's coat needs stripping twice yearly and regular brushing to maintain it in show condition, but many pet owners resort to clipping their terriers. The coat is usually left on in winter to provide extra warmth.

Feeding
Thirteen-20oz (369-587g) of a branded, meaty product with biscuit added in equal part by volume, or 1¾-3 cupfuls of a dry food, complete diet, mixed in the proportion of 1 cup of feed to ½ cup of hot or cold water.

Origin and history
The Welsh Terrier — like its close relation, the Irish Terrier — is of Celtic origin. In fact, two strains once existed side by side: that evolved by the Welsh from a purpose-bred, coarse-haired Black and Tan Terrier and an English variety achieved through crossing the Airedale and the Fox Terrier. These two types caused much argument while recognition for the breed was being sought. However, the English variety appears to have died out, and the true Celtic strain was presented in 1885. The Welsh Terrier Club was founded a year later. The following year the Welsh Terrier was awarded championship status by the Kennel Club. The first Welsh Terriers were taken to the United States in 1888, but they were not evident in any real numbers until after 1901.

SHOW STANDARD
Colour. The colour should be black and tan for preference, or black-grizzle and tan, free from black pencilling on the toes. Black below the hocks is a fault.
Head and skull. The skull should be flat and rather wider between the ears than the Wire-haired Fox Terrier. The jaw should be powerful, clean cut, rather deeper and more punishing (giving the head a more masculine appearance) than that usually seen on a Fox Terrier. Stop not too defined, fair length from stop to end of nose, the latter being black.
Body: Should exhibit good substance, a level topline and a strong, moderately short loin. The chest is moderately wide with good depth of brisket.
Tail. The tail should be well set on but not too gaily carried.
Feet. The feet should be small, round and cat-like.

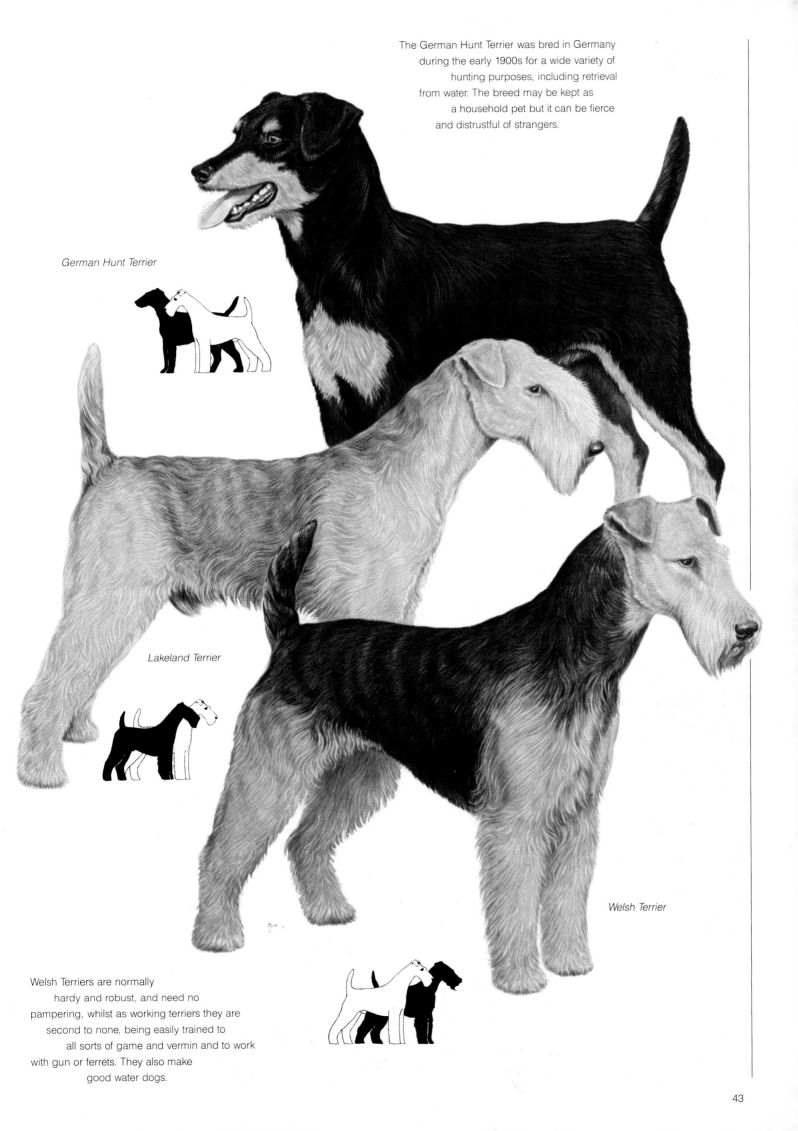

The German Hunt Terrier was bred in Germany during the early 1900s for a wide variety of hunting purposes, including retrieval from water. The breed may be kept as a household pet but it can be fierce and distrustful of strangers.

German Hunt Terrier

Lakeland Terrier

Welsh Terrier

Welsh Terriers are normally hardy and robust, and need no pampering, whilst as working terriers they are second to none, being easily trained to all sorts of game and vermin and to work with gun or ferrets. They also make good water dogs.

STANDARD DACHSHUND

(Variously known as Teckel, Dachel, Dacksel, Badger Hound)

Good points
- *Affectionate*
- *Brave*
- *Easy to look after*
- *Loyal family pet*
- *Sense of fun*
- *Watchdog with loud bark*

Take heed
- *Prone to disc trouble*
- *Self-willed*
- *Slightly aggressive with strangers, if unchecked*

The dachshund (or Teckle) was bred as a badger hound in its native Germany. What was needed was a short-legged hound with a keen sense of smell, coupled with courage and gameness and a dog that could burrow. This ability, if unchecked in today's Dachshund, will play havoc with your garden.

Some Dachshunds are still bred as hunting dogs and will bravely tackle an opponent larger than themselves, such as the badger. They would also defend their master until death. However, their role nowadays is mainly as a companion. They may be a little aggressive with strangers, if unchecked, but are affectionate and full of fun. Despite their short legs they can cope with as much exercise as you can give them. They have a loud bark for their size and are first-class watchdogs.

Size
Long-haired: middle weight up to 18lb (8.2kg) for dogs and 17lb (7.7kg) for bitches.
Smooth-haired: dogs should not exceed 25lb (11.3kg); bitches should not exceed 23lb (10.4kg).
Wire-haired: dogs should weigh 20-22lb (9-10kg) and bitches 18-20lb (8.2-9kg).

Exercise
Regular exercise is important, as the tendency to put on weight must be discouraged. This does not mean you must take your pet on 10 mile (16km) treks, but short, frequent walks are advisable with plenty of runs in a well-fenced garden or yard.

Grooming
The Dachshund's coat is easy to keep in condition. The smooth-coat needs only a few minutes' attention every few days with a hound glove and soft cloth. A stiff-bristled brush and comb should be used on the Long-hair and the Wire-hair.

Health care
Disc trouble can befall the Dachshund because of its long back and stubby little legs. Anyone who has seen a young dog paralysed, while otherwise in good health, will recognize the need to keep their pet's weight within the breed standard and to prevent it from leaping on and off furniture. Treatment varies from injections of

cortisone to an operation; some owners swear by an osteopath.

The Dachshund's teeth are prone to tartar. Regular scaling is recommended, but stains can be removed with a paste of water and cream of tartar, applied with a bit of cotton wool.

Feeding
Suggested would be 10oz (283kg) of a branded, meaty product with biscuit added in equal part by volume, or 1½ cupfuls of a dry food, complete diet, mixed in the proportion of 1 cup of feed to ½ cup of hot or cold water. A satisfactory menu for an adult may be based on ¾oz (21g) of food for each 16oz (454g) the dog weighs, from half to three-quarters of this amount being given as meat. Do not permit to become overweight.

Above: The Long-haired Dachshund's coat is easy to look after. A gentle brushing two or three times a week is sufficient.

Origin and history
The Dachshund was bred as a badger hound, or hunting dog, and is known to have existed before the sixteenth century and to have been derived from the oldest German breeds such as the Bibarhund.

When the German Dachshund Club was formed in 1888, the records that had been kept in the pre-existing German stud book did not always contain complete pedigrees or notations describing the coat lengths of the dogs entered in the stud book. Today there are three varieties, with miniatures of each type: the Smooth-hair, Wire-hair and Long-hair. The Wire-hair was introduced through crossing with the Scottish Dandie Dinmont and other terriers, the Long-hair by crossing the Smooth-hair with the spaniel and an old German gundog, the Stöberhund. The bandiness in the breed, due to a weakness in the tendons, has now been eradicated, as has exaggerated length.

In Europe during both world wars, the Dachshund, recognized as the national dog of the Teutonic Empire, was often discarded, shouted at or even stoned in the streets because of its German ancestry. Happily this sorry state of affairs has long since passed, and the sporty, lovable Dachshund is again popular.

The Dachshund breeds were imported by fanciers into the United States and dog shows and stud books were established.

SHOW STANDARD
Long-haired
General appearance. Form, colour, size and character are similar in all respects to those of the smooth Dachshund, except for the long, soft hair. The form is compact, short-legged and long, but sinewy and well muscled with bold head carriage and an intelligent expression. In spite of the shortness of the legs, the body should be neither too plump nor so slender as to have a weasel-like appearance. Height at shoulder should be half the length of the body measured from the breast bone to the set-on of the tail, and the girth of the chest double the height at the shoulder. The length from the tip of the nose to the eyes should be equal to the length from the eyes to the base of the skull. The tail should not touch the ground when at rest, neither should the leather (i.e. the ears) extend beyond the nose when pulled to the front.

Colour. Black and tan, dark brown with lighter shadings, dark red, light red, dappled, tiger-marked or brindle. In black and tan, red and dappled dogs the nose and nails should be black; in chocolate ones they are often brown.

Head and skull. Long and conical when seen from above, and in profile, sharp and finely modelled. Skull neither too broad nor too narrow, only slightly arched without prominent stop. Foreface long and narrow, finely modelled. Lips should be tightly drawn, well covering the lower jaw, neither too heavy nor too sharply cut away, the corners of the mouth slightly marked.

Tail. Set on fairly high, not too long, tapering and without too marked a curve; not carried too high; fully feathered.

Feet. Broad and large, straight or turned slightly outwards; the hindfeet smaller and narrower than

Above: A Smooth-haired Dachshund, carrying its head boldly as befits the fierce and relentless hunter that this breed is.

the forefeet. Toes close together and with a distinct arch to each toe; nails strong. The dog must stand equally on all parts of the foot.

Smooth-haired
General appearance. Long and low but with a compact and well-muscled body, not crippled, cloddy, or clumsy; bold carriage of the head and an intelligent expression.
Colour. Any colour other than white (except a white spot on the breast).

Nose and nails should be black. In red dogs a red nose is permissible but not desirable. In chocolate dogs and dapples the nose may be brown or flesh-coloured. In dapples large spots of colour are undesirabe, and the dog should be evenly dappled all over.
Head and skull. Long and appearing conical when seen from above; from a side view, tapering to the point of the muzzle.
Tail. Set on fairly high, strong and tapering but not too long and not too curved or carried too high.
Feet. The front feet should be full, broad and close-knit, and straight or very slightly turned outwards, the hindfeet smaller and narrower.

Wire-haired
General appearance. Low to ground, short-legged, the body

Above: The Wire-haired Dachshund has a distinctive beard which gives its face a rather squared-off appearance.

long but compact and well muscled. The head should be carried boldly and the expression be very intelligent. Despite its short legs, compared with the length of its body, it must not be awkward, cramped, crippled or lacking in substance.
Colour. All colours are allowed, but a white patch on the chest, though not a fault, is not desirable. The nose should be black, except in the case of chocolates when it may be brown or flesh-coloured.
Head and skull. Looked at from above or from the side, the head should taper uniformly to the tip of the nose and be clean cut. The skull is only slightly arched, being neither too broad nor too narrow, and slopes gradually, without marked stop, to a finely formed, slightly arched muzzle. The nasal bones and cartilage (septum) are long and narrow. The ridges of the frontal bones are well developed, giving prominence to the nerve bosses over the eyes. The jaw has extremely strong bones, is very long and opens very wide; it should not be too square.
Tail. Continues line of the spine; slightly curved; must not be carried too gaily or reach the ground when at rest.
Feet. The front feet are full, broad in front, straight or turned just a trifle outwards. The four toes forming the foot are compact and well arched and have tough pads; the fifth toe (dew-claw) is usually left on. The nails are strong and short.

First and foremost a sporting dog, the Smooth-haired Dachshund is remarkably versatile, being equally adaptable as a house-pet. The smooth, close coat is impervious to rain or mud. The breed's temperament and acute intelligence make it the ideal companion for town or country. It revels in plenty of exercise.

Smooth-haired Dachshund

Wire-haired Dachshund

The Long-haired Dachshund's thick, soft hair protects it against thorns, enables it to endure both cold and heat, and is rain-proof. The breed is especially suited to water work.

Long-haired Dachshund

WIRE FOX TERRIER

Good points
- First-rate companion
- Good with children
- Intelligent
- Smart appearance
- Trainable

Take heed
- Needs plenty of exercise
- Not entirely suited for apartment living

The Wire-haired Fox Terrier is, when well turned out, a delightful sight to see. It is intelligent, cheerful and easily trained; a first-rate children's companion with the typical terrier's 'get up and go'. Nowadays it is seen more frequently than the smooth-coated variety.

Size
A full-size, well-balanced dog should not exceed 15½in (39cm) at the withers — the bitch being slightly lower — nor should the length of back from withers to root of tail exceed 12in (30cm). Weight 18lb (8.2kg) in show condition, a bitch about 2lb (0.9kg) less with a margin of 1lb (0.45g) either way.

Exercise
The Wire-haired Fox Terrier will enjoy nothing more than going rabbiting with its master. It adores sniffing out vermin and is not afraid of a fight, despite its usual good nature. It adapts well to life as a household pet but really deserves a country home rather than a city one.

Grooming
Hand stripping is required in spring, summer and autumn — more frequently if it is the intention to show. Normally a frequent brushing will suffice, but watch the coat carefully as terriers are susceptible to eczema. Chalking is usual for a show.

Feeding
Recommended would be 6-13oz (170-369g) of a branded, meaty product with biscuit added in equal part by volume, or ¾-1½ cupfuls of a dry, complete food, mixed in the proportion of 1 cup of feed to ½ cup of hot or cold water.

Origin and history
The Wire-haired Fox Terrier is a separate breed from the smooth-coated, although in conformation the breeds are the same. The Wire undoubtedly derived from the wire-haired terriers around the British coalmining areas of Durham, Wales and Derbyshire, where it had existed for some time before gaining the attention of fanciers. It did not appear in the ring until 1872. For many years its popularity lagged behind the smooth variety, but now the position is reversed.

SHOW STANDARD
General appearance. The dog should be balanced: this may be defined as the correct proportions of a certain point or points when considered in relation to another point or points. The chief points for consideration are the relative proportions of skull and foreface; head and back; the height at the withers; and the length of the body from shoulder-point to buttock. The ideal of proportion is reached when the last two measurements are the same.

Colour. White should predominate. Brindle, red, liver or slaty blue are objectionable. Otherwise, colour is of no importance.

Head and skull. The top line of the skull shold be almost flat, sloping slightly and gradually decreasing in width towards the eyes. In a well-balanced head there should be little apparent difference in length between skull and foreface. If, however, the foreface is noticeably shorter, it amounts to a fault, the head looking weak and 'unfinished'. The nose should be black.

Tail. Should be set on rather high and carried gaily but not curled. It should be of good strength and substance and of fair length — a three-quarters dock is about right — because it affords the only safe grip when handling a working terrier. A very short tail is suitable neither for work nor for show.

Feet. Should be round, compact and not large. The pads should be tough and well cushioned, and the toes are moderately arched and turned neither in nor out.

A terrier with good-shaped forelegs and feet will wear its nails down short by contact with the road surface, the weight of the body being evenly distributed between the toe pads and the heels.

SMOOTH FOX TERRIER

Good points
- Alert and intelligent family pet
- Smart appearance
- Useful medium size

Take heed
- Needs plenty of exercise
- Not entirely suited for apartment living

The word terrier comes from the Latin word 'terra', meaning 'earth', the job of the terrier being to kill vermin and to worry or 'boot' the fox from its lair.

The Smooth Fox Terrier is arguably the smartest terrier bred for this purpose. It enjoyed almost unrivalled popularity just before and after World War II and is always a popular contender in the show ring, though it has been said that the elegance of this terrier has been attained at the expense of its former hunting ability. It makes an ideal family pet.

Size
About 16-18lb (7.3-8.2kg) for a dog and 15-17lb (6.8-7.7kg) for a bitch in show condition are appropriate weights.

Exercise
The terrier was once called 'the little athlete of the dog world' and deserves a chance to live up to that title. It will adjust to a regular trot around the park — on a lead, of course — but deserves the opportunity for frequent off-the-lead runs, preferably in the country.

Grooming
Frequent brushing with a stiff brush. Trimming is required a few weeks before a show, paying particular attention to the inside and outside of ears, jaw and muzzle. Usually a chalk block is used to ensure that the coat is snowy white.

Feeding
As for Wire Fox Terrier.

Origin and history
The Smooth Fox Terrier has been around in its present form for at least 100 years. Before then, almost all terriers that went to earth were known simply as fox terriers.

It was in 1862 at the Birmingham, England, National Dog Show that the breed first made its debut in the show ring. Its ancestors probably lived throughout the English counties of Cheshire and Shropshire. Another possible ancestor is the hound, the Beagle.

SHOW STANDARD
General appearance. The dog must present a generally gay, lively and active appearance; bone and strength in a small compass are essentials; but this must not be taken to mean that a Fox Terrier should be cloddy or in any way coarse. Speed and endurance must be looked to as well as power, and the symmetry of the Foxhound taken as a model. The Fox Terrier, like the Foxhound, must on no account be leggy, nor must it be too short in the leg. It should stand like a cleverly made hunter, covering a lot of ground, yet with a short back.

Colour.
White should predominate; and brindle, red or liver markings are objectionable. Otherwise this point is of no importance.

Head and skull. The skull should be flat and moderately narrow, gradually decreasing in width to the eyes. Not much 'stop' should be apparent, but there should be more dip in the profile between the forehead and the top jaw than in the Greyhound. The nose, towards which the muzzle must gradually taper, should be black.

Tail. Should be set on rather high and carried gaily, but not over the back or curled; it should be of good strength.

Feet. Should be round, compact and not large; the soles hard and tough; the toes moderately arched, and turned neither in nor out.

NB: In the United States, the Smooth-haired and the Wire-haired Fox Terriers were not considered separate breeds but were merely two varieties of the breed known as the Fox Terrier. With the exception of the difference in type of coat, the two are identical in conformation. In December 1984, however, AKC approved separate breed standards for the Smooth Fox Terrier and the Wire Fox Terrier.

JACK RUSSELL TERRIER

Good points
- Affectionate
- Handy size
- Sporty companion

Take heed
- Excitable in a pack
- Not yet a pedigree breed in the United States

The Jack Russell Terrier has become immensely popular in recent years. For some time persons who fancied the Jack Russell were disappointed on finding that the breed they sought and acquired could not be registered with the Kennel Club in the United Kingdom for it was not as yet a pedigreed dog. The Kennel Club, aware of efforts to standardize the breed but unable to accept it while there was so much variation in colour, size and form, finally accorded championship status to the Jack Russell.

Size
The Jack Russell Terrier Club of the United Kingdom has drawn up a breed standard aiming to produce a uniform type of Jack Russell Terrier allowing for two different heights: 11-15in (28-38cm) at the shoulder, and under 11in (28cm) at the shoulder.

Exercise
The Jack Russell Terrier will adapt well to life as a household pet provided regular walks are given. However, it is really in its element in the countryside, ferreting, facing badgers or after foxes.

Grooming
Frequently, with a stiff brush.

Feeding
As for Wire Fox Terrier. Increase the amount if the terrier is working.

Origin and history
Reverend Jack Russell, a sporting parson in Devonshire, England, who died almost 100 years ago, built up a strain of wire-haired fox terriers that would hunt with his hounds, go to ground and bolt the fox. The dogs were, in fact, hunt terriers. Jack Russell not only bred his unique hunt terriers but also judged terriers at West Country shows and was one of the earliest members of the Kennel Club. After many years the breed has been established and proper records of pedigree are kept.

SHOW STANDARD
The head should be strong-boned with powerful jaws, level bite and good, strong cheek muscles. Eyes should be almond shaped, and the small V-shaped, dropped ears carried close to the head. The back to be straight with a high-set tail. Hindquarters strong with good angulation. The coat is smooth but woolly; the colour is basically white with black, tan or traditional hound markings.

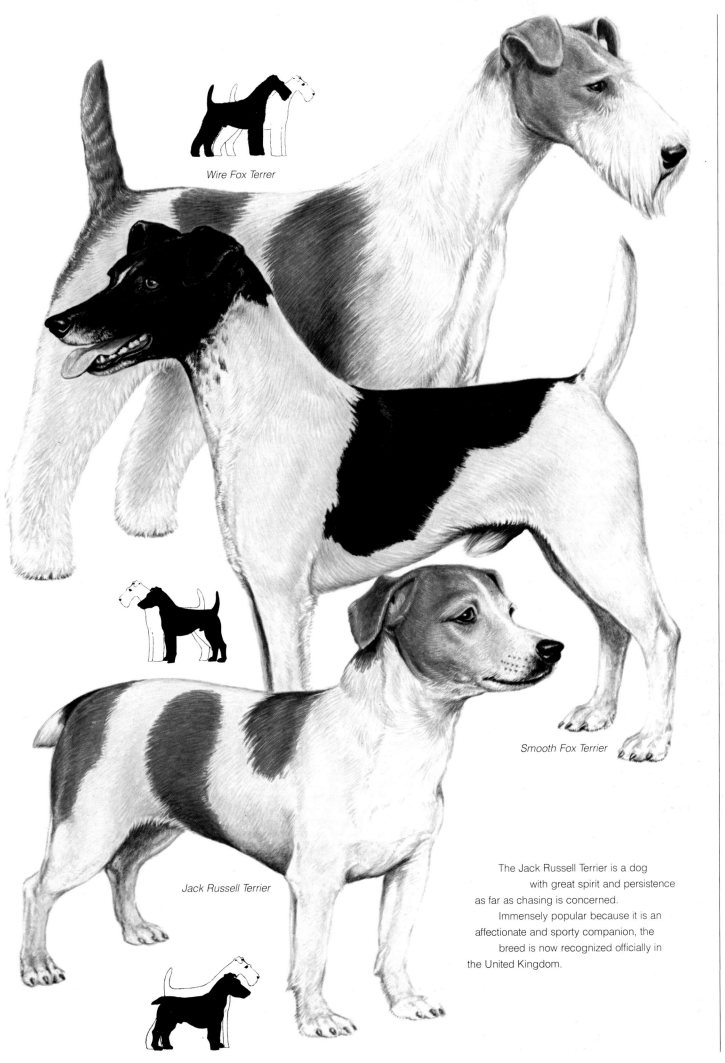

Wire Fox Terrer

Smooth Fox Terrier

Jack Russell Terrier

The Jack Russell Terrier is a dog with great spirit and persistence as far as chasing is concerned.
Immensely popular because it is an affectionate and sporty companion, the breed is now recognized officially in the United Kingdom.

DANDIE DINMONT TERRIER

Good points
- *Courageous*
- *Intelligent*
- *Keen sense of humour*
- *Excellent watchdog*

Take heed
- *Tends to be a one-person dog whose friendship and respect must be earned*

Although once popular as a badger and fox hunter, the Dandie Dinmont is now kept mainly as a household pet: indeed, they fare better indoors as a single pet than living with their fellows in kennels. They do, however, tend to be a little suspicious of strangers, giving all their devotion to their owner. They are excellent guard dogs with a bark that should deter any burglar.

Size
The height should be 8-11in (20-28cm) at the top of the shoulder. Length from top of shoulder to root of tail should be not more than twice the dog's height, but preferably 1-2in (2.5-5cm) less. The ideal weight for a dog in good working condition is as near 18lb (8.2kg) as possible.

Exercise
The Dandie Dinmont is an adaptable dog and will be happy whether running in the fields or enjoying the role of an old person's pet. It would, however, be unfair to keep this active, inquisitive breed in a home without a garden.

Grooming
Grooming is not a difficult task, the only equipment needed being a stiff brush and comb. Old hairs should be removed with finger and thumb, allowing the under-coat to come through. Incidentally, don't use a trimming knife because this will ruin the coat. Brush frequently and the Dandie Dinmont should always look immaculate.

Feeding
Recommended would be 6-13oz (170-369g) of a branded, meaty product with biscuit added in equal part by volume, or ¾-1½ cupfuls of a dry, complete food, mixed in the proportion of 1 cup of feed to ½ cup of hot or cold water.

Origin and history
Most Dandies can be traced back to the late 1700s to an individual named Piper Allan. Something of a character of his day, Allan had two Dandie Dinmonts called 'Charlie' and 'Peachem'. Also well known is James Davidson, who was renowned for his 'pepper and mustard' terriers, so called because of their colour. It was from Davidson that Sir Walter Scott acquired his dogs, and indeed it was from a character in his novel *Guy Mannering* that the breed received its name.

SHOW STANDARD
Colour. The colours are pepper or mustard. The peppers range from a dark bluish black to a light silvery grey, the intermediate shades being preferred; the body colour comes well down the shoulder and hips, gradually merging into the leg colour. The mustards vary from reddish brown to pale fawn, the head being creamy white, the legs and feet of a shade darker than the head. The claws are dark, as in other colours. Nearly all Dandie Dinmont Terriers have some white on the chest, and some have white claws. White feet are objectionable.
Head and skull. The head should be strongly made and large but not out of proportion to the dog's size; the muscles show extraordinary development, especially the maxillary. Skull broad between the ears, getting gradually less towards the eye, and measuring about the same from the inner corner of the eye to the back of the skull as it does from ear to ear. The forehead should be well domed. The head is covered with very soft silky hair, which should not be confined to a mere topknot; the lighter in colour and silkier it is the better. The nose is black.
Tail. Rather short, say 8-10in (20-25cm), and covered on the upper side with wiry hair of a darker colour than that of the body, the hair on the under side being lighter in colour and not so wiry with a nice feather about 2in (5cm) long, getting shorter as it nears the tip.
Feet. Flat feet are objectionable. The whole claws should be dark, but the claws of all vary in shade according to the colour of the dog's body. The feet of a pepper dog should be tan, varying according to the body colour from a rich tan to a pale fawn; those of a mustard dog are a darker shade than its head. Hindfeet should be much smaller than forefeet.

SKYE TERRIER

Good points
- *Beautiful in appearance*
- *Pleasant disposition*
- *Patient*

Take heed
- *Needs plenty of grooming*
- *Does not take kindly to strangers*

The Skye Terrier originated on the Isle of Skye in the Hebrides and is, despite its beautiful appearance, a relentless fighter if aroused. It is not a vicious dog but tends to give total trust and devotion to its owner and has little time for strangers. Considerable care has to be given to the grooming of this breed. If given the chance it is a valiant hunter, having been bred to hunt fox, otter and badger.

Size
Height 10in (25cm), total length 41½in (105cm), weight 25lb (11.3kg); bitch slightly smaller.

Exercise
It would be unfair to buy this gay little breed purely as a fashionable accessory, for it is tireless and enjoys nothing better than a long country walk and romp in fresh air.

Grooming
The Skye should be brushed frequently and combed once a week with a wide-toothed comb. Incidentally, the coat does not reach its full beauty until the third year.

Feeding
Recommended would be 13-20oz (369-587g) of a branded, meaty product with biscuit added in equal part by volume, or 1½-3 cupfuls of a dry, complete food, mixed in the proportion of 1 cup of feed to ½ cup of hot or cold water.

Origin and history
The Skye Terrier is a legend — not only in Scotland but throughout the world — because of the tale of 'Greyfriars Bobby', whose statue stands near Greyfriars churchyard, Edinburgh. Following his master's death, 'Bobby' would each day for the next 14 years visit the café that he had frequented with his master. There he would be given a bun before retracing his steps to his master's grave where he spent his days until his own death from old age. The statue was later erected in his memory.

The Skye evolved from the small earth dogs kept in Scotland to hunt foxes, badgers and other vermin. Although the Cairn and other breeds existed in the Highlands, it would seem that the Skye owes its appearance to no one, although the Highland terriers in early days were not separate breeds.

SHOW STANDARD
Colour. Dark or light grey, fawn, cream or black, with black points. In fact, any self colour allowing shading of the same colour and lighter under-coat, so long as the nose and ears are black. A small white spot on the chest allowed.
Head and skull. Head long with powerful jaws. Nose black.
Tail. When hanging, upper part pendulous and lower half thrown back in a curve. When raised, a prolongation of the incline of the back, not rising or curling up.
Feet. Large and pointing forward.

GLEN OF IMAAL TERRIER

Good points
- *Affectionate*
- *Courageous*
- *Excellent with children*
- *Good working dog*
- *Loyal*
- *Playful*

Take heed
- *Rarely seen in a show ring, so not a good choice for that purpose*

The Glen of Imaal Terrier originates from a valley of that name in the county of Wicklow in Ireland, where it was — and is — used as a working terrier to dispel fox and badger. It is still mainly to be found in Ireland, combining life as a working terrier with the role of pet and children's protector.

Size
Height not more than 14in (35.5cm); weight up to 35lb (15.9kg), less for bitches.

Exercise
Happiest when able to run in open spaces, this adaptable little dog will take to normal household life provided it has a garden to play in and is given regular walks.

Grooming
A good frequent brushing.

Feeding
As for Skye Terrier.

Origin and history
The Glen of Imaal Terrier is an Irish-bred working terrier and is still popular in its area of origin. But although its fame has long spread outside its native Ireland, where it received official breed recognition in 1933, it is not often seen in the show ring. It is also recognized by the Kennel Club but not by the American Kennel Club.

SHOW STANDARD (Taken from FCI Standard, Belgium, 1975)
General appearance. Medium long-coated dog of great strength for its size, active and agile, low to the ground. Movement should be free, not hackneyed in action but covering the ground effortlessly.
Colour. Blue brindle or wheaten but not toning to black.
Head and skull. The head should be of good width and fair length with a foreface of power bearing to the nose but showing no sign of the bottle head often seen in other breeds. There should be a pronounced stop.
Tail. The tail must be strong at the insertion, well set on, and carried gaily.
Feet. Compact, with strong, rounded pads.

CESKY TERRIER

The Cesky Terrier, sometimes known as the Bohemian Terrier, comes from Czechoslovakia and is not widely known. It is a useful short-legged terrier, hardy, healthy and extremely adaptable, being ideally suited as a house-pet.

Size
Dog: 11-14in (28-35.5cm) high, bitch slightly smaller.

Feeding
Six-13oz (170-369g) of a branded, meaty product with biscuit added in equal part by volume, or ¾-1½ cupfuls of a dry, complete food, mixed in the proportion of 1 cup of feed to ½ cup of hot or cold water. Step up the rations if the dog is in work.

Colour
The Cesky comes in two colours, blue grey and light coffee brown.

The coat of the Dandie Dinmont Terrier should be a mixture of hardish and soft hair, which gives a sort of crisp feel to the hand. The hair on the under part of the body is lighter in colour and softer in texture.

Cesky Terrier

Dandie Dinmont Terrier

Glen of Imaal Terriers that meet the high standard of gameness set by the breed club receive an award known as 'Teastors Misneac'.

Glen of Imaal Terrier

Skye Terrier

FRENCH BULLDOG

Good points
● *Affectionate and devoted pet*
● *Loves human company*

Take heed
● *Lubricate facial creases with petroleum jelly occasionally*

The French Bulldog is a devoted animal and makes the ideal family pet. It has a keen, clownish sense of humour, is intelligent and adapts well to town or country living. It is perhaps the healthiest of the bulldogs and does not suffer from the over developments or nasal difficulties of the Boston Terrier and the English Bulldog.

Size
The ideal weight is 28lb (12.7kg) for dogs and 24lb (10.9kg) for bitches, but soundness must not be sacrificed to smallness.

Exercise
Short, regular walks and scampers.

Grooming
Normal routine brushing.

Feeding
Thirteen-20oz (369-587g) of a branded, meaty product with biscuit added in equal part by volume, or 1½-3 cupfuls of a dry food, complete diet, mixed in the proportion of 1 cup of feed to ½ cup of hot or cold water.

Origin and history
Credit must go to the French for the development of this breed. It is, however, uncertain whether it derives from small English Bulldogs taken to France by Nottingham laceworkers in the nineteenth century or from crossings with dogs imported to France from Spain. In any event, this delightful animal is obviously the descendant of small bulldogs, and by the beginning of this century it had found favour in both the United Kingdom and the United States.

SHOW STANDARD
General appearance. A French Bulldog should be sound, active and intelligent, of compact build, medium or small, with good bone, a short smooth coat and the various points so evenly balanced that the dog does not look ill-proportioned.
Colour. The colours allowed are: (1) Brindle — a mixture of black and coloured hairs. This variety may contain white on condition that brindle predominates. (2) Pied — a dog in which the white predominates over the brindle. White dogs are classified with the pieds, but their eyelashes and eye-rims should be black. (3) Fawn — the fawn dog may contain brindle hairs but must have black eye rims and eyelashes.
Head and skull. Head massive, square and broad. Skull nearly flat between the ears with a domed forehead, the loose skin forming symmetrical wrinkles. Muzzle

Above: French Bulldogs love people and have a sense of fun. Moreover they adapt well to town or country living.

broad, deep and laid back with the muscles of the cheek well developed; nose and lips black. Stop well defined. Lower jaw should be deep, square, broad, slightly undershot and well turned up. Nose extremely short, black and wide with open nostrils and the line between well defined. Lips thick, the lower meeting the upper in the middle, completely hiding the teeth. The upper lip should cover the lower on each side with plenty of cushion but not so exaggerated as to hang much below the level of the lower jaw.
Tail. Very short, set low, thick at the root and tapering quickly towards the tip, either straight or kinked but never curling over the back. A good tail is placed so that it cannot be carried gaily.
Feet. Should be small, compact and placed in a continuation of the line of the leg with absolutely sound pasterns. The hindfeet are rather longer than the forefeet. Toes compact; knuckles high; nails short, thick and black.

MINIATURE BULL TERRIER

The Miniature Bull Terrier is a replica of its big brother the Bull Terrier in all respects except size. It is thus the gladiator of the dog world in miniature, perhaps more suited to apartment dwelling than its bigger counterpart. Miniatures are not easy to breed and are therefore rare and hard to obtain.

Headings relating to the Bull Terrier are identical for the Miniature except for:

Size
Height should not be more than 14 in (35.5cm). Weight should be not more than 20lb (9kg).

Feeding
Recommended would be 6-13oz (170-369g) of a branded, meaty product with biscuit added in equal part by volume, or 1½ cupfuls of a dry, complete food diet, mixed in the proportion of 1 cup of feed to ½ cup of hot or cold water.

Right: Boston Terrier pups should live indoors, free from draughts; but their daily walks on- or off-lead should not be ignored.

BOSTON TERRIER
(Formerly American Bull Terrier)

Good points
● *Affectionate*
● *Easy to look after*
● *Excellent guard*
● *Good family pet*
● *Odourless*
● *Good with children*
● *Obedient*
● *Playful nature*
● *Rarely sheds coat*
● *Handy size*

Take heed
● *Avoid draughts*
● *Not the easiest type to breed and/or produce for showing*
● *Watch out for eye trouble*

The Boston Terrier is a lively and attractive American breed. It is intelligent and trainable and makes a delightful companion, always ready for a walk or a game. However, achieving the desired markings can be a show aspirant's nightmare, and bitches frequently require caesarean section in whelping.

Size
Weight: not more than 25lb (11.3kg).

Exercise
This breed will happily settle for an on-the-lead walk if you do not have a garden to offer it more freedom of movement. It is essentially a pet dog and should not be confined in an outside kennel.

Grooming
Frequent brushing is needed. In the United States ears are cropped in some states according to state law. This practice is illegal in the United Kingdom. The coat rarely sheds.

Feeding
Recommended would be 6-13oz (170-369g) of a branded, meaty product with biscuit added in equal part by volume, or ¾-1½ cupfuls of a dry, complete food, mixed in the proportion of 1 cup of feed to ½ cup of hot or cold water.

Health care
The Boston is robust but, as in the case of the Pekingese and other round-eyed breeds, watch that foreign bodies do not penetrate and damage the eyes.

Origin and history
The Boston Terrier, sometimes called the 'American gentleman', can

trace its ancestry from the mating of a crossbred bulldog/terrier called Judge, imported to the United States from the United Kingdom in 1865. To later progeny were added a dash of English and Staffordshire bull terrier until the dog we know today evolved. At first it was known as the American Bull Terrier, but as a result of objections from other bull terrier clubs it was renamed the Boston Terrier after the city responsible for its development. The Boston Terrier Club of America was formed in Boston in 1891. Two years later the American Kennel Club admitted the breed to its stud book.

The male Boston is known as the American gentleman because of his gentle disposition, but even though he is not known as a fighter, the Boston is able to take care of himself and of those he loves.

SHOW STANDARD
General appearance. The Boston Terrier should be a lively, highly intelligent, smooth-coated, short-headed, compactly built, short-tailed, well-balanced dog of medium size, of brindle colour and evenly marked with white. The head should indicate a high degree of intelligence and should be in proportion to the size of the dog; the body rather short and well knit; the limbs strong and neatly turned; tail short; and no feature to be so prominent that the dog appears badly proportioned. The dog should convey an impression of determination, strength and activity, with style of a high order, carriage easy and graceful. The gait of the Boston Terrier is that of a sure-footed, straight-gaited dog, forelegs and hindlegs moving straight ahead in time with perfect rhythm, each step indicating grace and power.
Colour. Brindle with white markings; brindle must show throughout the body distinctly; black and white markings are permissible, but brindles with white markings are preferred. (Ideal colour shall be one in which the brindle colouring is evenly distributed throughout the body.) Ideal markings: white muzzle, even white blaze over head, collar, breast, part or whole of forelegs, and hindlegs below hocks.
Head and skull. Skull square, flat on top, free from wrinkles; cheeks flat; brow abrupt, stop well defined. Muzzle short, square, wide and deep, and in proportion to the skull; free from wrinkles; shorter in length than in width and depth, not exceeding in length approximately one-third of length of skull; width and depth carried out well to end, the muzzle from stop to end of nose on a line parallel to the top of the skull; nose black and wide with well-defined line between nostrils. The jaws broad and square. The chops of good depth but not pendulous, completely covering the teeth when mouth is closed.
Tail. Set on low; short, fine and tapering; straight or screw; devoid of fringes or coarse hair, and not carried above horizontal.
Feet. Round, small and compact, and turned neither in nor out; toes well arched.

A distinctive feature of the French Bulldog are the 'bat ears', which are not characteristic of the Bulldog proper. They should be of medium size, wide at the base, rounded at the top, set high and carried upright and parallel.

Miniature Bull Terrier

French Bulldog

Boston Terriers were bred in the Boston area in the 1870s, but it was not until 1893 that the breed club was officially recognized, having changed its name from the American Bull Terrier Club of Boston to the Boston Terrier Club.

Boston Terrier

MANCHESTER TERRIER

Good points
- Clean
- Good family dog
- Great sporting companion
- Long-lived
- Suitable for town or country

Take heed
- Tends to be a one-person dog

The Manchester Terrier is an ideal choice for those seeking a small, hardy dog that causes no trouble and makes a great sporting companion. It will fit well into family life but does tend to attach itself to one person.

It is long-lived and seldom ill. It is happiest if given a place by the fireside.

Size
Desired height: dog 16in (40.5cm); bitch 15in (38cm).

Exercise
The Manchester is in its element running free in the countryside. Town dwellers need not rule out this breed, however, if they can offer regular walks, off-the-lead runs and a garden.

Grooming
Manchesters do not like rain, despite its proverbial frequency in their place of origin, and should be rubbed with a towel if they get wet. Otherwise, a frequent brushing will keep this essentially clean animal looking smart. Its coat condition is always an indication of health.

Feeding
Six-13oz (170-369g) of a branded, meaty product with biscuit added in equal part by volume, or ¾-1½ cupfuls of a dry, complete food, mixed in the proportion of 1 cup of feed to ½ cup of hot or cold water.

Origin and history
The Manchester Terrier can trace its lineage back to the old hunting 'Black and Tan' Terrier, which, in the north of England, had the reputation of rat killer supreme.

The Manchester Terrier — once closely related to a white English terrier that seems to have disappeared, probably because of its tendency to deafness — has evolved as a reliable household pet. It retains its sporting instincts while fitting happily into a home that requires an alert, lively pet. It is usually good with children.

At one time the Manchester Terrier and the English Toy Terrier were shown as Black and Tan Terriers with a weight division. The English Toy Terrier is now separately classified in England, but in the USA, where the Manchester Terrier is popular, breeding of toys and standards is permitted. The toy variety may not exceed 12lb (5.4kg). The standard variety should be more than 12lb (5.4kg) but no more than 22lb (10kg).

A number of Manchesters were exported from the United Kingdom to the United States, Canada and Germany in the 1800s, and it is thought (see Dobermann Pinscher) that the Manchester contributed to the make-up of the Dobermann, certainly as far as its short, shiny black and tan coat was concerned. Earlier Manchesters had cropped ears, a practice that became illegal in the United Kingdom in 1895.

SHOW STANDARD
General appearance. The dog shall be compact in appearance with good bone and free from any resemblance to the Whippet.
Colour. Jet black and rich, mahogany tan distributed as follows: on the head, the muzzle to be tanned to the nose, the nose and nasal leather to be jet black. There shall be a small tan spot on each cheek and above each eye, the under-jaw and throat to be tanned with a distinct tan 'V'. In all cases the black should not run into the tan or vice versa, but the division between the colours should be clearly defined.
Head and skull. Long, flat in skull and narrow, level and wedge-shaped.
Tail. Short and set on where the arch of the back ends.
Feet. Small, semi-harefooted, strong with well-arched toes.

TIBETAN TERRIER

Good points
- Charming 'shaggy' appearance
- Happy disposition
- Hardy constitution
- Excellent companion
- Adaptable

Take heed
- No drawbacks known

The Tibetan Terrier is one of three small Tibetan breeds, the others being the Tibetan Spaniel and the Lhasa Apso, both of which are dealt with elsewhere. There is also a Tibetan Mastiff, which is a much larger breed.

The Tibetan Terrier, which in appearance resembles a small Old English Sheepdog, is in truth not a terrier at all, having no history of going to earth.

Size
Height at shoulders: dog should be 14-16in (35.5-40.5cm); bitches should be slightly smaller.

Exercise
The Tibetan Terrier enjoys an off-the-lead scamper and the freedom of a garden; otherwise normal, regular walks will suffice.

Grooming
Needs thorough brushing frequently.

Feeding
As for Manchester Terrier.

Origin and history
Bred in the monasteries of Tibet. Has a history as an all-purpose farm dog that first reached Europe at the beginning of this century, when both the Lhasa Apso and the Tibetan Terrier were referred to as Lhasa Terriers. The situation became somewhat confused, and in 1934 the Kennel Club formed the Tibetan Breeds Association.

The Tibetan Terrier standard is included in the Kennel Club's Utility group, and over the past ten years the breed has attracted quite a number of enthusiasts. The Tibetan Terrier was admitted to the American Kennel Club stud book in May 1973. The following autumn it was admitted to AKC's non-sporting group.

SHOW STANDARD
General appearance. A well-muscled dog, in general appearance not unlike a miniature Old English Sheepdog.
Colour. White, golden, cream, grey or smoke, black, parti-colour, and tricolour — in fact, any colour except chocolate or liver.
Head and skull. Skull of medium length, not broad or coarse, narrowing slightly from ear to eye, not domed but not absolutely flat between the ears. Nose, black.
Tail. Medium length, set on fairly high and carried in a gay curl over the back. Very well feathered. There is often a kink near the tip.
Feet. The feet should be large, round, heavily furnished with hair between the toes and pads.

BASENJI
(Variously known as Zande Dog, Belgian Congo Dog, Congo Bush Dog, Bongo Terrier, Congo Terrier, Nyam-Nyam Terrier)

Good points
- Adaptable to most climates
- Has no bark
- Clean
- Gentle with children
- Intelligent
- Odourless

Take heed
- Does not like rain
- Bitches may come into season only once a year
- Mischievous

The Basenji (the name is the translation of a native word meaning 'bush thing') is an interesting and attractive breed. Its main claim to fame is that it has no bark. But only the bark is absent; the Basenji will growl and whine like other breeds and can express itself feelingly with a distinctive chortle or yodel. The breed's vocal cords are present, and it is believed that training, over thousands of years, to hunt game silently may account for its characteristic quietness.

The breed is well known for its gentle disposition and love of children, though it can be aloof with strangers. It has great curiosity and mischievousness, and its advocates swear that it teases its owners into playing by rubbing a paw over its face.

Appealing features are its curling tail, high set and lying over to one side of the back, its habit of washing with its paw like a cat and its forehead full of 'worried' wrinkes.

Size
Ideal height: dog 17in (43cm) at the shoulder; bitch 16in (40.5cm); but an inch either way should not penalize an otherwise well-balanced specimen. Ideal weight: 24lb (10.9kg); bitch 21lb (9.5kg).

Exercise
The Basenji is a great hunter and if not exercised has a tendency to put on weight. It is fleet-footed, tireless and enjoys a daily walk and off-the-lead run. It is, incidentally, a breed that is particularly good with horses.

This is a breed that should not be kept in an outside kennel. It is essentially a house dog that loves to stretch out in front of the fire or to indulge in its strange habit of reclining in places off the ground. It is suitable for apartment living as long as it is given sufficient exercise.

Grooming
Regular use of a hound glove is recommended.

Feeding
About 20-26oz (587-737g) of branded dog food with an equal volume of biscuit, or 3-4 cupfuls of dry food, complete diet, mixed in the proportion of 1 cup of feed to ½ cup of hot or cold water. Green vegetables should be added to Basenji fare.

Origin and history
Dogs of the Basenji type are depicted in many of the carvings in the tombs of the Pharaohs, and it is believed that these dogs were brought as precious gifts by travellers from the lower reaches of the River Nile.

The Basenji almost disappeared from public view from Ancient Egyptian times until the mid-nineteenth century, when it was discovered by explorers in the Congo and southern Sudan.

The foundation stock recognized today derived from the Belgian Congo with further import from Sudan and Liberia. It is said that similar dogs are to be found in the Malayan jungle and north of Katmandu, but these do not appear to have been extracted from their homeland.

SHOW STANDARD
General appearance. The Basenji should be lightly built, finely boned, aristocratic-looking animal, high on the leg compared with its length, always poised, alert and intelligent.
Colour. Pure bright red, or pure black, or black and tan, all with white feet, chest and tail tip.
Head and skull. The skull should be flat, well chiselled and of medium width, tapering towards the nose, with only a slight stop. A black nose is greatly desired.
Body. The body is short and the back level. There is ample heart space between well-sprung ribs, and the deep, short-coupled brisket ends in a definite waist.
Tail. The tail should be high set with the posterior curve of the buttock extending beyond the root of the tail.
Feet. Small, narrow and compact, with deep pads; well-arched toes.

Tibetan Terrier

Manchester Terrier

Basenji

The first successful introduction
of the Basenji to Europe was
in 1937, the breed appearing
at Crufts in that year as the
Congo Terrier or Bush Dog. Successful
breeding from imported
specimens began in America in 1941.

WEST HIGHLAND WHITE TERRIER

Good points
- Easy to train
- Gets on well with other dogs
- Good with children
- Handy size
- Suitable for town or country

Take heed
- No drawbacks known

The West Highland White Terrier is a game, hardly little dog that originated in Argyll, Scotland. In recent years it has gained tremendous popularity because of its attractive appearance, sporting instincts and handy size. It gets on well with children and other dogs and makes the ideal family dog.

Size
About 11in (28cm) at the withers. There is no weight standard for this dog in the United Kingdom or the United States.

Exercise
The Westie will adapt to town or country. However, it will be happiest as a family pet allowed to share the comfort of the fireside but given adequate free runs in the countryside. Remember that it was originally used as a working terrier, and its job was to hunt fox and badger. It is also, of course, a good ratter. This breed will enjoy an energetic ball game.

Grooming
Although the Westie may be the ideal choice for someone who wants a healthy and active dog, it is perhaps not so ideal for the show aspirant who does not want to spend much time on grooming. The Westie's coat must be brushed and combed nearly every day and have surplus stripped twice a year. The neckline is particularly important, and straggly hairs should be removed from ears and tail. Ideally, the Westie's coat should be approximately 2in (5cm) in length with the neck and throat hair shorter. It is probably wise to ask the breeder to demonstrate what is required before you make your purchase and to let you have a grooming chart with full instructions. If you feel you cannot handle the task yourself, you can entrust it to a dog grooming parlour.

Feeding
Thirteen-20oz (369-587g) of a branded, meaty product with biscuit added in equal part by volume, or 2-3 cupfuls of a dry, complete food, mixed in the proportion of 1 cup of feed to ½ cup of hot or cold water. The Westie loves burrowing in the earth, often retrieving a long-discarded, much-loved bone; so do let it have the occasional marrow or chop bone to get its teeth into — but no splintery bones, please.

Origin and history
The first West Highland White Terrier clubs were formed in 1905, when breeds such as the Cairn Terrier and Skye Terrier, which in the past had all been classified as Small Highland Working Terriers, attained individual status.

It does appear that in the late 1800s there existed a white Scottish Terrier, or Scottie. A strain of this breed was bred by Colonel Malcolm of Poltalloch, from which the name Poltalloch Terrier was derived; they were also known as Roseneath Terriers.

SHOW STANDARD
General appearance. The general appearance of the West Highland White Terrier is that of a small, game, hardy-looking terrier, possessed of no small amount of self-esteem; with a varminty appearance; strongly built, deep in chest and back ribs; level back and powerful quarters on muscular legs, exhibiting in a marked degree a great combination of strength and activity.

Colour. Pure white.

Head and skull. The skull should be slightly domed and, when gripped across the forehead, should present a smooth contour. There should be only a very slight tapering from the skull at the level of the ears to the eyes. The distance from the occiput to the eyes should be slightly greater than the length of the foreface. The jaws should be strong and level. The nose must be black and should be fairly large, forming a smooth contour with the muzzle.

Tail. About 5-6in (12.5-15cm) long, covered with hard hair, no feather, as straight as possible, carried jauntily, not gay or carried over the back. A long tail is objectionable, and on no account should tails be docked.

Feet. The forefeet are larger than the hind ones, round, proportionate in size, strong, thickly padded and covered with short hard hair. The hindfeet are smaller and thickly padded. The under-surface of the pads of the feet and all nails should be black.

SCOTTISH TERRIER

Good points
- Straightforward and honest
- Fine guard
- Utterly loyal
- Home-loving

Take heed
- Has little time for strangers; best for a childless couple or unattached owner

The Scottish Terrier or Scottie has been aptly described as a gentleman. It is an honest dog that will not look for trouble but on finding it will always fight fairly. It is a devoted companion to its owner but has little time for strangers and is not the most suitable of dogs for a family with children or a couple intending to add to their family. It will fight fox or badger but enjoys itself just as much in an energetic ball game and likes nothing better than carrying a stick or a ball in its mouth. Altogether an attractive and sporty little animal.

Size
Weight: 19-23lb (8.6-10.4kg).
Height: 10-11in (25-28cm).

Exercise
The Scottie loves nothing more than being out of doors, and it would be wrong to deprive it of romps in the garden or regular, daily walks.

Grooming
The Scottie needs regular brushing and combing, particularly its fine beard, and should be trimmed in spring and autumn.

Feeding
Recommended would be 13-20oz (369-587g) of a branded, meaty product with biscuit added in equal part by volume, or 2-3 cupfuls of a dry, complete food, mixed in the proportion of 1 cup of feed to ½ cup of hot or cold water.

Origin and history
The Scottish Terrier, once known as the Aberdeen Terrier and generally known as the Scottie, has existed in various forms for many centuries, but it was not until after 1800 that line breeding began. The first Scottish Terrier Club was formed in Scotland in 1892, when a standard was laid down for the breed that has changed little up to the present.

SHOW STANDARD
General appearance. A Scottish Terrier is a sturdy, thick-set, short-legged dog of a suitable size to go to ground, alert in carriage and suggestive of great power and activity in a small compass.

Colour. Black, wheaten or brindle of any colour.

Head and skull. Without being out of proportion to the size of the dog, the head should be long, the length of skull enabling it to be fairly wide, yet retain a narrow appearance.

Tail. Of moderate length to give a general balance to the dog, thick at the root and tapering towards the tip, set on with an upright carriage or with a slight bend.

Feet. Of good size, well padded, toes well arched and close-knit.

SEALYHAM TERRIER

Good points
- Beautiful appearance
- Devoted
- Good with children
- Does not shed
- Good watchdog

Take heed
- Enjoys a scrap
- Needs lots of grooming
- Obstinate

The Sealyham was bred as a rat and badger hunter but has evolved into an elegant pet and show dog for those with time to devote to its coiffure.

The Sealyham is a game, lovable little terrier that becomes devoted to its owners and is reliable with children. However, it can be obstinate and snappy if not firmly, but kindly, disciplined when young.

Size
Weight: dog should not exceed 20lb (9kg); bitch should not exceed 18lb (8.2kg). Height should not exceed 12in (30cm) at the shoulder.

Exercise
This dog will adapt happily to regular walks around the park and off-the-lead runs. But give a Sealyham the chance and it will enjoy getting gloriously dirty in the wet, muddy countryside.

Grooming
The Sealyham needs hand stripping at least twice a year and regular combing with a wire comb to remove surplus hair. As mentioned elsewhere, stripping by the inexperienced can prove a disastrous experience for both owner and dog, so do have the job done professionally, or ask an expert to show you how. Clipping is excusable for the older dog but will ruin the coat for showing.

Feeding
Recommended would be 13oz (369g) of a branded, meaty product with biscuit added in equal part by volume, or 1½ cupfuls of a dry food, complete diet, mixed in the proportion of 1 cup of feed to ½ cup of hot or cold water. And it will just love bones.

Origin and history
The Sealyham takes its name from Sealyham in Haverfordwest, Wales, UK, where the breed was created in the mid-1800s. The Sealyham was derived from other terriers with proven ability as hunters of fox, badger and vermin. (Some say that the Sealyham owes its existence to a terrier imported into Wales from Belgium in the fifteenth century.) Haverfordwest formed the first Sealyham Terrier Club in 1908, and Fred Lewis, founder of the Sealyham Terrier Club, is said to have done much to improve the strain. The breed was recognized by the British and American kennel clubs three years later.

The Sealyham's popularity on the American show bench has remained fairly constant since it was first exhibited in San Mateo, California, in September 1911. The American Sealyham Terrier Club was founded on 15 May 1913 to promote the welfare of the breed and to encourage its advocates to enter their dogs in conformation shows and working trials.

SHOW STANDARD
General appearance. Should be that of a freely moving, active dog.

Colour. Mostly all white or white with lemon, brown, or badger pied markings on head and ears.

Head and skull. The skull should be slightly domed and wide between the ears. Head powerful and long with a punishing and square jaw. Nose black.

Tail. Carried erect.

Feet. Round and cat-like with thick pads.

The West Highland White Terrier's pure white coat is one of its most striking features. The outer coat consists of hard hair free from any curl. The under-coat, which resembles fur, is short, soft and close. The coat may be whitened with a chalk block for showing purposes.

West Highland White Terrier

Scottish Terrier

The Sealyham Terrier has been a very successful show dog around the world, especially in America where it made its show debut in California in 1911.

Sealyham Terrier

MINIATURE SCHNAUZER

Good points
● *Intelligent*
● *Obedient*
● *Long-lived*
● *Good with children*
● *Fine watchdog*

Take heed
● *No drawbacks known*

The Miniature Schnauzer is an attractive little dog with appealing bushy eyebrows. It is good-natured, adores children and is happiest living with the family indoors, rather than being relegated to an outside kennel. It is long-lived and easy to train and often does well in obedience competitions.

Size
The ideal height for bitches shall be 13in (33cm) and for dogs 14in (35.5cm).

Exercise
The Miniature Schnauzer can be kept in town or country and does not require a great deal of space, although it does enjoy a garden to romp in and looks forward to good walks and off-the-lead runs.

Grooming
This breed needs to be hand stripped in spring and summer — more often if a show career is envisaged. Have this professionally done, or get instructions from the breeder — the breed club is sure to have an instruction leaflet. Clumsy, inexperienced hands can ruin a good temperament. A good weekly brushing is essential and so is the removal of any dead hair in the under-coat.

Feeding
Recommended would be 6-13oz (170-369g) of a branded, meaty product with biscuit added in equal part by volume, or ¾-1½ cupfuls of a dry food, complete diet, mixed in the proportion of 1 cup of feed to ½ cup of hot or cold water.

Origin and history
The Miniature Schnauzer is a replica in miniature of its bigger brother, the Standard Schnauzer, there being some 4in (10cm) difference in height between them. There is strong support for the suggestion that the Miniature Schnauzer evolved through crossing the Standard Schnauzer with the little monkey-faced Affenpinscher, although a Pomeranian or even a Fox Terrier may have been used.

This miniature variety was bred in Germany for at least a century before finding its way to the United Kingdom in 1928, when a black bitch was imported. She was followed in 1930 by two pepper-and-salt champions. About this time the breed also began to gain popularity in the United States, where the breed is extremely popular nowadays. Its spread among British fanciers has been

Above: A Miniature Schnauzer, an appealing, good-natured breed that loves children, is easy to train and does well in obedience tests.

somewhat slower, but the breed has been awarded challenge certificates since 1935.

SHOW STANDARD
General appearance. The Miniature Schnauzer is a powerfully built, robust, sinewy, nearly square dog (length of body is equal to height at shoulder). Its temperament combines high spirits, reliability, strength, endurance and vigour. Expression keen and attitude alert. Correct conformation is of more importance than colour or other purely aesthetic points.
Colour. All pepper-and-salt colours in even proportions, or pure black.
Head and skull. Head strong and elongated, gradually narrowing from the ears to the eyes and thence toward the tip of the nose. Upper part of the head (occiput to base of forehead) moderately broad between the ears with flat, creaseless forehead and well-muscled but not too strongly developed cheeks. Medium stop to accentuate prominent eyebrows. The powerful muzzle formed by the upper and lower jaws (base of forehead to tip of nose) should end in a moderately blunt line with bristly, stubby moustache and chin whiskers. Ridge of nose straight and running almost parallel to the extension of the forehead. The nose is black and full. Lips should be tight and not overlapping
Tail. Set on and carried high; cut down to three joints.
Feet. Short, round and extremely compact with close-arched toes (cat's paws); deep or thickly padded, pointing forward. Dark nails and hard soles.

LUNDEHUND
(Puffin Dog; Puffin Hound)

Good points
● *Alert*
● *Active*
● *Excellent hunter*
● *Faithful companion*

Take heed
● *No drawbacks known*

The Lundehund has existed for centuries on two islands off the coast of northern Norway but is little known outside Scandinavia. For

many years it was impossible to export a breed member and this may still be the case. The breed is derived from the Miniature Elkhound.

Size
Weight approximately 13-14lb (5.9-6.4kg). Height: dog 12½-14in (31.5-35.5cm); bitch 12-13½in (30-34cm).

Exercise
This little dog is a hunter skilful at scaling rocks and precipes. Kept as a pet, it is happiest if exercised freely.

Grooming
Regular brushing with a stiff-bristled brush should be sufficient.

Feeding
Six-13oz (170-369g) of a branded, meaty product with biscuit added in equal part by volume, or ¾-1½ cupfuls of a dry, complete food, mixed in the proportion of 1 cup of feed to ½ cup of hot or cold water.

Origin and history
The Lundehund, or Puffin Dog, is a Spitz variety that received recognition in Scandinavia in 1943. Its job in life is to locate puffins' nests in rocks and crevices and to retrieve the eggs and birds, the puffin being a welcome addition to the islanders' meal table. Puffin-hunting is an art that has existed in Scandinavia for at least 400 years.

This dog has five functional toes on each foot (normally there are four); and in the upper part of the ears, the cartilage ends meet and can shut when the ears are partly raised. It is thought that this may prevent water penetrating and damaging the ear.

SHOW STANDARD
This breed is recognized in the United Kingdom but not in the United States. It is a small variety of Spitz. Colours: black, grey and various shades of brown with white. The coat is rather rough, dense and close to the body, and the tail, which is set on rather high, has a short dense coat, but no flag.

SCHIPPERKE

Good points
● *Affectionate*
● *Excellent guard*
● *Good with children*
● *Handy size*
● *Hardy*

Take heed
● *Needs affection and individual attention*

The Schipperke is a delightful breed that originated in Belgium, where its job was to guard canal barges when they had been tied up for the night. The name Schipperke is, in fact, Flemish for 'little captain'.

Apart from being an excellent guard dog, the Schipperke is a most affectionate animal, and it is particularly good with children. It is also hardy and long-lived. However, it needs individual attention and

likes to be treated as a member of the family; it also takes a while to accept strangers.

Size
The weight should be about 12-16lb (5.4-7.3kg).

Exercise
A Schipperke can walk up to 6 miles (10km) or more without any sign of fatigue; but it can manage with a great deal less exerecise if its owner lives in a town.

Grooming
The Schipperke has a dense hard coat that needs very little regular grooming.

Feeding
Feeding is no problem: a Schipperke will eat anything that is offered to it, and one good meal a day, perhaps with biscuit at night, will suffice. Recommended for its size would be 6-13oz (170-369g) of a branded, meaty product with biscuit added in equal part by volume, or ¾-1½ cupfuls of a dry, complete food, mixed in the proportion of 1 cup of feed to ½ cup of hot or cold water.

Origin and history
The Schipperke originated in Belgium but is often thought to be a Dutch dog, probably because Belgium and the Netherlands have been one country in the past. The breed is well over 100-years-old; some claim it to be nearer 200-years-old, but there are no records to support this theory.

How the breed evolved is subject to conjecture. Some classify it as a member of the Spitz family, others as the result of a terrier/Pomeranian cross. However, it seems likely that the Schipperke and the Groenendael have a common ancestor, the Schipperke closely resembling a smaller example of that other fine Belgian breed.

The Schipperke became a fashionable pet in 1885 when Queen Marie Henriette, wife of Leopold II, acquired a Schipperke at a show in Brussels. Three years later the breed made its way to the United States, and not long after that it was being shown in miscellaneous classes there, but the first American breed club was not formed until 1929.

SHOW STANDARD
General appearance. A small, cobby animal with a sharp expression and intensely lively, presenting the appearance of being always on the alert.
Colour. Should be black, but other whole colours are permissible.
Head and skull. Head foxy in type, skull not round but fairly broad, flat and with little stop. The muzzle should be moderate in length, fine but not weak, and well filled out under the eyes. Nose black and small.
Hindquarters. Fine compared to the foreparts; muscular and well-developed thighs; tail-less rump, well rounded. Legs strong and muscular, hocks well let down.
Feet. Should be small, cat-like and standing well on the toes.

Lundehund
(Puffin Dog)

The Miniature Schnauzer's coat
should be hard and wiry and
just short enough for smartness,
clean on the neck,
shoulders, ears and skull with
plenty of good hard hair
on the front legs.

Miniature Schnauzer

Schipperke

The Schipperke's coat
should be dense and harsh,
smooth on the head, ears
and legs, lying close on the
back and sides. It should be
erect and thick round the
neck, forming a mane and frill, and
there should be a good culotte on the
back of the thighs.

AMERICAN COCKER SPANIEL

Good points
- Adaptable to town or country living
- Beautiful
- Excellent family pet
- Intelligent
- Obedient

Take heed
- Needs lots of grooming
- Progressive retinal atrophy exists in this breed

The American Cocker Spaniel is an excellent hunter and excels in flushing out and retrieving birds. It is also extremely popular as a household pet and is an attractive, affectionate, adaptable animal and an excellent companion.

Size
The ideal height at the withers for an adult dog is 15in (38cm) and for an adult bitch 14in (35.5cm). Height may vary ½in (13mm) above or below this ideal. A dog whose height exceeds 15½in (39.5cm) or a bitch whose height exceeds 14½in (37cm) or an adult bitch whose height is less than 13½in (34cm) should be penalized.

Exercise
It must be remembered that the Cocker Spaniel was originally bred for hunting and, although it adapts happily to the role of companion and family pet, it will obviously fit in best with families who are prepared to give it two good walks a day and have a garden for it to romp in.

Grooming
The American Cocker with its luxuriant coat needs frequent brushing and combing and a bath and trim every eight to ten weeks. It is best to ask the breeder for advice or to visit a professional dog groomer because the skull and muzzle hair must be trimmed to precise accepted lengths with electric clippers. The neck and shoulders must also be scissored carefully with feathering left on the legs, ears and belly. Feet must also be trimmed. Obviously you may wish to attend to this ritual yourself, but it is advisable to be shown the procedure by an expert first.

Feeding
Recommended would be 13-20oz (369-587g) of a branded, meaty product with biscuit added in equal part by volume, or 2-3 cupfuls of a dry food, complete diet, mixed in the proportion of 1 cup of feed to ½ cup of hot or cold water.

Origin and history
The American Cocker is smaller than the English Cocker, has a much thicker coat and, although originating from England, has been bred along different lines in the United States. Its elegant trousers and length of coat are the simplest means of clear identification.

An American Cocker was first shown in America at Manchester, New Hampshire, in September 1883, and when permission was given by the American Kennel Club for the two varieties to be shown, there was great enthusiasm for the American Cocker.

SHOW STANDARD
General appearance. A very serviceable-looking dog with a refined head; standing on straight legs and well up at the shoulders; of compact body and wide, muscular quarters. The American Cocker Spaniel's sturdy body, powerful quarters and strong, well-boned legs show it to be a dog capable of considerable speed combined with great endurance. Above all it must be free and merry, sound, well-balanced throughout, keen to work, equable in temperament and with no suggestion of timidity.

Colour. Blacks should be jet black; shadings of brown or liver in the sheen of the coat are not desirable. Black and tan (classified under solid colours) should have definite tan markings on a jet black body. The tan markings should be distinct and plainly visible, and the colour of the tan may be from the lightest cream to the darkest red colour. The amount of tan markings should be restricted to 10 per cent or less of the colour of the animal; tan markings in excess of 10 per cent should be penalized. Tan markings not readily visible in the ring, or the absence of tan markings in any of the specified locations, should be penalized.

In all the above solid colours, a small amount of white on chest and throat, though not desirable, is allowed; but white in any other location should be penalized. Parti-colours: Two or more definite colours appearing in clearly defined markings are essential. Primary colour that is 90 per cent or more should be penalized; secondary colour or colours that are limited to one location should also be penalized. Roans are classified as parti-colours and may be of any of the usual roaning patterns. Tricolours are any of the above colours combined with tan markings. It is preferable that the tan markings be located in the same pattern as for black and tan.

Head and skull. There should be a good square muzzle with a distinct stop mid-way between the tip of the nose and the occiput. The skull should be well developed, cleanly chiselled, neither too fine nor too coarse. The cheek bones should not be prominent. The nose should be sufficiently wide to allow for the acute scenting power of this breed.

Body. The body is short and compact. The distance from the highest point of the shoulder blades to the ground is 2in (2.5cm) longer than the distance from the shoulder to the set on of the tail.

Tail. This should be set on slightly lower than the line of the back; it must be carried in line with the back and never cocked up. The tail should not be docked too long nor too short to interfere with its action.

Feet. Feet should be firm, thickly padded and cat-like.

ENGLISH COCKER SPANIEL

Good points
- Affectionate, gentle nature
- Excellent gundog
- Good with children
- Long-lived
- Merry temperament

Take heed
- Overfeeding will cause weight problems
- Keep ears out of feed bowl
- Progressive retinal atrophy exists in this breed.

The 'merry' Cocker, as it is called, makes an ideal family pet — a dog for Dad to take out shooting or for the children to romp with in the garden. It is manageable, intelligent and a good all-purpose gundog, second to none at flushing out game.

With correct diet and exercise the Cocker Spaniel proves to be one of the healthiest and most long-lived of dogs. Its beautiful, appealing eyes make it difficult to refuse it anything, and there are few breeds in the world to challenge its beauty as a pup.

Size
The weight should be about 28-32lb (12.7-14.5kg). The height at the withers should be: dog 15½-16in (39.5-40.5cm), bitch 15-15½in (38-39.5cm).

Above: The English Cocker Spaniel, here with pup, makes a gentle pet, but owners should be aware of potential eye problems.

Exercise
This is an active dog that needs regular exercise. It adores the country and is likely to return from a walk with tail wagging and covered with mud. So it is not perhaps the ideal choice for smart town dwellers, but it does enjoy home comforts, such as a place beside a warm fire.

Grooming
The Cocker requires frequent brushing and combing, care being taken that its coat does not become matted. Particular care must be exercised that the ears do not become tangled; and watch out that they do not flop into the feed bowl — a common occurrence. You might consider taping them back while the dog is eating.

Origin and history
The Cocker Spaniel is particularly popular in the United Kingdom. In the United States it is known as the English Cocker. It is also sometimes referred to as the 'merry' Cocker because of its happy, lively temperament and constantly wagging tail. Other titles bestowed upon it have been the Cocking Spaniel or Cocker, because of its one-time prowess at flushing out woodcock.

The Cocker Spaniel did however originate in Spain — whence the name 'spaniel' — and its ancestry can be traced back to the fourteenth century. It is believed to have been used in various countries in falconry. Today, however, it is in its element rabbit hunting, flushing out game for its master, then remaining motionless until a shot has been fired. It is also well able to retrieve and is an ideal choice for both working trials and dog training competitions.

Feeding
Recommended would be 13-20oz (369-587g) of a branded, meaty product with biscuit added in equal part by volume, or 2-3 cupfuls of a dry food, complete diet, mixed in the proportion of 1 cup of feed to ½ cup of hot or cold water. Obviously rations will need to be stepped up if the dog is taking vigorous exercise. This is a breed that will plead endearingly for titbits, which should be denied if the owner is to avoid an overweight pet.

SHOW STANDARD
General appearance. A merry, sturdy sporting dog. The Cocker Spaniel should be well balanced and compact and should measure about the same from the withers to the ground as from the withers to the root of the tail.

Colour. Various; in self-colours no white is allowed except on the chest.

Head and skull. There should be a good square muzzle with a distinct stop, which should be half-way between the tip of the nose and the occiput. The skull should be well developed, cleanly chiselled, neither too fine nor too coarse. The cheek bones should not be prominent. The nose should be sufficiently wide to allow for the acute scenting power of this breed — useful when flushing out game in the wild.

Body. The body is close-coupled, compact and firmly knit. The ribs are well sprung, and the depth of brisket should reach to the elbow. Dogs that are too long or that lack depth should be faulted.

Tail. The tail should be set on slightly lower than the line of the back; it must be carried in line with the back and never cocked up. The tail should not be docked too long nor too short to interfere with its action.

Feet. These should be firm, thickly padded and cat-like.

The most noticeable difference between the American and
English Cocker spaniels is one of size: bred to flush and retrieve
smaller game in America, the American Cocker
Spaniel is a correspondingly smaller breed. Both
breeds have achieved great success in the
show ring, the American being generally
shown with a more profuse coat
than the English breed.

American Cocker Spaniel

English Cocker Spaniel

SWEDISH VALLHUND
(Västgötaspets)

Good points
- Active
- Excellent drover/cattle dog
- Loyal

Take heed
- No drawbacks known

The Vallhund or Västgötaspets is a Swedish breed, similar in appearance to the Welsh Corgi. It is an active, intelligent worker and is rapidly gaining popularity in many parts of the world.

Size
Height: dog 13in (33cm), bitch 12.3in (31.2cm).

Exercise
Fares best if given plenty of exercise.

Grooming
Normal frequent brushing.

Feeding
Thirteen-20oz (369-587g) of a branded, meaty product with biscuit added in equal part by volume, or 2-3 cupfuls of a dry food, compete diet, mixed in the proportion of 1 cup of feed to ½ cup of water.

Origin and history
The Västgötaspets, to give it its Swedish name, looks something like a Cardigan/Pembroke Corgi cross. There is certainly a connection between the Corgi and this attractive breed, but it is impossible to determine whether it evolved as the result of Vikings taking Corgis to Sweden or if Swedish dogs brought to Britain developed the Corgi. The Swedes certainly claim credit for this fine little cattle dog, which owes its present development and recognition to Björn von Rosen.

PEMBROKE WELSH CORGI

Good points
- Devoted companion
- Excellent guard
- Fond of children

- Hardy
- Tireless

Take heed
- Needs training when young— the inherent tendency to nip must be discouraged

The Welsh Corgi (Pembroke) has, like the Cardigan, been worked in the south of Wales for many centuries. It has evolved as a popular and affectionate pet, particularly because it is a breed much favoured by the British royal family, whose pets have been known to take the occasional, much publicized nip.

Size
Weight: dog 20-24lb (9-10.9kg); bitch 18-22lb (8.2-10kg). Height: 10-12in (25-30cm) at the shoulder.

Exercise
Although traditionally a worker, the Pembroke adapts well to life as a domestic pet if given daily walks of average length. But beware: if you do not give sufficient exercise, this breed will soon lose its figure.

Grooming
Frequent brushing needed. The breed has a water-resistant coat.

Feeding
Give 6-13oz (170-369g) of a branded, meaty product with biscuit added in equal part by volume, or ¾-1½ cupfuls of a dry food, complete diet, mixed in the proportion of 1 cup of feed to ½ cup of hot or cold water.

Origin and history
The Welsh Corgi (Pembroke) has worked in southern Wales since the *Domesday Book* survey was instigated by William the Conqueror in the eleventh century. Its traditional task was to control the movement of cattle by nipping at their ankles and then getting quickly out of range. It has, however, a bolder temperament than the Cardigan.

Some say that the Pembroke derives from stock brought to Wales by Flemish weavers who settled in the locality and crossed their dogs with Welsh native stock; others point out the similarity that exists between the Welsh Corgi (Pembroke) and the Swedish Västgötaspets, suggesting that trading between the Welsh and the Swedes introduced the breed to Wales.

In any event, the Welsh Corgi (Pembroke) has been exhibited in Britain since 1925, receiving separate classification from the Welsh Corgi (Cardigan) in 1934. It is, perhaps, one of the best-known breeds in the United Kingdom because of its association with Her Majesty Queen Elizabeth II.

SHOW STANDARD
General appearance. Low-set, strong sturdily built, alert and active,

Left: The Vallhund closely resembles the Welsh Corgi in appearance. It was developed in Sweden as a fine cattle dog.

Above: Pembroke Welsh Corgis make most affectionate pets once their tendency to nip has been discouraged.

giving an impression of susbtance and stamina in a small space; outlook bold, expression intelligent and workman-like. The movement should be free and active, elbows fitting closely to the sides, neither loose nor tied. Forelegs should move well forward without too much lift, in unison with the thrusting action of the hindlegs.

Colour. Self-colours in red, sable, fawn, black and tan, or with white markings on legs, chest and neck. Some white on head and foreface is permissible.

Head and skull. Head foxy in shape and appearance with alert and intelligent expression; skull fairly wide and flat between the ears; moderate amount of stop. Length of foreface in proportion to the skull as 3:5. Muzzle slightly tapering. Nose black.

Tail. Short, preferably natural.

Feet. Oval, the two centre toes slightly in advance of the two outer ones; pads strong and well arched; nails short.

CARDIGAN WELSH CORGI

Good points
- Devoted companion
- Excellent guard
- Fond of children
- Hardy
- Quieter temperament than the Pembroke
- Tireless

Take heed
- This breed had eye defects in the past, so seek a veterinarian's advice if your choice gives you cause for concern

The Welsh Corgi (Cardigan) has been known and worked in the south of Wales for centuries. It is hardy, fond of children and tireless, and, despite its orginal task of nipping the heels of cattle to bring them into line, has a more equable temperament than the Pembroke and is less likely to nip the heels of unsuspectng visitors.

Size
Height as near as possible to 12in (30cm) at the shoulder. Weight: dog 22-26lb (10-11.8kg); bitch 20-24lb (9-10.9kg).

Exercise
Although traditionally a worker, the Cardigan adapts well to life as a domestic pet if given daily walks of average length. But beware: if you do not give sufficient exercises this breed will soon lose its figure.

Grooming
Frequent brushing needed. The breed has a water-resistant coat.

Feeding
Give 6-13oz (170-369g) of a branded, meaty product with biscuit added in equal part by volume, or ¾-1½ cupfuls of a dry food, complete diet, mixed in the proportion of 1 cup of feed to ½ cup of hot or cold water.

Health care
Avoid letting your pet jump from heights, especially if overweight; this could lead to painful spine trouble. See also the remarks above on eye defects (progressive retinal atrophy); fortunately, these have now been almost eradicated from the breed.

Origin and history
The Welsh Corgi (Cardigan) has worked in southern Wales since the *Domesday Book* survey was instigated by William the Conqueror in the eleventh century. Its traditional task was to control the movement of cattle by nipping at their ankles and then getting quickly out of range.

The breed first made its appearance in the British show ring in 1925, classified as one breed with the Welsh Corgi (Pembroke); it received separate classification in 1934. Welsh folklore contains many references to this dependable, ancient breed, which has perhaps missed out on popularity due to the British royal family's particular fondness for its Pembrokeshire cousin.

SHOW STANDARD
General appearance. Expression as foxy as possible; alertness essential; the body to measure about 36in (91.5cm) from point of nose to tip of tail.

Colour. Any colour except pure white.

Head and skull. Head foxy in shape and appearance. Skull fairly wide and flat between the ears, tapering towards the eyes, above which it is slightly domed. Muzzle should measure about 3in (7.5cm) in length (or in proportion to the skull as 3:5) and taper towards the snout. Nose black (except in blue merles), slightly projecting and in no sense blunt with nostrils of moderate size. Under-jaw should be clean cut and strong but without prominence.

Body. The body is long and strong, and there is a slight downward slope to the tail set. The chest is moderately broad with a prominent breast bone. Well-sprung ribs allow for good lungs. The waist is well defined.

Tail. Moderately long and set in line with the body (not curled over the back) and resembling that of a fox.

Feet. Round and well padded. All dew-claws removed. Rather large.

An ancient breed, the Swedish Vallhund has been part of the agricultural scene in the south and midlands of Sweden since time immemorial, but taken so much for granted that at the beginning of this century it had almost disappeared as a pure breed. Although it resembles the Pembroke Corgi in appearance, in contrast to the bright colours associated with that breed, this little dog has a grey, brownish-yellow or brindle coat.

Swedish Vallhund

Pembroke Welsh Corgi

Cardigan Welsh Corgi

A Selection of
MEDIUM DOGS

Medium-sized dogs are the most popular kind. The medium-sized dog is not, perhaps, so ostentatious as the animal of diminutive or gargantuan proportions, and so it tends to be accepted most readily as part of the average domestic scene.

The couple with a medium-sized house and a medium-sized garden might naturally choose a dog that conforms with their all-things-in-moderation life-style. In the eyes of its owners, the medium-sized dog is neither so small as to make them look ridiculous nor so large as to frighten away their visitors. Neither do medium-sized dogs cause them worry about providing exercise and space or anxiety over the cost of feeding. The medium-sized dog is also big enough to play tirelessly with the children once it is fully grown.

Medium-sized dogs are usually easiest to find and to cater for. Because their puppies are much sought after, breeders are rarely in short supply. Similarly, baskets, cots and other accessories are usually made with the average pet in mind.

There is a medium-sized breed to suit everyone. The man or woman with a wish to enter their pet in obedience competitions could not make a better choice than a Border Collie. A Whippet should satisfy the buyer who wants an elegant animal that can also share his sporting interests. There is a spaniel variety suitable for any huntsman. The traditional Bulldog could not be better for a man who is getting on in years and wants a dog that will not walk him off his feet. And the Beagle or the Basset Hound is ideal for any couple who want an amusing and affectionate pet; but since these are hounds they will give their owners the slip if possible and wander off, nose to the ground, on the trail of some scent-filled adventure. Breeds in all categories, however, be they medium, large or small, have their personality quirks.

Many philosophers believe that the middle course is often the best. Interestingly, it is believed that if dogs were allowed to breed without human interference, the average dog would eventually be a medium-sized animal between 35 and 45lbs (16 and 20kgs).

Below: The morose-looking Basset Hound is a popular pet with all the family.

PORTUGUESE WATER DOG
(Cao d'Agua)

Good points
- Excellent retriever
- First-rate swimmer
- Good watchdog
- Loyal

Take heed
- Suspicious of strangers

The Portuguese Water Dog is most commonly found in the Algarve area of its native Portugal, where it is a true fisherman's dog, acting virtually as a member of the crew and tackling a variety of tasks ranging from guarding the nets to diving and retrieving. It will actually catch an escaping fish in its jaws and swim back with it safely to the boat. It is loyal to its master but not very trustworthy with strangers.

Size
Height: dog 20-22½in (51-57cm); bitch 17-20½in (43-52cm). Weight: dog 42-55lb (19-25kg); bitch 35-48½lb (15.9-22kg).

Exercise
Revels in an active, outdoor life.

Grooming
The Portuguese Water Dog comes in two coat types, but as this is the only difference there is only one standard for the breed. There is a long-coated variety, which has a lion show trim reminiscent of the Poodle, and a short, curly-coated variety, which gives the animal an appealingly scruffy appearance, particularly as it is so often in water. Regular brushing is advised.

Feeding
Thirteen-20oz (369-587g) of a branded, meaty product with biscuit added in equal part by volume, or 1¾-3 cupfuls of a dry food, complete diet, mixed in the proportion of 1 cup of feed to ½ cup of hot or cold water.

Origin and history
This unusual dog, which is not only a fine fisherman but can also catch rabbits, has been known for centuries around the Iberian Peninsula, where it was bred for its task of retrieving fish and guarding nets. Formerly used throughout Portugal, it is almost limited today to the region of the Algarve, where fishing traditions continue very much as in the past. It is little known outside its country of origin. This breed should not be confused with the Portuguese Warren Hound (or Podengo), which is mainly found in northern Portugal, where it is used for rabbiting.

SHOW STANDARD
General characteristics. A medium-sized dog, very well proportioned, rugged and muscular. Its constant use as a water retriever accounts for the extraordinary muscular development.
Colour. Black, white and various shades of brown; also combinations

of black or brown with white. A white coat does not indicate albinism provided nose, mouth and eyelids are black.
Head and skull. The head is well proportioned and massive. Viewed in profile, the skull is slightly longer than the muzzle. The curve of the skull is rather more accentuated at the back than in front. The occiput is well defined. Viewed from the front the skull is domed with a slight concavity in the middle. The forehead is furrowed for two-thirds of the length of the parietal bones; the frontal bones are prominent.

The muzzle tapers from base to nose. The stop is well defined and lies slightly farther back than the inner corner of the eyes. The nose is wide with well-open nostrils, which are finely pigmented. Nose colour varies with coat colour. The lips are rather thick, especially in front. The inner mouth is well blacked, the powerful jaws are neither undershot nor overshot. The teeth are not visible when the mouth is closed; the canines are strongly developed.
Tail. Not docked; thick at the base, tapering gradually to the tip. It

Above: The long-coated Portuguese Water Dog is a rare breed.

should be set on neither too high nor too low. Extended, it should not reach below the hock. When the dog is on the alert, the tail should be held in a ring, the forepart of which does not lie beyond the rear limit of the loin. The tail is used actively in both swimming and diving.
Feet. The feet are round and rather flat. The toes should not be too long and should not be knuckled up.

The Portuguese Water Dog was once common in all the Portuguese and Spanish seaports. Used exclusively as a working dog on fishing boats, it was reputed to be a formidable fighter.

Portuguese Water Dog

BRITTANY

Good points
- *Affectionate*
- *Excellent pointer*
- *Good nose*
- *Tireless*
- *Loyal*

Take heed
- *A sensitive dog that needs kind handling*

The Brittany combines well the roles of hunter and companion. It has a natural talent for pointing and has been described as more like a setter than a spaniel. It has an excellent nose and can cope with difficult terrain. It is, however, a sensitive animal that expects, and deserves, every consideration from its master. It is easily distinguishable by its short, stumpy tail. This breed is relatively unknown in the United Kingdom, but has been successful in field trials in the USA.

Size
Height: maximum 20½in (52cm), minimum 18¼in (46.5cm); ideal for dog 19¼-20in (49-51cm), for bitch 18¾-19¾in (47.5-50cm).

Exercise
Relishes plenty of exercise.

Grooming
Regular brushing. Take care that foreign bodies do not lodge in ears, eyes or paws.

Feeding
Recommended would be 13-20oz (369-587g) of a branded, meaty product with biscuit added in equal part by volume, or 1¾-3 cupfuls of a dry food, complete diet, mixed in the proportion of 1 cup of feed to ½ cup of hot or cold water.

Origin and history
The Brittany probably originated either in Spain or in the Argoat Forests of Brittany. There is also a story that one of the red and white English Setters of a Breton count mated with a Breton bitch, thus starting the development of the Brittany.

SHOW STANDARD
General appearance. A medium dog, elegant but vigorous, compact and stocky. The movement is energetic, the expression intelligent and it has the general look of a fine spaniel.
Colour. Orange and white, maroon and white, black and white, tricolour or marked with one or the other of these colours.
Head and skull. Skull average length, rounded; hollow stop obvious although lightly falling in or sloping. Forehead shorter than the larger axis of the skull; straight or slightly curved, in the proportion of 3:2 to the skull. Nose a deep shade, according to the colour of the dog. Nostrils well open; nose a little angular. Lips thin and receding; upper lip slightly overlapping the lower.
Tail. Straight or drooping, if the animal is not in action; always short, about 4in (10cm); often a trifle crooked and ending in a tuft.
Feet. Closed toes, with a little hair between them.

WELSH SPRINGER SPANIEL

Good points
- *Loyal*
- *Willing*
- *Fine gundog*
- *Excellent nose*
- *Good water dog*
- *Makes good pet*
- *Tireless*

Take heed
- *Needs training or could become a destructive hunter*

The Welsh Springer Spaniel is a lively dog with plenty of enthusiasm and endurance. It is somewhere between the little Cocker Spaniel and the English Springer in stature. It is a tireless breed and, in common with most spaniels, provided it is given plenty of exercise and correct feeding it will live to a ripe old age.

Size
Dog up to 19in (48cm) in height at shoulder, and bitch 18in (46cm) approximately.

Exercise
Like most spaniels, the Welsh Springer is essentially a working animal and is not ideally suited for apartment life or for those with insufficient time to take it for lengthy walks.

Grooming
Similar care to other spaniels, regular brushing and combing required.

Feeding
See Brittany.

Origin and history
A dog that would seem to be a forerunner of the Welsh Springer Spaniel is mentioned in the earliest records of the *Laws of Wales*, circa 1300 AD. Indeed, it appears that even before that time a similar white spaniel with red markings had been associated with the region. The Welsh Springer Spaniel is, in fact, very similar to the Brittany and makes a first-class gundog and household pet.

SHOW STANDARD
General appearance. A symmetrical, compact, strong, merry, very active dog; not stilty (i.e. stiff in appearance); obviously built for endurance and hard work. A quick and active mover displaying plenty of push and drive.
Colour. Rich red and white only.
Head and skull. Skull proportionate, of moderate length, slightly domed with a clearly defined stop, and well chiselled below the eyes. Muzzle of medium length, straight, fairly square; the nostrils well developed and flesh-coloured or dark. A short, chubby head is objectionable.
Tail. Well set on and low, never carried above the level of the back; lightly feathered and lively in action.
Feet. Round with thick pads. Firm and cat-like, not too large or spreading.

POINTING WIRE-HAIRED GRIFFON

Good points
- *Easy to train*
- *Equable temperament*
- *Good companion*
- *Intelligent*
- *Good water dog*

Take heed
- *A reliable and careful, rather than speedy, gundog*
- *Needs plenty of exercise*

The Pointing Wire-haired Griffon is an intelligent, companionable dog that not only points, but also works well in water. It is an attractive, good-natured animal which performs its task slowly but surely. It is easily trained.

Size
Height: dog 21½-23½in (54.5-60cm), bitch 19½-21½in (49.5-54.5cm).

Exercise
Needs plenty of vigorous exercise.

Grooming
Regular brushing will keep the coat in good condition.

Feeding
See Brittany.

Origin and history
The Pointing Wire-haired Griffon was developed around 1874 by a Dutch sportsman named Edward Korthals. Korthals was a man of considerable breeding experience, who had managed the kennels of a German prince for many years, and it was his resolve to produce a dog with both courage and hunting ability. He achieved this by experimental crossings with French, Belgian and German gundogs until the Pointing Wire-haired Griffon was established — a pointer that was at home in water and, although not as swift a worker as other gundogs, a reliable and plucky worker. Some say that it is the ideal gundog for the older sportsman. It was first shown in the United Kingdom in 1888.

SHOW STANDARD (FCI)
Colour. Preferably steel grey with chestnut markings or uniformly reddish chestnut or roan. White and chestnut and white and orange are also acceptable.
Head and skull. Large, long with rough tufted hair, thick but not too long, very pronounced moustache and eyebrows, skull not too wide, muzzle long, strong and square, facial angle not too pronounced, nose invariably brown.
Tail. Carried horizontally or with the tip slightly raised; the hair abundant but not plumed. Usually it is docked.
Feet. Round and solid, the toes close and webbed.

Below: These Pointing Griffons are slow but reliable and plucky.

Although the Brittany was not officially recognized in France until 1907, from reports of hunting in the mid-1800s it appears that its progenitors were popular because of their excellent pointing and retrieving ability. It was introduced into the United States in 1931.

Brittany

Welsh Springer Spaniel

The Welsh Springer Spaniel, or starter as it is known in Wales, is an active, hard-working dog with a hardy constitution. Able to withstand a rigorous climate and having a long, water-resistant coat, it makes an excellent hunter for all seasons.

FIELD SPANIEL

Good points
- *Sensible*
- *Intelligent*
- *Excellent in the field*
- *Affectionate*
- *Docile temperament*

Take heed
- *No drawbacks known*

Field Spaniels are of similar origin to the Cocker, and it was not until 1892 that they were categorized as separate breeds. Afterwards the Cocker Spaniel improved dramatically and the Field Spaniel did not, becoming, in fact, extremely long-bodied and short-legged. However, the Field Spaniel Society was reformed in the United Kingdom in 1948 and — thanks to tremendous work and enthusiasm — a standard type has evolved that is breeding true. The breed is little known, although recognized, in the United States. The passing of the Field Spaniel would be a tragedy, as it is an extremely docile animal, excellent in the field and a fine house-pet. It is intelligent and also has a very steady temperament.

Size
Weight: about 35-50lb(15.9-22.7kg). Height: about 18in (46cm) to the shoulder.

Exercise
It would be a great pity to keep a Field Spaniel in an apartment or a city environment where it would not get the lengthy walks and runs that it needs and deserves.

Grooming
Regular brushing and combing will suffice, but take care that the coat does not become tangled or matted and that nothing becomes lodged between the toes.

Feeding
Recommended would be 13-20oz (369-587g) of a branded, meaty product with biscuit added in equal

Below: The Field Spaniel is a willing and tireless worker. Its steady temperament makes it a fine house-pet as well.

part by volume, or 1¾-3 cupfuls of a dry complete diet, mixed in the proportion of 1 cup of feed to ½ cup of hot or cold water.

Origin and history
The history of the Field Spaniel runs parallel with that of the the Cocker, and until the breeds were separated in 1892 they were shown as Field Spaniels under and over 25lb (11.3kg). The breed is recognized in the United States but there are few registrations.

SHOW STANDARD
General appearance. A well-balanced, noble sporting dog; built for activity and endurance; a combination of beauty and utility; unusualy docile.

Colour. The Field Spaniel should be a self-coloured dog in black, liver, golden liver, mahogany red, roan or any one of these colours with tan over the eyes and on the cheeks, feet and pasterns. Other colours, such as black and white, liver and white, red or orange and white, although they do not debar a dog, are a fault.

Head and skull. The head should be as characteristic as that of the English Bulldog or the Bloodhound; its very stamp and countenance should at once convey the impression of high breeding, character and nobility. Skull should be well developed with a distinct occipital protuberance that gives the character alluded to; not too wide across the muzzle, long and lean, neither snipy nor squarely cut; and in profile curving gradually from nose to throat; lean beneath the eyes, as a thickness here gives coarseness to the whole head. The great length of muzzle gives surface for the free development of the olfactory nerve, and thus secures the highest possible scenting powers. Nose should be well developed with open nostrils.

Tail. Well set on and carried low, if possible below the level of the back, in a straight line or with a slight downward inclination, never elevated above the back, and in action always kept low; nicely fringed with wavy feather of silky texture.

Feet. Not too small; round with short, soft hair between the toes; good, strong pads.

WACHTELHUND
(German Spaniel; German Quail Dog)

Good points
- *Excellent nose*
- *Good in water*
- *Fine retriever/gundog*
- *Hardy*

Take heed
- *No drawbacks known*

The Wachtelhund is a hardy breed bearing some resemblance to the English Springer Spaniel. It is little known outside Germany, where it has a sound reputation as a gundog and retriever.

Size
Height: 15½-19½in (39.5-49.5cm).

Exercise
Needs plenty of exercise.

Grooming
Normal frequent brushing.

Feeding
Thirteen-20oz (369-587g) of a branded, meaty product with biscuit added in equal part by volume, or 1¾-3 cupfuls of a dry food, complete diet, mixed in the proportion of 1 cup of feed to ½ cup of hot or cold water.

Origin and history
The Germans, when they produced the Wachtelhund, wanted to create a breed that could cope with waters and forest and also flush out and retrieve game. The breed was produced by the crossing of a number of small dogs. However, Harrap's *Champion Dogs of the World* credits the old German Stöber with the Wachtelhund's excellent nose.

The Wachtelhund, which is not recognized in either the United Kingdom or the USA, is usually dark brown in colour, and there can be white marks on chest and toes. It can also be white with brown spots, white and brown, or solid white.

SUSSEX SPANIEL

Good points
- *Loyal*
- *Tireless worker*
- *Intelligent*
- *Alert*

Take heed
- *Tends to be a one-person dog*

The Sussex Spaniel has been known in southern England for more than a century; it was very popular with Sussex farmers and thus its name was derived. The breed was first recognized by a Mr Fuller in 1795, when the breed was very much larger than at the present time. Later, another strain, called the Harvieston appeared, which had something of the Clumber and the Bloodhound about it. It is a pity that suddenly

the Sussex Spaniel does not enjoy greater popularity for it is a breed that makes a loyal companion, is active and alert and has an extremely good nose. This dog has a rich liver-coloured coat, which strangely loses something of its golden hue if the animal is kept indoors as a pet.

Size
Ideal weight: dog 45lb (20.5kg), bitch 40lb (18.1kg). Height: 15-16in (38-40.5cm).

Exercise
Like most spaniels, the Sussex is essentially a working animal and is not ideally suited for apartment life or for those with insufficient time to take it for long walks.

Grooming
A regular brush and comb is necessary, taking care — as with other spaniels — that the ears do not become tangled and that mud does not become caked between the paws or elsewhere in the coat.

Feeding
Recommended would be 13-20oz (369-587g) of a branded, meaty product with biscuit added in equal part by volume, or 1¾-3 cupfuls of a dry food, complete diet, mixed in the proportion of 1 cup of feed to ½ cup of hot or cold water.

Origin and history
The Sussex is essentially an English breed and has been shown since 1862, when breed members were exhibited at Crystal Palace, London. The breed was kept going between the two world wars by Mrs Freer of Fourclovers Kennels, who is owed tremendous credit for the survival of the breed. In the mid-1950s fresh blood was introduced by crossing the Sussex with the Clumber, which seems to have resulted in improved bone size and temperament.

SHOW STANDARD
General appearance. Massive and strongly built. An active, energetic, strong dog, whose characteristic movement is a decided roll, unlike that of any other spaniel.

Colour. Rich golden liver, hair shading to gold at the tips, and the gold predominating. Dark liver or puce is objectionable.

Head and skull. The skull should be wide and show a moderate curve from ear to ear, neither flat nor apple-headed, has a centre indentation and a pronounced stop. Brows frowning; occiput decided but not pointed. Nostrils well developed and liver colour. A well-balanced head.

Body. The entire body is characterized as long, low and level. The chest, which is round, particularly behind the shoulders, has good depth, width and girth. The shoulders are oblique. The back and loin are long and muscular in their depth and width.

Tail. Set low and not carried above the level of the back. Free action, thickly clothed with hair but no feather. Docked 5-7in (12.5-18cm).

Feet. Circular, well padded, well feathered between toes.

The coat of the Field Spaniel should be flat or slightly waved, silky in texture but sufficiently dense to be weather resistant. It must be glossy, and the chest, underbelly and behind the legs should be well feathered. Any tendency to curl or wiriness is a show fault.

Field Spaniel

Wachtelhund (German Spaniel)

Sussex Spaniel

BULL TERRIER

Good points
- Affectionate
- Can cope with most climates
- Excellent with children
- First-class guard
- Healthy
- Hardy

Take heed
- Best suited to country life
- Needs disciplining when young
- Needs plenty of exercise
- Powerful dog: you must be strong enough to hold on to the lead

The Bull Terrier, despite its somewhat doleful appearance, is a gentle dog and utterly reliable with children. However, if provoked by another dog, this terrier will fight to the death. The Bull Terrier never lets go. It is also a fine guard. It may let an intruder into your house, but one thing is certain: it won't let him out again. No one could call this a beautiful breed, but it has an attraction all its own.

Size
The standard has no height or weight limits: the Bull Terrier could be 70lb (31.75kg) in weight or half that. Maximum substance is required according to the size of the dog.

Exercise
The Bull Terrier is a powerful dog with boundless energy and should not be confined to apartment life. More suitable would be a happily controlled country life with plenty of opportunity to run free.

Grooming
Normal regular brushing.

Feeding
If the dog is 20-50lb (9-22.7kg) give it 13-20oz (369-587g) of a branded, meaty product with biscuit added in equal part by volume, or 1¾-3 cupfuls of a dry food, complete diet, mixed in the proportion of 1 cup of feed to ½ cup of hot or cold water.
If it is 50-100lb (22.7-45.4kg) in weight give 20-26oz (587-737g) of a branded, meaty product with biscuit added in equal part by volume, or 3-5 cupfuls of a dry food, complete diet, mixed in the proportion of 1 cup of feed to ½ cup of hot or cold water.

Health care
The Bull Terrier is a healthy, hardy dog. However, don't buy one without checking its hearing: Bull Terriers are often born deaf.

Origin and history
This terrier began life as a fighting dog and battled on, seemingly impervious to pain, until bull baiting was outlawed by the British parliament in 1835. Thereafter a dedicated band of fanciers determined to preserve the breed and refine it while preserving its strength and tenacity. They included James Hinks of Birmingham, Eng d, who, by crossing the Whi nglish Terrier

with the English Bulldog and Dalmatian, produced a new strain of white dogs he called English Bull Terriers. Following World War II, coloured Bull Terriers made their appearance. However, the breed as a whole has never regained the tremendous popularity it enjoyed in the 1940s as companion and friend. Perhaps this is all to the good, as there are today few individuals except first-class breeders producing sound, attractive stock, though a common criticism has been that some animals are much too whippety.

SHOW STANDARD
General appearance. The Bull Terrier is the gladiator of the canine race. It must be strongly built, muscular, symmetrical and active with a keen, determined and intelligent expression, full of fire and courageous but of even temperament and amenable to discipline. Irrespective of size, dogs should look masculine and bitches feminine.
Colour. For white, a pure white coat; skin pigmentation and markings on the head should not be penalized. For coloured, the colour should predominate. All other things being equal, brindle to be preferred.
Head. The head should be long, strong and deep, right to the end of the muzzle but not coarse. Viewed from the front it should be egg-shaped and compeltely filled. The nose should be black and bent downwards at the tip. The nostrils should be well developed. The under-jaw should be strong.
Tail. Should be short, set on low and carried horizontally. Thick at the root, it should taper to a fine point.
Feet. Round and compact with well-arched toes.

AMERICAN STAFFORDSHIRE TERRIER

Good points
- Excellent guard
- Fearless
- Good with children
- Docile
- Adapts readily to new homes

Take heed
- Needs discipline in youth
- Not always comfortable with other dogs
- Stubborn if not taken in hand while still young

The American Staffordshire Terrier is not to be confused with the English Staffordshire Bull Terrier, which is a lighter dog with smaller bones. At one time the American Kennel Club was allowing the American Staffordshire Terrier to be shown with the Staffordshire Bull and, indeed, crossbreeding of the two was allowed. However, although the American Staffordshire's ancestry does originate in England, it has evolved as a quite independent breed.

Size
Height and weight should be in proportion. A height of about 18-19in (46-48cm) at shoulders for the male and 17-18in (43-46cm) for the female is to be considered preferable.

Exercise
As for Staffordshire Bull Terrier.

Grooming
As for Staffordshire Bull Terrier

Feeding
As for Staffordshire Bull Terrier.

Origin and history
The American Staffordshire Terrier is of British origin derived from the traditional English Bulldog and an English terrier. The result was the Staffordshire Terrier, also known as the Pit Bull Terrier and later the Staffordshire Bull Terrier. Once it found its way to the United States in 1870, it became known variously as Pit Dog, Yankee Terrier and American Bull Terrier. The breed was recognized by the American Kennel Club in 1935 under the name of Staffordshire Terrier, which was revised in January 1972 to American Staffordshire Terrier.

SHOW STANDARD
General appearance. The American Staffordshire Terrier should give the impression of great strength for its size, a well put-together dog, muscular but agile and graceful, keenly alive to its surroundings. It should be stocky, not long-legged or racy in outline. Its courage is proverbial.
Colour. Any colour, solid, parti, or patched, is permissible, but all white, more than 80 per cent white, black and tan, and liver not to be encouraged.
Head and skull. Medium length, deep through, broad skull, very pronounced cheek muscles, distinct stop; and ears are set high. Jaws well defined. Upper teeth to meet tightly outside lower teeth in front. Nose definitely black.
Tail. Short in comparison to size, low set, tapering to a fine point; not curled or held over back. Not docked.
Feet. Of moderate size, well arched and compact.

STAFFORDSHIRE BULL TERRIER

Good points
- Excellent guard
- Fearless
- Good with children

Take heed
- Needs discipline in youth
- Stubborn if not taken in hand while still young

The Staffordshire Bull Terrier is a sound breed and an excellent family dog derived from the crossing of an English Bulldog with a terrier breed some time in the 1800s. Probably the partner of the Old English Bulldog in this match was the Old English Black and Tan

Terrier, which preceded the Manchester Terrier. It is, of course, an English breed, recognized by the Kennel Club in 1935 and subsequently recognized in the United States in 1975.
The Staffordshire Bull Terrier, in common with its close relation the Bull Terrier, is a surprisingly gentle dog beneath a somewhat fearsome exterior. It is a good guard dog but adores its family and is utterly reliable with young children.

Size
Weight: dog 28-38lb (12.7-17.2kg); bitch 24-34lb (11-15.4kg). Height (at shoulder): 14-16in (35.5-40.5cm).

Exercise
The Staffordshire Bull Terrier can't resist a fight with another dog if given the chance, so keep this breed on the lead when walking on a public thoroughfare. It is a first class ratter and a good companion in the field, but will adapt to life in a normal-sized house and garden as long as regular walks of a reasonable length are given.

Grooming
This breed requires little attention other than a frequent brushing.

Feeding
Recommended would be 13-20oz (369-587g) per day of a branded, meaty product with biscuit added in equal part by volume, or 1¾-3 cupfuls of a dry, complete food mixed in the proportion of 1 cup of feed to ½ cup of hot or cold water.

Origin and history
The Staffordshire Bull Terrier has a bloody history, for it was evolved for the purpose of the once popular sport of bull and bear baiting and later for fighting dogs. Fortunately, however, with the banning of these sports the Staffordshire was developed as a companion dog, and in the mid-1930s it was recognized by the Kennel Club as a pure breed, the standard being drawn up and a breed club formed in Cradley Heath, south Staffordshire.

SHOW STANDARD
General appearance. The Staffordshire Bull Terrier is a smooth-coated dog. It should be of great strength for its size and, although muscular, should be active and agile.
Colour. Red, fawn, white, black or blue, or any of these colours with white. Any shade of brindle or any shade of brindle with white.
Head and skull. Short, deep through, broad skull, very pronounced cheek muscles, distinct stop, short foreface, black nose.
Body. Close-coupled with a level topline. The front is wide, the brisket is deep and the ribs are well sprung. The loins, however, are rather light.
Tail. The tail should be of medium length, low set, tapering to a point and carried rather low. It should not curl much.
Feet. The feet of this breed shoud be well padded, strong and of medium size.

The ideal Bull Terrier must be well rounded in the body with a short strong back and a marked spring to the ribs. The shoulders, though powerful, must not be heavy. The legs must be strong boned but not coarse, the forelegs perfectly straight, the hindlegs very muscular in the thighs. The overall impression should be one of immense power and strength combined with supple agility.

Bull Terrier

American Staffordshire Terrier

From its history as a fearless fighter the modern Staffordshire Bull Terrier draws its characteristics of indomitable courage, high intelligence and tenacity which, coupled with its affectionate and trustworthy nature, make it an excellent all-purpose family pet.

Staffordshire Bull Terrier

KERRY BLUE TERRIER
(Irish Blue Terrier)

Good points
- First-class guard
- Good sporting dog or family pet
- Excellent with children

Take heed
- Loves a scrap and not averse to starting one

The Kerry Blue Terrier loves children and makes an ideal house-pet. It does, however, have a fine Irish temper when aroused. It needs firm but gentle training when young to curb its aggressiveness.

Size
Weight: 33-37lb (15-16.8kg); greater tolerance in the United States.

Exercise
Bred as a working dog, it needs and deserves plenty of exercise.

Grooming
Frequent brushing with a stiff brush and metal comb. You can easily learn to scissor trim the pet yourself. If you plan to show, however, there is a lot of work involved in show preparation.

Feeding
Thirteen-20oz (369-587g) of a branded, meaty product with biscuit added in equal part by volume, or 1¾-3 cupfuls of a dry food, complete diet, mixed in the proportion of 1 cup of feed to ½ cup of hot or cold water.

Origin and history
The Kerry Blue originates from the county of Kerry in southwestern Ireland. The Irish Terrier had a hand in its make-up, to which the Bedlington Terrier and Bull Terrier are also said to have contributed.

The Kerry started life as a hunter of badgers and foxes and has also done its share of otter hunting, being a keen, strong swimmer. It has guarded livestock and has seen army service during World War II. Now, however, it is predominantly kept as a popular pet and show dog. A Kerry Blue Terrier, Champion Callaghan of Leander, won the Best in Show award at Crufts in 1979.

SHOW STANDARD
General appearance. The typical Kerry Blue Terrier should be well upstanding, compact and well proportioned, showing a developed and muscular body.
Colour. Any shade of blue with or without black points. A shade of tan

Above: The Kromfohrländer, which is hardly known outside Germany.

Left: The Kerry Blue Terrier — a beautiful, well-proportioned dog kept as a popular pet and a show dog. Its coat, which can be any shade of blue, needs attention on a regular basis.

is permissible in puppies, as is also a dark colour up to the age of 18 months. A small, white patch on the chest should not be penalized.
Head and skull. Well-balanced, long, proportionately lean with slight stop, flat over the skull. Foreface and jaw very strong, deep and punishing; nose black; nostrils of due proportion.
Tail. Set on high to complete a perfectly straight back and carried erect.
Feet. Round and small. Toenails black.

KROMFOHR-LÄNDER

Good points
- Excellent temperament
- Good companion
- Guarding/hunting instincts
- Intelligent

Take heed
- No drawbacks known

The Kromfohrländer is a powerful dog with a long, wedge-shaped head, rectangular body and strong, sturdy legs. It was developed from a cross between a Griffon and a terrier.

This is a faithful and intelligent dog with guarding and hunting instincts. Regrettably it is little known outside Germany.

Size
Height at the withers 15-18in (38-46cm).

Exercise
This is a terrier with plenty of energy to unleash.

Grooming
Regular brushing.

Feeding
Thirteen-20oz (369-587g) of a branded, meaty product with biscuit added in equal part by volume, or 1¾-3 cupfuls of a dry food, complete diet, mixed in the proportion of 1 cup of feed to ½ cup of hot or cold water.

Origin and history
The Kromfohrländer has come into being only since the end of World War II. Legend has it that a group of American soldiers, accompanied by a medium-sized dog, passed through the Siegen area of Germany. There the dog was found a new home with a Frau Schleifenbaum, who already owned an English Wire-haired Terrier bitch. The resultant progeny from the first and subsequent litters were so pleasing that it was decided to develop a specific type, eventually known as the Kromfohrländer. In 1953 the breed received recognition by the German Kennel Club.

General appearance
There are three varieties of this attractive terrier; the short-haired rough-coat, rough-coat, and long-haired rough-coat. However, the rough-coat is by far the most popular. Colours are basically white with markings ranging from light to dark brown on the head or with a white star on a brown head. Markings should be regular.

An all-purpose dog, the Kerry Blue Terrier makes a first-class pet or working dog. It can be readily trained to the gun and, possessing an excellent nose, will track and retrieve like a gundog. Affectionate and gentle with its friends but a fearsome adversary, as companion and watchdog it has no equal.

Kerry Blue Terrier

Kromfohrländer

The Kromfohrländer is a powerful dog with a long, wedge-shaped head, rectangular body and strong, sturdy legs. Developed from a cross between a Griffon and a Terrier, it makes a lively, affectionate pet.

SOFT-COATED WHEATEN TERRIER

Good points
- *Hardy*
- *Not finicky about food*
- *Intelligent*
- *Excellent guard*
- *Gentle with children*

Take heed
- *No drawbacks known*

The Soft-coated Wheaten Terrier is an exceptionally intelligent, medium-sized dog, which is defensive without being aggressive. It is an excellent house guard but gentle with children. The Wheaten has strong sporting instincts, and some have been trained with success, for the gun.

Size
Weight: dog approximately 35-45lb (15.9-20.5kg). Height: dog approximately 18-19½in (46-49cm) measured at the withers. Bitch slightly less in both regards.

Grooming
The Wheaten's coat does not shed. Frequent combing should start from puppyhood, as regular grooming will keep the coat clean and tangle-free.

Fuzziness, not natural to the breed, can be aggravated by the use of a wire or plastic brush, and a medium-toothed metal comb should be used instead.

Bathing should be carried out as necessary: for showing, bathe the dog about three days before the event to avoid a fly-away appearance.

Ears, tail and feet need to be tidied, so do any long, straggly hairs underneath the body.

Feeding
About 13-20oz (369-587g) of a branded, meaty product with biscuit added in equal part by volume, or 1¾-3 cupfuls of a complete dry food, mixed in the proportion of 1 cup of feed to ½ cup of hot or cold water. Meat scraps and non-splintery bones are acceptable on occasion.

Origin and history
The origin of the Soft-coated Wheaten, like that of so many breeds, has been lost over time. However, from old pictures and records, the breed has been traced back at least 200 years in Ireland. There for many generations hardly a farm or smallholding did not boast an attendant Wheaten that was valued for its sterling qualities.

It is recorded that the Soft-coated Wheaten Terrier is the oldest Irish breed of terrier, said to be the progenitor of the Kerry Blue and Irish terriers. Legend tells us that a blue dog swam ashore from a ship wrecked in Tralee Bay about 180 years ago. This dog mated the native Wheaten, and from this originated the Kerry Blue. Wheaten-coloured pups have appeared in Kerry Blue litters from time to time.

There is no record of cross-breeding in the Wheaten, and it appears today to be much as it always has been.

SHOW STANDARD
General appearance. A medium-sized, compact, upstanding terrier well covered with a soft, wheaten-coloured, natural coat that falls in loose curls or waves.
Colour. A good clear wheaten, the shade of ripening wheat; a white coat and a red coat are equally objectionable. Dark shading on the ears is not untypical. Dark overall colour and the even darker markings often present in the immature coat clear by about 18 months, if not before.
Head and skull. Head moderately long and profusely covered with coat, which should fall forward over the eyes. The skull, while not being coarse, should be narrow. The nose should be black and large for the size of dog. Head in general, powerful without being coarse.
Tail. Docked. The tail of the fully grown dog should be about 4-5in (10-12.5cm) long. Set on high, carried gaily but never over the back. Not curled or too thick.
Feet. Strong and compact, turned neither in nor out. Good depth of pad. Toenails black.

BORDER COLLIE

Good points
- *Intelligent*
- *Loyal*
- *Ideal choice for obedience competitions*
- *Good family and/or working dog*

Take heed
- *This breed will herd anything, people included, if sheep and cattle are not available*

The Border Collie is a first-class, everyday working dog, famed for herding cattle and rounding up sheep. This is the star of sheepdog trials, the persistent winner of obedience competitions, the breed favoured by those who want a 'working' dog.

The Border Collie (the name refers to the England-Scotland border) was bred for speed, stamina and brains. It makes a first-class companion, is good with children and is one of the most trainable dogs.

Size
Dog about 21in (53cm); bitch slightly less.

Exercise
This is essentially a working dog that enjoys being out of doors, whether trotting at its master's heels on a routine walk, doing exercises at a dog training class or working on a farm. It will adapt to whatever role you have for it but is not ideally suited to town life.

Grooming
Brush regularly with a good pony dandy brush and comb. Inspect the ears for signs of canker and the ears and feet for foreign matter. Dead fur should be removed when grooming.

Feeding
About 13-20oz (369-587g) of a branded, meaty product with biscuit added in equal part by volume, or 1¾-3 cupfuls of a complete dry food, mixed in the proportion of 1 cup of feed to ½ cup of water.

Origin and history
The present-day Border Collie is descended from collies of the Lowland and Border counties of England and Scotland. They are working sheepdogs of a distinct, recognizable type, which have been exported to many countries of the world where sheep are farmed, and they are also excellent as guide dogs for the blind.

It was not until July 1976 that a standard for the breed was approved in the United Kingdom by the Kennel Club. This standard was a combination of several proposed standards submitted by interested bodies, including the recognized one from the Australian Kennel Club.

SHOW STANDARD
General appearance. The Border Collie should be a well-proportioned dog, the smooth outline showing gracefulness and perfect balance combined with sufficient substance to convey the impression that it is capable of enduring long periods of active duty.
Colour. A variety of colours is permissible.
Head and skull. Skull should be fairly broad, occiput not pronounced. Cheeks should not be full or rounded. The muzzle, tapering to the nose, should be moderately short and strong; and the skull and foreface should be approximately the same length. Nose black; nostrils well developed. Stop very distinct.
Tail. The tail should be moderately long, the bone reaching at least to the hock joint, set on low, well furnished and with an upward swirl towards the end.
Feet. Oval in shape; pads deep, strong and sound; toes moderately arched and close together. Nails short and strong.

STABYHOUN

Good points
- *Affectionate*
- *Easily trained*
- *Excellent guard dog*
- *Fine all-purpose sporting dog*

Take heed
- *No drawbacks known*

The Stabyhoun is one of the most popular dogs in its native Netherlands but is little known elsewhere in the world.

This is an excellent, all-purpose sporting dog, nowadays kept mainly as a companion house dog. It is reliable with children, has an affectionate nature, is easily trained and has an equable temperament.

It is a splendid retriever with a good nose.

Size
Dog up to 19½in (49.5cm) at the withers, bitch somewhat smaller.

Exercise
The Stabyhoun excels at working in the field as a retriever, doing the job for which it was bred. It adapts well to town life as long as it has ample opportunity to run free.

Grooming
The Stabyhoun should be groomed two or three times a week with a good pony dandy brush and a medium-toothed comb in order to remove dead fur. During these grooming sessions, inspect the ears for signs of canker or foreign matter and inspect the feet for dirt, thistles and the like.

Feeding
About 13-20oz (369-587g) of a branded, meaty product with biscuit added in equal part by volume, or 1¾-3 cupfuls of a complete dry food, mixed in the proportion of 1 cup of feed to ½ cup of water.

Origin and history
The Stabyhoun was recognized by the Dutch Kennel Club in 1942, but it has existed in the Netherlands since as long ago as 1800. It was bred in the Friesland district as an all-purpose gundog but was primarily a dispeller of vermin. Crossed with the Wetterhoun, it made a formidable ratter.

Above: The affectionate Stabyhoun.

SHOW STANDARD
General characteristics. A simple, robust pointer whose body is longer than it is high; the dog should appear neither too massive nor too fragile.
Colour. Dappled black, dappled blue, dappled brown, dappled orange.
Head. Lean; in good proportion to the rest of the body; longer than it is broad. Skull and muzzle are of equal length. The skull is slightly rounded, not narrow. The nose is black for brown and orange dogs. It is not divided; the nostrils are well open and large.
Tail. Long, reaching to the hocks. It is set on at medium height and hangs straight with the last third turned upward. In action, the tail is raised. It is covered all around with long hair, which is neither curled nor wavy and not too thick.
Feet. The hindfeet are round with strong pads.

As its name suggests, the coat of the Soft-coated Wheaten Terrier is exceptionally soft and silky, loosely waved or curly, and should be especially abundant on the head and legs. The length and texture of the coat remains the same throughout the year; there is no seasonal variation.

Soft-coated Wheaten Terrier

Because the Border Collie's background contains a mixture of other sheepdogs, there was considerable individual variation in type, and it was only during the 1970s that a standard for the breed was decided and official recognition granted.

Border Collie

SHAR-PEI
(Chinese Fighting Dog)

Good points
- *Excellent watchdog*
- *Loyal to owner*
- *Amiable unless provoked*
- *Highly intelligent*
- *Good with children*

Take heed
- *May be more susceptible to entropion and skin disease than are other breeds*

The Chinese Shar-Pei, once listed in the *Guinness Book of Records* as the rarest dog in the world, is now accepted for championship competition by kennel clubs in the United Kingdom and United States.

Descriptions of the Shar-Pei vary from a dog that looks as if its skin is several sizes too big for it, to a Bloodhound with wrinkles all over.

The Sharp-Pei has small, rectangular ears that point towards the eyes, a tail that forms a circle, its tip touching its base, and stiff short hair that stands up.

It is an extremely intelligent dog, an excellent guard and amiable unless provoked. It enjoys human companionship; it is also most affectionate.

In 1947, the tax on dogs in the People's Republic of China rose so steeply that few people could afford to keep them, and many were utilized as food. The Shar-Pei may have escaped this fate simply because it was not very tasty.

Size
Weight: 40-50lb (18.1-22.7kg).
Height: 18-20in (46-51cm) at the withers.

Exercise
The Shar-Pei — or perhaps, to give it its former name, the Chinese Fighting Dog — was used to hunt wild boar and to herd flocks. It is a breed more suited to those with large gardens or houses near areas where the Shar-Pei may unleash its energies. It needs good daily walks and off-the-lead runs.

Feeding
In their land of origin these dogs are undoubtedly fed on rice, a diet that has resulted in instances of rickets and other ailments associated with malnutrition. The Shar-Pei is a hardy dog and, if fed correctly, should have few health problems. The branded canned food requirement for a dog of its size is approximately 20oz (587g) per day, with the usual biscuit supplement.

Health care
The breed is susceptible to entropion, an eye disease that can cause blindness if the lashes penetrate the cornea. The disease is curable, and a veterinarian should be consulted at any sign of eye irritation.

A unique feature of this breed is that heat in the female can be at irregular intervals, and with some females the season may not occur until she is 15-months-old.

Origin and history
Works of art depicting a likeness to the Shar-Pei survive from the Han Dynasty (206 BC to 220 AD).

It is possible that the Shar-Pei originated in Tibet or the Northern Province of China about 20 centuries ago, when it was probably a much larger dog than it is now, weighing 85-165lb (38.6-74.8kg). Other sources maintain that the Shar-Pei is a descendant of the Service Dogs that, for thousands of years, lived in the Southern Province near the South China Sea.

Certainly, for hundreds of years it lived up to its name of Chinese Fighting Dog; it was provoked, and then matched against other dogs for the owner's profit. The loose skin of the Shar-Pei made it difficult for its opponent to get a firm grip on its body. It is said that drugs were used to heighten the breed's aggression, for it is basically a loving and gentle animal.

SHOW STANDARD
The following are points taken from the tentative standard.

General appearance. An active, compact, short-coupled, squarely built dog that stands firmly on the ground with the posture of a warrior.
Head and skull. Skull flat, broad and large with little stop. Occiput not pronounced. Profuse wrinkles on forehead and cheeks. Heavy dewlaps. Muzzle moderately long and broad with no tapering towards the nose.
Colour. Self-coloured. May be black, dark fawn, light fawn or cream-coloured. Fawn with dark eyes, blue-grey mask and black nose preferably.
Tail. Set very high. Thick and round at base, tapering to a fine point at the tip. Preferably, the tail should be curled tightly in a circle or loosely in a semi-circle carried to one side.
Feet. Moderate in size; compact and firm; toes well separated; knuckles high.

BULLDOG

Good points
- *Courageous*
- *Intelligent*
- *Good tempered*
- *Loves children*
- *Easy to groom*

Take heed
- *Best suited to a temperate climate — excessive heat causes heart attacks*
- *Snores*
- *Not built for strenuous exercise*
- *Difficult to breed*
- *Frequently needs caesarean sections*

The Bulldog, despite its somewhat ferocious appearance, has a docile temperament and generally adores children. It is quick to learn and will enjoy taking part in games. However, its build precludes any fast running, and it must never be allowed to rush about in hot weather, as its nose does not equip it for rapid breathing. It should never be shut in a car or other confined space unless plenty of fresh air is available.

This breed is not renowned for longevity. It can, however, be recommended warmly as a loyal guard and lovable family pet.

Size
Weight: dog 55lb (25kg); bitch: 50lb (22.7kg).

Exercise
The Bulldog will benefit from a good daily walk on a loose lead. If the owner lives in a safe, rural area or has a nearby enclosed park, the dog will enjoy being allowed off the lead so that it may amble at its own pace. But please don't drag it or let it over-exert itself as a pup. Experience will show just how much exercise it enjoys without tiring. But the Bulldog is not the breed for all-day hikers.

Grooming
A regular brushing with a fairly stiff brush and a rub down with a hound glove will keep the Bulldog in good condition.

Feeding
Thirteen oz (369g) of a branded dog food product with biscuit added in equal part by volume, or 1¾ cups of a dry food, complete diet, mixed in the proportion of 1 cup of food to ½ cup of hot or cold water.

Origin and history
This breed can be traced back to the Molossus, the fighting dog of the ancient Greek tribe at Athens called the Molossi. However, the Mastiff would seem to resemble this powerful breed more faithfully, which suggests that the Mastiff, Bulldog and Boxer may have a common ancestor. Certainly they were all fighting dogs; the Mastiff fought against both gladiators and wild beasts in the arenas of Rome, and the Boxer was known in Germany as 'Bullenbeisser' or bull baiter.

It is, however, the Bulldog that is generally associated with the unpleasant 'sport' of bull baiting — seizing the bull by the nose and holding it until it fell. The sport was promoted by a certain Earl Warren of Stamford, Lincolnshire, who, after enjoying the spectacle of two dogs fighting bulls in 1209, sought to bring such a sight to a wider audience.

When bull baiting became illegal in 1838, the Bulldog was in danger of extinction, for it appeared to have served its purpose. However, a Mr Bill George continued to breed Bulldogs, and to him a debt of gratitude is due in that the breed, despite its fearsome countenance, has developed into a much esteemed, reliable pet. The Bulldog Club, established in 1875, was the first specialist breed club to be set up in the United Kingdom. At the beginning of the twentieth century, New Yorkers paid very large sums of money for Bulldogs, when the breed became fashionable.

SHOW STANDARD
General appearance. The Bulldog is a smooth-coated, thick-set dog, rather low in stature but broad, powerful and compact. The head is strikingly massive and large in proportion to the dog's size, and the face is extremely short. The muzzle is very broad, blunt and inclined upwards.
Colour. The colour should be whole or smut (that is, a whole colour with a black mask or muzzle). The only colours (which should be brilliant and pure of their sort) are whole colours, viz, brindles, reds, fawns, fallows, white and also pied (i.e. a combination of white with any other of the foregoing colours).
Head and skull. The skull should be very large — the larger the better — and in circumference should measure (round in front of the ears) at least the height of the dog at the shoulders.
Tail. The tail, termed the 'stern', should be set on low, jut out rather straight, then turn downwards. It should be round, smooth and devoid of fringe or coarse hair. It should be moderate in length — rather short than long — and thick at the root, and taper quickly to a fine point.
Feet. The hindfeet, like the forefeet, should be round and compact, with the toes well split up and the knuckles prominent. The forefeet should be straight and turn very slightly outwards, of medium size and moderately round. The toes should be compact and thick, being well split up, making the knuckles prominent and high.

Below: Their good-tempered, placid intelligence makes Bulldogs excellent pets.

The Shar-Pei originated in the ancient Orient, where it was for centuries bred and trained as a fighting dog. It is believed that drugs were used to provoke the Shar-Pei to aggression, for it is basically an amiable and gentle dog.

Shar-Pei

The Bulldog should convey an impression of determination, strength and activity: qualities which have been said to reflect the true character of the British nation, of which the Bulldog has become a popular symbol.

Bulldog

KEESHOND

Good points
- Equable temperament
- Good watchdog
- Long-lived

Take heed
- Needs lots of grooming
- One-person dog

The Keeshond, the Netherlands' national dog, began life as a barge dog, and still has the knack of finding an out-of-the-way corner for itself. It is a loyal dog of sound temperament but needs a lot of grooming and tends to favour one member of the family. It is an excellent watchdog.

Size
Height: dog 18in (46cm), bitch 17in (43cm).

Exercise
Average requirements.

Grooming
Regular attention with a stiff brush. A choke chain should not be used on this breed or it will spoil the ruff.

Feeding
Recommended would be 13-20oz (369-587g) of a branded, meaty product with biscuit added in equal part by volume, or 1¾-3 cupfuls of a dry food, complete diet, mixed in the proportion of 1 cup of feed to ½ cup of hot or cold water.

Below: A Keeshond and her puppy. The abundant ruff on the adult model of this breed wants frequent attention, or else it will form mats that will spoil its appearance.

Origin and history
The Keeshond (plural Keeshonden) is pronounced Kayshond. It has a romantic history. During the period of uncertainty that preceded the French Revolution, the Dutch patriots were led by a man named Kees de Gyselaer, a dog lover who owned a little dog of this breed. The dog, named Kees, became the symbol of the patriots, and gave the breed its name.

The Keeshond has never become very popular outside the Netherlands, despite Mrs I. Tucker's Champion Volkrijk of Vorden being Best in Show at Crufts in 1957. It has, however, a staunch band of devotees who breed for soundness and quality. In common with other Spitz varieties, the Keeshond must originally have evolved in the Arctic Circle, and it has the traditional Spitz tail tightly curled over the back.

SHOW STANDARD
General appearance. A short, compact body; alert carriage, fox-like head. Small pointed ears and a well-feathered, curling tail, carried over the back. Hair very thick on the neck, forming a large ruff; head, ears and legs covered with short thick hair. Dogs should move cleanly and briskly (not lope like a German Shepherd Dog), but movement should be straight and sharp. Dogs should show boldly.
Head and skull. Head well proportioned to the body, wedge-shaped when seen from above; from the side showing a definite stop. Muzzle should be of medium length, neither coarse nor snipy.
Colour. Should be wolf, ash-grey; not all black or all white; markings should be definite.
Tail. Tightly curled; a double curl at

the end is desirable. Plume should be white on the top where curled with a black tip.
Feet. Round and cat-like with black nails.

HUNGARIAN PULI
(Puli; Hungarian Water Dog)

Good points
- Easily trained
- Fine guard
- Highly intelligent
- Loyal

Take heed
- Tends to be a one-person dog

The Hungarian Puli is a loyal, obedient dog and perhaps the best-known of the Hungarian sheepdogs outside its homeland. It is easily distinguishable by its long, dark, corded coat, which is not so difficult to groom as might be believed

Size
Height: dog 16-18in (40.5-46cm); bitch 14-16in (35.5-40.5cm). Weight: dog 29-33lb (13.1-15kg); bitch 22-29lb (10-13.1kg).

Exercise
Plenty of exercise is preferable, but this adaptable dog will fit in with city life, as long as it is at its owner's side.

Grooming
The coat hangs in long black cords, which in the adult dog reach to the ground, giving a tousled, unkempt look. The cords have to be separated by hand and regularly brushed and combed. Cleanliness is essential.

Feeding
Thirteen-20oz (369-587g) of a branded, meaty product with biscuit added in equal part by volume, or 1¾-3 cupfuls of a dry food, complete diet, mixed in the proportion of 1 cup of feed to ½ cup of hot or cold water.

Origin and history
The Puli is better known than other Hungarian sheepdogs, such as the Pumi, the Komondor and the Kuvasz, probably because in its

Above: The Puli's 'dreadlocks' are an awesome sight.

native land it directs the flock by jumping on or over the sheep's backs. It is said to have existed for 1,000 years, being a descendant of the sheepdogs brought to Hungary by the Magyars. It has proved itself as a fine water retriever and has done well in obedience and police work. Hungarian shepherds favour their dark colour, which is easily picked out among the flock.

SHOW STANDARD
General appearance. A lively, agile, intelligent, undemanding dog of medium size. It has a solid physique, lean and muscular throughout. The outline of the body and limbs is square. Examination of the individual parts of the body is difficult, because the Puli is completely covered with a thick, long, wavy coat that tends to mat. The head gives the impression of being round because of the long hair that comes down over the eyes, concealing the true shape. The shaggy tail, long and curled up about to the loins, makes it seem that the hindquarters slope upward. The precise body lines are hard to follow, as a glance will show; even the individual parts are difficult to see clearly because of the Puli's unique coat.
Colour. Today breeders are producing Pulis that are black or black with reddish or white ticking as well as several varieties of grey.
Head. Small and fine. From the front it appears round, whereas in profile it seems elliptical. The nose is relatively large and is black, like the eye-rims and lips. The bridge is shorter than the skull, its length being 35 per cent that of the head. The lips fit closely over the gums. The bridge is straight, the muzzle rounded. The jaws are equally developed with strong, regular teeth; and the jaws meet in a scissor bite. The lower canines are set slightly forward of the upper; the other teeth meet precisely. The stop is accentuated. The skull is rounded; the supra-orbital ridges are pronounced.
Tail. Carried over the loin, its hair mingles with the rump hair so that the tail is virtually invisible.

Keeshond

The re-establishment of
the Keeshond's popularity
after a considerable decline during
the nineteenth century was largely due
to the work in breeding and public
relations of Baroness van Hardenbroek
during the 1920s and '30s.

Hungarian Puli

FINNISH SPITZ
(Suomenpystykorva)

Good points
- Beautiful
- Brave
- Excellent guard/house-dog
- Faithful
- Good with children
- Hunter
- Home-loving
- Sociable

Take heed
- No drawbacks known

The Finnish Spitz is Finland's national dog. It is popular in Scandinavia as both a hunter (mainly of birds) and a show dog. It also has devotees in the United Kingdom, where it is kept mainly as a pet and show dog. It is a beautiful animal with the habit of cleaning itself like a cat.

Size
Height: dog 17½in (44.5cm), bitch 15½in (39.5cm).

Exercises
This is a real outdoor dog that likes to run free whenever possible. However, it also relishes its place by the fireside, so it should not be kept kennelled.

Health care
Although a hardy, healthy dog in adulthood, it can prove delicate as a pup, and this Spitz type is not the easiest to breed.

Grooming
Normal frequent brushing will keep the coat clean and handsome.

Feeding
Recommended would be 13-20oz (369-587g) of a branded, meaty product with biscuit added in equal part by volume, or 1¾-3 cupfuls of a dry food, complete diet, mixed in the proportion of 1 cup of feed to ½ cup of hot or cold water.

Origin and history
The Spitz was known for centuries in its own country prior to official recognition, when the Finnish Kennel Club gained acceptance by the FCI. It originates from the eastern zone of Finland and is mentioned in the country's epic the Kalevala.

Called the 'Finkie' by Lady Kitty Ritson, who pioneered the breed in the United Kingdom in the 1920s, it is related to the Russian Laika breed, a member of which was to orbit the Earth in an early space flight. It is a descendant of the earliest hunter dogs of Lapland and Scandinavia.

SHOW STANDARD
General appearance. Body almost square. Bearing bold. The whole appearance, and particularly the eyes, ears and tail, indicates liveliness.
Colour. On the back, reddish-brown or yellowish-red, preferably bright. The hairs on the inner sides of the ears, on the cheeks, under the muzzle, on the breast and abdomen, inside the legs, at the back of the thighs and under the tail are of a lighter shade. White markings on feet and a narrow white stripe on the breast can be permitted, also some black hairs on the lips and sparse separate hairs with black points along the back.
Head and skull. Medium sized

Below: Finnish Spitz puppies enjoying the sun; they can be delicate to raise, but will grow into beautiful pets or show dogs.

and clean cut, forehead slightly arched, stop pronounced. Muzzle narrow and clean cut, seen from above; from the sides, evenly tapering. Nose should be pitch black. Lips tightly closed and thin.
Tail. Curves vigorously from its root in an arch, forward, downward and backward, then pressing down against the thigh with its tip extending to the middle part of the thigh. Extended, the tail vertebrae usually reach to the hock joint.
Feet. Preferably roundish.

NORRBOTTEN SPITZ
(Norrbottenspets)
(See also Finnish Spitz)

Good points
- Excellent guard
- Good with children
- Happy nature
- Lively
- Strong herding instinct

Take heed
- No drawbacks known

The Norrbotten Spitz is named after Norrbotten, the northern region of Sweden from which it originates. It is Sweden's answer to the Finnish Spitz and the Norwegian Buhund, though smaller and lighter. It makes an excellent companion, house-dog and farmyard protector.

Size
Maximum height 16in (40.5cm).

Exercise
This dog is a natural herder that enjoys its freedom. However it adapts well to the life of a house-pet with regular walks.

Grooming
Normal frequent brushing will keep the coat clean and handsome.

Feeding
Thirteen-20oz (369-587g) of a branded, meaty product with biscuit added in equal part by volume, or 1¾-3 cupfuls of a dry food, complete diet, mixed in the proportion of 1 cup of feed to ½ cup of hot or cold water.

Origin and history
The Norrbotten Spitz is little known outside Sweden. It was declared extinct by the Swedish Kennel Club in 1948. Luckily this proved to be untrue, and there was an upsurge of interest in the 1960s, resulting in sufficient registrations for the breed to become re-established. Its Spitz origin probably derives from Finnish Spitz or Norwegian Buhund ancestry. The Norrbotten Spitz is not yet recognized in either the United Kingdom or the USA.

SHOW STANDARD
General appearance. This is a small dog, compact, but light in build, of the Spitz type with good carriage.
Colour. All colours are permissible, although preference is given to white as the base colour with russet or yellow markings. Each colour

area should be distinct from the others.
Tail. Set on high; curved, generally carried on the side, and when down, the tip reaches mid-thigh. The tail joints should not reach below the hock. A docked tail is permissible, but not desirable.

JAPANESE SPITZ

Good points
- Courageous
- Intelligent
- Loyal
- Lively

Take heed
- Tends to be a one-person dog
- Distrustful of strangers

The Japanese Spitz is a close relation of the Norrbotten Spitz, but the Japanese variety has developed as a separate breed in Japan, to which it was undoubtedly imported long ago. It has come upon the international scene not that long ago and is still comparatively rare. The Japanese Spitz is not accepted for championship competition by the American Kennel Club.

Size
Height: 12-16in (30-40.5cm); bitch, 10-14in (25-35.5cm).

Exercise
This dog is natural herder, and it enjoys its freedom. However, it adapts well to the life of a house-pet with regular walks or supervised runs in the country. In addition, a large, fenced-in yard or garden will afford the Japanese Spitz the needed opportunity to run at will.

Grooming
Normal frequent brushing will keep the coat clean and handsome.

Feeding
Thirteen-20oz (369-587g) of a branded, meaty product with biscuit added in equal part by volume, or 1¾-3 cupfuls of a dry food, complete diet, mixed in the proportion of 1 cup of feed to ½ cup of hot or cold water.

SHOW STANDARD
General appearance. Profuse, pure white off-standing coat. The dog should have a sharply pointed muzzle and triangular ears standing erect. The bushy tail is carried over the back. The body should be firm, strong and flexible. Fore- and hindquarters should be well proportioned and balanced.
Head and skull. Head of medium size without coarseness, moderately broad and slightly rounded. Skull broadest at occiput. Well defined stop. Cheeks rounded, full head not protruding; muzzle sharply pointed, neither too thin nor too long. Lips firm and tightly closed. The nose round, small and black.
Colour. Pure white.
Tail. Moderate in length; root set high; carried over the back.
Feet. Toes should be small, round and cat-like. Well padded with good pigment; nails should be hard and black or dark.

The Finnish Spitz is characterized by its courage, fidelity and eagerness to hunt. Its coat is short and close-lying on the head and legs (except on the backs of the thighs, where it is long and dense). The outer coat on the shoulders is considerably longer and coarser, particularly in males, and the under-coat short, soft and dense.

Finnish Spitz

Originally bred as a hunting dog, the Norrbotten Spitz is now known as an affectionate and lively house-dog. It is little known outside Sweden, where it was re-established in 1960.

Norrbotten Spitz

It is possible that the Japanese Spitz is a fairly long-coated version of the family popularly known as Japanese Large Size. Middle Size and Small Size dogs. It is still seldom seen outside Japan.

Japanese Spitz

BASSET HOUND

Good points
- *Equable temperament*
- *Good with children*
- *Ideal family pet*

Take heed
- *Needs lots of exercise*
- *Likes to wander*

The Basset Hound is an affable dog that gets on with most people and makes the ideal family pet. It does, however, retain strong hound instincts and will wander miles if a gate is left conveniently open. Basset owners are always telling folk about their Basset's roamings, often quite far afield, but it is up to owners to see that their properties are adequately fenced. Like the Beagle, the Basset has a mind of its own; it is eminently lovable, but not always obedient — unless it chooses!

Size
Height: 13-15in (33-38cm).

Exercise
Most important. If you can't give a Basset Hound plenty of exercise don't have one.

Grooming
Frequent brushing and combing. Pay attention to ears and toenails.

Feeding
Thirteen-20oz (369-587g) of a branded, meaty product with biscuit

Below: Lovable pets, Basset Hounds can be wilful at times. Moreover, they like to wander and need plenty of exercise.

added in equal part by volume, or 1¾-3 cupfuls of a dry food, complete diet, mixed in the proportion of 1 cup of feed to ½ cup of hot or cold water. Careful feeding in puppyhood is advocated for this fast-growing breed.

Health care
Choose the specimen with the straightest limbs, even if those knobbly knees seem attractive.

Origin and history
The Basset Hound is of French origin, being derived from the French Basset Artésien-Normand, which was imported to England and crossed with the Bloodhound. It is a slow but sure tracker, still used in the United Kingdom to hunt hare. Primarily, however, it is kept as a popular household pet. French sources maintain that the first Bassets appeared in a litter of normal long-legged hounds and that after breeding from these the Basset (which means 'dwarf') Hound appeared.

The earliest known mention of the use of the word 'Basset' to describe a breed of dog has been found in a late-sixteenth century text on hunting written by Fouilloux. An illustration shows a sportsman going out accompanied by his group of badger dogs or 'Bassets'.

SHOW STANDARD
General characteristics. A short-legged hound of considerable substance, well-balanced and full of quality. Action is most important. A smooth free action is desired with forelegs reaching well forward and hindlegs showing powerful thrust while the hound moves true both front and rear. Hocks and stifles must not be stiff in movement, nor

must any toes be dragged.
Colour. Generally black, white and tan, or lemon and white; but any recognized hound colour is acceptable.
Head and skull. Domed with some stop and the occipital bone prominent, of medium width at the brow and tapering slightly to the muzzle; the general appearance of the foreface is lean but not snipy. The top of the muzzle is nearly parallel with the line from stop to occiput and not much longer than the head from stop to occiput. There may be a moderate amount of wrinkle at the brows and beside the eyes, and the skin of the head should be so loose as to wrinkle noticeably when drawn forward or when the head is lowered. The flews of the upper lip overlap the lower substantially.
Tail. Well set on, rather long, strong at the base and tapering with a moderate amount of coarse hair underneath. When the hound is moving, the stern is carried well up and curves gently sabre-fashion over the back but is never curling.
Feet. Massive, well knuckled-up and padded. The forefeet may point straight ahead or be turned slightly outwards. In every case the hound must stand perfectly true, the weight being borne equally by toes with pads together so that the feet would leave the imprint of a large hound with no unpadded areas in contact with the ground.

BASSET GRIFFON VENDÉEN

Good points
- *Excellent family pet*
- *Friendly*
- *Likes human company*
- *Voice will deter unwelcome callers*

Take heed
- *Needs plenty of exercise*
- *Not suitable for apartments or tiny gardens*

The Basset Griffon Vendéen (Petit) is an ancient French hunting breed. As its name implies it is a short-legged (basset), rough-coated (griffon) hound, originating in the district of Vendée, and is one of the four breeds of Basset Hounds found in France. The others are the Basset Artésien Normand, the Basset Bleu de Gascogne and the Basset Fauve de Bretagne.

The Basset Griffon Vendéen (Petit) is a cheerful, active, busy little hound, intelligent and inquisitive. Its friendly nature and liking for human companionship make it an excellent family pet, and its deep resonant voice can act as a deterrent.

Size
Height: 13½-15in (34-38cm). A tolerance of ⅖in (1cm) is allowed.

Exercise
The Basset Griffon Vendéen (Petit) is an active, energetic breed needing plenty of exerise. It is not

recommended for life in small apartments or houses with tiny gardens unless great care, time and trouble can be given to its needs and well-being.

Grooming
Its rough coat needs little attention.

Feeding
Recommended would be 6-13oz (170-369g) of a branded, meaty product with biscuit added in equal part by volume, or ¾-1¾ cupfuls of a dry food, complete diet, mixed in the proportion of 1 cup of feed to ½ cup of hot or cold water.

Origin and history
The Griffon Vendéen (Petit), to quote Monsieur P. Doubigne, an expert on the breed, is a miniature Basset reduced in size and proportions, while retaining all the qualities of the breed: the passion for hunting, fearlessness in the densest coverts, activity and vigour. It was bred down from a larger variety, the Basset Griffon Vendéen (Grand), which was originally used for wolf hunting and is now used, in France, for hunting wild boar.

SHOW STANDARD
General appearance. A small hound, lively and vigorous, with a body of medium length. Tail carried proudly. Coat rough and long without exaggeration. Expressive head. Ears well turned, garnished with long hair, attached below the line of the eye, and not too long.
Colour. Unicolour; hare grizzle, grey or fawn, although this colour is not encouraged. Bicolour: orange and white; black and white; grey and white; tan and white. Tricolour: black, white and tan; white, hare and tan; white, grey and tan.
Head and skull. Skull slighty convex and of moderate length, not too wide, narrow below the eyes. Stop marked. Occipital bone shows.
Tail. Set high, strong at base and gradually tapering. Not too long, carried sabre fashion. Lively.
Feet. Not too strong; hard and tight-padded. Nails solid.

BASSET ARTÉSIEN NORMAND

The Basset Artésien Normand is virtually identical to the Basset Hound and has the same feeding and grooming requirements and general characteristics. It is of ancient French origin, descended from the old French Bloodhound and the St Hubert Hound. Its job was to trail deer and small game.

This breed found favour as a hunting dog in France but was adopted by the British, who crossed it with the Bloodhound to develop the Basset Hound, now so popular as a pet.

The breed stands 10-13in (25-33cm) high. Colours are white or white and orange. A tricoloured dog must be widely marked with tan on the head and a mantle of specks of black or badger colour.

The long ears of the Basset Hound should be set on low but not excessively so and never above the line of the eye. Narrow throughout their length and curling well inwards, they should reach at least to the end of a muzzle of correct length and be supple, fine and velvety in texture.

Basset Hound

Basset Griffon Vendéen

Basset Artésien Normand

WHIPPET

Good points
- ● *Clean*
- ● *Elegant*
- ● *Gentle and affectionate*
- ● *Good with children*

Take heed
- ● *Strong hunting instincts*

The Whippet is an excellent choice for those who want a dog that will combine the role of an affectionate and gentle pet with performance in the show ring. It has a peaceful temperament but can be a little nervous in strange surroundings.

Size
The ideal height for dogs is 18½in (47cm) and for bitches 17½in (44.5cm). Judges should use their discretion and not unduly penalize an otherwise good specimen.

Exercise
The Whippet is a racer, capable of 35-40 miles (56-64km) an hour. It will adapt to life as a family pet, but make sure that you can give it plenty of exercise.

Grooming
Needs little grooming, but the tail usually needs tidying up for show. Teeth should be scaled regularly.

Health care
Whippets are hardy, despite their delicate appearance, but should sleep indoors and be kept out of draughts.

Feeding
Recommended would be 6-13oz (170-369g) of a branded, meaty product with biscuit added in equal part by volume, or ¾-1¾ cupfuls of a dry food, complete diet, mixed in the proportion of 1 cup of feed to ½ cup of hot or cold water.

Origin and history
The Greyhound obviously had a hand in the Whippet's make-up, but there is some controversy as to whether the cross was with a terrier, a Pharaoh Hound or some other imported hound. The breed has been popular in the United Kingdom since the beginning of the century and was exhibited at Crufts as early as 1897. It was recognized by the Kennel Club in the United Kingdom five years later. The Whippet is also popular in the United States, where the standard allows for a slightly larger dog. It was designed for racing and coursing, in which it excels. Many Whippet owners derive immense pleasure from keeping a dog that not only satisfies their sporting interests but is also a popular show contender and loving household pet.

SHOW STANDARD
General appearance. Should convey an impression of beautifully balanced muscular power and strength combined with great elegance and grace. Symmetry of outline, muscular development and powerful gait are the main considerations; the dog being built for speed and work, all forms of exaggeration should be avoided. It should possess great freedom of action; the forelegs should be thrown forward and low over the ground like a thoroughbred horse, not in a hackney-like action. Hind legs should come well under the body, giving great propelling power. Movement should not be stilted, high stepping or mincing.
Colour. Any colour or mixture of colours.
Head and skull. Long and lean, flat on top, tapering to the muzzle, rather wide between the eyes; jaws powerful and clean cut. Nose black; in blues a bluish colour is permitted, and in livers a nose of the same colour; and in whites or parti-colours a butterfly nose is permissible.
Tail. No feathering. Long and tapering; when in action, carried in a delicate curve upward but not over the back.
Feet. Very neat, well split up between the toes; knuckles highly arched; pads thick and strong.

AUSTRALIAN KELPIE AND CATTLE DOG

Good points
- ● *Brave*
- ● *Excellent working dog*
- ● *Good companion*
- ● *Loyal*

Take heed
- ● *No drawbacks known*

The Australian Kelpie is a superb sheepdog descended from working imported Scottish stock. It is famed for the way it runs along the backs of sheep to reach the head of the flock. It is extremely fast and has an almost camel-like ability to go without water for lengthy periods. It is an attractive prick-eared dog with great intelligence and loyalty to its master.

The Australian Cattle Dog is an intelligent dog, amenable and first-rate at its job of driving cattle, sometimes covering vast distances. Like the Kelpie, it has an equable temperament and makes a loyal companion.

Size
Kelpie: weight 30lb (13.6kg); height 18-20in (46-51cm) at the shoulder. Cattle dog: weight 35lb (15.9kg). Height: 20in (51cm) at shoulder.

Exercise
The Australian Kelpie and the Australian Cattle Dog are accustomed to plenty of exercise in the great outdoors.

Grooming
These breeds will benefit from regular vigorous brushing.

Feeding
Thirteen-20oz (369-587g) of a branded, meaty product with biscuit added in equal part by volume, or 1¾-3 cupfuls of a dry food, complete diet, mixed in the proportion of 1 cup of feed to ½ cup of hot or cold water.

Origin and history
The Kelpie derives from Collies brought to Australia by early settlers. Its ancestry can be traced to a pup named Caesar, later mated to a bitch named Kelpie. Their offspring included the famous King's Kelpie, winner of the first ever sheepdog trials in Australia in 1872. The Scottish writer Robert Louis Stevenson refers to the 'Water Kelpie' in his famous adventure story *Kidnapped*, giving credence to the suggestion that Kelpies derived from the working Scottsh Collie.

The Australian Cattle Dog has emerged from crossings with the Old English Sheepdog (or Bobtail), Scottish Collies, Dingos and Red Bobtails.

STANDARD SCHNAUZER

Good points
- ● *Affectionate*
- ● *Lively and playful*
- ● *Good with children*
- ● *Intelligent*
- ● *Excellent watchdog*
- ● *Robust*

Take heed
- ● *Mistrustful of strangers*

The Schnauzer is a good-natured, lively dog that loves both children and games. However, it does not trust strangers. It is terrier-like — thus a great ratter, intelligent and an excellent guard.

Size
Ideal height: dog 19in (48cm); bitch 18in (46cm). Any variation of more than 1in (2.5cm) in these heights should be penalized.

Exercise
Enjoys regular walks and ball games but will adapt to country or apartment living.

Grooming
The Schnauzer should be brushed regularly and trimmed in spring and autumn.

Feeding
Recommended is 13-20oz (369-587g) of a branded, meaty product with biscuit added in equal part by volume, or 1¾-3 cupfuls of a dry food, complete diet, mixed in the proportion of 1 cup of feed to ½ cup of hot or cold water.

Origin and history
As the name implies, the Schnauzer is of German origin. There is a statue in Stuttgart, dated 1620, depicting a watchman with a dog similar in appearance to the Schnauzer of today.

The breed originated in Bavaria and Württemberg where it was esteemed as a ratter and a cattle driver. However, when cattle driving died out, the breed found its way to the city, where it gained popularity, coming to the attention of serious fanciers about 1900.

There are actually three kinds of Schnauzers that are bred and registered as distinct breeds — the miniature, the standard and the giant. From these three, the medium or standard is considered the prototype. (In the United States it is a member of the working group but was first classifed as a terrier.)

SHOW STANDARD
General appearance. The Schnauzer is a powerfully built, robust, sinewy, nearly square dog, the length of its body being equal to its height at the shoulders. Its temperament combines high spirits, reliability, strength, endurance and vigour. Expression is keen and attitude alert.
Colour. All pepper-and-salt colours in even proportions, or pure black.
Head and skull. Head strong and elongated, gradually narrowing from the ears to the eyes and forward from there to the tip of the nose. Upper part of the head (occiput to base of the forehead) moderately broad between the ears with flat, creaseless forehead and well-muscled but not too strongly developed cheeks. Medium stop to accentuate prominent eyebrows.

The powerful muzzle formed by the upper and lower jaws (base of the forehead to tip of the nose) should end in a moderately blunt line with bristly, stubbly moustache and chin whiskers. Ridge of the nose straight and running almost parallel to the extension of the forehead. The nose is black and full. Lips should be tight.
Tail. Set on and carried high; cut down to three joints.
Feet. Short, round, extremely compact, with close-arched toes (cat's paws), dark nails and hard soles. The feet also deep or thickly padded, pointing forward.

MEDIUM PINSCHER
(German Pinscher)

Good points
- ● *Alert guard*
- ● *Elegant appearance*
- ● *Lively pet*
- ● *Loyal to owner*

Take heed
- ● *Aggressive to strangers*
- ● *Fiery temperament*

The Medium Pinscher, previously known as the German Pinscher, is a very old breed, yet it is virtually unknown outide its homeland. This, the middle-sized of the pinschers, bears far more similarity to the Dobermann than to the Miniature Pinscher and, like the Dobermann, has its ears cropped in its native country. The tail is docked and the coat is smooth and glossy. Colour usually black with small tan markings or self red. There is also a most attractive and distinctive harlequin Pinscher.

The Medium Pinscher was bred as a ratter, but nowadays is mainly kept as an alert, lively pet. Height is 16-19in (40.5-48cm).

The coat of the Whippet should be fine, short and as closely textured as possible. Its chest should be very deep and its back broad, well muscled and arched over the loin.

Whippet

Medium Pinscher

Australian Kelpie

Standard Schnauzer

The Schnauzer breed was first shown in the United States at the beginning of the twentieth century, when some confusion was caused because both the Schnauzer and Dobermann were generally called pinschers.

SIBERIAN HUSKY

Good points
- *Adaptable*
- *Friendly*
- *Good with children*
- *Intelligent*
- *Reliable*

Take heed
- *Needs lots of exercise*

The Siberian Husky is perhaps the most friendly of all Arctic Spitz breeds. It has a long history of friendship with man, combining the roles of household companion with workmate, hauling the sled or herding. It is faithful and reliable.

Size
Height at the withers: dog 21-23½in (53-60cm); bitch 20-22in (51-56cm). Weight: dog 45-60lb (20.5-27.2kg); bitch 35-50lb (15.9-22.7kg). Weight should be in proportion to height.

Exercise
Famed for sled racing, remarkable endurance and great powers of speed, this is not a dog to keep confined in a small yard.

Grooming
Regular brushing will keep the coat in good condition.

Feeding
Recommended would be 20-33oz (587-936g) of a branded, meaty product with a handful of biscuit added, or 3-5 cupfuls of a dry food, complete diet, mixed in the proportion of 1 cup of feed to ½ cup of hot or cold water.

Origin and history
The Siberian Husky was bred by the nomadic Chukchi tribes of northeastern Asia. Their purpose in breeding the Husky from other local dogs was to produce a hardy animal of great endurance that would combine the roles of companion and hunter with that of a speedy sled dog that, at times, would be their only means of transport.

More recently, the Siberian Husky has been recognized as a show dog. It performed creditably as a search-and-rescue dog for the United States Air Force in World War II and has popularized the sport of sled racing in the USA and elsewhere in the world.

SHOW STANDARD
General appearance. A medium-sized working sled dog; quick and light on its feet, free and graceful in action with a moderately compact and well-furred body, erect ears and brush tail. The characteristic gait is smooth and seemingly effortless. Its body proportions and forms reflect a basic balance of power, speed and endurance. It should never appear heavy and coarse, nor light and fragile.The male should be masculine but never coarse; the bitches should appear feminine but without weakness of structure. Both sexes

Above: The Siberian Husky is a dog with great powers of speed and endurance. It was bred to hunt and haul sleds in northeastern Asia as well as to provide intelligent and reliable companionship. It is now famed for sled racing, popular in North America.

should be capable of great endurance. In proper condition, with firm and well-developed muscle, the Siberian Husky does not carry excess weight. Any appearance of excessive bone or weight; constricted or clumsy gait; straight or loose shoulders; weak pasterns; weak, sloping or roach back; straight stifles; feet soft and splayed,too large and clumsy, or too small and delicate, is undesirable.
Colour. All colours, including white, are allowed, and all markings. A variety of markings on the head is common, including many striking patterns not found in other breeds.
Head and skull. The head should be of medium size and in proportion to the body, neither clumsy nor too fine. It should be slightly rounded on top, tapering gradually from the widest point to the eyes. The muzzle should be of medium length and width, neither snipy nor coarse, and taper gradually to the rounded nose. The distance from the tip of the nose to the stop should be equal to the distance from the stop to the occiput. The stop should be clearly defined but not excessive, and the line of the nose straight from the stop to the tip. The nose should be black in grey, tan or black dogs; liver in copper dogs; and may be flesh-coloured in pure white dogs. In winter a pink-streaked 'snow nose' is acceptable.
Tail. The well-furred tail of round fox-brush shape should be set on just below the level of the top line, and should usually be carried over the back in a graceful sickle curve when the dog is at attention. When carried up, the tail should not curl too tightly, nor should it curl to either side of the body or snap flat against the back. The hair on the

tail should be of medium length and approximately the same length all round. A trailing tail is normal for the dog when it is either working or in repose.

SAMOYED

Good points
- *Beautiful*
- *Devoted to owner*
- *Obedient*
- *Intelligent*
- *Excellent watchdog*
- *Adaptable*

Take heed
- *Slightly independent*
- *That white coat sheds*

The Samoyed, or 'Sammy' as it is often called, is a beautiful, somewhat independent breed that should, according to its standard, show 'marked affection for all mankind'. These dogs adore the snow and are happiest in the wide open spaces. But having said that, I know of some living happily in semi-detached houses.

Size
Height at the shoulder: dog 20-22in (51-56cm); bitch 18-20in (46-51cm). Weight in proportion to size.

Exercise
Needs a liberal amount of exercise and, if possible, some obedience work, even if this is only weekly attendance at a dog training club.

Grooming
Regular brushing and combing and a towelling after getting wet. The under-coat sheds once a year; at such times it is best to comb out as much surplus hair as one can. Bathing helps, as this tends to loosen the hair.

Feeding
Recommended would be 20-33oz (587-936g) of a branded, meaty product with biscuit added, or 3-5 cupfuls of a dry food, complete diet, mixed in the proportion of 1 cup of feed to ½ cup of hot or cold water.

Origin and history
The Samoyed is a beautiful Spitz-type that takes its name from the Siberian tribe of the Samoyeds. It is a sled dog in its native country and is also used as a guard and herder of reindeer. Some Sammies were used by the explorer Nansen on his journey to the North Pole.

The breed came to the United Kingdom in 1889, and much of the present-day stock can be traced to the original pair. British stock has done much to popularize the breed in other countries of the world.

SHOW STANDARD
General apperance. The Samoyed, being essentially a working dog, should be strong and active and graceful. And as its work lies in cold climates, its coat should be heavy and weather-resistant. It should not be too long in the back, because a weak back would make the dog practically useless for its legitimate work; but at the same

Above: The Samoyed is a beautiful and devoted dog and is growing increasingly popular. Coming from a cold climate, its heavy and weather-resistant coat needs regular brushing and combing. It also needs plenty of exercise and should attend obedience classes.

time a cobby body, such as a Chow's, would also place it at a great disadvantage as a draught dog. Breeders should aim for a happy medium, viz. a body not long, but muscular, allowing liberty, with a deep chest and well-sprung ribs, a strong neck proudly arched, straight front and exceptionally strong loins. Both dog and bitch should give the appearance of being capable of great endurance but should be free from coarseness. A full-grown dog should stand about 21in (53cm) at the shoulder. On account of the depth of chest required, the legs should be moderately long; a very short-legged dog is to be deprecated. Hindquarters should be particularly well developed, stifles well angulated and any suggestion of unsound stifles or cow hocks severely penalized.
Colour. Pure white; white and biscuit; cream.
Head and skull. Head powerful and wedge-shaped with a broad flat skull; muzzle of medium length; a tapering foreface not too sharply defined. Lips black. Hair short and smooth before the ears. Nose black for preference, but may be brown or flesh-coloured. Strong jaws.
Body. The chest is deep, and the ribs are well sprung in order to allow proper movement for the shoulders. The back is straight to the loin, medium in length, neither long nor short-coupled. The breed just misses being square, its length being about 5 per cent greater than the height.
Tail. Long and profuse, carried over the back when alert; sometimes dropped down when at rest.
Feet. Long, flattish and slightly spread out. Soles well cushioned with hair.

It is claimed that the Samoyed is closer than any other modern breed to the primitive dog with no trace in the strain of either fox or wolf. The Samoyed's worldwide popularity was boosted when 28 Sammies helped Amundsen conquer the South Pole in 1911.

Samoyed

Siberian Husky

The coat of the Siberian Husky is double and medium in length, giving a highly furred appearance but never one so long as to obscure the clean-cut outline of the dog. The under-coat (which is normally absent during the shedding season) is soft and dense.

A Selection of
LARGE DOGS

Large dogs are magnificent, impressive and undoubtedly useful. They also often attract the wrong owners, reminding one of the old adage that there are no bad dogs, only bad owners.

The right reasons for wanting a large dog are that you like and admire them, you want to work a specific type at the task for which it was bred, you need a guard, you aim to enter obedience competitions or you wish to have a large, lovable pet for the family. Any of these reasons is acceptable, provided that you select a breed carefully, have adequate space and are able to give the dog the liberal feeding and exercise it will probably need.

Don't buy a large, ferocious-looking animal because you are a timid type and think that having a German Shepherd Dog on a chain will have the immediate effect of making you feel, and look, 10ft (3m) tall; or, if you've never owned a dog before, do not buy a German Shepherd Dog thinking it is some kind of super-charged burglar alarm. It is an intelligent animal that likes a job to do. It is loyal and affectionate, and although it has a guarding instinct don't leave it about the house all day getting bored.

The Rottweiler and Dobermann also make excellent guards, but settle for an Airedale bitch if you want your guard dog as a part-time children's nanny or leave the kids with a lovable, reliable St Bernard. Big dogs whelp easier than small ones and generally have large litters. Most are good-natured, but they benefit from firm, but kindly, discipline in puppyhood and attendance at dog training classes.

Large dogs — with a few noted exceptions — tend to resemble large, aggressive men who become putty in the little woman's hands and revel in companionship and fondling almost as much as in vigorous outdoor activity. A picture that will always remain in my memory is of a small child, fast asleep on a bench at Crufts, cuddled up to the protective, majestic body of an Irish Wolfhound. That massive dog was living up to its breed's reputation of 'gentle when stroked, fierce when provoked'. The little girl could not have been in safer company.

Below: The fierce-looking Irish Wolfhound, a very protective breed.

SALUKI
(Gazelle Hound)

Good points
- *Excellent guard*
- *Good companion*
- *Healthy*
- *Intelligent*
- *Odourless*
- *Reliable with children*

Take heed
- *Strong hunting instinct*
- *Not recommended for city dwellers*

The Saluki and the horse are prized Arab possessions. The Saluki is capable of great speed and is able to keep pace with the fleet-footed Arab stallions. It is still used in the Middle East for hunting the gazelle, but in the West it is kept mainly as an elegant companion, pet and show dog. It is intelligent and somewhat aloof but is a faithful, gentle companion, trustworthy with children. Care must be taken, particularly in country areas, that the Saluki is kept under control; despite its domestic role, it retains very strong hunting instincts.

Size
Height of dog should average 23-28in (58.5-71cm), bitch slightly smaller.

Exercise
Salukis need plenty of exercise, and ownership should not be contemplated by those without a large garden or other exercise area.

Grooming
Brush regularly with a soft brush, and use a hound glove. Combing of ear and tail fringes may be necessary.

Feeding
Recommended would be 13-20oz (369-587g) of a branded, meaty product with biscuit added in equal part by volume, or 1¾-3 cupfuls of a dry food, complete diet, mixed in the proportion of 1 cup of feed to ½ cup of hot or cold water.

Origin and history
The Saluki is one of the most ancient breeds of dog. Like the Afghan and Greyhound the Saluki is a sight hound that derives from the Middle East. The Saluki is said to take its name from Saluk in the Yemen, but its likeness is portrayed on the tombs of the Egyptian Pharaohs.

The breed did not gain recognition by the American Kennel Club until 1927. In the United Kingdom it was known long before, for a litter bred in London Zoo in 1836 was shown as the 'Persian Greyhound'. It was another 60 years before the Amherstia Foundation Kennels were started from two imported hounds. The breed was recognized in the United Kingdom by the Kennel Club in 1922.

SHOW STANDARD
General appearance. The whole appearance of this breed should give an impression of grace and symmetry. Its great speed and endurance, coupled with strength and activity, enable it to kill gazelle or other quarry over deep sand or rocky mountain. The expression should be dignified and gentle with deep, faithful, far-seeing eyes.
Colour. White, cream, fawn, golden, red, grizzle and tan, tri-colour (white, black and tan), and black and tan, or variations of these.
Head and skull. Head long and narrow; skull moderately wide between ears, not domed, the stop not pronounced, the whole showing great quality. nose should be black or liver. Eye colour is dark to hazel. The eyes, while large and oval, are not prominent.
Tail. Long, set on low and carried naturally in a curve; well feathered on the underside with long silky hair, not bushy.
Feet. Of moderate length, toes long and well arched, not splayed out, but at the same time not cat-footed; the whole strong and supple, well feathered between the toes.

Above: The Saluki has strong hunting instincts and must be kept under control in country areas. Its need for exercise count against it as a breed for city dwellers.

Although more often regarded in the West as a prize-winning show hound, the Saluki is the traditional hunting dog of the nomadic Bedouin tribes. Perfectly built for speed, lithe and sturdy and tough in constitution, this dog has always been a treasured possession of the tribesmen.

Saluki

STANDARD POODLE

Good points
- *Eye-catching appearance*
- *Good temperament*
- *Intelligent*
- *Recommended household pet*
- *Good sense of fun*
- *Splendid retriever*
- *Has stamina*
- *Useful in obedience competitions*
- *Usually good with children and other dogs*

Take heed
- *Do not make a clown or fashion model out of a fundamentally outdoor type*

The Poodle has a character full of fun. It is intelligent and obedient. In the United Kingdom it has proved a useful competitor in obedience competitions. It has a fondness for water, if the owner permits. The Standard Poodle is much favoured for the show ring where, exhibited in the traditional lion clip, it is a beauty to behold. It is also, debatably, the most difficult breed to prepare for the ring, involving the handler in a day's canine beauty treatment.

Size
Height: 15in (38cm) and over.

Exercise
This is a robust, healthy dog that loves the outdoors, has plenty of stamina and has lost none of its retrieving sporting instincts. It wil enjoy plenty of exercise.

Grooming
Use a wire-pin pneumatic brush and a wire-toothed metal comb for frequent grooming. The lion clip is an essential for the show ring, but pet owners generally resort to the more natural lamb clip with the hair a short uniform length. It is possible to clip your own dog with a pair of hairdressers' scissors. If despite the help which is usualy available from the breeder you find the task tedious, there are numerous pet and poodle parlours to which you should take your dog every six weeks. Bath regularly.

Feeding
Twenty oz (587g) of a branded, meaty product with biscuit added in equal part by volume, or 3 cupfuls of a dry food, complete diet, mixed in the proportion of 1 cup of feed to ½ cup of hot or cold water.

Origin and history
The Poodle was originally a shaggy guard, a retriever and protector of sheep, with origins similar to the Irish Water Spaniel and, no doubt, a common ancestor in the French Barbet and Hungarian Water Hound.

The Poodle may not be, as many suppose, solely of French origin. It originated in Germany as a water retriever; even the word poodle comes from the German 'pudelnass' or puddle. From this fairly large, sturdy dog, the Standard Poodle, the Miniature and the Toy have evolved.

The breed has been known in England since Prince Rupert of the Rhine, in company with his Poodle, came to the aid of Charles I in battle. The breed was favoured also by Marie Antoinette who, rumour has it, invented the lion clip by devising a style which would match the uniform of her courtiers. It is also popular in the United States.

SHOW STANDARD
General appearance. A very active, intelligent, well-balanced and elegant-looking dog with good temperament, carrying itself very proudly.
Colour. All solid colours. White and cream Poodles to have black nose, lips and eye rims; black toenails desirable. Brown Poodles to have dark amber eyes, dark liver nose, lips, eye rims and toenails. Apricot Poodles to have dark eyes with black points or deep amber eyes with liver points. Black, silver and blue Poodles to have black nose, lips, eye rims and toenails. Cream, apricot, brown, silver and blue Poodles may show varying shades of the same colour up to 18 months. Clear colours preferred.
Head and skull. Long and fine with slight peak at the back. The skull not broad and with a moderate stop. Foreface strong and well chiselled, not falling away under the eyes; bones and muscle flat. Lips tight fitting. Chin well defined but not protruding. The whole head must be in proportion to the size of the dog.
Tail. Set on rather high, well carried at a slight angle away from the body; never curled or carried over the back; thick at the root.
Feet. Pasterns strong; tight feet proportionately small, oval in shape, turning neither in nor out; toes arched; pads thick, hard and well cushioned.

IRISH WATER SPANIEL

Good points
- *Brave*
- *Easily trained*
- *Equable temperament*
- *Intelligent*
- *Loving*

Take heed
- *No drawbacks known*

The Irish Water Spaniel is a most attractive animal. It is loyal, intelligent and has a deeply affectionate nature. It is an excellent retriever and a strong, fearless swimmer, most useful for wildfowling.

Size
Height: dog 21-23in (53-58.5cm); bitch 20-22in (51-56cm).

Exercise
Needs plenty of exercise.

Grooming
Frequent brushing and weekly combing. Seek advice on stripping of unwanted hair. Take care that mud does not become caked in the toes.

Feeding
Approximately 13-20oz (369-587g) of a branded, meaty product with biscuit added in equal part by volume, or 1¾-3 cupfuls of a dry food, complete diet, mixed in the proportion of 1 cup of feed to ½ cup of hot or cold water.

Origin and history
It is not surprising that there is some resemblance between the Standard Poodle and the Irish Water Spaniel, because they are, or were, both water retrievers. This dog was developed in Ireland from several spaniel breeds towards the end of the nineteenth century. Unfortunately, perhaps,it has never gained immense popularity.

SHOW STANDARD
General appearance. The Irish Water Spaniel is a gundog bred for work in all types of shooting, and it is particularly suited for wildfowling. Its fitness for this purpose should be evident in its appearance; it is a strongly built, compact dog, intelligent, enduring and eager.
Colour. A rich dark liver with the purplish tint or bloom peculiar to the breed and sometimes referred to as puce-liver.
Head and skull. The head should be of good size. The skull high in dome, of good length and width sufficient to allow adequate brain capacity. The muzzle long, strong and somewhat square with a gradual stop. The face should be smooth and the skull covered with long curls in the form of a pronounced topknot growing in a well-defined peak to a point between the eyes. Nose large and well developed, dark liver colour. There should be an impression of fineness.
Tail. Peculiar to the breed, should be short and straight, thick at the root and tapering to a fine point. It should be low set, carried straight and below the level of the back and in length should not reach the hock joint. About 3-4in (7.5-10cm) of the tail at the root should be covered by close curls that stop abruptly; the remainder should be bare or covered by straight fine hairs.
Feet. Should be large and somewhat round and spreading; well covered with hair over and between the toes.

AMERICAN WATER SPANIEL

Good points
- *Equable temperament*
- *Excellent working dog*
- *Hardy*

Take heed
- *No drawbacks known*

The American Water Spaniel is little known outside its country of origin, where it has found great favour as a working gundog. It is a strong swimmer, an excellent waterfowler and an efficient retriever of most game.

Size
Height: 15-18in (38-46cm). Weight: dog 28-45lb (12.7-20.5kg); bitch, 25-40lb (11.3-18kg).

Exercise
Needs plenty of exercise.

Grooming
Regular brushing and weekly combing. Seek advice on stripping of unwanted hair. Take care that mud does not become caked in the toes.

Feeding
Thirteen-20oz (369-587g) of a branded, meaty product with biscuit added in equal part by volume, or 1¾-3 cupfuls of a dry food, complete diet, mixed in the proportion of 1 cup of feed to ½ cup of hot or cold water.

Origin and history
The American Water Spaniel is believed to have originated through the crossing of an Irish Water Spaniel with a smaller spaniel breed and/or with a Curly-coated Retriever.

In some parts of America it is still known as the Boykin Spaniel, after Whit Boykin, one of the pioneers of the breed in Boykin, South Carolina. It was recognized by the American Kennel Club in 1940 and has recently become recognized in the United Kingdom.

SHOW STANDARD
General appearance. Medium in size, of sturdy typical spaniel character, curly coat, an active muscular dog with emphasis placed on proper size and conformation, correct head properties, texture of coat and colour. Of amicable disposition; demeanour indicates intelligence, strength and endurance.
Colour. Solid liver or dark chocolate, a little white on toes or chest permissible.
Head and skull. Moderate in length, skull rather broad and full, stop moderately defined but not too pronounced. Forehead covered with short smooth hair and without tuft or topknot. Muzzle of medium length, square and with no inclination to snipiness. jaws strong and of good length, and neither undershot nor overshot, teeth straight and well shaped. Nose sufficiently wide with well-developed nostrils to ensure good scenting power.
Body. Sturdily constructed but not too compact or close-coupled. The shoulders are clean, muscular and sloping. The loins are slightly arched and well furnished. The brisket is deep but not too broad. Medium-length, well-boned legs.
Tail. Moderate in length, curved in a slightly rocker shape, carried slightly below level of back; tapered and covered with hair to tip; action lively.
Feet. Should harmonize with size of dog. Toes closely grouped and well padded.

The Poodle's potential for glamour has sometimes obscured
its essentially active and sporting character. Because its intelligence
enables it to be trained to perform complex
tricks, and because it can be
attractively clipped, it was formerly
employed as a circus dog.

Standard Poodle

Irish Water Spaniel

American Water Spaniel

ENGLISH SPRINGER SPANIEL

Good points
- *Excellent with children*
- *Good worker in the field*
- *Intelligent*
- *Loyal*
- *Good house-pet*

Take heed
- *Could develop skin trouble*
- *Could put on weight if under-exercised*

The English Springer Spaniel makes an excellent dual-purpose gundog and pet. It gives a good account of itself in obedience competitions and excels as a happy, efficient retriever.

Size
The approximate height should be 20in (51cm). The approximate weight should be 50lb (22.7kg).

Exercise
Needs plenty of exercise, or is likely to put on weight. Lack of exercise often leads to skin troubles, too.

Grooming
Frequent brushing. Take care that mud does not become caked in the paws and make sure that the ears are kept clean and tangle-free to prevent infection.

Feeding
Recommended would be 13-20oz (369-587g) of a branded, meaty product with biscuit added in equal part by volume, or 1¾-3 cupfuls of a dry food, complete diet, mixed in the proportion of 1 cup of feed to ½ cup of hot or cold water.

Origin and history
The English Springer is the oldest of the British spaniels except for the Clumber, but it has never gained the popularity of the smaller Cocker Spaniel. The Springer is favoured, in the main, by those with an interest in shooting and/or field trials. Incidentally, the English Springer was appreciated by the Americans as a 'bird' dog before it had even been recognized by the Kennel Club in London. There is some controversy as to whether the dog, originally called a Norfolk Spaniel, came from the county of Norfolk, England, or took its name from the famous Norfolk family. Certainly the name 'springer' is derived from its early task of 'springing' game for hunter's nets.

SHOW STANDARD
General appearance. The general appearance of the modern Springer is that of a symmetrical compact, strong, upstanding, merry and active dog, built for endurance and activity. It is the highest on the leg and the raciest in build of all British land spaniels.
Colour. Any recognized land spaniel colour is acceptable, but liver and white, black and white, or

Above: The English Springer Spaniel needs regular grooming and plenty of long energetic walks in order to keep trim.

either of these colours with tan markings is preferred.
Head and skull. The skull should be of medium length, fairly broad and slightly rounded, rising from the foreface, making a brow or stop, divided by a fluting between the eyes gradually dying away along the forehead towards the occiput bone, which should not be peaked. The cheeks should be flat, i.e. not rounded or full. The foreface should be of proportionate length to the skull, fairly broad and deep without being coarse, well chiselled below the eyes, fairly deep and square in flew but not exaggerated to such an extent as would interfere with comfort when retrieving. Nostrils should be well developed in this particular breed.
Tail. The stern should be low and never carried above the level of the back; well feathered and with a lively action.
Feet. Feet tight, compact, and well rounded with strong full pads.

CLUMBER SPANIEL

Good points
- *Even temperament*
- *Intelligent*
- *Reliable*

Take heed
- *Slow but sure worker*

The Clumber is the heaviest of the spaniels and is thought to be of French origin, brought about by crossing the Basset Hound with the Alpine Spaniel (which is now unfortunately extinct).

It is a brave, attractive and reliable dog; a slow but sure worker that excels for rough shooting and is an excellent retriever.

Size
Dog about 55-70lb (25-32kg); bitch about 45-60lb (20.5-27kg).

Exercise
This is essentially a working dog, best suited to country life, and needs plenty of exercise and off-the-lead runs in open spaces.

Below: Attractive and massive, Clumbers make reliable workers. The heaviest of spaniels, they are somewhat slow, but quite reliable.

Grooming
Routine brushing. Keep coat tangle-free and take care that mud does not become lodged between the toes.

Feeding
Recommended would be 20-33oz (587-936g) of a branded, meaty product with biscuit added, or 3-5 cupfuls of a dry food, complete diet, mixed in the proportion of 1 cup of feed to ½ cup of hot or cold water. Rations should be stepped up or decreased, according to the amount of work the dog is asked to do.

Origin and history
The Clumber Spaniel was fostered and promoted by the Duc de Noailles in the years before the French Revolution. The breed became renowned as beaters and retrievers in the field.

With the advent of war, the Duc de Noailles brought his dogs to England and entrusted them to the Duke of Newcastle at Clumber Park, from which the name is derived. The Duc de Noailles was killed in the revolution, but he left his mark for posterity by the legacy of his spaniels which remained safely in England.

SHOW STANDARD
General appearance. A dog with a thoughtful expression; very massive but active, it moves with a rolling gait which is somewhat characteristic of the breed.
Colour. Plain white with lemon markings, orange permissible; slight head markings and freckled muzzle; white body preferred.
Head and skull. Head large, square and massive, of medium length, broad on top with a decided occiput; heavy brows with a deep top; heavy muzzle, well-developed flew (pendulous upper lip), and level jaw and mouth; nose square and flesh coloured.
Tail. Set low, well feathered and carried about level with the back.
Feet. Large and round, well covered with hair.

The coat of the English Springer Spaniel should
be close, straight and weather-resistant without being coarse.
The dog's ears, which must be given special
attention in grooming, should be lobular
in shape, set close to the head in a line
with the eye, and of good length
and width, but not exaggerated.

English Springer Spaniel

Clumber Spaniel

KARELIAN BEAR DOG

Good points
- Brave
- Fine hunter
- Hardy
- Loyal to its owner

Take heed
- Does not get on with other dogs
- Unsuitable as a family pet

The Karelian Bear Dog is a sturdy hunter of bear and elk. It is a brave dog, loyal to its master. It does not get on with other dogs and can not, ideally, be recommended as a family pet.

Size
Height at shoulder: 21-24in (53-61cm) for dogs, 19-21in (48-53cm) for bitches.

Exercise
Needs plenty of exercise to stay in a healthy condition.

Grooming
Frequent brushing will keep the coat in good condition.

Feeding
Recommended would be 13-20oz (369-587g) of a branded, meaty product with biscuit added in equal part by volume, or 1¾-3 cupfuls of a dry food, complete diet, mixed in the proportion of 1 cup of feed to ½ cup of hot or cold water.

Origin and history
The Karelian Bear Dog is a Spitz belonging to the Russian breed of Laikas, but this type evolved in Finland. It is known throughout Scandinavia as a fearless hunter of bear and elk. (The Russians decreed, in 1947, that only four distinct types of Spitz should in the future be referred to as Laikas, and these are neither known nor exported outside the USSR.)

SHOW STANDARD
General appearance. The Karelian Bear Dog is an athletic and imposing dog, of robust build, strong and slightly longer than high; it has a thick coat, cocked ears and an introverted nature, and is brave and persistent. Its senses, particularly that of scent, are keen, and it is admirably adapted to big game hunting.
Colour. Black, preferably slightly brownish or dull, mostly with white markings or spots on the head, neck, chest, belly and legs.
Head. Shaped like a blunt wedge, fairly broad at the forehead and cheeks. Forehead slightly arched; stop gently sloping; slight protuberance above the eyes. The muzzle is high and its bridge is preferably straight, tapering slightly only towards the nose. Nose black and well developed.
Tail. Of medium length, usually arched; a full arch is most desirable.
Feet. Hindfeet slightly longer than forefeet. Paws thick, high and roundish: those of a born hunter.

ELKHOUND
(Norwegian Elkhound)

Good points
- Good household pet
- Odourless
- Reliable with children
- Sensible guard

Take heed
- Needs firm but gentle discipline in puppyhood

The Elkhound is a happy breed, loyal and devoted to its master, reliable with children. It has a great love of the outdoors, is energetic, and is not recommended for those unable to provide exercise.

Size
Height at shoulder: dog 20½in (52cm); bitch 19½in (49.5cm). Weight: dog 50lb (22.7kg); bitch 43lb (19.5kg).

Exercise
Needs plenty of exercise.

Grooming
Frequent brushing and combing.

Feeding
Thirteen-20oz (369-587g) of a branded, meaty product with biscuit added in equal part by volume, or 1¾-3 cupfuls of a dry food, complete diet, mixed in the proportion of 1 cup of feed to ½ cup of hot or cold water.

Origin and history
The job of the Elkhound was to seek out elk and hold them at bay until its master moved in for the kill. It has existed in Norway for centuries but was not considered a show prospect until 1877, the year in which the Norwegian Hunters' Association first held a show.

Today's Elkhound has been tailored to meet the ideal decided upon by various Scandinavian clubs and societies. When other Spitz breeds fell by the wayside, a Norwegian breed standard emerged for this national breed.

Above: The powerful Elkhound has a thick, weather-resistant coat that looks good in the show ring and wears well in the field.

SHOW STANDARD
General appearance. It has a compact and proportionately short body, a coat thick and abundant but not bristling and prick ears; tail tightly curled over back.
Colour. Grey of various shades with black tips to the long outer coat; lighter on the chest, stomach and legs, and the underside of the tail. Any distinctive variation from the grey colour is most undesirable, and too dark or too light a colouring should be avoided. Pronounced markings on legs and feet are also not desirable.
Head and skull. Broad between the ears; the forehead and back of the head are slightly arched with a clearly marked but not large stop. Muzzle moderately long, broader at the base and gradually tapering — whether seen from above or from the side — but not pointed; bridge of the nose straight, jaw strong with lips tightly closed.
Tail. Set high, tightly curled over the back but not carried on either side; hair thick and close.
Feet. Compact, oval in shape and not turned outwards; toes tightly closed; toenails firm and strong.

SWEDISH ELKHOUND
(Jämthund)

Good points
- Brave
- Equable temperament
- Excellent hunter

Take heed
- No drawbacks known, but remember it is essentially a hunter

The Swedish Elkhound is little known outside its native country, where its popularity surpasses that of the Norwegian Elkhound. It has great stamina and makes a bold and energetic hunter. It is also an excellent guard. It is loyal to its master, of a calm temperament and extremely agile.

Size
Height at shoulder: dog 23-25in (58.5-63.5cm), bitch 21-23in (53-58.5cm).

Exercise
Needs plenty of exercise to stay in tip-top condition.

Grooming
The thick coat wants regular brushing and combing.

Feeding
Thirteen-20oz (369-587g) of a branded, meaty product with biscuit added in equal part by volume, or 1¾-3 cupfuls of a dry food, complete diet, mixed in the proportion of 1 cup of feed to ½ cup of hot or cold water.

Origin and history
The Swedish Elkhound is similar to the Norwegian Elkhound. Yet despite continuing popularity in its country of origin, it is little known elsewhere — unlike the Norwegian Elkhound, which has had universal success in the show ring.

The breed was evolved by Swedish huntsmen who considered their local Spitz breeds superior to the Norwegian Elkhound for hunting. It is taller than the Norwegian dog, and the Swedes are adamant that it is also a better hunter.

SHOW STANDARD
General appearance. A large Elkhound of the Spitz type with erect ears and a well-curled tail, but not tightly so, carried high over the back. The breed is robust, compact and lean without heaviness; it should not look long. Courageous and energetic, this breed is at the same time calm and reflective.
Colour. Dark grey or light grey; parts of the muzzle, cheeks and throat are light grey or cream, and these are characteristic of the breed. Varicolour on legs, chest and belly and around the vent is allowed.
Head. Long, lean, relatively broad between the eyes. The skull is very slightly rounded. The stop is clearly defined but is not pronounced. The nose is broad, the bridge straight, wide and strong. The lips are close-fitting over the jaws. The muzzle is slightly shorter than the skull, tapering gently and uniformly to the nose. It should not, however, be pointed as seen either from above or in profile. The cheeks are flat. The teeth should meet in a level bite.
Tail. Set on high, of medium length and uniform thickness. It is well feathered but without fringe, it is carried curled up over the back, not too much to the side.
Feet. The Elkhound's feet are robust and straightforward, not turned out. There is also a slightly elliptical cast to the feet, and the toes are closed.

The Elkhound has a longish and coarse top-coat, dark at the tips with a light coloured, soft and woolly under-coat. About the neck and the front of the chest, where the coat is longest, it forms a kind of ruff which, allied to the dog's pointed and very mobile ears, expressive eyes and tightly curled tail, gives an alert and energetic appearance.

Elkhound

Karelian Bear Dog

The Karelian Bear Dog, named from Karelen province in eastern Finland, was recognized as a pure breed in 1935 and officially recognized by the FCI in 1946. Of striking and attractive appearance, it is widely shown in Finland.

The Swedish Elkhound survived the adoption of the Norwegian Elkhound as the official Scandinavian elk-hunting Spitz around the turn of the century, and was recognized as a separate breed in 1946.

Swedish Elkhound

ENGLISH FOXHOUND

Good points
- *First-rate hunter*
- *Lively*

Take heed
- *Noisy*
- *Does not make a suitable pet*

The Foxhound is not suitable as a household pet. It is almost always confined to a foxhunting pack. Hunt supporters often take on the role of puppy walker, in order to accustom a young hound to road hazards and livestock before returning it to its pack. Hounds are attractive, vivacious pups, but they are far too active and destructive for the average household. It is not possible in the United Kingdom to purchase a Foxhound as a pet. Hounds are always counted by the pack in couples: the huntsman will talk of having 30 couples of hounds.

Size
Height: dog 23in (58.5cm); bitch just a little less.

Exercise
Vigorous exercise is necessary. Foxhounds should have the stamina to spend all day running foxes with the hunt.

Grooming
Use a hound glove.

Feeding
Foxhounds are not fed as household pets, pack members being trencher-fed with horse flesh and an oatmeal mash called a 'pudding'. The leaner hounds are led to the trough first, so that they may eat their fill, and then the remainder are led in. They are not fed the day before a hunt.

Origin and history
The Foxhound is descended from the heavier St Hubert Hounds, brought to England by the Norman invaders, and from the now extinct Talbot Hounds. The Ardennes Hounds derived their name of Hubertus Hounds from the Bishop of Liege who later became St Hubert, patron saint of all hunters.

The Foxhound is never exhibited at ordinary dog shows but has its own events under the auspices, in the United Kingdom, of the Association of Masters of Foxhounds.

SHOW STANDARD
Colour. The Masters of Foxhounds declare that no hound can be a bad colour.
Head and skull. Skull broad.
Feet. The toes of the feet should be close together and not open.
Tail. Should be well put on at the end of good quarters, and these quarters should in no way end abruptly and be of the type that hound-men term 'chopped off behind'. A curly stern, although unsightly, will not be detrimental to the hound's hunting qualities.

AMERICAN FOXHOUND

Good points
- *First-rate hunter*
- *Lively*

Take heed
- *Noisy*
- *Does not make a suitable pet*

The American Foxhound is a lighter, racier-looking dog that the English Foxhound. It is exhibited in the show ring in the United States.

Size
Height: dogs should not be under 22in (56cm) nor over 25in (63.5cm); bitches should not be under 21in (53cm) nor over 24in (61cm). Measurements made across the back at the point of the withers, the hound standing in a natural position with its feet well under it.

Exercise
Needs plenty of vigorous exercise.

Grooming
Use a hound glove.

Feeding
Foxhounds are not fed as household pets, pack members being trencher-fed with horse flesh and an oatmeal mash called a 'pudding'. The leaner hounds are led to the trough first, so that they may eat their fill, and then the remainder are led in. They are not fed the day before a hunt.

Origin and history
The American Foxhound may have been derived from a pack of English Foxhounds taken from Britain to America by Robert Brooke in 1650, but some authorities say that the first mention of hound importations to America appears in the diary of one of De Soto's men. They are very fast, their quarry — the American red fox — being a speedier prey than its English counterpart. In about 1770, George Washington also imported English Foxhounds from Great Britain and received a gift from Lafayette of some excellent French specimens in 1785. The French and British breeds were crossbred, producing the Virginia Hounds, which have developed to form today's American Foxhound.

SHOW STANDARD
Colour. Any colour is acceptable.
Head and skull. The skull should be fairly long, slightly domed at occiput with cranium broad and full. Ears set on moderately low, long, reaching when drawn out nearly, if not quite, to the tip of the nose; fine in texture, fairly broad, with almost entire absence of erectile power — setting close to the head with the forward edge slightly turning to the cheek — round at tip.
Feet. Fox-like. Pad full and hard. Well-arched toes. Strong nails.
Tail. Set on moderately high and carried gaily but not turned forward over the back; slight curve and very slight brush.

HAMILTON HOUND
(Stövare)

Good points
- *First-rate hunter*
- *Lively*

Take heed
- *Noisy*
- *This breed does not make a suitable pet*

This medium-sized hound was named after Count Hamilton, who created the breed by crossing the English Foxhound with the best German hounds, including the Holstein Hound and the Hanoverian Haidbracke. It is the most popular hunting hound in Sweden. Count Hamilton was the founder of the Swedish Kennel Club.

Size
Height: dog 19½-23in (49.5-58cm); bitch 18-22½in (46-57cm).

Exercise
Requires plenty of strenuous exercise.

Grooming
Use a hound glove.

Feeding
As for English Foxhounds.

SHOW STANDARD
General appearance. The dog should be well built, giving an impression of strength and ruggedness and should have a tricolour coat.
Head and skull. Long, rectangular and lean. The skull is moderately arched and broad, the occipital protruberance is not prominent. The stop is not pronounced. The nose is always black, fairly large, and with wide nostrils. The bridge is straight and parallel to the line of the skull. The upper lips should be full but not excessively pendulous. The muzzle is robust, rectangular and quite long. The zygomatic arch should not be overly prominent. The teeth are strong and should be without any defect; they should close in a scissors bite.
Tail. Set on high, almost as a continuation of the backline; when down it should reach the hocks. Thick at the root, it tapers towards the tip; it should be carried straight out or slightly curved.
Feet. They should be strong and directed forward with elastic and well-closed toes and large pads. Wolf feet are not desirable.

HARRIER

Good points
- *First-rate hunter*
- *Lively*

Take heed
- *Noisy*
- *This breed does not make a suitable pet*

The Harrier bears some similarity to the Beagle but more closely resembles the Foxhound, with which it has been so interbred that few purebred Harriers exist today. It is slower than the Beagle and Foxhound and is generally used to hunt the hare on both foot and horseback, although it is also used for foxhunting.

Size
Height varies from 18-22in (46-56cm).

Exercise
Needs liberal amounts of exercise.

Grooming
Use a hound glove.

Feeding
As for English Foxhounds.

Origin and history
The Harrier is extremely popular in the United States but is, in fact, an ancient British breed whose first pack was recorded in the year 1260. This pack, the Penistone, was established by Sir Elias de Midhope and existed for over five centuries. The word 'harrier' is Norman French for 'hunting dog', and at one time all hunting dogs in Britain were known as Harriers. The breed is similar in appearance to the Foxhound. Primarily used for fox and rabbit hunting, it has an additional, unexpected chore in South America and Sri Lanka, where it is used for leopard hunting. Harriers are exhibited in dog shows in the United States. It is also popular with American drag hunts.

SHOW STANDARD
(American Standard)
The points of the modern Harrier are very similar to those of the English Foxhound. The Harrier, however, is smaller than the English Foxhound, and the most popular size is 19-21in (48-53cm). They should be active, well balanced and full of strength and quality with shoulders sloping into the muscles of the back, clean and not loaded on the withers or point.

The back is level and muscular, not dipping behind the withers or arching over the loin. The elbow's point set well away from the ribs, running parallel with the body and not turning outwards. Deep, well-sprung ribs, running well back with plenty of heart room and a deep chest.

Good straight legs with plenty of bone running well down to the toes but not overburdened, inclined to knuckle over very slightly but not exaggerated in the slightest degree. Round cat-like feet and close toes turning inwards. Hindlegs and hocks stand square with a good sweep and muscular thigh to take the weight off the body.

The head should be of medium size with good bold forehead, and plenty of expression; head must be well set up on a neck of ample length, not heavy; stern should be set well up, long and well controlled.

The tail, which should not be carried too gaily, is set in a continuation of the spine and extends without curvature.

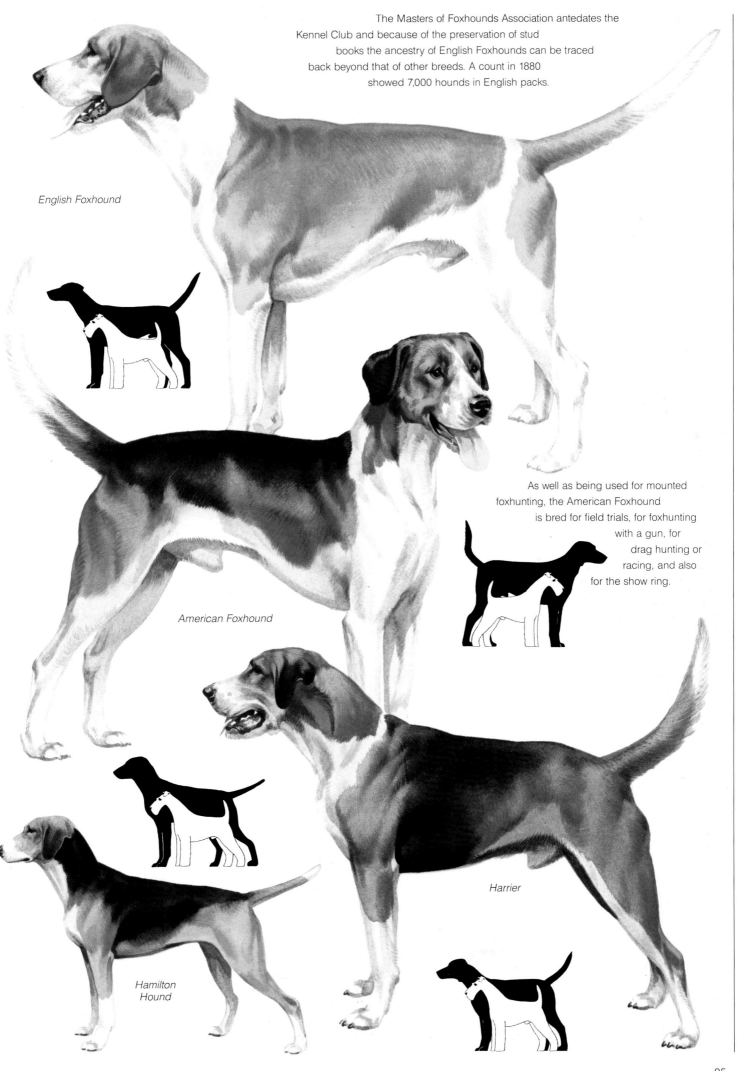

The Masters of Foxhounds Association antedates the Kennel Club and because of the preservation of stud books the ancestry of English Foxhounds can be traced back beyond that of other breeds. A count in 1880 showed 7,000 hounds in English packs.

English Foxhound

American Foxhound

As well as being used for mounted foxhunting, the American Foxhound is bred for field trials, for foxhunting with a gun, for drag hunting or racing, and also for the show ring.

Harrier

Hamilton Hound

PHARAOH HOUND

Good points
- *Affectionate*
- *Excellent hunter*
- *Full of fun*
- *Good with children*
- *Intelligent*
- *Odourless*

Take heed
- *Not suitable for town life*
- *Wary of strangers*

The Pharaoh Hound is one of the oldest domesticated dogs in recorded history. Two hounds hunting gazelle are depicted on a circular disc dating back to around 4000 BC, certainly before the First Dynasty.

The dog, and particularly the hunting dog, played an intimate part in the daily life of kings and nobles in Ancient Egypt. It is therefore not surprising to find dogs frequently depicted in the reliefs carved on the tomb walls of these men.

The Pharaoh Hound is a medium-sized hound, elegant, powerful and swift. It is intelligent, affectionate and full of fun; it is also very good with children but is a little diffident at first with strangers. Out hunting it is keen and fast. Unlike the Greyhound, it hunts by both scent and sight.

Size
Height: dog 22-25in (56-63.5cm); bitch ideally 21-24in (53-61cm). Overall balance must be maintained.

Exercise
This is a breed that needs plenty of exercise. It is unsuitable for town or apartment living.

Grooming
The silky, smooth coat needs little attention for a smart appearance.

Feeding
This is a hardy and healthy breed, yet on the Island of Gozo (near Malta) to which it is believed the Pharaoh Hound was brought by Phoenicians, it was fed almost entirely on a meat-free diet of soup and goat's milk. Nowadays it enjoys a more traditional canine diet, but care must be taken that it does not become overweight.

Recommended would be 13-20oz (369-587g) of a branded, meaty product with biscuit added in equal part by volume, or 1¾-3 cupfuls of a complete, dry food mixed in the proportion of 1 cup of feed to ½ cup of hot or cold water.

Origin and history
It is thought that the Phoenicians took these hounds with them when they settled on Malta and Gozo. The preservation of the breed, which has changed little in 5,000 years, can be accredited to Malta, where it is known to have existed for over 2,000 years. In Malta, Pharaohs are bred for rabbit hunting and are known by the Maltese as 'kelb-tal-fenek' (rabbit dog).

In 1935 the Harvard-Boston expedition, under Dr George Reisner, working in the great cemetery west of the Pyramid of Cheops at Giza, found an inscription recording the burial of a dog named 'Abuwtiyuw'. The burial was carried out with all the ritual ceremonies of a great man of Egypt, by order of the kings of Upper and Lower Egypt.

Like other Egyptian nobles, the dog was in constant attendance, a daily fact in the life of the king. Whenever a dog died, the monarch ordered that it be buried ceremonially in a tomb of its own, in order that, like human beings buried in this way, its 'ka' might enter the afterlife as an honoured spirit. Thus, after death, its future existence might be assured to continue attendance on the king.

SHOW STANDARD
General appearance. The Pharaoh Hound is medium-sized, of noble bearing with clean-cut lines. It

Below: Elegant and alert, a Pharaoh Hound bitch is seen here with her two puppies. This breed is very affectionate and full of fun. It is the oldest in recorded history and has hardly changed in 5,000 years.

is graceful yet powerful and very fast with a free, easy movement and an alert expression.

Colour. Tan or rich tan with white markings allowed as follows: white tip on tail is desirable; white on chest (called the 'star'); white on toes; slim white blaze on centre line of face permissible. Flecking or white other than as above is undesirable.

Head and skull. Skull long, lean and well chiselled. Foreface slightly longer than skull. Only slight stop. Top of skull parallel with the foreface. The whole head represents a blunt wedge when viewed in profile and from above.

Tail. Medium set, fairly thick at the base and tapering (whip-like), reaching just below the point of the hock in repose. Carried high and curved when the dog is in action. The tail should not be tucked between the legs. A screw tail is a fault.

Feet. Strong, well knuckled and firm, turning neither in nor out. Paws well padded. Dew-claws may be removed.

IBIZAN HOUND

Good points
- *Excellent with children*
- *Good gundog*
- *Kind disposition*
- *Seldom fights*
- *Wonderful house-pet*
- *Strong and resilient*
- *Good watchdogs*

Take heed
- *No drawbacks known*

The Ibizan Hound is a kind dog loved by children, in whom it seems to inspire confidence. It is easily hurt, however, and due to its acute hearing must not be shouted at. It has great stamina and can, according to the natives of Ibiza, hunt by day or by night, singly or in pairs. But it is not a dog to go off on its own and not return. They willingly retrieve and are often taken hunting on the island without guns.

Size
Weight: 49-50lb (22.2-22.7kg). Height: 22-28in (56-71cm), for a dog, less for a bitch.

Exercise
It would be unkind to keep this hound in a confined space, for it is a tireless dog, able to retrieve and to jump great heights. It is an excellent companion for a sportsman. It must not be kennelled; ideally it should be kept as a companion in the home.

Grooming
The Ibizan needs a good brush every so often but is not difficult to maintain in good condition.

Feeding
Recommended would be 13-20oz (369-587g) of a branded, meaty product with biscuit added in equal part by volume, or 1¾-3 cupfuls of a dry food, complete diet, mixed in the proportion of 1 cup of feed to ½ cup of hot or cold water. The

addition of raw fish and fruit to the diet of the Ibizan is beneficial.

Origin and history
We know that hounds like the Ibizan were owned by the pharaohs of Egypt because hunting dogs of this type were drawn on rock, stone and papyrus as early as 3000 BC. Indeed, bones of similar hunting dogs have been found from about 4770 BC. The dogs of the pharaohs probably spread through trade to neighbouring lands. On the invasion of Egypt by the Romans, their neighbours the Carthaginians and the Phoenicians were driven out to the island of Ibiza in the ninth century BC, where they lived for about a century. The hounds that they brought with them remained on Ibiza for the next 3,000 years. Although some fine hounds have recently been taken from Ibiza to Majorca, the purest hounds are still found on Ibiza. They retain all the colours shown in the Egyptian drawings, i.e. spotted red and lion on white, or any of these singly.

The Ibizan reached the United States in 1956 when a pair of hounds was imported by a Rhode Island couple. That autumn the first Ibizan litter was born. Those eight puppies plus several other imports constituted the foundation stock of the breed in the United States. The Ibizan was admitted to the AKC stud book in 1978 and to competition the following year.

Above: The noble head of the Ibizan Hound. This ancient breed makes a sensitive and gentle pet, especially for children.

SHOW STANDARD
General appearance. Tall, narrow, finely built, large erect ears.

Colour. White, chestnut, or lion solid colour, or any combination of these.

Head and skull. Fine, long flat skull with prominent occipital bone. Stop not well defined, slightly convex muzzle, the length of which from the eyes to the tip of the nose should be equal to the length from the eyes to the occiput. Nose flesh coloured, should protrude beyond the teeth, jaw very strong and lean.

Tail. Long, thin, low set, reaching well below the hock, when passed between the legs and round the flank should reach the spine; may be carried high when excited.

Feet. Well-arched toes, thick pads, light coloured claws. Front feet may turn slightly outwards. Dew-claws should not be removed in front No hind dew-claws.

At the beginning of this century the Ibizan Hound was common as a hunting dog on the Spanish mainland. Although generally used for coursing rabbit and hare, in some regions it would hunt stag and bear, and was also used as a gundog. More recently it has become popular throughout southern Europe and is seen frequently in large numbers at all the major shows. The modern Ibizan Hound very closely resembles its ancestors of almost 50 centuries ago.

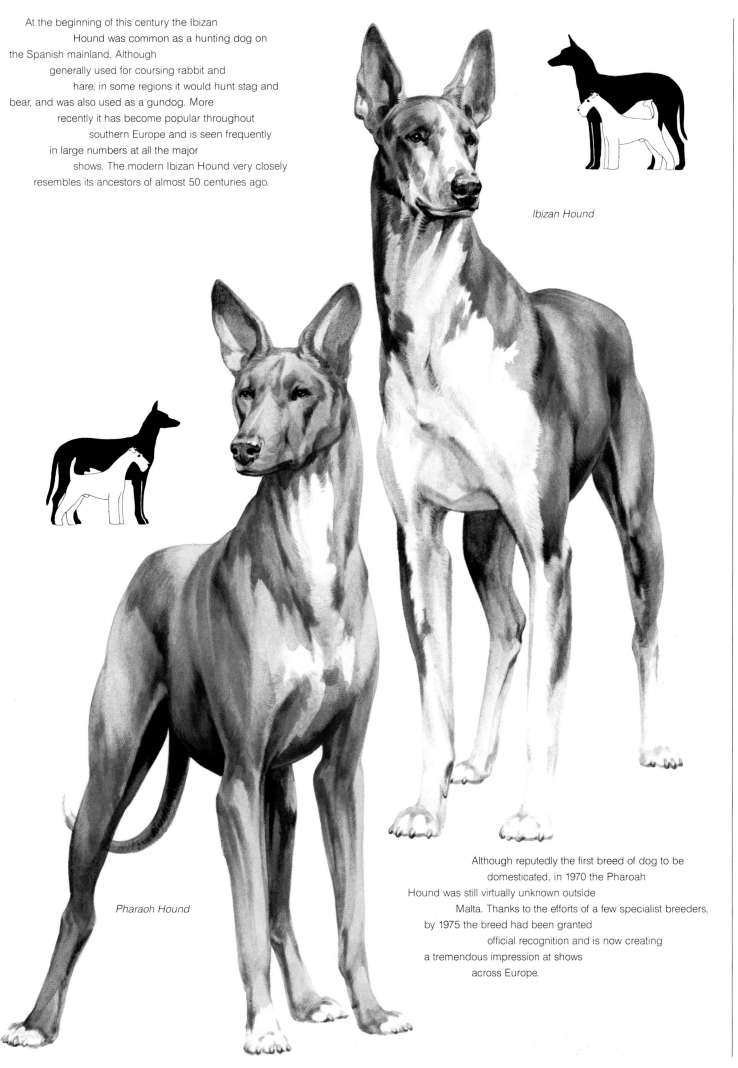

Ibizan Hound

Pharaoh Hound

Although reputedly the first breed of dog to be domesticated, in 1970 the Pharoah Hound was still virtually unknown outside Malta. Thanks to the efforts of a few specialist breeders, by 1975 the breed had been granted official recognition and is now creating a tremendous impression at shows across Europe.

AFGHAN HOUND

Good points
- *Beautiful in appearance*
- *Loyal and affectionate*
- *Good with children who do not tease*

Take heed
- *Independent*
- *Needs plenty of exercise*
- *Not suitable for apartments*
- *Needs daily grooming*
- *Must have firm, loving handling*
- *Can be fiery tempered, particularly in adolescence*

The Afghan is dignified, aloof and fond of comfort. Though it enjoys nothing more than surveying the scene from a cosy armchair, the Afghan is not the ideal choice for apartment dwellers or those with a small house and garden. For despite its beautiful house manners, the Afghan is basically a hunting dog, warmly affectionate to its owners and usually trustworthy with children. But it is independent in character and often quite fiery in temper, particularly in adolescence.

It is impossible to show an Afghan too much affection, and it shouldn't be bullied. But it is important to maintain superiority from the first, especially during showing and training sessions, or later you may suffer the indignity, and physical near-impossibility, of publicly wrestling with a powerful creature armed with a mouthful of large teeth.

Size
Ideal height: dog 27-29in (68.5-73.5cm), bitch approximately 2-3in (5-7.5cm) smaller.

Exercise
Afghans need free running to keep fit and happy. Their original task was to hunt wolves and gazelles in the deserts of Afghanistan, so a stroll in the park or a run up and down a suburban garden will not be enough to subdue their boundless energy. A puppy, from the first, should be allowed unrestricted exercise in its waking hours. This should be in a safe enclosed place. An adult should have a minimum of half an hour's free galloping a day, as well as disciplined walking on the lead.

Grooming
Daily grooming is important to prevent the dog's thick coat from matting; the well-groomed Afghan is a delight to behold, the neglected specimen an abomination. Indeed, this breed is definitely not for those with little time on their hands for grooming and exercising.

The only type of brush capable of getting through an Afghan's coat is one with an air cushion behind the tufts. The best of all is a real bristle brush — made for humans. The nylon version is cheaper, but remember to use a coat lubricant with this, otherwise static electricity will build up and cause the hair to become brittle. An air-cushioned brush with steel pins is excellent and is not expensive.

Feeding
Recommended would be 20-33oz (587-936g) cans of a branded, meaty product with biscuit added, or 3-5 cupfuls of a dry food, complete diet, mixed in the proportion of 1 cup of feed to ½ cup of hot or cold water.

Origin and history
The Afghan is an ancient breed reputed to have existed thousands of years ago in the Middle East. Present-day experts believe that it was crossed with the Saluki.

A papyrus found in Sinai dated at 3000 BC was, from early translations, thought to refer to a Cynocephalus, or monkey-faced hound; this could have been the forerunner of the Afghan, which because of its facial resemblance is often called a 'monkey dog'. However, later work on the translation confirmed belief that it referred not to a dog but to a hound-faced baboon.

At any rate a Greyhound-like dog was destined to find its way, perhaps through Persia, to Afghanistan, where it grew a long, shaggy coat for protection against the harsh climate and found favour with the royal and aristocratic families of that land.

The Afghan Hound Breed Club was formed in the United Kingdom in 1926, the same year as the breed was officially registered for the first time by the American Kennel Club. The Afghan began making strides in the United States in 1931 when Zeppo Marx and his wife imported an English bitch named 'Asra of Ghazni' and a dog named 'Westmill Omar'. The Marxes eventually sold this pair, who went on to form the cornerstone of the breed in America.

SHOW STANDARD
General appearance. The Afghan Hound should be dignified and aloof with a certain keen fierceness. The Eastern or Oriental expression is typical of the breed; the Afghan looks at, and through, one. The gait of the Afghan Hound should be smooth and springy with a style of high order. The whole appearance of the dog should give the impression of strength and dignity combining speed and power. The head must be held proudly.
Colour. All colours are acceptable. (You will see the breed in fawns, silvers, grey and tan grizzles and black and tan.)
Head and skull. Skull long, not too narrow with a prominent occiput. Foreface long with punishing jaws and slight stop. The skull should be well balanced and surmounted by a long topknot. Nose preferably black, but liver is no fault in light-coloured dogs.
Tail. Not too short. Set on low with a ring at the end. Raised when in action. Sparsely feathered.
Feet. Forefeet strong and very large in both length and breadth and covered with long thick hair; toes arched. Pasterns long and springy, especially in front, and pads well down on the ground. Hindfeet long, but not quite so broad as the forefeet, and covered with long thick hair.

GREYHOUND

Good points
- *An aristocrat, built for speed*
- *Adaptable*
- *Affectionate*
- *Good with adults and children — rarely snaps unless teased*
- *Loyal*

Take heed
- *It is the Greyhound's natural instinct to chase small, fast-moving objects*
- *Has a tendency to rheumatism and arthritis*

The Greyhound is one of the most ancient breeds and, some say, the most misunderstood. Although built for speed and used for racing and coursing, the Greyhound is basically lazy. It adapts well to life as a family pet and will enjoy nothing better than lazing on a settee or mattress, which is what it will have done for many hours when living in racing kennels. It is a good-natured, friendly and affectionate dog and is very gentle with children.

Good pet homes are always needed for ex-racing Greyhounds. Those with a love for the breed may consider making enquiries at their local track or (in the United Kingdom) of the National Greyhound Racing Club's Retired Greyhound Trust, to discover where dogs are available.

The retired Greyhound racer is not an aged animal. It is unlikely to be more than three- or four-years-old and may be as little as 18 months if it has proved unsuitable for racing. But remember that it will require a period of de-training. There is no overnight magic formula for preventing the Greyhound from chasing cats and other small moving objects, because this is its natural instinct. And out of doors this dog must be kept on a lead at all times.

Size
Dog 28-30in (71-76cm); bitch 27-28in (68.5-71cm). There is no standard desired weight.

Exercise
Three or four short walks every day will be sufficient. Although the Greyhound must never be exercised off-the-lead in a public place, it will enjoy the opportunity to run free in open country, away from sheep and other livestock. It is a highly sensitive creature and will learn to respond quickly to the tone of voice, which helps greatly in obedience training.

Speed enthusiasts may like to know that the Greyhound has clocked in at 37 mph (60 kph).

Grooming
Regular use of a hound glove will keep the coat shining.

Feeding
A retired Greyhound is like every other dog in that it responds best to a regular routine, especially where feeding and exercise are concerned. During their racing careers they are fed twice daily, in the early morning and in mid-afternoon, and exercised four times a day. There is no need to continue this routine once the Greyhound has settled in a new home, but it is kind to allow it to adapt gradually to its new lifestyle.

The canned food requirement for a Greyhound is between 20-33oz (587-936g) of a branded dog food per day, mixed with 10-16oz (284-454g) of biscuit meal and moistened with bone stock, for Greyhounds are used to sloppier food that most breeds. They should also be pampered with a thick slice of brown bread crumbled into ½pt (0.28l) of milk at breakfast time and a small drink of milk with two large-sized dog biscuits at bedtime.

Health care
A retired Greyhound may at first be restless in its new surroundings. It must be remembered that the home is a very different environment from a racing track, and it is unlikely that a retired racing Greyhound, when it leaves the track, will have seen home appliances such as television sets or mirrors. Care must also be exercised if Greyhounds have to be anaesthetized for any reason.

Origin and history
The Greyhound is a pure breed: that is, it has not evolved from crossings with other types. Indeed, it seems unlikely that this breed has altered materially since early Egyptian times, as proved by a carving of a Greyhound in an Egyptian tomb in the Nile Valley, circa 2900 BC.

The Greyhound has been known for centuries in England. Laws enacted at a Parliament held at Winchester in 1016 stipulated that 'No meane person may keepe any greihounds'.

The breed came to North America long before 1776. One of the most famous Greyhound owners was General George A. Custer, who might have enjoyed a longer life had he been able to run as swiftly as his dogs.

SHOW STANDARD
General appearance. The general appearance of the typical Greyhound is that of a strongly built, upstanding dog of generous proportions, muscular power and symmetrical formation with a long head and neck, clean well-laid shoulders, deep chest, capacious body, arched loins, powerful quarters, sound legs and feet and supple limbs.
Colour. Black, white, red, blue, fawn, fallow or brindle, or any of these colours broken with white.
Head and skull. Long, and of moderate width; flat skull, slight stop. Jaws powerful and well chiselled.
Tail. Long, set on rather low, strong at the root, tapering to tip, carried low and slightly curved.
Feet. Moderate in length with compact well-knuckled toes and strong pads.

The Greyhound has been used for coursing game for many centuries, probably since Roman times. More recently its development has proceeded along three distinct lines: the larger and rather narrow show dog; the smaller, agile coursing hound; and the lean and muscular track-racing dog.

Greyhound

Afghan Hound

The Afghan Hound must surely be the most glamorous dog in the world: the star of any show with its remarkably long, flowing coat and sweeping grace.

AIREDALE

Good points
- Attractive, sporty appearance
- Intelligent
- Faithful guard
- Loyal to owner
- Good with children
- Sound temperament

Take heed
- That hard, wiry coat ought to be hand stripped
- Can be over-protective

The Airedale is the king of the terriers and the largest of the terrier group. It is a splendid-looking animal with plenty of stamina and combines ideally the roles of family pet and guard.

Prior to World War I, the Airedale worked as a patrol dog with dock and railway police. It served during the war in the Russian Army and the British Army. It also worked for the Red Cross, locating the wounded and carrying messages. Indeed, at that time its abilities as a messenger and guard were considered superior to those of the German Shepherd Dog. The Airedale also took part in World War II but was gradually superseded by the German Shepherd Dog, the Dobermann, the Boxer and others.

Size
Height: dogs 24in (61cm) at the shoulder, bitches slightly less. Weight: approximately 55lb (25kg).

Exercise
One of the useful features about this dog is that although large it will adapt easily to living in a reasonably confined space, provided that it has at least two good 20-minute walks and an off-the-lead run every day. Alternatively, it will be in its element running with horses in the country and squelching, with wagging tail, through muddy fields.

Grooming
The Airedale needs frequent grooming with a stiff brush, and if you plan to enter the dog in the show ring, it is essential that its coat is regularly hand stripped. Ask the breeder to show you how this is done and don't be ashamed if you eventually resort to having the job done by a skilled canine beautician. If you do not plan to show, you need to have your Airedale stripped only in spring and summer for coolness and neatness, but allow it to keep its thick coat for winter protection.

Feeding
The Airedale needs at least 13-20oz (369-587g) cans of a branded, meaty dog food every day, plus a generous supply of biscuit meal. It will also appreciate the occasional large dog biscuit.

Watch the Airedale's weight. If it shows signs of becoming too heavy, reduce the supply of biscuit meal. Its girth will depend on how active a life the dog leads.

Incidentally, the old adage 'give a dog a bone' can be misleading. Almost all dogs will gnaw a bone with relish, but whereas one may show no after-effects, the fatty content may make another very sick. The owner must be guided by experience.

Origin and history
The Airedale is named after the valley of Aire in Yorkshire from which its ancestors came. It was originally called the Waterside, or working terrier. The forerunner of the present-day Airedale was kept for vermin control by Yorkshire gamekeepers, and it was probably crossed with the Otterhound.

In the late 1800s the Fox Terrier enjoyed immense popularity, and much thought and care went into the breeding and development of this bigger terrier as an attractive and, at the same time, useful dog. It was soon adopted as a companion, but — when given the chance — can still prove itself as an expert ratter and ducker. It can also be trained to the gun. I can recall a family Airedale coming to the rescue when we kept a rather fierce Muscovy Drake; the dog would round it up and carry the bird gently back to the pen in its mouth.

SHOW STANDARD
General appearance. Keen of expression, quick of movement, on the tip-toe of expectation at any moment. Character is denoted and shown by the expression of the eyes and by the carriage of the ears and tail.
Colour. The head and ears, with the exception of dark markings on each side of the skull, should be tan, the ears being of a darker shade than the rest. The legs up to the thighs and elbows also should be tan, the body dark grizzle.
Head and skull. The skull should be long and flat, not too broad between the ears, and narrowing slightly to the eyes. The skull should be free from wrinkles with stop hardly visible and cheeks level. Both the jaws should be deep, powerful, strong and muscular, as strength of foreface is an essential characteristic of the Airedale, but there must be no excess development of the jaws to give a rounded or bulging appearance to the cheeks, as 'cheekiness' is not desired. Lips should be tight, and the nose black.
Body. The shoulders are long. The chest is deep but not broad. The depth of the chest is approximately level with the elbows. The body is short, strong and level. The ribs are well sprung. The loins are muscular and of good width. There is little space between the last rib and the hip joint. The hindquarters are strong and muscular with no droop.
Tail. The tail should be set on high and carried gaily but not curled over the back. It should be of good strength and substance and of fair length.
Feet. These should be small, round and compact with a good depth of pad, well cushioned and the toes moderately arched, not turned either in or out.

DOBERMANN
(Dobermann Pinscher; Dobermann)

Good points
- Alert
- Brave
- Loyal
- Ideal guard
- Intelligent

Take heed
- Stands aloof from those outside the family circle
- Likely to be the victor in any battle

The Dobermann is a strong, alert guard that will enjoy the comforts of its master's fireside and protect him and his family with its life. It is unlikely to have to give its life, however, for the Dobermann generally gets the better of any opponent and is one of the best guard dogs in the world. It is an aloof animal that takes its responsibilities seriously, is skilled at tracking and makes a fine police dog.

Size
Ideal height at withers: dog 27in (68.5cm); bitch 25½in (65cm). Considerable deviation from this ideal to be discouraged.

Exercise
Certainly at least 40 minutes each day, which must include a ten-minute off-the-lead run.

Grooming
The Dobermann, with its short coat, needs little grooming other than a frequent rub down with Turkish towelling to remove loose hairs.

Feeding
Recommended would be 20-33oz (587-936g) cans of a branded, meaty product with biscuit added in equal part by volume, or 3-5 cupfuls of a dry food, complete diet, mixed in the proportion of 1 cup of feed to ½ cup of hot or cold water. Yeast tablets are beneficial at meal-times, especially during winter; also cod liver oil. These dogs fare well on raw meat, which keeps them in excellent condition, but the choice of whether to feed meat, cooked or raw, must be left to the prefernce of the individual dog and its owner. And owners who choose raw meat had better be able to add the proper vitamins and minerals in the proper amounts to their dogs' food.

Origin and history
Louis Dobermann of Apolda, in Thuringia, Germany, was a tax collector during the 1880s. Having a penchant for fierce dogs, he decided to breed the ideal animal to accompany him on his rounds. It was a relatively easy task for him, as he was keeper of the local dog pound, with access to numerous strays. He had in mind a medium-to large-sized dog, short-coated (thus easily maintained) with courage, alertness and stamina.

The existing German Pinscher was considered to be both aggressive and alert, so it was around this breed that Louis

Above: A delightful ten-week-old Dobermann lazing on a summer's afternoon.

Dobermann blended his stock, introducing the Rottweiler — a dog with great stamina and tracking ability — and, it is believed, the Manchester Terrier, which at that time was a much larger animal. No doubt it is from the Manchester that the Dobermann obtained its gleaming coat and black and tan markings. Possibly the Pointer was also used.

SHOW STANDARD
General appearance. The Dobermann is a dog of good medium size with a well-set body, muscular and elegant. It has a proud carriage and a bold, alert temperament. Its form is compact and tough and, owing to its build, capable of great speed. The gait is light and elastic. The eyes show intelligence and firmness of character, and the Dobermann is loyal and obedient. Shyness or viciousness must be heavily penalized by show judges.
Colour. Colours allowed are definite black, brown or blue with rust red markings. Markings must be sharply defined, appearing above each eye and on the muzzle, throat and forechest, on all legs and feet and below the tail. White markings undesirable.
Head and skull. Must be proportionate to the body, long, well filled under the eyes and clean cut. Its form, seen from above and from the side, must resemble a blunt wedge. The upper part of the head should be as fat as possible and free from wrinkle. The top of the skull should be flat with a slight stop, and the muzzle line should extend parallel to the top line of the skull. The cheeks must be flat and the lips tight. The nose should be solid black in black dogs, solid dark brown in brown dogs and solid dark grey in blue dogs.
Tail. Should be docked at the first or second joint, and should appear to be a continuation of the spine without material drop.
Feet. Forefeet should be well arched, compact and cat-like, turning neither in nor out. All dew-claws to be removed. Long, flat deviating paws and weak pasterns should be penalized. Hindfeet should be well arched, compact and cat-like, turning neither in nor out.

The frequency with which the Airedale has been judged best of
all breeds at major shows worldwide must be attributed to the perfection of
type attained in this breed. Yet, to be shown
to its full advantage, a potential champion
requires long hours of brushing, trimming
and shaping of its thick, wiry coat.

Airedale

Dobermann

Although in the past the Dobermann's
public image has been marred by its
rather sharp and fiery temperament, today
such traits have largely been bred out.
Owners are also encouraged to attend
organized training programmes
to train their dogs to obedience
work, which reduces the dog's
aggression and therefore further
improves its reputation.

BEARDED COLLIE

Good points
- *Devoted pet*
- *Good with children*
- *Intelligent*
- *Natural herder*
- *Playful*

Take heed
- *Needs plenty of exercise*

The Bearded Collie is not so well known as other collies in the United Kingdom, and was almost extinct after World War II. Now, however, numbers of this delightful breed are increasing. It is a lovable dog, ideally suited for family life but retaining its herding capabilities. It is easily trained, reliable with children and a lively playmate.

Size
Ideal height at the shoulder: dog 21-22in (53-56cm), bitch 20-21in (51-53cm).

Exercise
Not suitable for a confined existence. Needs plenty of exercise, including off-the-lead runs.

Grooming
Frequent brushing. Bathing and chalking are necessary for show.

Feeding
Thirteen-20oz (369-587g) of a branded, meaty product with biscuit added in equal part by volume, or 1¾-3 cupfuls of a dry food, complete diet, mixed in the proportion of 1 cup of feed to ½ cup of hot or cold water.

Origin and history
The lovable Beardie bears a keen resemblance to the Old English Sheepdog, or Bobtail, and is reckoned to be one of the oldest herding dogs in Scotland. It is said to be of Polish origin, being derived from purebred Polish Lowland Sheepdogs — two bitches and a dog were exchanged on a trading voyage to Scotland in 1514, for a ram and ewe. It has also been said to have Magyar (Hungarian) blood.

Luckily the survival of the breed was assured when Mrs G. Willison, of the former Bothkennar Kennels, acquired a Beardie bitch puppy (then without pedigree) in 1944, and, after a fruitless search for a Beardie dog, found one playing with its owners on the beach at Hove, Sussex. They were willing to sell, and from this pair, 'Jeannie' and 'Bailie', all today's Beardies are descended.

SHOW STANDARD
General appearance. An active dog with a long, lean body and none of the stumpiness of the Bobtail. Though strongly made, it shows plenty of daylight under the body and does not look too heavy. The face should have an enquiring expression. Movement should be free and active.
Colour. Slate grey or reddish fawn, black, all shades of grey, brown and sandy with or without white collie markings.
Head and skull. Broad, flat skull with ears set high; fairly long foreface with moderate stop. Nose should be black except with brown or fawn coats, when brown is permitted.
Tail. Set low, should be moderately long with abundant hair or brush; carried low when the dog is quiet with an upward swirl at the tip; carried gaily when the dog is excited, but not over the back.
Feet. Oval in shape, soles well padded, toes arched and close together; well covered with hair, including between the pads.

A dog that bears a fairly strong resemblance to the Beardie is the Dutch Schapendoes, which has Beardie blood in its veins, as well probably as that of the Bergamasco, Puli and Briard. It is a popular sheepdog, guard and house-dog in the Netherlands but is little known in other countries.

Below: A Dutch Schapendoes, a relative of the Bearded Collie.

SMOOTH COLLIE
(Smooth-haired Collie)

Good points
- *Affectionate*
- *Easily trained*
- *Excellent pet*
- *Loves children*
- *Loyal*
- *Intelligent*

Take heed
- *Not too keen on strangers*

The Smooth Collie is like the Rough Collie in temperament. It makes an ideal family pet and is hardy and simple to groom. It is identical to the Rough-haired except in coat (see Show Standard).

Size
Height at shoulder: dog 22-24in (56-61cm); bitch 20-22in (51-56cm). Weight: dog 45-65lb (20.5-29.5kg); bitch 40-55lb (18.1-25kg).

Exercise
Normal daily exercise with off-the-lead runs when possible. The breed has plenty of energy.

Grooming
Frequent brushing will keep the coat in good condition.

Feeding
Recommended would be 20-33oz (587-936g) of a branded, meaty product with biscuit added, or 3-5 cupfuls of a dry food, complete diet, mixed in the proportion of 1 cup of feed to ½ cup of hot or cold water.

Origin and history
Every Smooth Collie and Rough Collie can trace its origin to a tricolour dog called 'Trefoil', born in 1873; and until 1974 the Smooth-haired did not have a separate standard in the United Kingdom, except for the coat. However, while the Rough-haired has maintained international popularity, the Smooth-haired is seldom seen and might have become extinct were it not for the determined efforts of dedicated breeders.

SHOW STANDARD
General appearance. The Smooth Collie should appeal instantly as gifted with intelligence, alertness and activity. It should stand with dignity, and its movements, governed by perfect anatomical formation with no part out of proportion, should be smooth and graceful. It should give the appearance of a dog capable of working.
Colour. The three recognized colours are: sable and white, tri-colour and blue merle.
Head and skull. The head properties are of great importance and must be considered in proportion to the size of the dog. When viewed from both front and profile, the head should bear a general resemblance to a well-blunted, clean wedge, being smooth in outline. Whatever the colour of the dog, the nose must be black.
Tail. Should be long with the bone reaching at least to the hock joint. To be carried low when the dog is quiet but with a slight upward swirl at the tip. It may be carried gaily when the dog is excited but never over the back.
Feet. Should be oval with soles well padded. Toes arched and close together. Hindfeet slightly less arched.

ROUGH COLLIE
(Rough-haired Collie)

Good points
- *Affectionate*
- *Easily trained*
- *Excellent pet*
- *Loves children*
- *Loyal*

Take heed
- *Not keen on strangers*

No breed causes so much consternation to buyers and those giving breed information as the collie. People tend to have a fixed idea of the type of collie they want, be it Rough, Smooth, Border, Old English or Bearded; and, having written to enquire about a collie, they expect the recipient of their letter to be on the same wavelength. If it's a dog like the film star 'Lassie' that you want, you are thinking of a Rough Collie, sometimes erroneously called a Scottish Collie; the Sheltie, or Shetland, is a 'Lassie' in miniature.

The Rough Collie makes an ideal family pet, being biddable, affectionate and loyal. It is hardy and, despite its thick coat, relatively simple to groom.

Size
Height at shoulder: dog 22-24in (56-61cm); bitch 20-22in (51-56cm). Weight: dog 45-65lb (20.5-29.5kg); bitch 40-55lb (18.1-25kg).

Exercise
Normal daily exercise with off-the-lead runs when possible.

Grooming
Frequent brushing. Don't be afraid to vacuum clean with the smallest brush, if it gets muddy. But get the dog accustomed to the noise of the machine first.

Feeding
As for Smooth Collie.

Origin and history
The Rough Collie is generally spoken of as a Scottish breed. In fact, its ancestors were introduced into England and Scotland from Iceland 400 years ago. But it was as guardians of the flock that they acquired their name in Scotland, where sheep with black faces and legs were known as colleys. Queen Victoria kept a Rough Collie at Balmoral in 1860, and in the same year a breed member was exhibited in a Birmingham show.

SHOW STANDARD
General appearance. The Rough Collie should instantly appeal as a dog of great beauty, standing with impassive dignity with no part out of porportion to the whole.
Colour. Sable and white, tricolour and blue merle. (1) Sable — any shade from light gold to rich mahogany or shaded sable. (2) Tricolour — predominantly black with rich tan markings about the legs and head. (3) Blue merle — predominantly clear, silvery blue, splashed and marbled with black.
Head and skull. The head properties are of great importance and must be considered in proportion to the size of the dog. When viewed from the front or the side, the head bears a general resemblance to a well-blunted, clean wedge, being smooth in outline. Whatever the colour of the dog, the nose definitely must be black.
Body. Firm, hard and muscular. The shoulders are well sloped, and behind them the ribs are well rounded. The chest is deep, extending to the elbows.
Tail. Should be long with the bone reaching at least to the hock joint. To be carried low when the dog is quiet but with a slight upward swirl at the tip. It may be carried gaily when the dog is excited but not over the back.
Feet. Should be oval in shape with soles well padded, toes arched and close together. The hindfeet slightly less arched.

Although intended as a sheep herder, the Bearded Collie is not as popular with the shepherd as some of the other collies. Temperamentally it appears to be more suited to simple cattle driving than heavy, persuasive sheep steering.

Bearded Collie

Smooth Collie

Both Rough and Smooth collies make good house-pets, but they are probably at their happiest when given the freedom of the fields and open country.

Rough Collie

GERMAN LONG-HAIRED POINTER
(Langhaar)

Good points
- Easily trained
- Equable temperament
- Excellent gundog
- Good with children
- Makes a good household pet
- Obedient

Take heed
- Needs plenty of exercise

The German Long-haired Pointer (or Langhaar) is, alas, almost extinct. It is a healthy dog with a good temperament, much endurance and the swimming and hunting ability of all pointers. It is energetic and immensely loyal to its master.

Size
Height 24-25in (61-63.5cm) at the shoulder

Exercise
Should be allowed plenty of exercise.

Grooming
Brush the coat regularly to keep it in good condition.

Feeding
Recommended would be 20-33oz (587-936g) of a branded, meaty product with biscuit added, or 3-5 cupfuls of a dry food, complete diet, mixed in the proportion of 1 cup of feed to ½ cup of hot or cold water.

Origin and history
This type varies in appearance from other pointers in that it resembles the setter in appearance. This is not surprising, because the Long-haired Pointer evolved as the result of crossing Dutch and French spaniels and local German breeds with the Gordon Setter, which at the time was greatly favoured by German huntsmen. It is an attractive dog, of great endurance, but its numbers are sadly dwindling in favour of the Wire-haired Pointer.

SHOW STANDARD (FCI)
General appearance. A dog of robust, muscular build but with a distinguished general appearance. The expression is one of intelligence and nobility, the character lively without any nervousness.
Colour. Usually self-coloured, light brown or dead leaf. The presence of red and black is penalized.
Head and skull. Long, lean, quite broad, divided into equal length for skull and muzzle; the upper part of the head is slightly rounded. It is the head which gives import and distinction to the general appearance. The nose is flat, more or less deep brown in colour.
Tail. Well set on, carried horizontally, sometimes slightly curved upward, the tail may be slightly docked if it is too long or if it is out of proportion with the rest of

the body; the long hair at the midpoint of the tail should be a good fringe.
Feet. Well closed, of moderate length, moderately round.

GERMAN WIRE-HAIRED POINTER
(Drahthaar)

Good points
- Easily trained
- Equable temperament
- Excellent gundog
- Good with children
- Makes a good household pet
- Obedient

Take heed
- Needs plenty of exercise
- Slightly more aggressive than other pointer types

In its native country the German Wire-haired Pointer is known as the Drahthaar (literally translated, this means 'wire haired'). It is perhaps more spirited and aggressive than its fellow pointers with stronger guarding instincts and a hardy physique. It is an excellent gundog.

Size
Dog 24-26in (61-66cm), bitch smaller, not less than 22in (56cm).

Exercise
Needs plenty of exercise to discharge its abundant energy.

Grooming
Brush the coat regularly and inspect the footpads and ears.

Feeding
Follow the instructions for the German Long-haired Pointer.

Origin and history
The German Wire-haired Pointer is identical to the Short-haired except in coat. There are , however, some differences in background, and although the English Pointer undoubtedly contributed to its development, the Wire-haired was also derived from other hunting breeds. It is mentioned in German medieval documents.

SHOW STANDARD
General appearance. A medium-sized hunting dog of noble bearing; very harsh hair completely covers the skin; intelligent expression; devoted and energetic.
Colour. Solid liver, liver and white spotted, liver and white spotted and ticked, liver and white ticked, black and white. Colour unimportant.
Head and skull. The head should be of medium length with a long, strong muzzle.
Tail. Starts high and thick, growing gradually thinner. Docked by half its length. When the dog is quiet, tail should be carried down; when the tail is moving horizontally it is never held high over the back or bent.
Feet. Compact, close-knit, round to spoon-shaped, well padded; should turn neither in nor out. Toes well arched, heavily nailed.

GERMAN SHORT-HAIRED POINTER

Good points
- Easily trained
- Equable temperament
- Excellent gundog
- Good with children
- Makes a good household pet
- Obedient

Take heed
- Needs plenty of exercise

The German Short-haired Pointer is a good all-round sporting dog. It is affectionate and good with children. It is, however, happiest when in the wide open spaces and is excellent at working wildfowl and most types of game. It is a first-rate swimmer.

Size
Dog 23-25in (58.5-63.5cm); bitch 21-23in (53-58.5cm).

Exercise
Needs plenty of exercise.

Grooming
Brush the coat regularly.

Feeding
As German Long-haired Pointer.

Origin and history
The German Short-haired Pointer is of Spanish origin. It was bred from dogs imported into Germany and crossed with local hounds and, probably, with the English Foxhound for speed, the Bloodhound for nose and the English Pointer for its excellent pointing ability.

It was admitted to the American Kennel Club's stud book in 1930; the first show for pointers was held 11 years later.

SHOW STANDARD
General appearance. A noble, steady dog showing power, endurance and speed, giving the immediate impression of an alert and energetic (not nervous) dog whose movements are well co-ordinated. Neither unduly small nor conspicuously large nor of medium size and, like the hunter, 'With a short back, but standing over plenty of ground'.
Colour. Solid liver, liver and white spotted, liver and white spotted and ticked, liver and white ticked, black and white.
Head and skull. Clean-cut, neither too light nor too heavy but well proportioned to the body. The skull sufficiently broad and slightly rounded. Nose solid brown, wide nostrils well opened and soft.
Tail. Starts high and thick, growing gradually thinner. Docked to medium length by two-fifths to half its length. When the dog is quiet, tail should be carried down; and when moving horizontally, never held high over the back or bent.
Feet. Compact, close-knit, round to spoon-shaped, well padded; should turn neither in nor out. Toes well arched, heavily nailed.

POINTER

Good points
- Equable temperament
- Obedient
- Good with children
- Easily trained
- Excellent gundog
- Makes a good household pet

Take heed
- Needs plenty of exercise

The Pointer is famed for its classic pose, 'pointing' with its nose and tail in the direction of the game that has been shot. It is a friendly dog and makes an ideal household pet, getting on well with other animals, and children. But it does need a generous amount of exercise.

Size
Desirable hight: dog 25-27in (63.5-68.5cm); bitch 24-26in (61-66cm).

Exercise
Needs plenty of exercise. The more it runs outside the house, the more it will lie about quietly indoors.

Grooming
Brush the coat regularly.

Feeding
As German Long-haired Pointer.

Origin and history
There is some controversy about whether the Pointer originated in Spain or was produced in England through crossings of Bloodhounds, Foxhounds and Greyhounds. A great authority on the breed, William Arkwright of Sutton Scarsdale, England, spent his life travelling the world to check on the history and development of the breed. He believed that it originated in the East, found its way to Italy, then to Spain (where it developed its classic head) and thence to England and South America. Arkwright on Pointers is still the bible of the breed.

SHOW STANDARD
Head and skull. The skull should be of medium breadth and in proportion to the length of the foreface; the stop well defined; pronounced occipital bone. Nose and eye rims dark but may be lighter in the case of a lemon and white dog. The nostrils wide, soft and moist. The muzzle somewhat concave, ending on a level with the nostrils, giving a slightly dish-faced appearance. The cheekbones should not be prominent. Well-developed, soft lip.
Colour. The usual colours are lemon and white, orange and white, liver and white, and black and white. Self-colours and tri-colours are also correct.
Tail. Of medium length, thick at the root, growing gradually thinner to the point. It should be well covered with close hair and carried level with the back with no upward curl. When the dog is moving, the tail should lash from side to side.
Feet. Oval, with well-knit, arched toes, well cushioned underneath.

Used originally for hawking and falconry, the German Long-haired Pointer is a powerful animal and a versatile gundog. Particularly useful for work with gamebirds, it is also very good in close coverts.

German Long-haired Pointer

German Wire-haired Pointer

German Short-haired Pointer

Pointer

Handsome rather than glamorous: with its deep chest, straight bones and beautifully proportioned body the Pointer is the epitome of the working gundog.

IRISH SETTER
(Red Setter)

Good points
- Affectionate
- Beautiful
- Excellent with children
- Hunting ability

Take heed
- Lively
- No good as a guard; it loves everybody

The Irish Setter is a first-class gundog that combines this work admirably with the role of family pet. It is happiest as a house-dog and has great need of affection, which it returns a hundredfold. It is intelligent and utterly reliable with children. It is, however, high spirited and lively and should not be confined in close quarters or kept by those who cannot provide adequate exercise. It often strikes up a good relationship with horses.

Size
The Americans look for a tall dog, 25-27in (63.5-68.5cm) high, but in the United Kingdom no height is specified.

Exercise
An exuberant dog that needs lots of exercise, either working or running in the wide open spaces.

Grooming
Regular brushing, claw clipping and inspection of ears.

Feeding
Recommended would be 20-33oz (587-936g) of a branded meaty product with biscuit added, or 3-5 cupfuls of a dry food, complete diet, mixed in the proportion of 1 cup of feed to ½ cup of hot or cold water.

Origin and history
The Irish Setter has evolved from the crossing of Irish Water Spaniels, Springer Spaniels, the Spanish Pointer and English and Gordon setters. Its name was settled by the Ulster Irish Setter Club in 1876. Synonymous with the breed is the name of Edward Laverack, who, prior to his death in 1877, spent a lifetime improving the breed.

SHOW STANDARD
General appearance. Must be racy, full of quality and kindly in expression.
Colour. Rich chestnut with no trace whatever of black; white on chest, throat, chin or toes, or a small star on the forehead, or a narrow streak or blaze on the nose or face not to disqualify.
Head and skull. The head should be long and lean, not narrow or snipy, and not coarse at the ears. The skull oval (from ear to ear), having plenty of brain room and with well-defined occipital protuberance. Brows raised, showing stop. Muzzle moderately deep, and fairly square at the end. From the stop to the point of the nose should be long, the nostrils wide and the jaws of nearly equal length; flews not pendulous. The colour of the nose should be dark mahogany, dark walnut or black.
Tail. Of moderate length, proportionate to the size of the body; set on rather low, strong at the root and tapering to a fine point; to be carried as nearly as possible on a level with or below the back.
Feet. Should be small and very firm; toes strong, close together and arched.

ENGLISH SETTER

Good points
- Adaptable
- Beautiful
- Can live in house or kennel
- Reliable gundog

Take heed
- Not a loner, thrives in company of humans or of other dogs

The English Setter is the most distinctive of the three varieties: Irish, Gordon and English. It has a gentle nature that makes it the ideal companion for children, at the same time being an excellent gundog. As it needs lots of exercise, it is not a suitable companion for a flat dweller. It also requires a fair amount of grooming.

Size
Height: dog 25½-27in (65-68.5cm); bitch 24-25in (61-63.5cm). Weight: dog 60-66lb (27.2-30kg); bitch 56-62lb (25.4-28kg).

Exercise
Needs at least ten minutes of exercise a day as a three-month-old pup and a hour in adulthood to keep it in top condition. Trains well to the gun.

Grooming
You will need trimming scissors and a fine steel comb for frequent grooming, also a good stiff brush for the coat. Take care that the feathering on the legs does not become tangled. The silky hair under the ears should be removed and also the hair under the throat and below the ear down to the breast bone. Care must also be taken to remove hair that forms between the dog's pads. Any straggly hairs have to be plucked from the body before the dog goes into the show ring. The English Setter is always bathed before a show and the coat is combed flat when it is dry. American competitors are trimmed more heavily than those exhibited in the United Kingdom.

Feeding
Same as for Irish Setter.

Origin and history
It is generally agreed that the English Setter evolved from spaniels. Credit for the breed is given to Edward Laverack (1815-1877), who in his work The Setter wrote: 'this breed is but a Spaniel improved'. The Setting Spaniel, accepted by many modern authorities as the forerunner of the English Setter, was used as far back as the sixteenth century for setting partridges and quails. Through interbreeding, Laverack affected the strain so that it acquired not only the standard of excellence in the nineteenth century but that on which the present-day English Setter was built. To quote Sylvia Bruce Wilmore, writing in Dog News magazine: 'About the time the Laverack strain of English Setter was at its zenith, Mr R.L. Purcell Llewellin purchased a number of Mr Laverack's best show dogs of the pure Dash-Moll and Dash-Hill Laverack blood. He crossed these with entirely new blood which he obtained in the north of England represented by Mr Slatter's and Sir Vincent Corbet's strain, since referred to as the Duke-Kate-Rhoebe. The Llewellin strain of English Setter became immensely popular at the turn of the century, their reputation spreading to the United States and Canada where they dominated field trials for a quarter of a century, thus firmly establishing the line of breed in America.'

SHOW STANDARD
General appearance. Of medium height, clean in outline, elegant in appearance and movement.
Colour. The colour may be black and white, lemon and white, liver and white or tricolour (that is, black, white and tan); those without heavy patches of colour on the body, but flecked all over, are preferred.
Head and skull. Head should be long and reasonably lean with a well-defined stop. The colour of the nose should be black or liver, according to the colour of the coat.
Tail. The tail should be set on almost in line with the back; medium length not curly or ropy, to be slightly curved or scimitar-shaped but with no tendency to turn upwards; the flag or feather hanging in long pendent flakes.
Feet. The feet should be very close and compact, and well protected by hair between the toes.

GORDON SETTER

Good points
- Affectionate
- Equable temperament
- Excellent gundog
- Good with children

Take heed
- Not suitable for a guard dog

The Gordon Setter is a fine gundog, a bird-finding dog, used to silent trekking. It does not fit the role of guard, although it will not accept strangers as readily as the Irish Setter, which could well lick the face of a burglar while presenting him with some item 'retrieved' from its mistress's wardrobe.

The Gordon makes an excellent family pet and is trustworthy with children. It does enjoy an active working life, however, and is not really suitable for apartments.

Size
Weight about 65lb (29.5kg); bitch, 24½in (62cm), about 56lb (25.4kg). Shoulder height for dog, 26in (66cm).

Exercise
Ensure that it has plenty of exercise; this is a dog for outdoors.

Grooming
Regular brushing and monthly nail clipping.

Feeding
Recommended would be 20-33oz (587-936g) of a branded, meaty product with biscuit added, or 3-5 cupfuls of a dry food, complete diet, mixed in the proportion of 1 cup of feed to ½ cup of hot or cold water.

Origin and history
The Gordon is a true Scot, bred at Gordon Castle, Banffshire, the seat of the Duke of Richmond and Gordon. It is the only native Scottish gundog and was originally known as the Gordon Castle Setter. Credit must go to the 4th Duke of Richmond and Gordon for establishing the breed in the late 1770s, using probably the collie and the Bloodhound.

Daniel Webster, United States' statesman and orator, imported Gordon Setters in 1842. Webster was attracted to the breed by its beauty and superior hunting ability. Additional imports from Scandinavian countries were used to develop an American strain of Gordons.

SHOW STANDARD
General appearance. A stylish dog, built on galloping lines, having a thoroughbred appearance consistent with its build, which can be compared to a weight-carrying hunter. Must have symmetrical conformation throughout, showing true balance. Strong, fairly short and level back. Shortish tail. Head fairly long, clearly lined and with an intelligent expression; clear colours and long flat coat.
Colour. Deep shining coal black with no sign of rustiness, lustrous tan markings of a rich chestnut red, i.e. the colour of a ripe horse-chestnut as taken from the shell. Black pencilling allowed on toes, also a black streak under the jaw. Tan markings: two clear spots over the eyes, not over ⁴/₅in (2cm) in diameter; on the sides of the muzzle, the tan should not reach above the base of the nose.
Head and skull. Head deep rather than broad but definitely broader than the muzzle, showing brain room. Nose big and broad with open nostrils and black in colour.
Tail. Fairly short, straight or slightly scimitar-shaped; should not reach below the hocks. Carried horizontal or below line of back. Thick at the root, tapering to a fine point. The feather or flat, which starts near the root, should be long and straight, and grow shorter uniformly to the point.
Feet. Oval with close-knit, well-arched toes, plenty of hair between. Full toe pads and deep heel cushions.

Setters are elegant and efficient gundogs. The name arises from the traditional practice of training such dogs to sit when they have located game by scent and sight, hence the term 'sitting' or 'setting' dogs.

Irish Setter

English Setter

Gordon Setter

GERMAN SHEPHERD DOG
(Alsatian)

Good points
- Devoted to owner
- Excellent worker/herder
- Favoured for obedience competitions
- Loyal
- Supremely intelligent
- Protective

Take heed
- Tendency to over-guard
- Not a lap dog, but a worker that needs a task in life

The German Shepherd Dog has one of the largest followings in the world. It is also the breed that rouses the strongest emotions in the public. They either worship the German Shepherd or abhor it. If a smaller breed takes a nip out of the postman's trousers, the misdeed may go unreported; but if a German Shepherd is involved, the headlines are likely to be: 'German Shepherd Dog savages postman'.

The German Shepherd is one of the most courageous and intelligent of dogs, debatably the most intelligent. Breed members have fought bravely, and many lost their lives in two world wars. They have been, and still are, used, as guide dogs for the blind (US 'seeing eye dogs'), police dogs and military dogs. Certainly they are a very popular guard. It is this strong guarding instinct that can be their undoing, however, for a German Shepherd protecting a toddler may menace a stranger at the garden gate. It could also turn nasty through sheer boredom if acquired as a mere pet dog. The German Shepherd deserves a job to do, whether it be in the public service or competing eagerly in obedience and working trials.

Size
The ideal height (measured to the highest point of the shoulder) is 22-24in (56-61cm) for bitches and 24-26in (61-66cm) for dogs. The

Below: A German Shepherd puppy with soft under-coat. When the puppy matures, its outer coat will be dense and harsh.

proportion of length to height varies between 10:9 and 10:8.5.

Exercise
Needs plenty of exercise, off-the-lead runs and, if possible, obedience exercises. It will excel at the local dog training club in 'scent' and 'retrieve'. Remember that this breed is used to sniff out illegal drug shipments and to detect the elusive 'black box' amid the wreckage strewn over many miles after plane crashes.

Grooming
Brush frequently.

Feeding
Give 20-33oz (587-936g) of a branded, meaty product with biscuit added, or 3-5 cupfuls of a dry food, complete diet, mixed in the proportion of 1 cup of feed to ½ cup of hot or cold water.

Health care
This is a healthy, hardy breed. However, its popularity over the years has encouraged indiscriminate breeding, resulting in loss of temperament and form. Take care when purchasing a German Shepherd Dog to acquire only from registered HD-free stock. HD is an abbreviation for hip dysplasia, a malformation of the hip joint that can result in the dog's being crippled before middle age. Reliable vendors do not breed from affected stock. Many people feel this defect came about through over-emphasis on that desired show dog crouch.

Origin and history
The German Shepherd Dog is sometimes associated, rightly or wrongly, with the Bronze Age wolf, perhaps an unfortunate suggestion in that it wrongly associates the breed with wolf-like tendencies. Certainly around the seventh century a sheepdog of this type, but with a lighter coat, existed in Germany; and by the sixteenth century the coat had appreciably darkened.

The breed was first exhibited at a dog show in Hanover in 1882. Credit for the formation of the breed is widely assigned to a German fancier named von Stephanitz, who did much to improve its temperament and appearance.

The German Shepherd Dog was introduced into the United Kingdom following World War I by a small band of dedicated fanciers who had seen the breed working in Germany. These included the late Colonel Baldwin and Air Commodore Alan Cecil-Wright, president of the Kennel Club. It was thought inappropriate at that time to glorify an animal bearing a German prefix, so, as the breed had come from Alsace, it became known in the United Kingdom as the Alsatian. Only in 1971 did the Kennel Club relent and agree to the breed being known once more as the German Shepherd Dog.

SHOW STANDARD
General appearance. In general, the German Shepherd is a well-

Above: The German Shepherd Dog's balance and agility enable it to get over this barrier easily at a working trial.

proportioned dog showing great suppleness of limb, neither massive nor heavy, but at the same time free from any suggestion of weediness. It must not suggest the Greyhound type. The body is rather long, strongly boned with plenty of muscle, obviously capable of endurance and speed and of quick and sudden movement. The gait should be supple, smooth and long-reaching, carrying the body along with the minimum of up-and-down movement.

Colour. The colour of the German Shepherd is in itself not important; it has no effect on the character of the dog or on its fitness for work and should be a secondary consideration for that reason. All-white or near white dogs, unless possessing black points, are not desirable, however. The final colour of a young dog can be ascertained only when the outer coat has developed.

Head and skull. The head is proportionate to the size of the body, long, lean and clean cut, broad at the back of the skull but without coarseness, tapering to the nose with only a slight stop between the eyes. The skull is slightly domed, and the top of the nose should be parallel to the forehead. The cheeks must not be full or in any way prominent, and the whole head, when viewed from the top, should be much in the form of a V, well filled in under the eyes. There should be plenty of substance in the foreface with a good depth from top to bottom. The muzzle is strong and long and, while tapering to the nose, it must not be carried to such an extreme as to give the appearance of being overshot. It must not show any weakness or be snipy or lippy. The lips should be tight fitting and clean. The nose must be black.

Tail. When at the rest the tail should hang in a slight curve and reach at least as far as the hock. During movement and excitement it will be raised, but under no circumstances should the tail be carried past a vertical line drawn through the root.

Feet. The feet should be round, the toes strong, slightly arched and held close together. The pads should be firm, the nails short and strong. Dew-claws are neither a fault nor a virtue but should be removed from the hindlegs at four to five days old, as dew-claws are liable to spoil the gait.

BELGIAN SHEPHERD DOG
(Groenendael [Belgian Sheepdog] Laekenois, Malinois [Belgian Malinois], Tervueren [Belgian Tervuren]).

Good points
- Alert and agile
- Excellent guard
- Handy, medium size
- Intelligent
- Physically robust

Take heed
- Best suited to the open spaces, does not take kindly to apartment living
- Needs firm but kind handling

There are four types of Belgian Shepherd Dog — the Groenendael, the Laekenois, the Malinois and the Tervueren — all of which are similar to the German Shepherd.

Basically, they are hunting and herding dogs, but they have also served as Red Cross messengers in wartime, are vigilant guards and kindly protectors of children.

Size
The desired height for the dog is 24-26in (61-66cm) and for the bitch 22-24in (56-61cm). This applies to all four types.

Exercise
The Belgian Shepherd Dog is a working dog that excels in defending master and property. It is oblivious to bad weather and enjoys being out of doors, so adequate exercise is vital.

The breed has done well in working trials and in various obedience competitions; a Belgian Shepherd Dog, in the hands of an experienced trainer, will soon learn all that is required of it. Conversely, rough handling will benefit neither owner nor dog, but may turn a forthcoming, eager pup into a nervous animal.

Grooming
Little grooming is needed other than a good surface brushing. Bathing is not recommended, even for exhibition, unless the dog has got its coat into a filthy condition. As it has a double coat, combing out the under-coat will result in a dog with only half a coat.

Feeding
The Belgian Shepherd Dog should be fed similarly to other dogs of its size. Basic daily rations might be 20-26oz (587-737g) of branded dog food with an equal volume of biscuits, or 3-4 cupfuls of a dry food, complete diet, mixed in the proportion of 1 cup of feed to ½ cup of hot or cold water.

Origin and history
At the end of the nineteenth century there were shepherd dog varieties of all colours and sizes in Belgium, but in about 1890, Monsieur Rose of the Café du Groenendael discovered a black, long-coated bitch among one of his litters.

Later, he bought a similar dog

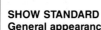

The characteristic expression of the German Shepherd Dog gives the impression of perpetual vigilance, fidelity, liveliness and watchfulness, alert to every sight and sound with nothing escaping attention. The German Shepherd Dog possesses highly developed senses, mentally and temperamentally.

German Shepherd Dog

Belgian Shepherd Dog (Groenendael)

The black-coated Belgian Shepherd Dog has received high praise for its working abilities.

from a Monsieur Bernaert and, by selective breeding and strict culling, eventually produced the Groenendael.

The origin of the modern Belgian Shepherd Dog dates from 1891, when a collection of shepherd dogs of all colours and sizes was gathered at the Brussels Veterinary University. It was decided to recognize three varieties: the rough-coated black; the smooth-coated fawn with black mask; and the wire-haired darkish grey. Since then there have been various additions to and subtractions from these types, but they have now been settled into four varieties: the Groenendael (long-coated black); the Tervueren (long-coated other than black); the Malinois (smooth-coated); and the Laekenois, or de Laeken (wire-coated).

It should be mentioned that in America only the Groenendael is known as the Belgian Shepherd Dog or Belgian Sheepdog; the Malinois and the Tervueren are registered as separate breeds, and the Laekenois — the rarest of the four — is not recognized. Incidentally, the breeds are known in America as the Belgian Malinois and the Belgian Tervuren, the latter with a slightly different spelling.

SHOW STANDARD
Belgian Shepherd Dog (Groenendael); Belgian Sheepdog.
General appearance. A medium-sized dog, well proportioned, intelligent, hardy and bred to withstand adverse weather. It should be alert and attentive with a lively and enquiring mien.
Colour. Black or black with limited white as follows: small to moderate patch or strip on chest, between the pads of the feet and on the tips of the hind toes. Frosting (white or grey) on the muzzle.
Head and skull. The head should be finely chiselled, long (but not excessively so) and gaunt. The skull and muzzle should be roughly equal in length with at most a slight bias in favour of the muzzle, giving the impression of a balanced whole. The skull should be of a medium width in proportion to the length of the head with a flattened rather than rounded forehead and the centre line not very pronounced; seen in profile it should be parallel to an imaginary line extending the muzzle line. The muzzle should be of medium length, tapering gradually towards the nose. The nose should be black with well-flared nostrils. Moderate stop.
Coat. The outer coat should be long, straight and abundant. It should not be silky or wiry; the texture should be of medium harshness. The under-coat should be extremely dense. The hair should be shorter on the head, the outside of the ears and the lower part of the legs. The opening of the ear should be protected by hair. The hair should be especially long and abundant around the neck, like a ruff, particularly in the male. There should be a fringe of long hair down the back of the forearm and long and abundant hair evident on the hindquarters and the tail. The

male should be longer coated than the female.
Tail. The tail should be firmly set, strong at the base and of medium length. At rest the dog should carry it hanging down with the tip slightly bent backwards at the level of the hock; on the move the dog should lift it, accentuating the curve towards the tip; however, it should under no circumstances curl up or bend to one side.
Feet. No specific requirements are laid down in the standard.

The four varieties of Belgian Shepherd Dog vary only in coat and colour. These are the standards for the other three varieties:

Laekenois
Coat. The coat should be rough, dry, untidy-looking and not curly. Any sprinkling of fluffy, fine hair in locks in the rough coat is inadmissible. The length of the coat should be about 2.4in (6cm) on all parts of the body. The hair around the eyes and that on the muzzle should be fairly long. It is essential, however, that the hair around the muzzle should not be so long as to make the head appear square or heavy. The tail should not be plumed.
Colour. Reddish fawn with black shading, principally on the muzzle and tail.

Malinois
Coat. The hair should be very short on the head, the exterior of the ears and the lower parts of the legs, short on the rest of the body, and thicker on the tail and around the neck, where it should resemble a ridge or collar, beginning at the base of the ear and extending to the throat. In addition the hindquarters should be fringed with longer hair. The tail should be thick and bushy. The coat should be thick, close and of a good firm texture with a wool under-coat.
Colour. Dark fawn with considerable black overlay; washed-out fawn or grey is highly undesirable, as is patchy black overlay or the total absence of black overlay. Black shading on muzzle and ears is desirable.

Tervueren
Coat. The outer coat should be long, straight and abundant. It should not be silky or wiry; the texture should be of medium harshness. The under-coat should be extremely dense. The hair should be shorter on the head, the outside of the ears and the lower part of the legs. The opening of the ear should be protected by hair. The hair should be especially long and abundant around the neck, like a ruff, particularly in the male. There should be a fringe of long hair down the back of the forearm, and long and abundant hair evident on the hindquarters and the tail. The male should be longer coated than the female.
Colour. All shades of red, fawn and grey with black overlay. The coat should be characteristically double-pigmented, wherein the tip of each light-coloured hair is blackened. On

mature males this blackening should be especially pronounced on the shoulders, back and rib section. The face should have a black mask, not extending above the line of the eyes, and the ears should be mostly black. The tail should typically have a darker or black tip. A small to moderate white patch or strip is permitted on the chest, between the pads of the feet and on the tips of the hind toes. Frosting (white or grey) on the muzzle. Beyond the age of 18 months, a washed-out colour or a colour too black should be considered a fault.

HOLLANDSE HERDER
(Dutch Shepherd Dog)

Good points
● *Excellent guard*
● *Hardy*
● *Intelligent*
● *Sound temperament*

Take heed
● *No drawbacks known*

The Hollandse herder was bred in the Netherlands as a sheepdog but nowadays is kept mainly as a companion and guard. It is relatively unknown outside its native country, where it is used as a police dog, as a guide dog for the blind (seeing eye dog) and occasionally for farmyard duties. It comes in three coat types: short-haired, long-haired and wire-haired. The long-haired variety is almost extinct, and the wire-haired is not greatly favoured; the short-haired type is the one most widely known.

Size
Height at the withers: dog 23-25in (58.5-63.5cm); bitch 21½-24½in (54.5-62cm). In the case of the long-haired only, the minimum is lowered to 21½in (54.5cm) for dogs, 21in (53cm) for bitches.

Exercise
Needs plenty of exercise to keep in good health, basically because of its origins as a working dog. As a consequence it is not well suited to a confined city existence.

Grooming
Regular brushing will keep the coat in good condition. The short-haired variety does not require as much attention as do the wire-haired or the long-haired dogs. The latter two must be brushed two or three times a week if their coats are to remain handsome.

Feeding
Recommended would be 20-33oz (587-936g) of a branded, meaty product with biscuit added, or 3-5 cupfuls of a dry food, complete diet, mixed in the proportion of 1 cup of feed to ½ cup of hot or cold water.

Origin and history
The Hollandse Herder is closely related to the Belgian Shepherd Dog, and they are of similar origin. It has, however, developed as a

separate breed in its native Netherlands, where it has always been extremely popular.

SHOW STANDARD
General appearance. A solid, sturdy dog, not too heavy; muscular, strong, symmetrical, always attentive and always in movement. The Dutch Shepherd has an intelligent expression and shows great aptitude for working with sheep.
Colour. Short-haired: Yellow, chestnut, brown, gold and silver streaked. The streaks should be sharp and distributed well over the entire body, as well as on the back of the thighs and tail. The streaking must involve the hair from root to tip. Too much black in the outer coat is a fault. The mask should be black.
Wire-haired: Yellow, red-brown, ash blue, streaked, grey-blue, pepper-and-salt.
Long-haired: Chestnut, gold or silver streaked.
Head. In good proportion to the body without being coarse, it gives the impression of leanness. Of moderate length, rather narrow (but not of the Greyhound type), more or less conical in shape. The muzzle is a little longer than the skull. The bridge is straight and parallel to the skull line; the stop is barely perceptible. The head of the wire-haired variety is squarer than for the short-haired. The tip of the nose is invariably black. The lips are well closed over the gums. The teeth are strong and regular and meet in a scissor bite.
Tail. In repose the tail is carried low with a slight curve, the tip not reaching the hocks. In action it is carried high but not rolled and without tending to either side.
Feet. Close, with well-arched toes; nails preferably black. The pads are soft and elastic, preferably black in colour.

Below: A short-haired Hollandse Herder, showing its streaked coat. Bred originally as a sheepdog, it is now used as a companion/guard.

The Belgian Shepherd Dog breeds are similar in size and appearance to the German Shepherd Dog. The four breeds began to take their final form during the 1890s. They all take their names from villages in Belgium.

Belgian Shepherd Dog (Malinois)

Belgian Shepherd Dog (Laekenois)

Belgian Shepherd Dog (Tervueren)

DALMATIAN

Good points
- *Equable temperament*
- *Loyal*
- *Reliable with children*

Take heed
- *Needs ample exercise*

The Dalmatian has a happy nature, is loyal and devoted to its owners and rarely fights. It is easily trained and fairly simple to present in show. It is generally long-lived and has a lively youth. Remember that it was bred to run with horse and carriage and has the need and stamina for plenty of exercise.

Size
Overall balance of prime importance, but the ideal height for a dog is 23-24in (58.5-61cm), for a bitch 22-23in (56-58.5cm).

Exercise
Don't buy a Dalmatian unless you can give it plenty of exercise. It is in its element running behind a horse but an active, open-air country life will suffice.

Grooming
Frequent brushing; occasional bathing.

Health care
Some Dalmatians suffer from deafness. Check that a pup can hear before buying.

Feeding
Recommended would be 20-33oz (587-936g) of a branded, meaty product with biscuit added, or 3-5 cupfuls of a dry food, complete diet, mixed in the proportion of 1 cup of feed to ½ cup of hot or cold water.

Origin and history
The Dalmatian has an obscure background and heritage, but even though people disagree about the breed's origins, everyone concurs that the Dalmatian has remained essentially unchanged for centuries.

The earliest verifiable references place the Dalmatian in the province of Dalmatia, a region along the Adriatic in western Yugoslavia, some time in the middle of the eighteenth century. (From 1815 to 1919 this region was a province of Austria.)

From this area the breed was exported eventually to other parts of the world, and it has acquired different nicknames in the process. In the United Kingdom it is known as the Carriage Dog or the Plum Pudding Dog, and in the United States it is often called the Firehouse Dog.

SHOW STANDARD
General appearance. The Dalmatian should be a balanced, strong, muscular, active dog of good demeanour. Symmetrical in outline, free from coarseness and lumber, capable of great endurance with a fair amount of speed.
Colour. The ground colour should be pure white. Black-spotted dogs should have dense black spots and liver-spotted dogs liver-brown spots. The spots should be round and well defined, 0.4-0.8in (1-2cm) in diameter, as well distributed as possible. Spots on the extremities should be smaller than those on the body.
Head and skull. The head should be of fair length; the skull flat, reasonably broad between the ears but refined. The nose in the black-spotted variety should always be black, in the liver-spotted variety always brown.
Tail. In length reaching approximately to the hocks. Strong at the insertion, gradually tapering towards the end; it should not be inserted too low or too high; free from coarseness and carried with a slight upward curve, never curled; preferably spotted.
Feet. Round, compact with well-arched toes (cat feet) and round, tough, elastic pads. Nails black or white in the black-spotted variety, brown or white in the liver-spotted variety.

WEIMARANER

Good points
- *Does not shed*
- *Excels in obedience competitions*
- *Fine gundog*
- *Good temperament*
- *Needs little brushing*

Take heed
- *Likes to have a job of work to do*

The Weimaraner (or Silver Ghost) is an excellent gundog that originally hunted big game. It is obedient and eminently trainable, excelling in obedience competitions, and has been used as both police dog and guard. It makes a good pet but is happiest when given a job to do.

Size
Height at withers: dog 24-27in (61-68.5cm), bitch 22-25in (56-63.5cm).

Exercise
Needs plenty; has boundless energy. No need to rule out town living, but it is essential that the Weimaraner has lots of supervised freedom.

Grooming
Needs very little brushing for its sleek, virtually self-cleaning, coat. Clip nails when necessary.

Feeding
Recommended would be 20-33oz (587-936g) of a branded, meaty product with biscuit added, or 3-5 cupfuls of a dry food, complete diet, mixed in the proportion of 1 cup of feed to ½ cup of hot or cold water.

Origin and history
The Weimaraner burst upon the British scene in the early 1950s, since when it has become popular as a family pet, show dog and contender in obedience competitions. It is also well thought of in the United States, the best stock being available there and in the United Kingdom. But the Weimaraner is in fact no newcomer, having been purpose-bred as a gundog at the court in Weimar, Germany, towards the end of the eighteenth century. Bloodhounds, pointers and the old St Hubert Hounds are said to have assisted in its make-up. Its silver-grey colour is extremely distinctive feature of this breed.

SHOW STANDARD
General appearance. A medium-sized grey dog with light eyes, it should present a picture of great driving power, stamina, alertness and balance.
Colour. Preferably silver-grey; shades of mouse or roe grey are admissible. The colour usually blends to a lighter shade on head and ears. A dark eel stripe frequently occurs along the back. The whole coat gives an appearance of metallic sheen.
Head and skull. Moderately long and aristocratic with moderate stop and slight median line extending back over the forehead. Expression should be keen, kind and intelligent.
Tail. Docked at a point such that the tail remaining shall just cover the scrotum in dogs and vulva in bitches. The thickness of the tail should be in proportion to the body, and it should be carried in a manner expressing confidence and sound temperament. In the long-haired Weimaraner the tip of the tail should be removed.
Feet. Firm and compact. Toes well arched; pads closed and thick. Nails short, grey or amber in colour. Dew-claws allowable on imported dogs only.

BOXER

Good points
- *Brave*
- *Clownish*
- *Good guard*
- *Loves children*
- *Loyal*

Take heed
- *Enjoys a scrap*

The Boxer is a delightful animal that takes longer than most to grow up. It loves children and is a faithful protector of the family. However, it is an exuberant, fairly powerful dog, deserving a reasonable-sized home and garden and owners prepared to spend the necessary time on exercising and training. It has served in the armed forces and as a guide dog for the blind (seeing eye dog). Its tail is docked, and when pleased it tends to wag its whole body with pleasure.

Size
Height at the withers: dog 22-24in (56-61cm); bitch 21-23in (53-58.5cm. Weight: dogs around 23in (58.5cm) should weigh about 66lb (30kg); and bitches of about 22in (56cm) should weigh about 62lb (28.1kg).

Exercise
Good daily walks and off-the-lead runs are recommended.

Grooming
Regular brushing is required.

Feeding
Recommended would be 20-33oz (587-936g) of a branded, meaty product with biscuit added, or 3-5 cupfuls of a dry food, complete diet, mixed in the proportion of 1 cup of feed to ½ cup of hot or cold water.

Origin and history
The Boxer is traceable to the old holding dogs of Molossus or Mastiff type, which the Cimbrians took into battle against the Romans. Like the Bulldog, its jaw is undershot, a trait common in bull baiters. The Brabant bull baiter, from which the English Bulldog evolved, also played its part in the evolution of the Boxer, which retains its fighting spirit to this day.

Until dog-fighting and bull baiting were outlawed by most civilized countries in the middle of the nineteenth century the Boxer, like other dogs of his type, was employed in these sordid diversions. The modern-day Boxer has lost none of the courage he displayed in less enlightened times, but he has nonetheless become a member of polite society.

SHOW STANDARD
General appearance. The Boxer is a medium-sized, sturdy, smooth-haired dog of short, square figure and strong limb. The musculation is clean and powerfully developed and should stand out plastically from under the skin. Movement should be alive with energy. Its gait, though firm, is elastic; the stride free and roomy; the carriage proud.
Colour. The permissible colours are fawn, brindle and fawn in various shades from light yellow to dark deer red. The brindle variety should have black stripes on a golden yellow or red-brown background. The stripes should be clearly defined.
Head and skull. The head imparts to the Boxer a unique individual stamp peculiar to the breed. It must be in perfect proportion to the dog's body; above all it must never be too light. The muzzle is the most distinctive feature. The greatest value is to be placed on its being of correct form and in absolute proportion to the skull. The nose, broad and black, very slightly turned up. The nostrils should be broad with a naso-labial line between them. The two jawbones should not terminate in a normal perpendicular level in the front, but the lower jaw should protrude beyond the upper jaw and bend slightly upwards. The Boxer is normally undershot. The upper jaw should be broad where attached to the skull and maintain this breadth except for a very slight tapering to the front.
Tail. Attachment should be high. The tail should be docked and carried upwards and should be not more than 2in (5cm) long.
Feet. Should be small with tightly arched toes (cat feet) and hard soles. The rear toes should be just a little longer than the front toes but similar in all other respects.

Weimaraner

The Weimaraner should indicate the ability to work hard in the field. Movement should be effortless and ground-covering should indicate smooth co-ordination.

Dalmatian

Boxer

Boxers in America and certain European countries may have their ears cropped, a practice that makes them ineligible for competition in some areas of the world.

GOLDEN RETRIEVER

Good points
- *Excellent gundog*
- *Gentle with children*
- *Sound temperament*
- *Readily trained*
- *Loyal*

Take heed
- *No drawbacks known*

The Golden Retriever cannot be too highly recommended as a breed to suit all the family. It will romp with the children, enjoy a day's shooting with the man of the house and happily accompany the mistress on a shopping trip or for a session at the dog training club. This is a trustworthy breed whose individuals are happiest sharing the fireside with their family. They love to retrieve and will enjoy nothing better than carrying the newspaper home or wandering around the house with an old, chewed slipper. They are often used as guide dogs (seeing eye dogs) for the blind.

Size
The average weight in good hard condition should be: dog 70-80lb (31.8-36.3kg); bitch 60-70lb (27.2-31.8kg). Height at shoulder: dog 22-24in (56-61cm); bitch 20-22in (51-56cm).

Exercise
Needs at least an hour's exercise every day, free runs and ample garden. A large, fenced-in yard is a virtual necessity.

Below: A Golden Retriever with pups. The ideal pet for all the family, it is comfortable either at home or working in the field.

Grooming
Regular brushing will keep the coat in good condition.

Feeding
Recommended would be 20-33oz (587-936g) of a branded, meaty product with biscuit added, or 3-5 cupfuls of a dry food, complete diet, mixed in the proportion of 1 cup of feed to ½ cup of hot or cold water.

Origin and history
There is some controversy as to the origin of this breed. Did it, as many believe, develop from a troupe of Russian shepherd dogs found by Lord Tweedmouth performing in a Brighton circus in 1860, or did it begin with a litter of golden-haired pups of retriever/spaniel ancestry born on his Scottish estate? Romanticists believe the tale that Lord Tweedmouth was so greatly impressed with the Russian shepherd dogs that he brought the entire troupe and bred from them, adding Bloodhound blood to develop the nose.

SHOW STANDARD
General appearance. Should be a symmetrical, active, powerful dog, a good level mover, sound and well put together with a kindly expression, not clumsy or long in the leg.
Colour. Any shade of gold or cream, but neither red nor mahogany. The presence of a few white hairs on the chest is permissible. White collar, feet, toes or blaze should be penalized. Nose black.
Head and skull. Broad skull, well set on a clean and muscular neck; muzzle powerful and wide; not weak-jawed; good stop.
Tail. Should not be carried too gaily or curled at the tip.
Feet. Round and cat-like, not open or splay.

LABRADOR RETRIEVER

Good points
- *Equable temperament*
- *Excellent gundog*
- *Good family pet*
- *Kind with children*

Take heed
- *No drawbacks known*

Like the Golden Retriever, the Labrador Retriever cannot be too highly recommended as a breed tailor-made to suit the whole family. It is an excellent retriever, can be trusted with the children and will give a good account of itself in obedience training competitions. The Labrador Retriever is a breed much favoured as a guide dog (seeing eye dog) for the blind.

Size
Height: dog 22-22½in (56-57cm); bitch 21½-22in (54.5-56cm).

Exercise
Needs an hour a day at least, free runs and an ample garden. A large, fenced-in yard is recommended.

Grooming
Regular brushing will keep the coat in good condition.

Feeding
Recommended would be 20-33oz (587-936g) of a branded, meaty product with biscuit added, or 3-5 cupfuls of a dry food, complete diet, mixed in the proportion of 1 cup of feed to ½ cup of hot or cold water.

Origin and history
The Labrador Retriever came to the United Kingdom with fishermen from Newfoundland (not Labrador) in the 1830s. The dog's task in those days was to land the nets of the fishermen; their ability to swim has survived. Among the most

Above: A yellow Labrador Retriever and her pup. In 1991 this versatile and popular breed was the most registered in the United States.

popular British gundogs, they are also much sought after as family pets in many parts of the world.

SHOW STANDARD
General appearance. The Labrador should be a strongly built, short-coupled, very active dog, broad in the skull, broad and deep through the chest and ribs, broad and strong over the loins and hindquarters. The coat is close and short with a dense under-coat and free from feather. The dog must move neither too wide nor too close in front or behind; it must stand and move true all round on legs and feet.
Colour. Generally black or yellow but chocolate is also permitted. The coat should be free from any white markings, but a small white spot on the chest is allowable. the coat should be of a whole colour and not of a flecked appearance.
Head and skull. The skull should be broad with a pronounced stop so that the skull is not in a straight line with the nose. The head should be clean cut without fleshy cheeks. The jaws should be medium length, powerful and free from snipiness, the nose wide and the nostrils well developed.
Tail. A distinctive feature of the breed, it should be very thick towards the base, gradually tapering towards the tip. Of medium length and practically free from any feathering, the tail is clothed thickly all round with the Labrador's short, thick, dense coat, thus giving the peculiar 'rounded' appearance that has been described as the 'otter' tail. It may be carried gaily but should not curl over the back.
Feet. Should be round and compact with well-arched toes and well-developed pads.

Golden Retrievers were first shown under that name in the United Kingdom in 1913 and first registered in the United States in 1925. Since that time, the breed has undergone an explosion in popularity, both as a gentle and trustworthy pet and as a reliable and intelligent working dog.

Golden Retriever

Recognized by the Kennel Club as a distinct breed in 1903, the Labrador Retriever has been much celebrated around the world for its intelligence, even temperament and all-round ability

Labrador Retriever

CHESAPEAKE BAY RETRIEVER

Good points
- First-class retriever
- Sportsman's favourite
- Usually good with children

Take heed
- Occasionally aggressive

The Chesapeake Bay is a favourite with American sportsmen but has to date few devotees in the United Kingdom. It is an excellent swimmer and an unsurpassed retriever of wild duck. It is generally good with children but can be a little headstrong and difficult to train. Distinguishing features are the breed's yellow eyes and webbed feet. It has a water-resistant coat.

Size
Weight: dog 65-75lb (29.5-34kg); bitch 55-65lb (25-29.5kg). Height: dog 23-26in (58.5-66cm); bitch 21-24in (53-61cm).

Exercise
Needs plenty of hard exercise to stay in good condition.

Grooming
Normal brushing is sufficient.

Feeding
Recommended would be 20-33oz (587-936g) of a branded, meaty product with biscuit added, or 3-5 cupfuls of a dry food, complete diet, mixed in the proportion of 1 cup of feed to ½ cup of hot or cold water.

Origin and history
This is an American retriever whose parent stock is of British origin. An English brig went aground off the coast of Maryland in 1807 and was rescued by an American ship, the *Canton*. Aboard the brig were two pups, which were named 'Canton', after the rescue ship, and 'Sailor'. They were subsequently trained to retrieve duck and were crossed with many of the dogs, most of which were of nondescript origins, that were used for retrieving at that time. The original dogs, 'Canton' and 'Sailor', are said to have been Newfoundland in origin. Americans seem to want to retain the Chesapeake Bay Retriever as a sporting dog, which is why it has not found its way into many homes as a pet. People either rave about the merits of the Chesapeake Bay or are completely put off by their oily coats, not unpleasant oily odour and yellow-orange eyes.

SHOW STANDARD
General appearance. Should show a bright and happy disposition and have an intelligent expression. Its outlines are impressive and indicative of a good worker.
Colour. Any colour varying from dark brown to faded tan or dead-grass colour of any shade from tan to dull straw.
Head and skull. Broad, round with medium stop; nose medium; muzzle pointed but not sharp; lips

thin, not pendulous.
Tail. Of medium length, in the dog 12-15in (30-38cm), in the bitch 11-14in (28-35.5cm). It should be fairly heavy at the root. Moderate feathering on tail and stern is permissible.
Feet. Well-webbed hare feet of good size. Toes well rounded and close; the pasterns slightly bent.

CURLY-COATED RETRIEVER

Good points
- Beautiful
- Equable temperament
- Excellent guard
- Fine swimmer
- Good nose/retriever
- Stamina
- Intelligent

Take heed
- No drawbacks known

The Curly-coat is an excellent worker on land and in water and will retrieve any game. It is a hardy dog, of good temperament and fine appearance.

Size
Weight: 70-80lb (31.8-36.3kg). Height: 25-27in (63.5-68.5cm).

Exercise
Thrives on liberal amounts of vigorous exercise.

Grooming
Don't brush and comb this breed. Just damp the coat down and massage with circular movements. Seek advice on trimming.

Feeding
As for Chesapeake Bay Retriever.

Origin and history
The Curly-coat was one of the earliest British retrievers. It was exhibited at dog shows in England as early as 1860 and was depicted in many sporting prints beforehand. Its popularity seems to have waned since the beginning of World War I and, despite its superb working ability, it has never been in great demand since. The early Labrador obviously played a part in its make-up and, to hazard a suggestion, the Water Spaniel, which with its tight curly coat it resembles.

SHOW STANDARD
General appearance. A strong, smart, upstanding dog, showing activity, endurance and intelligence.
Colour. Black or liver.
Head and skull. Long, well-proportioned flat skull; jaws strong and long but not inclined to snipiness. Nose black in the black-coated variety with wide nostrils. Coarseness of head to be deprecated, and so should wry, undershot bites, or overshot bites with a noticeable gap.
Tail. Moderately short, carried fairly straight and covered with curls; tapering towards the point: gay tail not desirable.
Feet. Round and compact with well-arched toes.

HOVAWART

Good points
- Excellent guard
- Home-loving
- Fond of children
- Loyal
- Obedient

Take heed
- Slow to mature
- Tends to be a one-person dog

The Hovawart is an old German breed that, like so many of similar origin, was not bred for a specific purpose. It is, and always has been, just a loyal companion dog and protector of the home.

It is generally obedient, loves children and has utter loyalty to its master, tending to be a one-person dog, although defending the entire family with its life.

Size
Height: 25-27in (63.5-68.5cm). Weight: 65-90lb (29.5-40.8kg); bitches less.

Exercise
Normal regular exercise.

Grooming
Regular brushing will keep the coat in good condition.

Feeding
As for Chesapeake Bay Retriever.

Origin and history
The Hovawart was already a popular companion dog in Germany during the Middle Ages. In fact, the name Hovawart means 'house guard'. It resembles the Kuvasz in stature and looks like a large collie. The breed seems to have suffered a period of unpopularity, but after World War I such specimens as could be found were crossed with Leonbergers and Newfoundlands to perpetuate a once famous breed.

SHOW STANDARD
General appearance. A robust working dog of medium weight, the Hovawart is strong and highly weather resistant, a good runner and jumper, brave, attentive and quick to react. It is a splendid guard dog. Sexual characteristics should be clearly evident. The voice is deep, full and powerful.
Colour. Black, black and tan (small white ticking permissible), flaxen (with a dark shade preferred). Eyes, nose and nails to be of a colour consistent with the basic colouring of the coat but not too light.
Head. Strong, with a broad, convex forehead. The muzzle is straight, neither too long nor too short. Maximum muzzle length should be equal to the distance from the occipital bone to the stop. Tight lips, well-formed muzzle. Teeth should be strong with a scissor bite. A pincer (level) bite is allowed but is counted a fault in show.
Tail. Reaches beyond the hocks but not to the ground, well feathered, carried low in repose and high when the dog is excited.
Feet. Hard pads on the forefeet.

FLAT-COATED RETRIEVER

Good points
- Easy to train
- Good with children
- Hardy
- Natural retriever

Take heed
- No drawbacks known

The Flat-coated Retriever enjoyed a renewed popularity after attaining the coveted Best in Show award at Crufts in 1980. It is a natural retriever, used for picking up game. It is hardy and easily trained and makes a good household companion if you wish, being very good with children.

Size
Should be 60-70lb (27.2-31.8kg).

Exercise
Thrives on plenty of exercise.

Grooming
Regular brushing and tidying up.

Feeding
As for Chesapeake Bay Retriever.

Origin and history
The Flat-coat probably owes its evolution to the Labrador Retriever, the collie and certain spaniels. It was at one time known as the Wavy-coated Retriever, and it is thought that collie blood was introduced to produce the Flat-coat. Prior to World War I the Flat-coat was perhaps the best-known gundog in the United Kingdom. It was overshadowed in the post-war era by the Golden Retriever and Labrador Retriever, whose appeal has remained constant, not, however, to the detriment of the quality of the Flat-coat breed.

SHOW STANDARD
General appearance. A bright, active dog of medium size with an intelligent expression, showing power without lumber and raciness without weediness.
Colour. Black or liver.
Head and skull. The head should be long and nicely moulded; the skull flat and moderately broad. There should be a depression or stop between the eyes, slight and in no way accentuated, so as to avoid giving either a down or a dish-faced appearance. The nose of a good size with open nostrils. The jaws should be long and strong with the capacity for carrying a hare or pheasant.
Body. The topline is strong and level. The chest, which is deep and moderately broad, has a well-defined brisket and a prominent forechest. The croup is somewhat sloped, and the rump is fairly broad.
Tail. Short, straight and well set on, carried gaily but never much above the level of the back.
Feet. Should be round and strong with toes close and well arched; the soles thick and strong.

Curly-coated Retriever

Chesapeake Bay Retriever

Flat-coated Retriever

Hovawart

JAPANESE AKITA

Good points
- *Easily trained*
- *First-class guard*
- *Good temperament*
- *Intelligent*

Take heed
- *No drawbacks known*

The Japanese Akita, the best known of the Japanese Spitz breeds, arrived on the international scene in the early 1980s. The breed is now exhibited in the United Kingdom and America, and the Japanese have done much to improve their purebred stock. Bred as a hunter of wild boar, deer and even black bear. The Akita is undoubtedly capable of ferocity, but it is easily trained and generally has an equable temperament.

Size
Height: dog 21-24in (53-61cm), some bigger; bitch 19-21in (48-53cm). Weight: 85-110lb (38.6-49.9kg).

Exercise
Does not require a great deal of exercise. Incidentally, it has webbed feet and is a fine swimmer and a good water dog.

Grooming
Normal brushing.

Feeding
Recommended would be 20-33oz (587-936g) of a branded, meaty product with biscuit added, or 3-5 cupfuls of a dry food, complete diet, mixed in the proportion of 1 cup of feed to ½ cup of hot or cold water.

Origin and history
The Akita resembles a smooth-coated Chow and is the largest of the known Japanese Spitz breeds. It is bred in its native land as a hunter of wild boar and deer and is obviously related to the Icelandic breeds. However, it has bred true in Japan's Akita province for more than 300 years, and its exact origin is obscure.

SHOW STANDARD (FCI)
General appearance. A solidly-built dog, well proportioned with an imposing appearance of great distinction. Prudent, docile, intelligent without sacrificing an impetuous temperament.
Colour. Salt and pepper, reddish salt and pepper, black pepper, streaked, white or white with markings.
Head. The skull is large with a broad forehead; the medial furrow is well marked. The stop is well defined. The cheeks are well formed. The muzzle is strong and pointed, the bridge straight and short. The teeth are solid and must meet in a bite free from overshot effects. The nose is large and black (white dogs may have a pink nose). The lips are rather thin and well fitted over the gums.
Tail. The tail is stout and strong,

reaching the hocks when straight. It is carried over the back in a ring which can be shifted from one side to the other. Sometimes the tail is a screwtail, at others a spiral curl; in either case the curl should be a complete turn.
Feet. The feet are large, with close toes. The nails are hard and dark. Pads should be hard and rugged.

CHOW CHOW

Good points
- *Beautiful*
- *Good endurance*
- *Loyal*
- *Odourless*

Take heed
- *Formidable opponent*
- *Needs firm gentle handling*
- *Strong willed*
- *One-man dog (but will accept owner's family)*

The Chow Chow, whose name is perhaps derived from the Chinese Choo Hunting Dog, is a member of the Spitz family known for over 2,000 years. It is lion-like in appearance and famed for its blue-black tongue. It is free of odour and makes an incredibly loyal companion, tending to devote itself to one member of the family though accepting and returning the affection of other household members. It needs quiet but firm handling: with its aloof temperament it is unlikely to deign to walk at your heel without persuasion. It does not take kindly to strangers and is a fearsome fighter if provoked.

Size
Minimum height for Chows is 18in (46cm), but in every case balance should be the outstanding feature and height left to the discretion of the judges.

Exercise
Most Chow owners seem to manage with regular on-the-lead walks, with runs in permitted areas. However, mindful of the Chow's prowess as a hunter of wolves, game and anything that moves, it seems unfair to keep it in confined surroundings or to deprive it of the open spaces that it relishes.

Grooming
About five or ten minutes' brushing a day and about half an hour each weekend with a wire brush should maintain the Chow gleaming.

Feeding
Recommended would be 13-20oz (369-587g) of a branded, meaty product with biscuit added in equal part by volume, or 1¾-3 cupfuls of a dry, complete food, mixed in the proportion of 1 cup of feed to ½ cup of hot or cold water. Perhaps not surprisingly, they also do well on rice or on tripe, chicken and lean beef.

Origin and history
Although there are other black-mouthed dogs, the Chow is the only dog with a blue-black tongue, although small bears — to which it

has some resemblance — share this characteristic. Reputed to be the original Lama's Mastiff, the Chow Chow must be one of the oldest members of the Spitz family and was bred variously for its flesh — which in many parts of Asia is considered a delicacy — and for its fur and as a useful hunter of game. In early Chinese writings, it was known as the Tartar Dog, or Dog of Barbarians. The first breed members imported into England, in 1760, were exhibited in a zoo. Sadly, a reputation for ferocity has come down with the Chow, yet it is an affectioante, devoted animal. It is unlikely to fight unless provoked, but then it will be a formidable opponent. The Chow Chow Club was formed in the United Kingdom in 1895, and today around 600 or 700 breed members a year are registered with the Kennel Club, and interest in the breed is constantly growing.

SHOW STANDARD
General appearance. An active, compact, short-coupled and well-balanced dog, well knit in frame with tail carried over the back.
Colour. Whole-coloured black, red,

Above: The beautiful, lion-like Chow is a one-person dog, but it keeps on friendly terms with the rest of the household. Delightful as a puppy, the adult Chow can be single-minded and aloof but is a stunning sight in the show ring.

bue, fawn, cream or white, frequently shaded but not in patches or parti-coloured (the underpart of tail and back of thighs are frequently of a light colour).
Head and skull. Skull flat and broad with little stop, well filled out under the eyes. Muzzle moderate in length, broad from the eyes to the point (not pointed at the end like a fox). Nose should be black, large and wide (with the exception of creams and whites, in which case a light-coloured nose is permissible, and in blues and fawns a self-coloured nose); but in all colours a black nose preferred.
Body. The back is short, straight and strong. The chest is broad, deep and muscular.
Tail. Set high and carried well over the back.
Feet. Small, round and cat-like, standing well on the toes.

Outside its native country, the Japanese
Akita is especially popular in the United
States: many specimens were brought back
by American servicemen at the end of
World War II.

Japanese Akita

Now appreciated in the
Western world mainly as
an outstandingly
successful show
dog, the Chow
Chow is an ancient
breed with great
scenting and hunting ability.
It was first exhibited
in the United States in 1890.

Chow Chow

ALASKAN MALAMUTE

Good points
- *Affectionate*
- *Fast and strong*
- *Fine sled dog*
- *Loves children*
- *Sociable*

Take heed
- *No drawbacks known*

The Alaskan Malamute is an Arctic Spitz-type little known outside Alaska and the United States. It is a sociable dog, capable of being driven in sled races by children. It is highly prized as a sled dog and capable of immense speed. Don't be put off by the wolfish appearance; the kindly expression is genuine.

Size
Height: dog 25-28in (63.5-71cm); bitch 23-26in (58.5-66cm). Weight: 85-125lb (38.6-56.7kg).

Exercise
Needs plenty of vigorous exercise to stay healthy.

Grooming
Regular brushing will keep the coat in good condition.

Feeding
Recommended would be 20-33oz 587-936g) of a branded, meaty product with biscuit added, or 3-5 cupfuls of a dry food, complete diet, mixed in the proportion of 1 cup of feed to ½ cup of hot or cold water.

Origin and history
The Alaskan Malamute is named after a native tribe called the Mahlemuts. The origin of the dogs is obscure, but the breed is obviously closely related to other Spitz-types, such as the Samoyed.

SHOW STANDARD
General appearance. The breed is primarily a working sled dog of the Arctic used for hauling heavy freight, and therefore it should be a heavily boned and powerfully built animal, not too compact and never appearing low on the leg.
Colour. From light grey through the intermediate shadings to black, or from gold through the shades or red to liver, always with white on the underbody, feet, parts of legs and part of mask markings. The markings on the face should be either cap-like or mask-like: combination of cap and mask is not unusual. A white blaze on the forehead, a white collar or a spot on the nape is acceptable. Heavy mantling of unbroken colour is

Below: Prized for its sled-pulling skill, the Alaskan Malamute is also a very sociable dog — as its kind, gentle expression implies.

acceptable but broken colour extending over the body in spots or uneven splashings is undesirable. The only solid colour allowable is the all white.
Head and skull. The head should be broad and powerful, not coarse, and in proportion to the size of the dog. The skull should be broad between the ears, gradually narrowing to the eyes; moderately rounded between the ears, flattening on top as it approaches the eyes and rounding off to the cheeks, which should be moderately flat. There should be a very slight but perceptible stop. The muzzle should be large in proportion to the size of the skull, scarcely diminishing in width or depth from the stop. Nose black except in dogs coloured red and white, when it should be brown.
Tail. Moderately high set and follows the line of the spine at the start. Well furred and carried over the back when the dog is not working; not tightly curled to rest on the back, nor short furred and carried like a fox brush but with the appearance of a waving plume.
Feet. Large and compact; tight-fitting toes, well arched; thick, tough pads; toenails short and strong. There should be a protective growth of hair between the toes.

ESKIMO DOG
(And Greenland Dog)

Good points
- *Beautiful*
- *Can become devoted*
- *Endurance*
- *Excellent sled dog*
- *Strong*
- *Fine guard*

Take heed
- *Suspicious of strangers*

The Eskimo Dog is one of several regional sled dogs of different names, few of which are well known outside the polar area. It is hardy and accustomed to fending for itself, living in the open and often having to find its own food.

The Greenland Dog is so similar that controversy rages as to whether they should be classified separately. Usually the Eskimo Dog

Above: Strong, beautiful and obviously built to endure hard work in a cold climate, these Greenland Dogs appear eager to get moving.

is a little shorter in the back than the Greenland and is weightier generally but without extra height.

Size
Height at shoulder: dog 23-27in (58.5-68.5cm); bitch 20-24in (51-61cm). Weight: dog 75-105lb (34-47.6kg); bitch 60-90lb (27.2-40.8kg).

Exercise
These dogs are accustomed to pulling sleds and hauling fishing boats ashore. They would soon get bored just snoozing by the fireside all day. Consider this if you consider acquiring either of these — or any other — working breeds.

Grooming
Regular brushing will keep the coat in good condition.

Feeding
Recommended would be 20-33oz (587-936g) of a branded, meaty product with biscuit added, or 3-5 cupfuls of a dry food, complete diet, mixed in the proportion of 1 cup of feed to ½ cup of hot or cold water.

Origin and history
These polar Spitz breeds no doubt originated in eastern Siberia and shared a common task and ancestry with the Alaskan Malamute, Siberian Husky and Samoyed. To quote the American explorer Peary, 'There is, in fact, only one sled dog'.

SHOW STANDARD
Colour. All known dog colours or combinations of these colours.
Head and skull. Well proportioned, broad and wedge-shaped with a moderate stop. Strong, flat skull and powerful jaws. Black or brown nose and lips. Muzzle of medium length, gently tapering to the nose.
Tail. Large and bushy. Set high and curled loosely over the back, falling to one side or the other.
Feet. Rather large, well spread and strong with strong nails. Thick pads well intersected with fur.

The Eskimo Dog is recognized by the Canadian Kennel Club as a separate breed, and the FCI recognize the closely related Greenland Dog. Both are Arctic hauling dogs.

Eskimo Dog

The Alaskan Malamute is a tremendously powerful sled dog known for generations in its native Alaska. It has survived as a pure breed and is particularly popular in the United States for winter sports.

Alaskan Malamute

OTTERHOUND

Good points
- *Appealing*
- *Easy to groom*
- *Friendly*
- *Gentle with children*
- *Waterproof coat*

Take heed
- *Essentially a hound rather than a house-pet, and not ideally suited to suburban living*

With otter hunting now outlawed in the United Kingdom, the Otterhound could have faced extinction had not the last Master of the Kendal and District Otterhounds in the Lake District set up the Otterhound Club to ensure the survival of the breed. Without the continued interest of breeders and the show world, the Otterhound would certainly have died out.

The Otterhound is an amiable, friendly animal, gentle with children and responsive to affection. However, one should not lose sight of the fact that it was a pack hound bred to kill, a background that does not ideally equip it as a household pet.

Size
Height: dogs should stand approximately 27in (68.5cm) at the shoulder; bitches approximately 24in (61cm). Weight: dogs 75-115lb (34-52.2kg); bitches 65-100lb (29.5-45.4kg).

Exercise
The Otterhound needs a lot of exercise. A feature of this breed is the existence of webbing between the toes. This gives the Otterhound a decided advantage in the water. Most dogs can swim, but the Otterhound excels in that ability and is as much at home in the water as it is on land.

Grooming
A thorough brush and comb once a week should be sufficient to keep the Otterhound's coat in good condition. There is natural oil in the coat, and if you are bathing the animal for a show, it is advisable to do this a week beforehand to allow the coat to regain its correct texture. However, the head hair can be bathed the day before a show because this is of a finer texture.

Particular attention must be paid to the ears, as they are inclined to collect wax and can become a source of irritation to the animal. Care should be taken to inspect the ears regularly.

Feeding
The Otterhound is a large dog and will need 20-33oz (587-936g) of a good branded, meaty diet to which biscuit should be added, or 3-5 cupfuls of a dry food, complete diet, mixed in the proportion of 1 cup of feed to ½ cup of hot or cold water.

Origin and history
The Otterhound is an extremely old breed, and its origins are somewhat obscure. Some say it descended from the old Southern Hound, and others see the Bloodhound in its ancestry. Today it is most like some of the French hounds, such as the Griffon Nivernais or Griffon Vendéen, and it is quite possible that the Otterhound springs from the same origins as these French breeds.

Otter hunting was one of the earliest field sports in England, and King John, Henry II and Elizabeth I all kept Otterhound packs long before foxes were thought worthy to be hunted. Many monasteries also kept Otterhounds to protect their fishponds from the nightly ravages of otters.

SHOW STANDARD
General appearance. A big, strongly built hound, straight-limbed, rough-coated with majestic head, strong body and loose, long-striding action. For a long day's work in water, the rough double coat and large feet are essential. As the animal must also gallop on land, it has to be free-moving. The Otterhound requires no trimming for exhibition. Handling and presentation are natural.

Colour. Any recognized hound colour is permissible, with the exception of the liver and white and a white-bodied hound with black and tan patches distinctly separated. Usually, whole-coloured grizzle, sandy, red, wheaten or blue, but these may have slightly white markings on head, chest, feet and tail tip. White hounds may have slight lemon, blue or badger pied markings. Also black and tan, blue and tan, black and cream or occasional liver and tan. Pigment should harmonize, though not necessarily blend, with coat colour: i.e. a tan hound may have a brown nose and eye-rims.

Head and skull. Clean and very imposing, it is deep rather than wide with clean cheekbones. Skull nicely domed, not coarse or overdone, rising from a distinct though not exaggerated stop to a slight peak at the occiput. There is no trace of scowl or bulge in the forehead, the expression being open and amiable. The muzzle should be strong and deep with a good wide nose bone ending in wide nostrils, the distance from nose-end to stop being slightly shorter than that from stop to occiput. Plenty of lip and flew, though not exaggerated. The whole head, except for the nose bone, should be well covered with rough hair, ending in slight moustaches and beard, both being part of the natural face hair. A slight butterfly nose should not disqualify an otherwise good hound.

Legs and feet. Forelegs should be strongly boned, straight from elbow to ground with strong, slightly sprung pasterns. Feet should turn neither in nor out, being large, round, well knuckled and thickly padded with web in evidence. They are compact when standing but capable of spreading. The hindfeet should be only slightly smaller than the forefeet.

Tail (stern). Should be set high and carried up when alert or on the move but must never curl over the

Above: As comfortable in the water as on land, the Otterhound is more at home as a hunter than as a household pet.

back, though it may droop when standing. Thick at the base, tapering to a point and reaching to the hock; carried straight or in a slight curve, the hair under the stern being rather longer and more profuse than that on the topside.

ITALIAN SPINONE

Good points
- *Affectionate*
- *Fine retriever of waterfowl*
- *Hardy*

Take heed
- *No drawbacks known*

The Italian Spinone is an ancient breed of gundog, much appreciated by Italian horsemen for its ability to work in marshy and wooded country. It has a soft mouth and will point and retrieve. It has a good nature and is well established in its own country.

Size
Height: dog 23½-25½in (60-65cm); bitch 21½-23½in (54.5-60cm).

Exercise
Needs plenty of vigorous exercise in order to remain in good condition physically and temperamentally.

Grooming
The Spinone's hard, thick, somewhat curly coat needs brushing two or three times a week, especially after the dog has been in water.

Feeding
Recommended would be 20-33oz (587-936g) of a branded, meaty product with biscuit added, or 3-5 cupfuls of a dry food, complete diet, mixed in the proportion of 1 cup of feed to ½ cup of hot or cold water.

Origin and history
The Spinone originated in the French region of Bresse but later found its way to Piedmont in Italy. Its evolution is attributable to the French Griffon, French and German pointers, the Porçelaine, Barbet and Korthals Griffon. What has emerged is a reliable gundog with a pleasing appearance, somewhere between a Pointer and a Foxhound.

Although the Spinone is accepted for championship competition by the Kennel Club, the breed can be shown only in the miscellaneous classes in the United States.

SHOW STANDARD
General appearance. The Spinone has a body that is square in outline. It is a solid, vigorous country dog with strong bone and well-developed muscle; the breed is characterized by its excellent fast trotting gait. The breed's facial expression is intelligent and shows power and courage. Its eyes are expressive with a markedly sweet, almost human expression. It is exceptionally hardy and enters nonchalantly into brambles and deep, cold water; for such work it is protected by its thick skin and hard, thick coat.

Colour. Permissible colours include: white; white with orange markings; solid white peppered with orange; white with brown markings; white speckled with brown hairs (brown roan) with or without larger brown markings.

Head and skull. The head is large with fairly broad, domed skull; the stop is not accentuated, but the muzzle is well developed and square.

Tail. Thick at the base and set on as a continuation of the croup line; carried horizontally or down; should be docked at 6-10in (15-25cm) from the root.

Feet. Compact and round with well-closed toes that are well arched and covered with short, thick hair, even including the spaces between the toes.

Otterhound

Italian Spinone

The Italian Spinone's coat
is particularly rugged and
harsh to the touch, a much-
needed protection for the dog
when it is retrieving game
from densely wooded terrain.

ROTTWEILER

Good points
- *Good temperament*
- *Intelligent*
- *Makes a good household companion/guard*
- *Reliable working dog*

Take heed
- *Responds best to kind, firm handling — not being chained or kennelled in a yard*

The Rottweiler is a German working dog of high intelligence and good temperament. It has been a draught dog and herder, and is still used as guard, police dog, sled dog and mountain rescue dog. In many countries it is sought after as a companion/pet and guard. It is a popular contender in the show ring and does well in obedience tests.

Size
Height at shoulder: dog 25-27in (63.5-68.5cm); bitch 23-25in (58.5-63.5cm).

Exercise
Regular walks and runs.

Grooming
Regular brushing will keep the coat in good condition.

Feeding
Recommended would be 20-33oz (587-936g) of a branded, meaty product with biscuit added, or 3-5 cupfuls of a dry food, complete diet, mixed in the proportion of 1 cup of feed to ½ cup of hot or cold water.

Origin and history
The Rottweiler is a butcher's dog. It comes from the German town of Rottweil in Württemberg, where it is known as the Rottweiler Metzgerhund or Rottweil butcher's dog.

It was known in the Middle Ages as a hunter of wild boar and later as a revered and trusted cattle dog as well as a draught dog that would draw carts for butchers and cattle dealers. Just before World War I its abilities were recognized as a police dog and guard.

Thelma Gray of the Rozavel Kennels introduced the breed into the United Kingdom in 1936. It was developing a following until World War II, when breeding ceased, and it was not until a Captain Roy-Smith, serving with the Occupation Army in Germany, brought home a dog and bitch that a sound breeding programme was re-established. Since then a few breed devotees have produced many good specimens.

SHOW STANDARD
General appearance. The Rottweiler is an above average-sized, stalwart dog. Its correctly proportioned, compact and powerful form permits feats of great strength, manoeuvrability and endurance. Its bearing displays boldness and courage; and the tranquil gaze manifests good nature and devotion.
Colour. The animal is black with clearly defined markings on the cheeks, muzzle, chest and legs, as well as over both eyes and the area beneath the tail. The markings range from rich tan to mahogany brown.

Head and skull. The head is of medium length; the skull between the ears is broad. The forehead line is moderately arched as seen from the side. The occipital bone is well developed but not conspicuous. Cheeks are well muscled but not prominent with the zygomatic arch well formed. The skin on the head should not be loose, although it is allowed to form a moderate wrinkle when the dog is attentive. Muzzle fairly deep with topline level and length not more than that from stop to occiput.

Tail. Carried horizontally; short, strong and not set too low. It should be docked at the first joint.

Feet. Strong, round and compact with the toes well arched. The hindfeet are somewhat longer than the front ones. The pads should be very hard, and the toenails short, dark and strong. Rear dew-claws are removed.

RHODESIAN RIDGEBACK

Good points
- *Affectionate*
- *Obedient*
- *Good with children*
- *Superior intelligence*
- *Sense of fun*

Take heed
- *No drawbacks known*

The Rhodesian Ridgeback is a handsome, muscular, medium-sized dog of the hound group with a short, tan-coloured coat, pendulous ears and a long, uncropped tail.

The breed is named after the line of hair, shaped like the blade of a broadsword, that grows in the reverse direction along the back with two crowns at the shoulder and the point towards the tail. This ridge is a very distinctive marking that is not found in any other breed of dog.

Although the ridge may appear to be a superficiality, created for the show ring or as a talking point, in fact it is far from recent and has come down through the centuries by way of the African Hottentot Hunting Dog.

The Rhodesian Ridgeback is of a quiet temperament and rarely barks; it enjoys spending hours curled up lazily in the corner of a room, stretched out in the summer sun or basking in front of an open fireplace. Although its exploits as a hunter of African game first brought it recognition, the breed was developed as a dual-purpose dog, as a hunter and a gentle guardian of the families of the early white settlers. More and more people are discovering the tranquil temperament of this breed, its affectionate dispostiion and desire for human companionship. The Ridgeback likes nothing better than to lean against you or to sit on your

Above: A Rhodesian Ridgeback and her pup. The ridge that gives the breed its name can be seen on the puppy's back.

feet. And if you own a diamond, this is just the dog to guard it.

Size
The desirable weight is: dog 80lb (36.3kg), bitch 70lb (31.75kg), with a permissible variation of 5lb (2.3kg) above and below these weights. A mature Ridgeback should be a handsome, upstanding animal; dogs should be of a height of 25-27in (63.5-68.5cm) and bitches 24-26in (61-66cm). Minimum bench standard: dog 25in (63.5cm), bitch 24in (61cm).

Exercise
This large, sleepy and apparently slow-moving animal with its characteristic love of lazing, contrasts sharply with its action when alerted. In a flash, it is converted into a graceful streak of rhythmic motion. This is a pet that should have a large garden to run in and deserves a master able to give it a good walk every day.

Grooming
Regular grooming with a hound glove, coupled with correct feeding and plenty of exercise, will keep the Ridgeback in healthy and gleaming condition.

Feeding
About 20-33oz (587-936g) of branded dog food complemented by biscuit should be sufficient for your Ridgeback. Or, if you prefer, 3-5 cupfuls of a dry food, complete diet, mixed in the proportion of 1 cup of feed to ½ cup of hot or cold water. And of course, like most breeds, the Ridgeback will enjoy the occasional bone.

Remember that suggested quantities are only a guide and should be increased or decreased according to the desired weight of your dog. Watch it carefully, and if it appears to be putting on undue weight, cut down on the biscuit.

Origin and history
Long before Europeans settled in southern Africa, the members of the Hottentot tribe had as a companion who accompanied them on their hunting expeditions an animal that has since been called the Hottentot Hunting Dog. The distinct characteristic of this dog is the ridge of hair growing in the reverse direction along its back.

During the sixteenth and seventeenth centuries, Dutch, Boers, Germans and Huguenots migrated to southern Africa. As these people were pioneers in a new and uncivilized country teeming with fierce wild animals, they brought with them their own European medium- and large-sized working and hunting dogs. Probably by chance, the white settlers' dogs became crossed with the tough Hottentot Hunting Dogs, and the superior quality and vigour of their offspring were quickly recognized, the presence of the ridge identifying the most desirable dogs.

This blending of the best qualitites of many European breeds with those of the Hottentot Hunting Dog formed the immediate ancestor of today's Ridgeback, which has many of the characteristics usually associated with other hounds.

SHOW STANDARD
General appearance. The Ridgeback should be a strong, muscular, active dog, symmetrical in outline and capable of great endurance with a fair amount of speed. Movement should be similar to the Foxhound's gait.
Colour. Light wheaten to red wheaten. Head, body, legs and tail should be of a uniform colour. A little white on the chest is permissible but excessive white hairs here, on the belly or above the paws should be penalized. White toes are undesirable. Dark muzzle and ears are permissible.
Head and skull. Should be of a fair length, the skull flat and rather broad between the ears, and should be free from wrinkles when in repose. The stop should be reasonably well defined and not in one straight line from the nose to the occiput bone, as required in a bull terrier. The nose should be black or brown in keeping with the colour of the dog. No other colour of nose is permissible. A black nose should be accompanied by dark eyes: a brown nose by amber eyes.
Body. The shoulders are sloping, clean and muscular. The chest, which should not be too wide, is nonetheless deep and capacious. The ribs are moderately well sprung, but they never should be rounded like the hoops of a barrel. This construction would suggest a lack of speed. The back is powerful. The loins are strong, muscular and somewhat arched.
Tail. Should be strong at the insertion and generally tapering towards the end, free from coarseness. It should not be inserted too high or too low and should be carried with a slight curve upwards.
Feet. The feet should be compact with well-arched toes and round, tough elastic pads protected by hair between the toes and pads.

Because the Rottweiler was long used
by butchers in the region of Rottweil,
southern Germany, to drive cattle to
market (and to guard its newly enriched
master when the cattle had been sold)
it was known there as the Rottweiler
Metzgerhund, or Rottweil butcher's dog.
As a show dog it was established in the
United States a little earlier than in
the United Kingdom, the breed being
recognized by the American
Kennel Club in 1935, and it is
steadily increasing in
international popularity.

Rottweiler

The characteristic ridge of hair
along the back of the Rhodesian
Ridgeback should be clearly defined,
tapering and symmetrical, and extend
from immediately behind the
shoulders to the haunches.
It must have an average width of
2in (5cm), and contain two
identical crowns, the lower
edges of which must not extend
down the ridge further
than one-third of its length.

Rhodesian Ridgeback

BOUVIER DES FLANDRES

Good points
● *Can be kept as a pet*
● *Easily trained*
● *Impressive guard*
● *Loyal to owner's family*
● *Trustworthy*

Take heed
● *Not suited for town or apartment living*
● *One-person family dog*

The Bouvier des Flandres is a Belgian cattle dog, hardy, trustworthy and — when its ears are cropped, as in its country of origin — looking the epitome of ferocity. It can be kept as a pet but tends to be a one-person dog, though that means guarding its family as well.

Size
Weight: dog 77-88lb (34.9-39.9kg); bitch 59½-77lb (27-34.9kg). Height: dog 24½-27in (62-68.5cm); bitch 23-25½in (58.5-65cm).

Exercise
Needs plenty of exercise. Not ideally suited to town life.

Grooming
Regular brushing will keep the coat in good condition.

Feeding
Recommended would be 20-33oz (587-936g) of a branded, meaty product with biscuit added, or 3-5 cupfuls of a dry food, complete diet, mixed in the proportion of 1 cup of feed to ½ cup of hot or cold water.

Origin and history
The Bouvier was derived from a number of working Belgian breeds. It was developed with an eye towards producing a good all-purpose dog, suitable for the rough shoot, for herding, and for work as a draught dog. It was not until 1912 that a meeting was held to discuss a possible standard for the Bouvier. No agreement was reached, and devotees had to wait until after World War I for a standard to be drawn up by the Club National Belge du Bouvier des Flandres and for efforts to be made to improve future stock of the breed.

SHOW STANDARD
General appearance. Rather short-legged and cobby, the body set on well-muscled, strong legs, giving the impression of great strength without clumsiness.
Colour. Usually fawn or grey, often brindled or shaded. Black is also permissible, and no colour shall have preference. Light, washed-out shades are undesirable.
Head and skull. The head should appear big, the moustache and beard making it appear even more so in proportion to the body and height. When handled it should be found to be well chiselled. Well developed and flat, the skull should be slightly broader than it is long. The lines of the underside of the skull and the top should be parallel.

The proportion of the length of the skull to the muzzle should be 3:2. A very slight furrow in the forehead. The stop not very deep, but appearing so, due to the heavy eyebrows. The muzzle broad, strong and bony, rectangular when seen from the front, gradually narrowing towards the nose, but never becoming pointed. The circumference, measured just in front of the eyes, should be approximately equal to the length of the head. Extending the foreface in a slightly convex line towards its tip, the nose should be very well developed, rounded at its edges and always black. Nostrils wide. Cheeks flat and clean.
Tail. Docked to two or three vertebrae. It should continue the normal line of the vertebral column and be carried gaily when moving. Dogs born without a tail should not be faulted for this.
Feet. Short, round and compact. Toes tight and well arched. Nails black, strong. Thick, hard pads.

BRIARD

Good points
● *Easy to train*
● *Family pet and/or farm worker*
● *Gentle nature*
● *Intelligent*
● *Amiable*

Take heed
● *No drawbacks known*

The Briard is the best known of the four French sheepdogs — the others being the Beauceron, the Picardy and the Pyrenean Mountain Dog — although the latter won Best in Show at Crufts in 1970. Briards are good-natured and can be kept happily either as an affectionate family pet or for work around the farm; quite a number are finding their way into the show ring.

Size
Height: dog 23-27in (58.5-68.5cm); bitch 22-25½in (56-65cm).

Exercise
Regular, and not just a walk around the park.

Grooming
Although the Briard is reputed to take pride in keeping itself clean, that task should be augmented by frequent, careful grooming from its devoted owner(s).

Feeding
Recommended would be 20-33oz (587-936g) of a branded, meaty product with biscuit added, or 3-5 cupfuls of a dry food, complete diet, mixed in the proportion of 1 cup of feed to ½ cup of hot or cold water.

Origin and history
The Briard is thought to have originated in the Brie area of France, where it is also known as the Berger de Brie or Chien de Brie. It has been known since the twelfth century. There is an entertaining fourteenth century French legend of how the Briard was given its name. In the year 1371 Sir Aubry de Montdidier was assassinated. His killer was hunted down by his dog, and it was ordained by the king that a battle should take place between the man, named Macaire, and the dog. The battle took place on the Isle of Notre Dame, and the dog proved the victor. Macaire then admitted his crime and was beheaded. It is likely that from then on the Briard became known as the Chien d'Aubry, and a shield sculpted in stone was placed in the church at Montdidier, bearing a likeness of a dog's head that looks similar to the Briard of today. Those who do not believe that the Briard originated in Brie claim that the name Briard is a distortion of Chien d'Aubry.

SHOW STANDARD
General appearance. A dog of rugged appearance; supple, muscular and well proportioned, gay and lively.
Colour. All solid colours are correct except those mentioned below. The darker shades are preferred. Incorrect colours are white, chestnut, mahogany and bicolour. Bicolour should not be confused with the slightly lighter shading at the extremities due to the beginnings of uneven pigmentation. This lighter shading should be of the same tone as the rest of the coat, e.g. light fawn on dark fawn, light grey on dark grey. Occasional white hairs through the black coat are acceptable and do not designate a bicolour.
Head and skull. Head strong, fairly long with a well-defined stop placed exactly mid-way in the length of the head. The head should carry hair forming moustache, beard and eyebrows that slightly veil the eyes. The muzzle should be neither narrow nor pointed. The nose should be large square, and always black, no matter what colour the dog. The forehead slightly rounded, the skull rectangular in shape.
Tail. Long, well covered with hair and with an upward hook at the tip that forms the letter 'J'. Carried low and deviating to neither one side nor the other. The bone of the tail should reach at least to the point of the hock.
Feet. Strong and slightly rounded, about mid-way between a cat foot and a hare foot. Nails should always be black. Pads should be firm and hard, and the toes close together.

Below: A Briard suckles her pups. This French sheepdog is used for herding, and it also makes an affectionate family pet. It is good-natured, easy to train and is very successful as a show dog.

The name of the Bouvier des Flandres
stems from the French word for a cowherd
or oxherd, reflecting its function
as a working dog in the later nineteenth
century. The fact that the Bouvier's
coat — rough, tousled and
unkempt in appearance —
requires regular brushing
is perhaps reflected in another
early name for the breed:
Vuilbaard or 'dirty beard'.

Bouvier des Flandres

It is believed that the Briard was
first brought into
North America by either the
Marquis de Lafayette or
Thomas Jefferson, both heroes of
the American Revolution of the
late eighteenth century. No litter was registered with the AKC
until 1922; foundation of the Briard Club
followed in 1928

Briard

HUNGARIAN VIZSLA

Good points
● *First-class gundog*
● *Makes an excellent family pet*

Take heed
● *No drawbacks known*

The Vizsla is Hungary's national dog and one of the purest breeds in the world. It is an excellent all-purpose gundog with a keen nose, well able to point, set and retrieve. Despite its hunting abilities it adapts happily to life as a family pet, and its temperament is sound.

Size
Height at withers: dog 22½-25in (57-63.5cm); bitch 21-23½in (53-60cm). Weight: 48½-66lb (22-30kg).

Exercise
Needs plenty of vigorous exercise.

Grooming
Regular brushing will keep the coat in a healthy condition.

Feeding
Recommended would be 20-33oz (587-936g) of a branded, meaty product with biscuit added, or 3-5 cupfuls of a dry food, complete diet, mixed in the proportion of 1 cup of feed to ½ cup of hot or cold water.

Origin and history
The Hungarian Vizsla was no doubt developed by the Magyar nobles and great care has been taken to avoid introducing new blood. It is a pure breed of outstanding ability and quality.

SHOW STANDARD
General appearance. A medium-sized dog of distinguished appearance, robust and not too heavily boned.
Colour. Russet gold. Small white marks on chest and feet, though acceptable, are not desirable.
Head and skull. The head should be gaunt and noble. The skull should be moderately wide between the ears with a median line down the forehead and a moderate stop. The muzzle should be a little longer than the skull and, although tapering, should be well squared at the end. The nostrils well developed, broad and wide. The jaws strong and powerful. The lips should cover the jaws completely and be neither loose nor pendulous. The nose should be brown.
Body. The body is strong and well proportioned with a short back and high withers.
Tail. Of moderate thickness, set rather low with one-third docked off. Whilst the dog is moving it should be held horizontally.
Feet. Rounded with toes short, arched and well closed. A cat-like foot is desirable, and hare foot is objectionable. Nails short, strong and a shade darker in colour than the coat; dew-claws should always be removed.

Above: The Hungarian Vizsla is one of the purest breeds remaining in the world and is an excellent, all-purpose gundog.

SLOVAKIAN KUVASZ
(Tsuvatch)

Good points
● *Brave*
● *Intelligent*
● *Keen, alert watchdog*
● *Acute hearing*

Take heed
● *Predominantly a working dog and guard*

The Slovakian Kuvasz is a lively and intelligent dog, ever watchful, and with acute hearing. Its characteristics are similar to those of the Hungarian Kuvasz.

Size
Height at shoulder is around 24in (61cm), but should not exceed 28in (71cm) for a dog, 26in (66cm) for a bitch.

Exercise
Needs plenty of vigorous exercise to stay healthy.

Grooming
Regular brushing is necessary to keep the coat in good, clean condition.

Feeding
Thirteen-20oz (369-587g) of a branded, meaty product with biscuit added in equal part by volume, or 1¾-3 cupfuls of a dry food, complete diet, mixed in the proportion of 1 cup of feed to ½ cup of hot or cold water.

Origin and history
The Slovakian Kuvasz is little known outside its own country. It would seem to be related to the Hungarian Kuvasz and bears resemblance also to the Owczarek Podhalanski, an ancient Polish herding breed. Indeed, Bo Bengtson and Ake Wintzell in their *Dogs of the World* suggest that the three breeds could be said to be local varieties in their respective countries of the same herding breed. The Polish and Slovakian types are sometimes known as 'Tatry' dogs, after the mountain range that stretches through both countries and where each has existed for a long time.

SHOW STANDARD
There is not a recognized standard in the United Kingdom for this breed. However, the most desirable colour is certainly pure white. (White animals were always desired by huntsmen, as their colour would distinguish them from their prey.)

HUNGARIAN KUVASZ

Good points
● *Excellent guard*
● *Loyal*

Take heed
● *Tends to be a one-person dog*

The Hungarian Kuvasz may be kept as a pet and is loyal and devoted to its owner and family. It is, however, essentially a guard and will be ever watchful for intruders. It is an intelligent dog, and its name comes from a Turkish word meaning 'guardian of the peace'. It is a natural herder and has been used for big game hunting. However, its role in life is predominantly that of protector.

Size
Height at withers: dog 28-29½in (71-75cm); bitch 26-27½in (66-70cm). Weight: dog 88-115lb (39.9-52.2kg); bitch 66-93lb (30-42.2kg).

Exercise
Needs plenty of exercise to stay healthy.

Grooming
Regular brushing will keep the coat in good condition.

Feeding
Recommended would be 20-33oz (587-936g) of a branded, meaty product with biscuit added, or 3-5 cupfuls of a dry food, complete diet, mixed in the proportion of 1 cup of feed to ½ cup of hot or cold water.

Origin and history
The Kuvasz has existed in Hungary for centuries, and as early as the 1490s it was protecting Hungarian nobility against possible assassins. It became known as the guard dog of the privileged, only the high-born being permitted to keep one. It is a breed that has to date attained greater popularity in the United States than in the United Kingdom, where there are very few.

SHOW STANDARD
General appearance. A big dog of nobility and power. The various parts of the body are well proportioned, neither excessively long nor too compact. The body outline is roughly square. The muscles are lean, the bone structure is strong without coarseness. Joints are lean. The regular positioning of the limbs, the deep chest, the slightly hollowed croup, allow the Kuvasz to work tirelessly. The teeth are very strong. The coat is rough and wavy in a way that characterizes the breed.
Colour. Most often this is white, although the less common ivory is acceptable at present.
Head. The most attractive feature of the Kuvasz, the head denotes nobility and power. The nose is pointed and black, as are the inner lips and eye-rims. The bridge is long, broad and straight. The lips fit closely to the gums and have a saw-toothed closure. The muzzle tapers from base to nose but must not be too pointed at the tip. The forehead medial furrow continues to the muzzle. The teeth are well developed, regular and strong; the jaws close in a scissor bite. The stop is gently sloping and broadly curved. The skull is long but not pointed, of medium width, with a broad occiput. The ears are set on fairly high, close to the rather flat skull. The supra-orbital ridges are of moderate development.
Tail. Set on quite low, a continuation of the croup. It hangs down approximately to the height of the hocks; the tip is curved slightly upward but without forming a ring. When the Kuvasz is excited or alerted, the tail is held above loin level.
Feet. The hindfeet are longer than the forefeet but just as strong. The pads are tight and elastic, the nails well developed and slate grey in colour. Dew-claws must be removed.

Below: The Hungarian Kuvasz is a natural herder and makes an excellent guard. It has also been used for big game hunting.

A dog resembling the Hungarian
Vizsla is shown on a Magyar rock carving
dating from around 1000 AD, but the
Vizsla became known outside its native
country only after World War II, when
many dogs were taken out of Hungary
by refugees.

Hungarian Vizsla

Slovakian Kuvasz (Tsuvatch)

A grave decline in the indigenous
Hungarian Kuvasz breed, caused by two world wars
and a Communist takeover, has fortunately been
outweighed by increased
interest abroad in
recent years.

Hungarian Kuvasz

BERNESE MOUNTAIN DOG
(Bernese Sennenhund)

Good points
- Beautiful
- Easily trained
- Excellent watchdog
- Good with other animals and people
- Suitable as a pet

Take heed
- No drawbacks known, but it is a big dog to have around the place

The Bernese Mountain Dog is the most internationally known of the four Swiss mountain dogs, the others being the Great Swiss Sennenhund (or Mountain Dog), the Appenzell Sennenhund and the Entlebuch Sennenhund. It is used as both draught dog and companion in its country of origin, but elsewhere it is gaining popularity as pet and show dog. It is easy to train despite its size and strength, is loyal, affectionate and docile with both other animals and humans. It is a beautiful dog with something of the Collie in its appearance.

Size
Height at the withers: dog 25-27½in (63.5-70cm); bitch 23-26in (58.5-66cm).

Exercise
Needs a reasonable amount of exercise and is not ideally suited to town life.

Grooming
Regular brushing will keep the coat in good condition.

Feeding
Recommended would be 20-33oz (587-936g) of a branded, meaty product with biscuit added, or 3-5 cupfuls of a dry food, complete diet, mixed in the proportion of 1 cup of feed to ½ cup of hot or cold water.

Origin and history
The Bernese has been used as both herder and draught dog for

Above: Two Bernese puppies showing the white tips to their tails.

centuries, and many a visitor to Switzerland returns with a snapshot of a Sennenhund pulling a milk cart. The types of Sennenhund are named after the regions in which they were found. These have Mastiff characteristics and are believed to have Molossian ancestry. The St Bernard, Rottweiler and Newfoundland are also related.

SHOW STANDARD
General appearance. Above medium size; a strong, active working dog; alert, well boned and of striking colour.
Colour. Jet black with rich reddish brown on the cheeks, over the eyes, on all four legs and on the chest. Slight to medium-sized symmetrical white head marking (blaze) and white chest marking (cross) are essential. Preferred but not essential are white paws, the white not reaching higher than the pastern, and a white tip to the tail. A few white hairs at the nape of the neck and a white anal patch are

Below: The Bernese has been a draught dog for centuries.

undesirable but tolerated.
Head and skull. Strong with flat skull and slightly developed furrow; well-defined stop; strong, straight muzzle; lips slightly developed.
Tail. Bushy, reaching just below the hock. When the dog is alert, may be carried gaily, but should not curl or be carried over the back.
Feet. Short, round and compact.

OLD ENGLISH SHEEPDOG

Good points
- Excellent with children
- Gets on well with other animals
- Sound temperament

Take heed
- No drawbacks known

The Old English Sheepdog, or Bobtail, is an extremely popular breed. It is a devoted friend and guardian of children and has a sound, sensible temperament. It will live contentedly in a fairly small house despite its bulky appearance.

Size
Height: dog 22in(56cm) and upwards; bitch slightly less.

Exercise
Regular walks of average length — perhaps two good walks of 20 minutes duration per day; and, of course, you need a garden.

Grooming
Daily brushing and weekly combing with a steel comb. The hair is brushed forward to cover the eyes. I don't know how, but it *can* see! White parts are powdered for showing.

Health care
Check the ears for canker, and take care that dead, matted hair does not accumulate around the feet. Some Bobtails are born with that stumpy tail; otherwise it is docked to a length of 2in (5cm).

Feeding
Recommended would be 20-33oz (587-936g) of a branded, meaty product with biscuit added, or 3-5

cupfuls of a dry food, complete diet, mixed in the proportion of 1 cup of feed to ½ cup of hot or cold water.

Origin and history
The Old English Sheepdog is often, for obvious reasons, known as the Bobtail. How it came to England is a subject of conjecture, for the breed is said to have evolved through the crossing of the Briard with the large Russian Owtscharka, a dog related to the Hungarian sheepdogs. It was used in England as a cattle dog and guard but nowadays is kept mainly as a much loved pet. Because of the Bobtail's reliability with children, a number have found their way into schools for handicapped youngsters. The first breed club for the Old English Sheepdog was established in the United Kingdom in 1888 and the standard has altered little in the intervening years.

SHOW STANDARD
General appearance. A strong, compact-looking dog of great symmetry; absolutely free of legginess; profusely coated all over; very elastic in a gallop but in walking or trotting it has a characteristic ambling or pacing movement; its bark should be loud, with a peculiar 'pot casse' ring in it. All round, it is a thick-set, muscular, able-bodied dog with a most intelligent expression, free of all Poodle or Deerhound character.
Colour. Any shade of grey, grizzle, blue or blue merle with or without white markings; any shade of brown or sable is considered distinctly objectionable and not to be encouraged.
Head and skull. Skull capacious and rather squarely formed, giving plenty of room for brainpower. The parts over the eyes should be well arched, and the whole well covered with hair. Jaw fairly long, strong, square and truncated; the stop should be defined to avoid a Deerhound face. Nose always black, large and capacious.
Tail. Puppies requiring docking should have the operation performed within a week of birth, preferably within four days.
Feet. Small and round; toes well arched, pads thick and round.

Bernese Mountain Dog

The coat of the Old English
Sheepdog should be profuse
and of good, hard
texture; not straight, but
shaggy and free
from curl.

Old English Sheepdog

TIBETAN MASTIFF

Good points
- *Excellent guard dog*
- *Reliable temperament unless provoked*

Take heed
- *No drawbacks known*

The Tibetan Mastiff bears a strong resemblance to the St Bernard. It is an excellent guard dog. Being good-natured unless provoked, it can be kept happily as a companion/guard.

Size
Height at shoulder: dog 25-27in (63.5-68.5cm); bitch 22-24in (56-61cm).

Exercise
Needs regular vigorous exercise.

Grooming
Frequent brushing will keep the coat in good condition.

Feeding
Recommended would be 20-33oz (587-936g) of a branded, meaty product with biscuit added, or 3-5 cupfuls of a dry food, complete diet, mixed in the proportion of 1 cup of feed to ½ cup of hot or cold water.

Origin and history
The Tibetan Mastiff is regarded as a British breed, but it originated in Central Asia, where its job was to guard flocks. Like other mastiffs,it is likely to have descended from the Greek Molossus.

SHOW STANDARD
General appearance. A powerful, heavy-boned dog, docile and aloof. A good guard dog.
Colour. Black and tan, or golden.
Head and skull. Broad, massive head and smooth face. Perfectly level mouth with powerful jaws. Muzzle of mastiff type but lighter than that of the English Mastiff.
Tail. Set on high, curled over back to one side; very thick and bushy.
Feet. Smooth, large, strong and compact.

PYRENEAN MOUNTAIN DOG
(Great Pyrenees)

Good points
- *Can be kept indoors or outdoors*
- *Easy to train*
- *Family protector*
- *Gets on well with other animals*
- *Intelligent*

Take heed
- *A working dog, happiest with a job to do*
- *Does not like strangers taking liberties*
- *Needs plenty of space*

The Pyrenean Mountain Dog is a natural shepherd dog bred to guard flocks in the Pyrenees. Nonetheless it has become a popular household pet with those who have the space and income to keep such a large dog. Mr and Mrs Prince's Bergerie Knur won Best in Show at Crufts in 1970.

Pyrenean Mountain Dogs are hardy and good-natured and become devoted to the entire family. They are not keen on approaches from strangers, however, and accidents have occurred when show visitors have been tempted to give a pat.

Size
Height at shoulder: dog at least 28in (71cm); bitch at least 26in (66cm). Weight: dog at least 110lb (49.9kg); bitch at least 90lb (40.8kg).

Exercise
Normal requirements. Strangely, for such a big fellow, the Pyrenean will adapt to town or country and be content with walks of average length.

Grooming
Regular brushing will keep the coat in good condition.

Feeding
Recommended would be 20-33oz (587-936g) of a branded, meaty product with biscuit added, or 3-5 cupfuls of a dry food, complete diet, mixed in the proportion of 1 cup of feed to ½ cup of hot or cold water.

Origin and history
The Pyrenean was a royal favourite in the French court before the revolution. It has never regained the same popularity, though it is widely known and frequently exhibited. It comes from the area from which it takes its name and was once used to guard sheep and also fortresses, wearing a spiked collar like that of the mastiff. The breed became known when shepherds found a ready market for their pups with tourists.

SHOW STANDARD
General appearance. The Pyrenean should possess great size, substance and power, giving an impression of an immensely strong yet well-balanced dog. These qualities should be accompanied by a certain elegance resulting from a combination of the attractive coat, the correct head and a general air of quiet confidence. It is of the utmost importance that nervousness or unprovoked aggression should be heavily penalized by judges.
Colour. Mainly white with patches of badger, wolf-grey or pale yellow, and white. These colours are of equal merit, and judges should show no preference for either. Areas of black hair, where the black goes right down to the roots, are a serious fault. The coloured markings can be on the head, the ears and at the base of the tail; a few patches on the body are permitted. The nose and eye-rims should be black. The presence of liver pigmentaion or pink is to be considered a serious fault.
Head and skull. It is very important that the head should give an impression of strength with no sign of coarseness; it should not be too heavy in proportion to the size of the dog. The top of the skull, as viewed from front and side, should show a definite curve so as to give a somewhat domed effect, and the breadth of the skull at its widest point should be about equal to the length from occiput to stop. The sides of the head should be nearly flat and of a good depth. There should be no obvious stop and only a slight furrow so that the skull and muzzle are joined by a gentle slope. The muzzle should be strong, of medium length, and with a slight taper near its tip. The nose should be absolutely black. When viewed from above, the head should have the general form of a blunt V, well filled in below the eyes.
Tail. Should be thick at the root, tapering gradually towards the tip; for preference, should have a slight curl. It should be of sufficient length to reach below the hocks, and the thick coating of fairly long hair should form an attractive plume. In repose, the tail should be carried low with the tip turned slightly to one side, but as the dog becomes interested the tail rises, and when the animal is fully alert, the tail should be curled high above the back in a circle.
Feet. Short and compact, the toes being slightly arched and equipped with strong nails.

Below: Pyrenean Mountain Dogs can adapt happily to town living.

Tibetan Mastiff

Although now seldom seen
in the United Kingdom, the Tibetan Mastiff
was quite well known
during the nineteenth century when
King George IV
imported the breed.

In keeping with its great
size and dignity, the
gait of the Pyrenean
Mountain Dog should
be unhurried, giving observers the
impression of a powerful
animal moving steadily and smoothly, yet well able
to produce bursts of speed.

Pyrenean Mountain Dog

BORZOI

Good points
● *Aloof*
● *Beautiful and graceful*
● *Intelligent*
● *Faithful*

Take heed
● *A dignified dog, not ideal as a children's playmate.*

The Borzoi is an animal of great beauty and grace used in Russia from the seventeenth century for wolf hunting and coursing. Today it is often regarded more as a fashion accessory: the fur-clad silent film star accompanied by two Borzois was not a rarity.

They are dignified, good-natured animals but somewhat aloof and not likely to enjoy playing wild games with children.

Size
Height at shoulder: dog from 29in (73.5cm) upwards; bitch 27in (68.5cm) upwards.

Exercise
The Borzoi needs a great deal of exercise, but remember that this dog is a hunter: it is essential that it should be allowed to run only when far from livestock.

Feeding
Recommended would be 20-33oz (587-936g) of a branded, meaty product with biscuit added, or 3-5 cupfuls of a dry food, complete diet, mixed in the proportion of 1 cup of feed to ½ cup of hot or cold water.

Origin and history
The Borzoi was maintained for centuries by the Czars and noblemen of Imperial Russia for hunting the wolf. During the fifteenth and sixteenth centuries it was crossed with the sheepdog to provide strength, and later with various hounds to obtain more speed. However, it was from the strain developed by the Grand Duke Nicolai Nicolayevitch that the present-day standard evolved. Information on Borzois from the former USSR was sketchy. There would appear to be more Borzois in fashionable major cities of the world such as New York, London and Paris.

SHOW STANDARD
General appearance. A very graceful, aristocratic and elegant dog, possessing courage, muscular power and great speed.
Head and skull. Head long and lean; well filled in below the eyes. Measurement equal from the occiput to the inner corner of the eye and from the inner corner of the eye to the tip of the nose. Skull very slightly domed and narrow; stop not perceptible, inclining to Roman nose. Head fine so that the direction of the bones and principal veins can be clearly seen. Bitch's head should be finer than the dog's. Jaws long, deep and powerful; nose large and black, not pink or brown, nicely rounded, neither cornered nor sharp. Viewed from above the skull should look narrow, converging very gradually to tip of nose.
Tail. Long, rather low set. Well feathered, carried low, not gaily. In action may be used as a rudder but not rising above level of back. From the level of the hocks may be sickle-shaped but not ringed.
Feet. Forefeet rather long, toes close together; well arched, never flat, turning neither in nor out. Hindfeet hare-like, i.e. longer and less arched.

BLACK AND TAN COONHOUND

Good points
● *Fine nose*
● *Good temperament*
● *Strong and hardy*

Take heed
● *No drawbacks known*

The Black and Tan Coonhound is a fast, hardy, strong working hound that, like the Bloodhound, does not kill its prey. It is similar to the Bloodhound in appearance, but you can detect the Coonhound by its lack of wrinkles, which are characteristic of the Bloodhound.

Size
Height at the shoulder: dog 25-27in (63.5-68.5cm); bitch 23-25in (58.5-63.5cm).

Exercise
It is a working dog and needs plenty of vigorous exercise.

Grooming
Regular grooming with a hound glove. Frequent ear inspection is advocated.

Feeding
Recommended would be 20-33oz (587-936g) of a branded, meaty product with biscuit added, or 3-5 cupfuls of a dry food, complete diet, mixed in the proportion of 1 cup of feed to ½ cup of hot or cold water.

Origin and history
The Black and Tan Coonhound is essentially an American breed. It is a close relation of the Bloodhound, being identical in size and often in colour. It traces back from the Talbot Hound to the Bloodhound and the Virginia Foxhound. The Black and Tan is one of six types of Coonhound recognized in the United States and used for hunting opossum and racoon. It is a working hound not often seen at shows.

SHOW STANDARD
General appearance. The Black and Tan Coonhound is fundamentally a working dog, capable of withstanding the rigours of winter, the heat of summer and the difficult terrain over which it is required to work. Judges are asked by the club sponsoring the breed to place great emphasis upon these factors when evaluating the merits of the dog. The general impression should be that of power, agility and alertness. The expression should be alert, friendly, eager and aggressive. The dog should immediately impress with its ability to cover the ground with powerful, rhythmic strides.
Colour. Coal black with rich tan markings above the eyes, on the sides of the muzzle and on chest, legs and breeching; black pencil markings on the toes.
Head and skull. Should be cleanly modelled with a medium stop occurring mid-way between occiput bone and nose. The head should measure 9-10in (23-25cm) in males and 8-9in (20-23cm) in females. Viewed in profile, the line of the skull is practically on a parallel plane to the foreface or muzzle. The skin should be devoid of folds or excess dewlap. The flews should be well developed with a typical hound appearance. Nostrils well open and always black. Skull should tend towards an oval outline. Teeth should fit evenly with a slightly scissor bite.
Tail. Strong with base slightly below level of back line, carried free and, when in action, at approximately a right angle to the back.
Feet. Should be cat-like with compact, well-arched toes and thick, strong pads.

BLOODHOUND

Good points
● *Charming to look at*
● *Good with children*
● *Great tracker and trailer*
● *Ideal family pet — if you have room*

Take heed
● *No drawbacks known*

The Bloodhound is a delightful animal with a nose that is second to none. It follows its quarry but does not kill. Indeed, it is loved by children, who can accompany it on the lead, and is often kept as a family pet. Bloodhounds are popular show dogs, but individuals are still often called in by police for tracking purposes; a number have appeared in films.

Size
Height: dog 25-27in (63.5-68.5cm); bitch 23-25in (58.5-63.5cm). Weight: dog 90lb (41kg); bitch 80lb (36kg).

Exercise
Needs plenty. These dogs have to gallop. Best to join a Bloodhound club if you become an owner, and take part in organized events.

Grooming
Regular grooming with a hound glove. Frequent ear inspection is advocated.

Health care
Bloodhounds are subject to torsion (stomach gases building into a bloat). A large proportion are affected, and it can prove fatal if not treated by a vet within minutes. Best to be aware of this and ready to seek immediate help.

Feeding
Recommended would be 20-33oz (587-936g) of a branded, meaty product with biscuit added, or 3-5 cupfuls of a dry food, complete diet, mixed in the proportion of 1 cup of feed to ½ cup of hot or cold water.

Origin and history
The Bloodhound is said to have been brought to England by William the Conqueror in 1066 and to be one of the oldest and purest of hound breeds. Bloodhounds in the United Kingdom are popular show ring contenders.

SHOW STANDARD
General appearance. The expression is noble and dignified and characterized by solemnity, wisdom and power. The gait is elastic, swinging and free, the stern being carried high, scimitar fashion.
Colour. The colours are black and tan, liver and tan (red and tan) and red. The darker colours are sometimes interspersed with lighter or badger-coloured hair and sometimes flecked with white.
Head and skull. The head is narrow in proportion to its length and long in proportion to the body, tapering only slightly from the temples to the muzzle. Thus (when viewed from above and in front) it has the appearance of being flattened at the sides and of being nearly equal in width throughout its length. In profile the upper outline of the skull is in nearly the same plane as that of the foreface. The length from the end of the nose to the stop (mid-way between the eyes) should not be less than that from the stop to the occipital protuberance (peak). The brows are not prominent, although owing to the deep-set eyes, they may have that appearance. The foreface is long, deep and of even width throughout with a square outline when seen in profile. The head is furnished with an amount of loose skin, which in nearly every position appears superabundant. More particularly, when the head is carried low, the skin falls into loose pendulous ridges and folds, especially over the forehead and sides of the face. The nostrils are large and open. In front, the lips fall squarely, making a right angle with the upper line of the foreface; behind them form deep, hanging flews, and, being continued into the pendant folds of loose skin about the neck, constitute the dewlap, which is very pronounced.
Body. The neck is long, and the shoulders are muscular. The back and loins are strong, the latter being deep and slightly arched. The ribs are well sprung, and the chest is well let down between the forelegs. The legs are straight and large in bone. The feet are strong and well knuckled up. The hocks are well bent and let down and squarely set. The gait is elastic, swinging and free.
Tail. The stern is long and thick, tapering to a point, set on high with a moderate amount of hair underneath. It should be carried scimitar fashion but not curled over the back or corkscrew at any time.
Feet. Should be strong and well knuckled up.

Borzoi

Black and Tan Coonhound

Bloodhound

The Bloodhound's
extremely long ears
must receive regular
attention. Thin and soft to the touch,
they are set on very low and fall
in graceful folds, the lower parts curling inwards
and backwards.

IRISH WOLFHOUND

Good points
- *Marvellous with children*
- *Good guard*
- *Happiest as a house-dog*

Take heed
- *Gentle when stroked, fierce when provoked*

The Irish Wolfhound, variously known as the Wolfdog, the Irish Greyhound and the Great Dog of Ireland, is a gentle giant, fierce only when provoked. It is intelligent, intensely loyal and slow to anger. Irish Wolfhounds do, nonetheless, have a mind of their own, so firm, gentle discipline is advocated in puppyhood.

Size
The minimum height and weight of dogs should be 31in (78.5cm) and 120lb (54.4kg); of bitches 28in (71cm) and 90lb (40.8kg). Anything below this should be heavily penalized. Great size, including height at shoulder and proportionate length of body, is the target to be aimed for. Ideally the breed should average 32-34in (81-86cm) in dogs, showing the requisite power, activity, courage and symmetry.

Exercise
Despite its size, the Irish Wolfhound does not require more exercise than smaller breeds, but it should have ample space in which to gambol. Let it have unrestricted play during puppyhood, but do not force it to take lengthy walks, rather allowing it to 'muscle up' by its own joyful activity. Irish Wolfhounds are usually taught both to walk and to move at the trot while being led; as they are so powerful, obedience is essential.

Grooming
Brush regularly and remove long,

Below: Irish Wolfhound puppies need firm but gentle discipline because members of the breed have minds of their own.

straggly hairs from ears, neck and underside with finger and thumb. This is a natural-looking breed that is not difficult to groom.

Feeding
At least 33oz (936g) of a branded, meaty product with biscuit added, or 5 cupfuls of a dry food, complete diet, mixed in the proportion of 1 cup of feed to ½ cup of hot or cold water.

Origin and history
The Irish Wolfhound is the national dog of Ireland, and its original role was to kill wolves. It is spoken of in many legends, but it almost certainly came from Greece with the invading Celts, circa 279 BC. The best-known story of an Irish Wolfhound concerns the dog Gelert, given as a gift to Llewellyn, Prince of Wales, by King John of England around 1210. Prince Llewellyn went hunting, leaving the faithful Gelert in charge of his baby son. On his return he could see only Gelert, with blood on its mouth, and, thinking it had killed the child, he drew his sword and slew the dog. It was only then that he saw, nearby, the body of a wolf, and heard the happy chuckle of his child. Gelert had killed the wolf and saved the child. Full of remorse, Prince Llewellyn ordered a statue to be erected in memory of Gelert, and the dog's name has lived on through the centuries.

SHOW STANDARD
General appearance. The Irish Wolfhound should not be quite so heavy or massive as the Great Dane; but it should be more so than the Deerhound, which in general type it should otherwise resemble. Of great size and commanding appearance; very muscular, strongly though gracefully built, movements easy and active; head and neck carried high; the tail carried with an upward sweep with a slight curve towards the extremity.
Colour. The recognized colours are grey, brindle, red, black, pure white, fawn or any colour that appears in the Deerhound.
Head and skull. Long; the frontal bones of the forehead very slightly raised, very little indentation

between the eyes. Skull not too broad. Muzzle long and moderately pointed.
Tail. Long and slightly curved; of moderate thickness and well covered with hair.
Feet. Moderately large and round, turned neither inwards nor outwards. Toes well arched and closed. Nails very strong and curved.

DEERHOUND
(Scottish Deerhound)

Good points
- *Graceful and beautiful*
- *Happy to be with humans and to please*
- *Loving*
- *Sound temperament*

Take heed
- *No drawbacks known, if you have sufficient space*

The Deerhound is a creature of grace and beauty, mentioned frequently in the novels of Sir Walter Scott. It is strong and healthy, anxious to please and asks no more than to be its owner's devoted companion.

Size
Weight: dog 85-105lb (38.5-47.6kg); bitch 65-80lb (29.5-36.3kg). Height at shoulder: dog not less than 30in (76cm); bitch 28in (71cm).

Exercise
Needs a great deal of exercise.

Grooming
Requires very little trimming, just removal of extra shaggy hairs for show, and regular brushing. Its coat is weather-resistant, and this breed rarely feels the cold — in fact, it seems to prefer it.

Feeding
Recommended would be 20-33oz (587-936g) of a branded, meaty product with biscuit added, or 3-5 cupfuls of a dry food, complete diet, mixed in the proportion of 1 cup of feed to ½ cup of hot or cold water. Will need extra feed if used for coursing.

Origin and history
The Deerhound was purpose-bred to hunt with its master by day and to grace his sumptuous dining hall at night. With the advent of breech-loading rifles, the need for the hunting Deerhound ceased, as did its popularity. In the United Kingdom it is now kept only by devotees of the breed. It is said that once you have owned a Deerhound, never again do you wish to own another breed. It is truly a gentle giant.

The breed has much of the Greyhound in its make-up, and it seems that until the nineteenth century the Irish Wolfhound and the Deerhound were of a similar type. Today it is easy to distinguish between the two, the Deerhound being a sleeker, lighter dog.

SHOW STANDARD
Colour. Much a matter of fancy.

Above: The graceful Deerhound makes a devoted companion. Its agility and beauty are matched by its willingness to please.

But there is no doubt that the dark blue-grey is the most preferred, because quality tends to follow this colour. Next come the darker and lighter greys or brindles, the darkest being generally preferred. Yellow and sandy red or red-fawn, especially with black points, i.e. ears and muzzle, are also in equal estimation, this being the colour of the oldest-known strains, the McNeil and Cheethill Menzies. White is condemned by all the old authorities; a white chest and white toes, which occur in a great many of the darkest dogs, are not so greatly objected to, but the less the better, as the Deerhound is a self-coloured dog. A white blaze on the head or a white collar should be heavily penalized. In other cases, an attempt should be made to get rid of white markings. The less white the better, but a slight white tip to the stern occurs in the best strains.
Head and skull. The head should be broadest at the ears, tapering slightly to the eyes, with the muzzle tapering more decidedly to the nose. The muzzle should be pointed but the lips level. The head should be long, the skull rather flat than round with a very slight rise over the eyes but with nothing approaching a stop. The skull should be coated with moderately long hair, which is softer than the rest of the coat. The nose should be black (though in some blue-fawns the colour is blue) and slightly aquiline. In the lighter coloured dogs, a black muzzle is preferred. There should be a good moustache of rather silky hair, and a fair beard.
Tail. Should be long, thick at the root, tapering and reaching to within about 1½in (4cm) of the ground. When the dog is still, the tail is dropped perfectly straight down or curved. When in motion, it should be curved; when excited, in no case to be lifted out of the line of the back. It should be well covered with hair on the inside, thick and wiry; on the underside, longer; and towards the end, a slight fringe is not objectionable. A curl or ring tail is very undesirable.
Feet. Moderately large and round, turning neither inward nor outward. Should be close and compact with well-arranged toes. Nails strong.

After a history spanning some 2,000 years the Irish Wolfhound was almost extinct as a breed by the mid-nineteenth century. It was restored by Captain George A. Graham of the British Army who in 1885 was able to supervise the establishment of the first standard for the breed.

Irish Wolfhound

The Deerhound should be shaggy but not over-coated, and never wooly. The hair on the body, neck and quarters should be harsh and wiry, about 3-4in (7.5-10cm) long; that on the head, breast and belly is much softer.

Deerhound

MAREMMA SHEEPDOG

Good points
- *Has stamina*
- *Beautiful*
- *Intelligent*
- *Natural guarding instinct*

Take heed
- *Will treat its master as an equal — this breed is not renowned for obedience*

The Italian Sheepdog, known in the United Kingdom as a 'Maremma', has a double name in Italy. There are two regions claim it as their own — the Maremma (that is, the land that follows the coast roughly from Cecina down to Rome) and the mountains of Abruzzi. In the past some people called the breed Pastore Abruzzese, others called it Pastore Maremmano, thinking that there was a difference between them. About 20 years ago, following a meeting in Florence, the late Professor Giuseppe Solaro drew up the present breed standard; and as both regions were so proud of their sheepdog, it was decided that henceforth it should have the double name of Pastore Maremmano Abruzzese, which made everybody happy.

The task of this breed was never to work sheep, as would the German Shepherd Dog, but to defend the flocks from wolves, bears and thieves.

The Maremma is a dog that cannot tolerate discipline and, although it becomes fond of its master, it would consider it a weakness to show it. The dog will guard the entrance to its master's home but will not lie across his feet. It will not forget kindness or forgive injury and will protect the family.

Size
Some latitude in size is permitted, with a minimum height of 25½in (65cm) for a dog and 23½in (60cm) for a bitch.

Exercise
Exercise is a necessity for the breed's well-being in its formative years, but excessive exercise is not a vital need when the animal is mature. Rather than covering a long distance, their daily walks should be made as varied and interesting as possible, and — despite the fact that they are not particularly obedient — it is important that they should have some off-the-lead freedom. Walking on a hard surface will help to keep the dog's nails in condition. Rain will not have an adverse effect on the Maremma's coat. All it needs after a soaking is a good rub down. The dog will clean itself and soon be gleaming white again.

Grooming
Grooming should be carried out regularly, preferably with a wire dog brush and the occasional use of a good cleansing powder. A bath should be given once a year — more often if absolutely necessary — but this is a scrupulously clean breed that attends to its toilet fastidiously. During grooming the ears should be checked carefully for any possible sign of infection.

Feeding
The diet of the Maremma must contain adequate calcium, which can be given in either tablet or powder form. It is very necessary because of the extraordinary growth rate of Maremma puppies. Two meals daily are recommended for the breed with perhaps some 'goodnight' biscuits. Recommended would be 20-33oz (587-936g) of a branded canned product with biscuit added, or 3-5 cupfuls of a dry food, complete diet, mixed in the proportion of 1 cup of feed to ½ cup of hot or cold water.

Origin and history
It is believed that the Maremma sheepdog may have evolved from the ancient white working dog of the Magyars, and they have been bred exceedingly true to type on the Maremma plains and hills by Tuscan farmers.

The first known record of what is believed to be the Maremma was made 2,000 years ago. Columbella (about 65 AD) mentioned a white dog, and Marcus Varro (116-27 BC) gives a standard for a sheepdog that would seem to describe the Maremma of today.

SHOW STANDARD
General appearance. The sheepdog of central Italy is of large size. It is lithe, strongly built, of outdoor appearance, and, at the same time, majestic, distinguished, sturdy, courageous without being aggressive, lively and intelligent. Any tendency to nervousness to be penalized by show judges. Movement should be free and active, giving the impression of a nimble dog, able to move easily over rough ground and to turn quickly.

Head and skull. The head should appear large and of conical shape but in proportion to the size of the body. The skull should be rather wide between the ears and should narrow towards the facial area. The occipital ridge should be very slightly less than that of the cranial area. The muzzle should tend to converge without showing snipiness. The jaws should be powerful, and there should be plenty of substance in the foreface. The lips should be little developed, close fitting and not pendulous. Pigmentation of the lips and nose should be black.

Tail. The tail should be set low and carried low in repose but should curl into the horizontal at hock level in normal carriage. It may be carried above the level of the back in excitement. It should be well provided with thick hair.

Another Italian Sheepdog, little known outside its country of origin, is the Bergamasco, or Bergamaschi Herder, a working dog descended from the herding dogs of Roman times which have lived and worked for centuries in northern Italy.

KOMONDOR

Good points
- *Hardy*
- *Loyal*
- *Excellent guard*
- *Seldom sheds*
- *Has little doggie odour*
- *Good with other animals (in family)*

Take heed
- *Will not tolerate teasing*
- *Wary of strangers*

The Komondor (pronounced Koh-mohn-dorh — the plural is Komondorok) is a large white dog of imposing bearing, very strong and agile for its size. Nobody can mistake a grown dog for any other breed. It is covered with a full coat falling in tassels or cords and looks like an old-fashioned string mop.

This is a loyal dog whose purpose in life is to guard the property and charges in its care. It does not attack without provocation but trespassers will not be tolerated.

Size
Weight: dog about 110-135lbs (49.9-61.2kg); bitch about 80-110lb (36.3-49.9kg). Height: dog average 31½in (80cm), minimum 26in (66cm); bitch average 27½in (70cm), minimum 23½in (60cm). Of the Komondor it can be said that there is no maximum height, but height should always be taken into consideration with the overall picture of the dog, which should be strong and well balanced and give the impression of vast strength.

Exercise
Puppies are large and active and require a lot of exercise for good development. A grown dog is maintained in good condition on a moderate amount of exercise. In a city this will have to be given on a lead.

Grooming
The Komondor has a thick, heavy, double coat; the shorter under-coat is woolly and soft, the outer-coat longer, coarse and wavy. The combination of the two types of hair forms naturally into tassel-like cords, the cords being a type of controlled matting. The coat feels felty to the touch. It is unique, and once you get used to the adult coat, it is a pleasure to maintain and to live with. It is never brushed or combed. It forms naturally with the owner aiding by controlling the size of the cords in areas where matting is too large: this must usually be done on the ears and the area behind them and especially in areas where limbs join the body.

Bath the Komondor when it gets dirty, wetting the coat thoroughly and using a canine shampoo; rinse thoroughly and wring with towels. A grown dog will take a long time to dry. Cords do not come out when you wash the dog; indeed, they will tighten up with age and washing. The dog requires standard care for eyes, pads and nails. If the eyes or ears run, this can cause staining on the coat.

Feeding
Recommended would be 20-33oz (587-936g) of a branded canned product with biscuit added, or 3-5 cupfuls of a dry food, complete diet, mixed in the proportion of 1 cup of feed to ½ cup of hot or cold water.

Remember that working dogs need more energy than a house dog of the same size. The same general feeding pattern should be used for working dogs, but most of their extra energy can be provided by biscuit, and it is better to increase this part of the diet more than the meat part.

Origin and history
The Komondor has been called the king of the three breeds of working dogs that for ten centuries have been native to the sheep and cattle regions of Hungary. This shaggy-coated dog's story most likely begins with the Aftscharka, a breed first encountered by the Huns when they passed through the southern steppes of Russia. Although remarkably similar to the massive, long-legged Russian herdsman's dog, today's Komondor is a more compact specimen.

The Magyars, who have bred the Komondor for more than a thousand years, are too busy attending to their herds and flocks to concern themselves with keeping track of who begat whom among their magnificent dogs. But pedigrees are of no moment, for the Magyars do not allow their dogs to mate with any but their own kind.

Otherwise, the history of purebred dogs in Hungary is not unlike that of other countries. Reliable records go back scarcely a century. The Hungarian Kennel Club and the Hungarian Komondor Club exercise diligent control over the registration of the Komondor. (The American Kennel Club's standard is, in fact, a translation of the Hungarian.) The salient points describing the strength and the protective features of the Komondor should be maintained, as they are its defining characteristics.

SHOW STANDARD
General appearance. A large muscular dog with plenty of bone and substance. Powerful in conformation.

Colours. Always white. Ideally the skin should be grey; pink skin is acceptable if there is no evidence of albinism.

Head and skull. The head should look somewhat short in comparison with the wide forehead. The skull should be slightly arched when viewed from the side. Stop moderate, muzzle slightly shorter than the length of the skull. Broad, rather coarse muzzle, not pointed. Nostrils wide. Nose black, though a dark grey or dark brown nose is acceptable (but not desirable).

Tail. Continuation of rump line, should reach down to the hocks, slightly curved at tip; when excited, raised in line with body.

Feet. Strong, large and compact; well-arched toes. Claws strong, grey or black; toes slightly longer on hindfeet. Pads hard, elastic and dark.

An ancient Italian breed, believed to have first been
recorded some 2,000 years ago, the Maremma
Sheepdog is an excellent guard, intelligent and
fearless, but extremely independent and difficult
to discipline. It was shown in the United Kingdom in the
nineteenth century, but then disappeared from the show
ring until the 1930s.

Maremma Sheepdog

Although still quite rare outside
Hungary, the Komondor is being
increasingly shown
throughout Europe and in the
United States. Its unique corded coat is fairly slow
to form; the adult coat starts to replace
the soft fluffy, puppy coat at 6-9 months
but may not be fully formed until the age of two.

Komondor

BULLMASTIFF

Good points
● *Affectionate*
● *First-class guard*
● *Good with children*

Take heed
● *Remember its ferocious past; if you have one, make sure it is trained and temperamentally sound*

The Bullmastiff is an extremely strong breed, obtained through crossing the Mastiff with the English Bulldog. At one time it had an almost unequalled reputation for ferocity, but today's specimens tend to be lovable and trustworthy, despite their power and size.

Size
Height at shoulder: dog 25-27in(63.5-68.5cm); bitch 24-26in (61-66cm). Weight: dog 110-130lb (49.9-59kg); bitch 90-110lb (40.8-49.9kg).

Exercise
Needs regular exercise. A child or lightweight adult would not be able to hold on to the lead.

Grooming
Regular brushing will keep the coat in good condition.

Feeding
Recommended would be 20-33oz (587-936g) of a branded, meaty product with biscuit added, or 3-5 cupfuls of a dry food, complete diet, mixed in the proportion of 1 cup of feed to ½ cup of hot or cold water.

Origin and history
The Bullmastiff is said to have been evolved 200 or 300 years ago by crossing the Mastiff with the Bulldog. It was developed to serve as a guard dog against poachers, the bulk of the dog weighing down intruders without actually harming them. It was not until later that they attained their reputation for ferocity, despite novelist Charlotte Brontë's loving references to her Bullmastiff 'Tartar'. Nowadays the breed has become a big softie whose appearance alone would deter. However, such large dogs need skilful handling.

SHOW STANDARD
General appearance. The Bullmastiff is a powerfully built, symmetrical dog, showing great strength, but it is not cumbersome.
Colour. Any shade of brindle, fawn or red, but the colour to be pure and clear. A slight white marking on the chest is permissible but not desirable. Other white markings are a fault. A dark muzzle is essential, toning off towards the eyes, with dark markings around the eyes giving expression. Dark toenails are desirable.
Head and skull. The skull should be large and square viewed from every angle with fair wrinkle when interested but not when in repose. The circumference of the skull may equal the height of the dog measured at the top of the shoulder; it should be broad and deep with good cheeks. The muzzle is short — the distance from the tip of the nose to the stop should be approximately one-third of the length from the tip of the nose to the centre of the occiput — broad under the eyes and nearly parallel in width to the end of the nose; blunt and cut off square, forming a right angle with the upper line of the face, and at the same time proportionate with the skull. Under-jaw broad to the end. Nose broad with widely spreading nostrils when viewed from the front; flat, not pointed or turned up in profile. Flews not pendulous and not hanging below the level of the bottom of the lower jaw. Stop definite.
Tail. Set high, strong at root and tapering; reaching to the hocks, carried straight or curved but not hound fashion. Crank tails a fault.
Feet. Not large, rounded toes; well arched (cat feet); pads hard. Splay feet a fault.

NEAPOLITAN MASTIFF

Good points
● *Excellent guard*
● *Friendly*

Take heed
● *Likes to have a job to do*
● *Make sure the specimen you buy is physically sound*

The Neapolitan Mastiff is a large, imposing dog, usually depicted wearing a spiked collar. It is an excellent guard but is reputed to have a docile and friendly temperament, being unlikely to attack except on command.

Size
Height: dog 25½-28½in (65-72.5cm), bitch 23½-27in (60-68.5cm). Weight: 110-150lb (49.9-68kg).

Exercise
Like most dogs of its size, it is happiest when given a job to do and with a reasonable area in which to exercise. Obviously, it should not be considered by anyone who cannot meet these needs.

Grooming
Regular brushing will keep the coat in good condition.

Feeding
Recommended would be 20-33oz (587-936g) of a branded, meaty product with biscuit added, or 3-5 cupfuls of a dry food, complete diet, mixed in the proportion of 1 cup of feed to ½ cup of hot or cold water.

Origin and history
One scientific classification of the Neapolitan Mastiff puts it in the Molossoid group. It is a guard and defence dog, a police dog and a tracker, of Italian origin, more specifically Neapolitan. Whether Italy's Mastiff ever did battle in the arenas of Rome is debatable, but geographical evidence gives credence to this theory.

SHOW STANDARD
General appearance. The large Neapolitan Mastiff is strongly built, vigorous, of rustic but at the same time majestic appearance. It is robust and courageous, intelligent in expression, and having good mental balance, with a docile, unaggressive character. It is a matchless defender of its master and his property. The general conformation is that of a heavy mesomorph with a body longer than the height at the withers.
Colour. Permissible are black, lead, mouse grey, streaked, sometimes with small white spots on the chest or on the tip of the toes.
Head. Massive with a broad, short skull. The total length of the head is about 35 per cent of the height at the withers; the length of the muzzle should be one-third of the total length of the head. The skin is abundant, forming wrinkles and folds.
Tail. Thick at the root, robust and slightly tapered towards the tip. In repose the tail should be carried as a sabre tail: that is, hanging for the first two-thirds of its length and slightly curved in the lower third. It is never carried straight up or curled over the back, but horizontal or very slightly above the backline when the dog is in action. Its length is equal to or slightly more than the distance to the hock. It is docked to about two-thirds of its length.
Feet. Oval (hare feet) with close, arched toes; the pads are lean and hard and dark in colour. The nails are strong, curved and dark.

MASTIFF

Good points
● *Brave*
● *Excellent guard*
● *Intelligent*
● *Loyal*
● *Quietly dignified*

Take heed
● *Likes to have a job to do*
● *Like many large breeds, the Mastiff is prone to hip dysplasia*

The Mastiff is a large, powerful dog that makes a formidable guard and loyal companion, becoming devoted to its owners. It is suspicious of strangers, and happiest when given a job to do.

Size
Height at shoulder: dog 30in (76cm), bitch 27½in (70cm).

Exercise
Regular normal exercise, but preferably with a purpose.

Grooming
Regular brushing will keep the coat in good condition.

Health care
The Mastiff is a fair prospect for hip dysplasia, which is physically painful for the dog and is economically painful for its owner. Do not buy a Mastiff puppy unless both of its parents are certified to be free of hip dysplasia, and the breeder has the certificates.

Origin and history
The Mastiff is an ancient breed that was treasured by the Babylonians, fought in the arenas of Rome and has lived in Britain since the time of Julius Caesar. In the Middle Ages the Mastiff was used as a guard dog and also for hunting. St Bernard blood has been introduced in an effort to restore the Mastiff to something of the size of its early splendour. Numbers today are fairly low, though the author has come across one or two guarding the traditional British public house with powerful dignity.

SHOW STANDARD
General appearance. Large, massive, powerful, symmetrical and well-knit frame. A combination of grandeur and good nature, courage and docility. The head in general outline gives a square appearance when viewed from any point. Breadth is greatly to be desired, and should be to the length of the whole head and face in the ratio of 2:3. Body should be massive, broad, deep, long and powerfully built, set on legs wide apart and squarely set. Muscles sharply defined. Size is greatly prized, if combined with quality. Height and substance are important if both points are proportionately combined.
Colour. Apricot or silver, fawn or dark fawn-brindle. In any case, muzzle, ears and nose should be black with black around the orbits and extending upwards between them.
Head and skull. Skull broad between the ears; forehead flat but wrinkled when excited. Brows slightly raised. Muscles of the temples and cheeks well developed. Arch across the skull of a rounded, flattened curve with a depression up the centre of the forehead, from the median line between the eyes to half-way up the sagittal suture. Face or muzzle short, broad under the eyes and keeping nearly parallel in width to the end of the nose; truncated, i.e. blunt and cut off squarely, forming a right angle with the upper line of the face; of great depth from the point of the nose to under-jaw. Under-jaw broad to the end. Nose broad with widely spreading nostrils when viewed from the front; flat (not pointed or turned up) in profile. Lips diverging at obtuse angles with the septum and slightly pendulous so as to show a square profile. Length of muzzle to whole head and face in the ratio of 1:3. Circumference of muzzle (measured mid-way between the eyes and nose) to that of the head (measured before the ears) in the ratio of 3:5.
Tail. Put on high up and reaching to the hocks or a little below them; wide at root and tapering to the end; hanging straight in repose but forming a curve with the end pointing upwards (but not over the back) when the dog is excited.
Feet. Large and round. Toes well arched up. Nails black.

Bullmastiff

Neapolitan Mastiff

Mastiff

The Neapolitan Mastiff is only rarely seen outside its native Italy, where it has a strong and enthusiastic following and is regularly shown. In spite of its forbidding appearance, which is sometimes accentuated by close-cropped ears, it is a gentle, friendly animal.

The Mastiff should have a wide chest, deep and well let down between the forelegs, with arched, well-rounded ribs. The dog's girth should be one-third greater than its height at the shoulder, and its back and loins wide and muscular.

GIANT SCHNAUZER

Good points
- *Easy to train*
- *Excellent with children*
- *Fearless*
- *Fine guard*
- *Good-natured*
- *Playful*

Take heed
- *Slow to mature*
- *Wary of strangers*

The Giant Schnauzer is the largest of the three Schnauzer varieties (the others being Miniature and Standard) with which it shares the qualities of good humour, intelligence and devotion. It has been used for security and as a messenger in the armed services; it works well in obedience competitions and is a good ratter — ratting was, after all, the Schnauzer's original job. However, this giant variety is little seen in the United States or the United Kingdom, where the Miniature variety is popular but the Standard Schnauzer less so.

Size
Height: dog 25½-27½in (65-70cm); bitch 23½-25½in (60-65cm).

Exercise
Needs plenty of vigorous exercise.

Grooming
This is a breed that requires a certain amount of care if it is to do its owner justice. Frequent grooming with a wire brush or glove is necessary, and those quizzical whiskers have to be combed. The coat has to be stripped with a serrated stripping comb or the dead hair plucked out with finger and thumb. Ask the breeder for a grooming chart or at least a demonstration before tackling the job yourself — especially if your heart is set on the show ring.

Feeding
Recommended would be 20-33oz (587-936g) of a branded, meaty product with biscuit added, or 3-5 cupfuls of a dry food, complete diet, mixed in the proportion of 1 cup of feed to ½ cup of hot or cold water.

Origin and history
Descended from German sheepdogs and cattle dogs, the largest Schnauzer was evolved through interbreeding with the smaller Schnauzer varieties. It was first shown in Munich in October 1909 under the name 'Russian bear Schnauzer', the breed being classified as a working dog in 1925.

SHOW STANDARD
General appearance. The Schnauzer is a powerfully built, robust, sinewy, nearly square dog (length of body equal to height at shoulder). Its temperament combines high spirits, reliability, strength, endurance and vigour. Expression keen and attitude alert. Correct conformation is of more

Above: The bristly moustache and chin whiskers of the Giant Schnauzer require combing on a frequent basis.

importance than colour or other purely aesthetic points.

Colour. All pepper-and-salt colours in even proportions or pure black.

Head and skull. Head strong and elongated, gradually narrowing from the ears to the eyes and thence forward towards the tip of the nose. Upper part of the head (occiput to base of forehead) moderately broad between the ears with flat, creaseless forehead and well-muscled but not too strongly developed cheeks. Medium stop to accentuate prominent eyebrows. The powerful muzzle formed by the upper and lower jaws (base of forehead to tip of nose) should end in a moderately blunt line with a bristly, stubby moustache and chin whiskers. Ridge of the nose straight and running almost parallel to the extension of the forehead. The nose is black and full. Lips tight and not overlapping.

Tail. Set on and carried high; cut down to three joints.

Feet. Short, round, extremely compact with close-arched toes (cat's paws), dark nails and hard soles. The feet deep or thickly padded, pointing forward.

GREAT DANE

Good points
- *Devoted*
- *Gets on with other animals*
- *Good-natured*
- *Easy to train*
- *Family dog*

Take heed
- *Not the dog to have a rough and tumble with — it might take you seriously*
- *Not renowned for longevity*

The Great Dane is a wonderful companion, devoted to the family, slow to anger and ready to accept other pets. Despite its size it does not object to apartment life, provided it has plenty of walks. It is easily trained. Regrettably this is a breed that is not renowned for its longevity.

Size
Minimum height: dog 30in (76cm); bitch 28in (71cm). Weight: dog 120lb (54.4kg); bitch 100lb (45.4kg).

Exercise
Regular exercise on hard ground.

Grooming
Regular grooming with a body brush. *NB*: the Great Dane needs warm sleeping quarters.

Feeding
Recommended would be 20-33oz (587-936g) of a branded, meaty product with biscuit added, or 3-5 cupfuls of a dry food, complete diet, mixed in the proportion of 1 cup of feed to ½ cup of hot or cold water.

Origin and history
The Great Dane has existed in the United Kingdom for many centuries and is thought to be a descendant of the Molossus hounds of Roman times. In the Middle Ages they were used to chase wild boar, to bait bulls and to guard their master.

Interest in the breed was roused in Germany in the 1800s by Bismarck, who had a penchant for the Mastiff. By crossing the Mastiff of southern Germany and the Great Dane of the north early devotees produced a Dane similar to the type known today. It was first exhibited at Hamburg in 1863, being shown under the separate varieties of Ulmer Dogge and Dänisch Dogge. In 1876, it was decided that they should be shown under the single heading of Deutsche Dogge, and they were acclaimed as the national dog of Germany. This breed is sometimes referred to as the Apollo of the dog world.

SHOW STANDARD
General appearance. the Great Dane should be remarkable in size and very muscular, strongly though elegantly built; the head and neck should be carried high and the tail in line with the back or slightly upwards but not curled over the hindquarters. Elegance of outline and grace of form are most essential to a Dane; size is absolutely necessary, but there must be that alertness of expression and briskness of movement without which the Great Dane character is lost. It should have a look of dash and daring, of being ready to go anywhere and do anything. The action should be lithe, springy and free, the hocks move freely, and the head be carried high except when galloping.

Colour. Brindles must be striped, ground colour from the lightest yellow to the deepest orange, and the stripes must always be black; eyes and nails preferably dark. Fawns, varying from lightest buff to deepest orange; darker shadings on the muzzle and ears and around the eyes are by no means objectionable; eyes and nails preferably dark. Blues, varying from light grey to deepest slate. Black. (In all the above colours, white is admissible only on the chest and feet, but it is not desirable even there. The nose is always black, except in blues. Eyes and nails preferably dark.) Harlequins, pure white ground with preferably black patches (blue patches are permitted), having the appearance of being torn. In harlequins, wall eyes, pink noses or butterfly noses are permissible but not desirable.

Head and skull. The head, taken altogether, should give the idea of great length and strength of jaw. The muzzle or foreface is broad and the skull proportionately narrow, so that the whole head, when viewed from above and in front, has the appearance of equal breadth throughout. The entire length of head varies with the height of the dog; 13in (33cm) from the tip of the nose to the back of the occiput is a good measurement for a dog of 32in (81cm) at the shoulder. The length from the end of the nose to the point between the eyes should be about equal to, or preferably of greater length than, that from this point to the back of the occiput. The skull should be flat and have a slight indentation running up the centre, the occipital peak not prominent. There should be a decided rise or brow over the eyes but no abrupt stop between them; the face should be well chiselled, well filled in below the eyes with no appearance of being pinched; the foreface long, of equal depth throughout. The cheeks should show as little lumpiness as possible, compatible with strength. The underline of the head, viewed in profile, should run almost in a straight line from the corner of the lip to the corner of the jawbone, allowing for the fold of the lip, but with no loose skin to hang down. The bridge of the nose should be very wide with a slight ridge where the cartilage joins the bone. (This is a characteristic of the breed.) The nostrils should be large, wide and open, giving a blunt look to the nose. A butterfly or flesh-coloured nose is not objected to in harlequins. The lips should hang squarely in front, forming a right angle with the upper line of the foreface.

Body. The long, sinewy neck is firm and clean with a high arch. The chest is quite broad, deep and well muscled. The ribs are well sprung and flattened at the side to allow for proper movement. The back is short and tensely set. The belly is well shaped and tightly muscled. The gait is characterized by a long, springy, easy stride with no rolling of the body.

Tail. Should be thick at the root and taper towards the end, reaching to or just below the hocks. It should be carried in a straight line level with the back; when the dog is in action, the tail may be slightly curved towards the end, but in no case should it curl or be carried over the back.

Feet. These should be cat-like, and should turn neither in nor out. The toes well arched and close; nails strong and curved. Nails should be black but light nails are permissible in harlequins.

As a herd dog in Germany in the later nineteenth century, the Giant Schnauzer was known as the Münchener, since the finest specimens were found in the Munich-Augsburg region. Its progress as a show dog has been impeded, especially in the United States, by the long-continuing popularity of the German Shepherd Dog.

Giant Schnauzer

Great Dane

The coat of the Great Dane should be short, dense and sleek-looking: it should never incline to roughness. In the United Kingdom the dog's ears should be small, set high on the skull, and carried slightly erect with the tips falling forward.

ST BERNARD

Good points
● *Adores children*
● *Easy to train*
● *Supremely intelligent*

Take heed
● *Not known for its longevity*
● *Well known for the occurrence of hip dysplasia*

The St Bernard is a gentleman; powerful, but considerate. It adores children and is loyal and affectionate, coupled with which it is supremely intelligent and proves very easy to train.

Size
The taller the better, provided that symmetry is maintained; thoroughly well proportioned and of great substance.

Exercise
Do not give the young St Bernard too much exercise. Short, regular walks are advocated rather than long, tiring ones.

Grooming
Regular brushing will keep the coat in good condition.

Feeding
Recommended would be 20-33oz (587-936g) of a branded, meaty product with biscuit added, or 3-5 cupfuls of a dry food, complete diet, mixed in the proportion of 1 cup of feed to ½ cup of hot or cold water.

Origin and history
The St Bernard is a descendant of the ancient Molossian dogs. It is

Below: A young St Bernard needs regular exercise but should not be taken for long, tiring walks that compromise its development.

named after the St Bernard Hospice in the Swiss Alps, to which it was introduced between 1660 and 1670, and where it became famous for rescuing climbers. One dog, Barry, is credited with saving 40 lives between 1800 and 1810. The first St Bernard to come to the United Kingdom arrived in 1865. The breed had a boost in popularity in the 1950s, when a St Bernard played a prominent role in the British film 'Genevieve', and it was also associated by almost everyone with advertisements for brandy.

SHOW STANDARD
General appearance. Expression should show benevolence, dignity and intelligence. Movement is most important, but St Bernards have often failed in this respect, the hindlegs being especially prone to faults.
Colour. Orange, mahogany brindle, red brindle; white with patches on the body of any of the above-named colours. The marking should be as follows: white muzzle, white blaze up the face, white collar around the neck, white chest, white forelegs, feet and end of tail; black shadings on face and ears.
Head and skull. Large and massive, circumference of skull being rather more than double the head length from nose to occiput. Muzzle short, full in front of the eye and square at nose end. Cheeks flat; great depth from eye to lower jaw. Lips deep but not too pendulous. From nose to stop perfectly straight and broad. Stop somewhat abrupt and well defined. Skull broad, slightly rounded at the top with somewhat prominent brow. Nose large and black with well-developed nostrils.
Tail. Set on rather high; long and in long-coated variety well feathered; carried low when in repose, and when excited or in motion should not be curled over the back.

Feet. large and compact with well-arched toes; dew-claws should be removed.

NEWFOUND-LAND

Good points
● *Excellent guard, but fierce only when provoked*
● *Fine swimmer*
● *Marvellous with other animals and children*

Take heed
● *No drawbacks known*

The Newfoundland is a gentle giant, a protector of children and family that gets on well with other animals and makes a thoroughly reliable companion and guard. It is slow to attack unless provoked.

Size
Average height at shoulders: dog 28in (71cm); bitch 26in (66cm). Weight: dog 140-150lb (63.5-68kg); bitch 110-120lb (49.9-54.5kg).

Exercise
Regular exercise on hard ground will keep the Newfoundland fit.

Grooming
Regular brushing with a hard brush.

Feeding
Recommended would be 20-33oz (587-936g) of a branded, meaty product with biscuit added, or 3-5 cupfuls of a dry food, complete diet, mixed in the proportion of 1 cup of feed to ½ cup of hot or cold water.

Origin and history
The Newfoundland is the traditional life-saving dog, an animal with the overpowering instinct to carry anything in the water safely ashore. It originates from the northeast of Canada, into whose protective harbours fishing boats of other nations have habitually come to avoid bad weather. It is believed that ships' dogs mated with the local working dogs, whose ancestors probably included American Indian dogs and Basque sheepdogs, to produce the Newfoundland. Particularly famous is the Landseer variety, with black and white markings; it is so named because of its portrayal by the British painter Sir Edward Landseer (1802-73).

Above: The excellent swimming Newfoundland is a life-saving dog and will rescue almost anything from the water.

SHOW STANDARD
General appearance. The dog should impress the eye with its strength and great activity. It should move freely on its legs with the body swung loosely between them, so a slight roll in gait should not be objectionable. Bone is massive throughout but not to give a heavy, inactive appearance.
Colour. These are the only permitted colours: (1) Dull jet black — a slight tinge of bronze or a splash of white on chest and toes is acceptable; black dogs having only white toes, white chest and white top of tail should be exhibited in classes for blacks. (2) Brown — can be chocolate or bronze; should in all other respects follow the black; a splash of white on chest and toes is acceptable; brown dogs to be exhibited in classes for blacks. (3) White with black markings only (Landseers) — for preference a black head with a narrow blaze, an evenly marked saddle and a black rump extending on to the tail; beauty in markings to be taken greatly into consideration; ticking is not desirable.
Head and skull. Head should be broad and massive, the occipital bone well developed; there should be no decided stop; the muzzle should be short, clean cut, rather square in shape and covered with short, fine hair.
Body. The topline is level from the withers to the croup, and the back is broad, strong and well muscled along the same line. The chest is full and deep, and the brisket reaches down at least to the elbows. The layback of the shoulder blade is the same as in the much smaller Pug — 45 deg.
Tail. Should be of moderate length, reaching down a little below the hocks. It should be of fair thickness and well covered with hair but not to form a flag. When the dog is standing still and not excited, the tail should hang downwards with a slight curve at the end; but when the dog is in motion, it should be carried up, and when excited, straight out with only a slight curve at the end. Tails with a kink are very objectionable.
Feet. Should be large and well shaped. Splayed or turned-out feet are objectionable.

In both the United Kingdom and the United States St Bernard clubs are among the oldest established speciality clubs: that of America was founded in 1888, the year after the Zurich Congress set an International Standard for the perfection of the breed.

St Bernard

Newfoundland

*Below: A German Shepherd Dog
has its tartar build-up removed with
careful use of a moist cotton bud
dipped in tooth powder.*

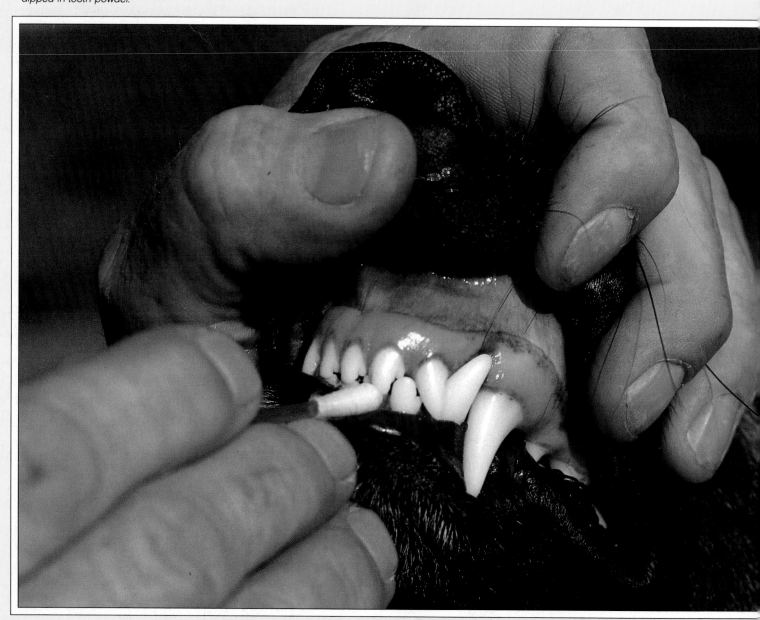

146

Part Two

PRACTICAL SECTION

Essential information for everyone who owns a dog or is thinking of buying one.

Dogs have been domesticated for roughly 12,000 years. Believed to have been the first animals domesticated by humankind, dogs had been bred in the pursuit of a wide range of skills and temperament for many centuries before they began to be bred for conformation alone. Their desire to please is a function of their background and of the social hierarchy in which they evolved.

In the modern-day family hierarchy, dogs are quite willing to allow us humans to become 'top dogs' in their lives. Yet it is a sad fact that many well-meaning people bring puppies into their homes without really considering their responsibilities or the basic needs they must provide for if the pet is to lead a happy, healthy life.

A puppy is like a new-born baby: it needs care and attention, especially during its first few months of life; it needs a basket and a corner it can call its own, where it can rest and recover from over-curious children; and it needs good-quality food and the right sort of exercise for its growing body. And, as it matures, it will benefit from discipline and sensible training, so that it can become a responsible and well-loved companion for its owners.

Just as expectant mothers and anxious fathers-to-be need sound, practical advice to help them prepare for their 'happy event', so prospective dog owners should know something of the tasks and possible problems that will face them. It is to provide such basic advice that this part of the book has been prepared. It consists of six chapters written by acknowledged experts in the dog world.

The first chapter raises the all-important question of what sort of dog to choose and suggests some of the points the would-be dog owner should consider before finally making a choice. This is followed by a detailed account of how to feed and exercise a dog to keep it in tip-top condition. The all-important subject of training is covered in the third chapter by an experienced dog trainer and veterinarian who recommends that basic discipline should be instilled in the very young pup by the owner acting as a substitute 'pack leader'. All the standard training routines are described and clearly illustrated, including general advice on the use of whistles and hand signals.

Grooming and health care are the subjects of the next chapter, which explains first how to keep a dog looking smart and then how to safeguard its health; this chapter includes sections on vaccinations, regular health checks, common diseases and ailments, first-aid measures and the correct way to give medicines.

For owners with their sights set on entering their dogs in the show ring, Chapter 5 gives detailed information on how shows are organized, what all those confusing terms really mean, how to buy, care for and train a show dog, and how to make show day an enjoyable and trouble-free experience for owner and dog alike. How to breed dogs is covered in the final chapter, which details the breeding cycle of the bitch, the timing and mechanism of mating, how the owner can assist at the time of birth, aftercare of the puppies and advice on the various forms of contraception available.

1

CHOOSING
A
DOG

There are few more pleasurable outings than going to buy a pup; yet too many irresistible and eager-to-please puppies, bought more out of whim than wisdom, are languishing in cages in animal shelters, waiting for a second chance to make some fortunate human happy. Such puppies come to grief for many reasons: The persons who bought them gave too little thought to a breed's disposition and exercise needs, they did not consider the wishes of other family members, or they ignored the regulations of a landlord or other authority.

Granted, there are times when a change in circumstances is unavoidable and even those dogs bought with the best intentions cannot always remain with their original owners. Misfortunes aside, however, prospective dog owners must realize when choosing a dog that they are assuming responsibility for a life — a life that will need proper feeding, exercise, comfort, veterinary care and, most important of all, love. Without the latter no dog can reach its true potential and no human can enjoy the matchless devotion of a happy and well-adjusted canine companion.

Think before you buy
There are several questions to consider before choosing a dog. Will one of the toy breeds be better suited for your house or apartment than a medium- or a large-sized dog? Do you have the patience and time to devote to a long-haired dog that will need regular maintenance? Would you be happier with a short-haired breed that will look smart on one or two brushings a week? Do you want a lap dog or a guard dog? Do you have room and energy enough to keep a dog that will

Above: A happy Bernese Mountain dog and its owner: this is clearly an ideal pet-owner relationship based on mutual trust and affection.

Left: English Setter puppies look adorable, but they will later need plenty of exercise. Consider such factors before purchasing.

need considerable exercise?

Breeds like the Golden, the Labrador and other retrievers are ideal all-purpose dogs for a family in which Dad may want a companion to take on a day's shooting, the kids want a dog to romp with, and Mum wants a sizeable dog for protection around the house and for company on walks. A few of the larger breeds, like the Airedale, do not need a great deal of space despite their size. What's more, they look sufficiently forbidding to the uninvited guest.

Toy dogs are devoted companions and, in spite of their diminutive size, make excellent watchdogs that behave as if they

would defend their homes without a thought for their own safety. They are superb dogs for town dwellers, the elderly and those who do not cherish the thought of long daily treks in the outback. Toys are not, however, always as readily house trained as larger dogs are; nor are they always suitable for young children who may treat them as playthings, not realizing that what is fun for a small child may be painful for an even smaller dog.

Boxers adore children and so do St Bernards, Old English Sheepdogs and the smaller Cavalier and King Charles spaniels — to name but a few of the other breeds that are fond of youngsters. In fact, most dogs have an affinity for children, especially when dog and child grow up together from puppyhood.

In your search for a dog, do not fret if you meet one whose personality holds little appeal. You may not get on with all kinds of people. Similarly, there will be dogs whose temperaments and characteristics clash with yours — and others with which you will develop an immediate and lasting rapport.

A pet or a show dog?
If you have decided on a certain breed of dog, you should then decide — if you have not done so already — what function you expect that dog to fulfil. Will its responsibilities be limited to lounging by the fireside, barking at strange noises in the vicinity of your house and accompanying you on daily walks through the fields and trips to the post office? Will you expect it, in addition, to flush game on brisk autumn days? Or do you hope that it will come back to home and hearth trailing clouds of glory from the show ring?

Persons who want a dog solely for companionship most often choose a 'pet-quality' animal. The term pet-quality — a rather condescending designation — is applied to dogs that have some cosmetic liability that argues against their breeding or showing success. A pet-quality dog may have a nose that is a bit too long or a muzzle that is not broad enough or hocks that are not sufficiently angulated or some other 'fault' or minor constellation of faults that do not amount to anything as far as its life expectancy or ability to provide true-blue companionship are concerned.

If you want a dog to assist you on game-slaying expeditions, you should look for breeds — or strains within breeds — that are apt to be skilled in, because they have been bred for, the killing fields. A hunter looking for a Labrador Retriever, for example, would not be interested in the same kind of Labrador as a person who wants a dog for the show ring.

Although breeders generally ask prospective buyers whether they want a show dog or a pet, persons who are looking for a show dog should make that clear when they go to inspect pups. Many first-time buyers who were not interested in showing when they purchased their puppies suddenly become flush with pride in their dogs and mistakenly assume they are likely show candidates simply because they are pedigreed. In truth, the majority of pedigreed dogs are not show-quality — if by 'show-quality' one means 'good enough to earn their championships'. Disappointment and even recriminations can follow when naive owners who have purchased a pet-quality dog at a pet-quality price enter a show and discover that their dog falls well below the standard for its breed.

Although puppies are ready to leave their mothers between eight and ten weeks of age, most breeders are hard put to determine which animals have show potential at such a tender age. Therefore, breeders usually hold on to promising pups in the hope that they will develop along show lines. If you want to be certain of purchasing a show dog, you may have to dispense with the joys and tribulations of coping with those first six months or so of puppyhood.

A dog or a bitch?

Some people — because of personal inclination or prior experience — prefer male or female dogs as pets; but either sex, when given love and attention, will make a charming companion. The cost of spaying a female dog is one-third to one-half more than the cost of neutering a male, but cost is a small consideration compared to function in choosing a dog of either sex.

Only those persons interested in breeding dogs should consider keeping an unspayed female or an unneutered male. Aside from the possibility that they threaten to increase the surplus animal population, there are other

reasons why they make less suitable pets.

Bitches come into season twice a year and each of those 21-day 'heats' can seem like an eternity. Not only are you liable to find a motley crew of male dogs hanging about your yard, but your complacent and devoted bitch will turn into an escape artist and indulge in various ploys in an attempt to get outside to meet them. She will also 'spot', or drip blood, onto your floors and their coverings during this time.

Whole males, which may be said to be always in season, are less manageable than their neutered brethren, more likely to run off in search of a mate, more apt to make sexual advances at your guests and more inclined to 'lift their legs' on the furniture.

Where to buy a puppy

Though it is possible to find an acceptable puppy in a pet shop, you are better advised to buy from a small-volume breeder who specializes in the breed of your choice. A breeder who raises a few litters a year is more likely to have taken the time to socialize those puppies correctly than a commercial kennel that deals in several breeds and raises a dozen or so litters at a time or a pet shop owner that sells hundreds of puppies a year. Puppies that are not handled often enough between the ages of three and ten weeks are less likely to develop into well-adjusted adults than pups that are handled frequently. Thus, the smaller the kennel, the more user-friendly the puppies it produces.

Breeders advertise in the specialist dog magazines, in the classified sections of local newspapers, on bulletin boards in veterinary offices, in grooming shops and pet food stores. Prospective buyers can also meet dog breeders by visiting dog shows, which are advertised in newspapers and magazines.

Above: A puppy's day comprises eating, sleeping, eliminating and playing. This Yorkie pup has seized a captured sock by the neck.

Below: A pleasant setting for a bright summer's afternoon: A dog-proof quoit and a child-proof pup in a walled-in garden.

Above: If man has a better friend, you could not prove it here. The Springer Spaniel is all eyes, tongue, attention and willingness.

A healthy puppy

A puppy's eyes should be bright and clear, its nose cool and slightly damp, its ears free of wax or dirt, its body soft and smooth, perhaps a little lean, but not skinny. Its coat should be free of bald patches, scabs, or tiny specks of black dirt, and the area around its tail free of dirt or discolouration.

How much will a puppy cost?

Price is normally a function of quality, supply, demand, geography and the age of the puppy. A show-quality dog in London, New York, or southern California is going to cost more — a lot more — than a pet-quality dog of the same breed in the smaller towns of the United Kingdom or the United States.

You can estimate what you might expect to pay for a pet-quality dog in a number of breeds by reading the 'Pets' section of the classified columns in the newspaper. The price of a show-quality dog, which is some multiple of the price of a pet, can best be determined by talking to several persons working with the breed(s) in which you are interested.

The purchase price is not the only cost encountered in buying a puppy. New owners also have to pay for a veterinary inspection (a wise investment even if the puppy comes with a health certificate) and, perhaps, for any additional vaccinations a puppy may require. Anyone buying a puppy from a breeder who lives beyond driving distance must pay to have the puppy shipped by plane. Shipping costs vary with the length of the flight, the method of shipping and the airline involved.

The buyer also must pay for the carrier in which the puppy is shipped. Carriers that meet airline specifications can be purchased at dog shows, pet shops or at some airline cargo offices. Secure, durable carriers cost £25 and upwards in the United Kingdom ($25 and upwards in the USA).

Collecting your dog

You will need to have bought puppy supplies before bringing your new pup home. These include a secure collar and lead (or a puppy harness); a sturdy glass, ceramic or metal food dish and water bowl; a placemat to protect the floor or carpet where your puppy will eat; dry and canned food that provide 100 per cent complete nutrition for puppies or for all stages of a dog's life; a stack of newspapers in case your puppy is not completely housetrained; a crate in which your puppy will sleep; a bed made of material that will withstand chewing; a brush, comb, nail clippers and other grooming implements; toys that are sturdy enough to stand up to a puppy's enthusiastic attention and that do not have any attachments that a puppy could chew off and swallow; and a fenced-in yard if you plan to allow your pupy to play outdoors unattended.

Before bringing your puppy home, make sure that your house is puppy-proof. All electrical cords within puppy's reach should be wrapped in heavy tape or covered with plastic tubing; all unused electrical sockets should be closed with plug-in socket guards; all cleaning agents should be secured in cabinets that can be closed or locked tightly; and all bins should be closed snugly.

Below: A Golden Retriever being 'stacked' at home. Stacking is the art of positioning a dog in such a manner as to reflect its good points while concealing its defects from a legally sighted judge who is standing a short distance away.

2

FEEDING AND EXERCISE

A dog's condition is a reflection of its genetic make-up and its owner's diligence. Dogs that are free from inherited defects have been bequeathed, through good fortune or their breeders' diligence, genes governing sound conformation. Dogs that carry the correct weight for their breed and size are being fed and exercised properly. Dogs that are thin are overworked or underfed by thoughtless owners. Dogs that are too heavy are ill-served by persons who allow them to lie about too much then try to put a little spice into their lives by putting too much food in their bowls.

The hand that holds the scoop

People can exercise greater control over their dogs' weight than they can over any other aspect of their pets' lives. The best-trained dog will resist a command on occasion; the most amicable dog may, for no apparent reason, snap at a visitor; and accidents will happen, no matter how thoroughly housetrained a dog may be; yet even the most determined eater cannot feed itself — as long as its owner does not leave food, opened or unopened, within reach. With discipline — and the help of companies that manufacture reduced-calorie dog foods — any owner can maintain his or her dog at its proper, most healthful weight.

How much should your dog weigh?

Most of the breed standards contained in the profile section of this book suggest recommended weights (and/or heights) for adult dogs and bitches of the breeds they describe. Since breeders should be familiar with the standards for their dogs, breeders should also be able to tell you how

Above: Although puppies will share a plate of food, each dog deserves its own bowl to ensure that it is getting the proper nutrition.

Left: A Labrador Retriever puppy has played itself into a temporary state of rest — most likely to be followed by another state of play.

much a dog or bitch ought to weigh. Equally important, a breeder should be able to tell you, approximately, what a dog or bitch ought to weigh at various stages of puppyhood and adolescence and the age at which dogs of either sex attain their mature weight.

Getting started

Whether you acquire an eight-week-old flurry of feet and kisses or a stately and reserved adult, there is a direct and incontrovertible connection between what you put into the dog's bowl and the quantity of muscle and fat that show up on its bones. Before you decide how often and how much to feed your dog, find out what kind of food it is used to eating. If its diet has been

sound, continue with the product(s). A sound diet may consist of commercially prepared foods that provide 100 per cent complete and balanced nutrition for puppies or for all stages of a dog's life, or it may consist of home-cooked rations to which the necessary vitamins and minerals — in the correct amounts and proportions — have been added. If you want to switch foods — which you probably will want to do if you buy a puppy that has been raised on a homemade diet and you would prefer to leave the measuring and stirring to the pet food companies — mix a balanced new food in with the puppy's regular menu in a three-parts-old-to-one-part-new ratio. Every three or four days increase the new food while decreasing the old until the changeover is complete.

Once your dog has attained its adult weight, you can prevent it from exceeding that weight if you weigh your dog once a month and feed accordingly. Whenever your dog gains a pound (or several pounds, depending on its size), reduce its calorific intake by 20 per cent. Weigh your dog again in a month. If the diet has worked, continue feeding the reduced amount for another month and weigh your dog once more. If its weight has dropped below the recommended ideal, increase its rations slightly. If its weight remains at the optimum, keep feeding the reduced amount. If you have several dogs and you want to put one on a diet, you may have to feed that dog separately.

Diet dog food, called 'lite' in the USA, is another way to keep a dog trim. This food contains 20-33 per cent fewer calories than does regular food. Lite and other special-diet foods should be fed only to those overweight, ill, or geriatric dogs whose veterinarians recommend them.

What to feed you dog

Reading a dog food label is like squinting at the last line of type on an eye examination chart. You cannot be certain if you are seeing what you think you are seeing, and even when you are certain, you are reading letters, not words. Letters like m-e-n-a-d-i-o-n-e s-o-d-i-u-m b-i-s-u-l-f-i-t-e.

Fortunately, there are only a few words that a person needs to recognize in order to read a dog food label: '"Brand X" supplies complete and balanced nutrition for all stages of a dog's life'. In the United Kingdom standards are monitored by the Feeding Stuffs Department at the Ministry of Agriculture and they enforce EEC directives. In the United States claims are substantiated 'by tests performed in accordance with the protocols established by the Association of American Feed Control Officials (AAFCO)'.

Different pet food companies speak different dialects on their labels. Instead of 'complete and balanced', some labels say '100 per cent complete and balanced'. In

place of 'all stages of a dog's life', some labels say 'for the growth and maintenance of dogs'. And for 'protocols' some labels substitute 'procedures'. Whatever the case, the label should vouchsafe that the food inside the package has been tested on the inside of a dog.

Let the buyer be aware, however, that all dog food — even the nutritionally balanced kind — is not suitable for all stages of a dog's life. Some food provides complete and balanced nutrition for adult dogs only, or for the maintenance but not the growth of dogs. Such food would not be appropriate for growing puppies, pregnant or lactating bitches, or dogs with age- or disease-related dietary needs.

In the United States not every brand of dog food that promises to deliver complete and balanced nutrition was tested in AAFCO-approved feeding trials. Thus, some labels say, '"Brand X" meets or exceeds the minimum nutritional levels established by the National Research Council (NRC) for all stages of a dog's life'.

What the label does not say is that the food meets or exceeds NRC nutritional levels *before* your dog eats it. What becomes of that

nutrition after it is eaten is anyone's guess. Therefore, the best nutritional guarantees are the ones that say a product was actually fed to dogs and has passed the AAFCO requirements.

Dry, semi-moist, or canned?

Dog food is manufactured in three categories: dry, semi-moist and canned. Dry food is less expensive, easier to store and more convenient to use than is canned food. Dry food also helps to reduce dental tartar to some extent. Canned food is generally more palatable and, since it is three-quarters moisture, is a better source of water than are other foods. (Dry food contains roughly 10 per cent water, semi-moist food about 35 per cent.)

With three categories of food from which to choose, dog owners should not allow their dog to beat around the bowl at meal-time. Indeed, fussy eaters are made, not born. Two surefire ways to turn up your dog's nose at meal-times are by feeding him the same food all

Below: A stainless steel bowl is strong enough to withstand a puppy's attentions and is easy to clean after the puppy has eaten.

the time or by feeding him people food. Give your dog an assortment of foods and brands. The diversity will sharpen his appetite.

Because it is more convenient and economical, dry food — mixed with a tablespoon or so of canned food for additional flavour — is preferred by many dog owners. But no matter what your dog is fed, it should always have clean water available in a clean bowl.

Generic, regular, or 'high-octane'?

In addition to having three categories of dog food from which to select, the dog owner can choose generic, regular, or, in American parlance, 'high-octane' brands and prices. High-octane brands, generally known as super-premium foods, are more expensive and turn a greater profit for their purveyors. But does your dog get more nutritional miles to the gobble? Some authorities think not: 'Most pet food companies have gourmet brands, usually with higher quality ingredients and higher palatability, but that doesn't make them any better', says animal nutritionist Quinton R. Rogers, Ph.D.

Proponents of super-premium foods claim that their higher digestibility results in lower faecal volume and less faecal odor. What's more, the price of super-premium brands might be higher than the price of regular foods, but the cost of using super-premium brands is not necessarily greater because one feeds less of a super-premium food than of the regular variety.

Snacks and treats

Many dog owners resort to snacks and treats to cajole their dogs into eating, but these owners are feeding their insecurities as well as their dogs. Not only are snacks nutritionally deficient on a full-time basis, your dog is soon going to want them all the time.

You can feed some foods to your dog all of the time and you can feed all foods to your dog some of the time, but nutritional wisdom is the better part of knowing which time is which. Again, let the label be your guide. If the label says they are intended 'for intermittent or supplemental use only', then use them intermittently. Do not allow snacks and treats to comprise more than 5-10 per cent of its diet.

How much and when should you feed?

Like people, dogs need progressively fewer calories as they grow older. A ten-week-old puppy requires 83 per cent more dry food, 100 per cent more semi-moist food or 100 per cent more canned food than does a 20-week-old puppy. Compared to an active adult, the ten-week-old puppy needs 206 per cent more dry food, 250 per cent more semi-moist food or 200 per cent more canned food.

EXERCISE

Unfortunately, the idea that all dogs need a great deal of exercise in order to remain healthy has attained much currency. Thus, the

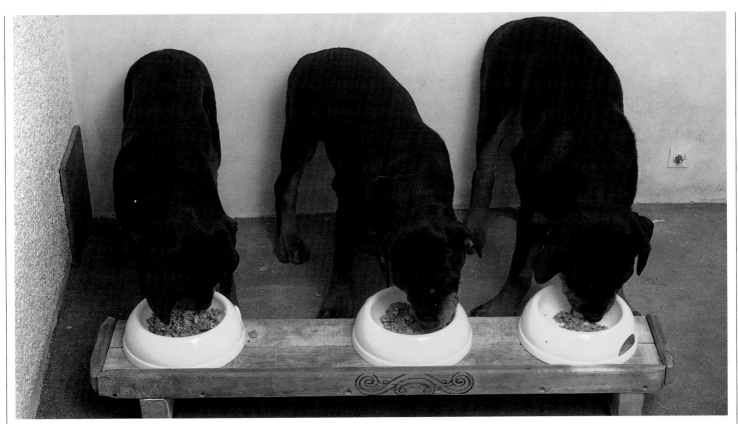

unattractive prospect of plodding around the streets in sensible shoes and foul-weather gear on a wet winter night with a bored dog on the end of a lead deters many otherwise qualified people from seeking canine companionship.

But truth to be told, most dogs are as adaptable as humans in their exercise requirements and, generally speaking, neither human nor dog really enjoys road walking in bad weather. That said, we must also acknowledge that some breeds — particularly those that have been bred for hunting or coursing — will not be happy in an apartment or a small house in town.

Otherwise, the majority of dogs need activity and interest in their lives more so than they need to rack up a prescribed amount of mileage each day. Although dogs and humans are usually the fitter for walking several miles a day, many people seldom achieve this target, yet they manage to remain healthy nevertheless. Dogs are the same.

Being the obliging creatures that they are, dogs will accompany their owners in whatever form of exercise an owner might wish to take. Yet many dogs survive surprisingly well on moderate exercise. For example, a dog imported into a country where quarantine regulations are in force must spend several months in quarantine kennels. There its exercise is limited to a kennel run that is less generous in its dimensions than the smallest garden, patio or yard. Yet dogs routinely come out of quarantine in good show condition. This has been evidenced by the prizes that have been won by some dogs almost immediately after they had cleared the necessary restrictions.

During quarantine each dog receives generous attention from staff members employed at the quarantine facility. Also, dogs take a great interest in watching the staff go about their duties every day. Dogs further have ample opportunity to race up and down in

their runs in response to the actions of neighbouring dogs. In short, their days are not boring, and that is largely the secret of maintaining good health in less than ideal exercise conditions such as those that are found in quarantine kennels. Therefore, owners who cannot provide a great deal of space for a dog but who are willing and able to provide that dog with attention and exercise on a regular basis should not be discouraged from getting a dog. Instead, they should seek out a breed that fits their living conditions.

There is a firm conviction among owners and non-owners alike, especially among the latter, that it is civically irresponsible to walk a dog through the streets so that it can pass urine against other people's gateposts or deposit faeces at the entrance to buildings. In many places, owners who allow their dogs these liberties are subject to fines. There is no doubt that such regulations will multiply in the future,

Above: These glaring plastic bowls are environmentally incorrect and may retain odours even if washed thoroughly after meals.

and quite rightly so. Elimination should take place on the owner's property or some other place from which the owner can conveniently clear the faeces. If a dog is taught to eliminate in its own garden, then daily walks may be taken solely for pleasure, and pleasure they should be for owner and dog as well.

One deprivation that does seem cruel is denying free outdoor access to dogs that are kept in apartments. Even the smallest dog should have the freedom to go in or out on occasion, to sit in sun or shade, to hunt moles or play at

Below: In this Irish Setter puppy feeding mêlée, the tyke at upper left may need assistance in getting to the pan before it is empty.

Daily Feeding Guidelines*

	Dry	Semi-moist	Canned
Puppies:			
10 wks	1.1oz (31g)	1.4oz (40g)	3.6oz (102g)
20 wks	0.6oz (17g)	0.7oz (20g)	1.8oz (51g)
30 wks	0.45oz (13g)	0.6oz (17g)	1.40z (40g)
40 wks	0.36oz (10g)	0 4oz(11g)	1.20z (34g)
Adults			
Inactive	0.32oz (9g)	0.4oz(11g)	1.0oz (28g)
Active	0.36oz (10g)	0.4oz (11g)	1.20z (34g)
Pregnant	0.45oz (13g)	0.6oz (17g)	1.4oz (40g)
Lactating	1.00oz (28g)	1.3oz (37g)	3.3oz (93g)

*Adapted from Nutrient Requirements of Dogs, National Research Council (USA), 1986.

Ounces are per pound of body weight. Note these amounts may be lower than those specified in the feeding instructions on the package.

jungles. The dog that can only be taken out on a lead, however dutiful its owner may be in this regard, spends all its time under human domination. A tiny patch of garden, securely fenced, provides some element of novelty and pleasure in a dog's routine; and it provides the much needed opportunity for a dog to be an independent animal, instead of a perpetual extension of its owner. Free but secure outdoor access is essential to the physical and mental well-being of any dog.

Most dogs like to keep busy, especially small terriers and breeds that were bred to function as guard dogs. They enjoy having access to all the rooms of a house or apartment and dashing from one door to another to ward off imagined intruders. Because two dogs will exercise each other in these pursuits, and in play fights or trials of strength of many kinds, persons with enough room for more than one dog should consider the possibility of adding another member to the family.

Dogs are amazingly adaptable. They can walk for miles on fine, sunny days and do little by way of exercise for the next few days. But this attribute must not be abused by their owners, especially when a dog is young or in ill-health. Young puppies and old, arthritic dogs must not be over-exercised to suit their owners' schedules. And certain breeds such as the Boxer, Bullmastiff, Bulldog, Boston, Pug and other brachycephalic (short faced) dogs must not be asked to take a lot of exercise on hot, humid days. Such breeds wilt easily under stress in hot weather, and for them a long walk is a liability on a warm day.

Exercising puppies

Puppies should not be exercised to excess while they are very young because overexertion can damage immature bones and ligaments. There is a great temptation, especially among children who have a new puppy, to take their newly acquired pet out and show it off to their friends. Apart from the risk involved to growing limbs in this adventure, allowing a child to tug a dog along on a lead is the quickest way to instil bad lead habits in that dog. Puppies are best taught lead control by an adult in a garden. In any case, they should not be out on public ground until their course of primary inoculations is completed when they are three-and-a-half to four-months-old.

Unfortunately, this advice conflicts with the perceived need to accustom a puppy to traffic noise and to meeting new people. The best compromise between these needs is for an adult to carry the

Left: A Poodle puppy at home with food, water, a surrogate friend, a comfortable bed and a few Royal headlines for amusement.

Below: Labrador Retrievers take to water so readily that one suspects they may have had gills at some stage in their development.

puppy in his or her arms for short journeys through busy places so that road walking holds fewer terrors when the dog is old enough to be on the lead.

Avoid formal exercise for large-breed puppies until they are six-months-old. Moreover, it is much better for their development if you can stop them from jumping and climbing stairs and banks during their first six months. It is all too easy to get their shoulders overdeveloped in an ugly way through too much exercise at too young an age.

Other forms of activity
There are several valuable kinds of alternative exercise that are beneficial to dogs. Swimming is an excellent activity for building or toning muscles, especially for helping a bitch regain her figure after she has whelped a litter. Teaching a minimal water retrieve is a lot of fun with any breed and, in addition to building a dog's muscles, familiarity with water may save its life one day.

Teaching a dog to jump over low obstacles is a great game that children can play with their dogs, but dogs that must be kept in compounds or fenced gardens should not be encouraged to jump too high or to scale fences or other obstacles.

Agility tests of all kinds can be devised by sensible older children. These games, which include teaching a dog to crawl under a weighted tarpaulin, to climb short ladders, to jump through a

suspended car tyre, and to catch thrown articles, can fill many hours, and they offer the opportunity for humans and dogs to become far better acquainted and more closely bonded to each other. (A safety note: A rubber quoit is a safer toy to play catch with than is a ball. The latter, if it is too small, may become lodged in a dog's throat and lead to tragedy.)

On stormy and rainy days, there is much activity possible within the home. Play 'hide and seek' with your dog, creeping surreptitiously upstairs, then calling it to come and find you and praising it when it tracks you down.

Make sure you conduct all play with laughter and a merry voice. This will help your dog to learn the differences between situations, principally those in which you both

Above: Cavalier King Charles Spaniel puppies play with a bone, something they may do for hours.

are enjoying a good romp, those that call for aggression and guarding, and those in which you want your dog to perform (or to stop performing) some action in response to your voice.

Animals employ distinctive body movements and, perhaps, scent to signal a desire to engage in play with one another. Humans have to make their purpose clear by their tone of voice. You can use your

Below: An owner demonstrates the correct way to extend a greeting to a puppy: hand open, palm up, under the puppy's chin.

dog's power of scent discrimination, however, by playing a game of 'hunt the slipper' in which you hide the slipper in increasingly difficult places, or by devising a treasure hunt that consists of pieces of biscuit hidden about the house. You can also train your dog to choose which hand holds the goody.

The beginning of training
Simple, elementary obedience tasks are best taught indoors. A dog can learn the commands 'sit', 'beg', 'down', 'stand' and 'down and roll' from someone sitting in a chair. First, though, the person doing the training must teach the animal to concentrate its attention on one person by talking to it, calling it and offering a small food reward.

Where a large covered space is available, one or two active adults can play countless games with a dog, and this kind of exercise involves more profitable interaction with the dog than lead walking. Far more behaviour control is possible when a dog is part of a three-cornered football game than when it is ambling at your side for the third mile of a forced march on a damp road. Play in a confined area develops an attachment between dog and owner. Thus, when you take your dog on a country ramble, it is more likely to stay within range as it walks and to come back when you call.

The less energetic or chairbound person can still do a lot for the dog, especially the young puppy or the old and arthritic dog that is also disinclined to move around. Begin by moving your hands gently all over the dog's body. While you are at your leisure, you will have the opportunity to detect lumps in the skin if they arise, to find knots or tangles in the coat or to see the signs of visitation by fleas or ticks.

Next massage the muscles of the hind- and forelimbs of the elderly dog to increase the blood supply. Examine the feet and nails, teeth and ears, not as a deliberate imposition on its dignity and liberty, which the dog may resent, but as a pleasurable grooming activity of the kind in which monkeys and other animals indulge. You may discover conditions that need attention to make life more comfortable for an old dog, and you will accustom the puppy to having sensitive areas handled, making its future veterinary visits easier.

If you have a growing puppy, it may benefit from having its jaw or ears massaged regularly in the way you hope they will develop. Use your fingers to disentangle knots in the coat instead of pulling at them with the comb you employ in normal grooming. Some corded coats can be encouraged into locks while the dog lies on your lap. Incidentally, a dog's smell at close quarters serves to indicate the animal's state of health.

Having built a close relationship with your dog and having helped it to develop a number of skills during the winter season, you will find your subsequent walks in good weather provide far more pleasure for you and your dog.

3

TRAINING YOUR DOG

Many a would-be dog owner day-dreams of proudly owning a 'wonder' dog like a keen-nosed St Bernard, able to find people lost in deep snow; a beast with the brains of the movie dog Lassie; or a powerful bodyguard such as a German Shepherd (Alsatian). Before you choose your own dog, stop for a minute and think why you really want one at all. For most of us the answer is simple: companionship and understanding. Whatever its breed, shape, size or sex, this is what keeping a dog is all about. If you are thinking of choosing a dog of a particular breed just because it looks beautiful or as 'one-upmanship' to impress the neighbours, I suggest you grow prize roses or put in a new swimming pool instead: you are likely to get more satisfaction and suffer fewer disappointments.

It is essential for the sake of your household and friends that you have some control over your animal. It is equally essential for your pet to learn that it cannot please only itself on its passage through life; dogs that do are insufferably anti-social. Also they do not get the full enjoyment from life that dogs deserve.

Any kind of dog can be trained to a certain degree, but if you want one that will win obedience competitions or act as a shooting companion, make sure you choose a breed with the appropriate mental or physical capacity. Mongrels or cross-breeds are doubtful prospects for such purposes. The expert may be able to get just what he wants from dogs of unknown breeding, but there are few experts about.

Think dog!
Training should be based on 'thinking dog'. I cannot over-emphasize the importance of this

Above: After a dog has been taught to walk at its owner's side, teaching it to turn is a simple extension of that lesson.

Left: While pointing with his right hand, the owner exerts pressure on the lead with his left hand to hold the dog in a sitting position.

phrase. The difference between a dog and a human being is that a person is capable of analysing and sifting complex thoughts, whereas a dog is highly developed in the fields of stamina, scent, eyesight and hearing, but designed to learn only simple things. The trouble with humans as trainers usually stems from their inability to use their superior brainpower from the dog's point of view. They do not realize that training is relatively simple once they anticipate a dog's reactions to a given set of circumstances instead of expecting the creature to behave as they would.

Above all, owners must realize that wild dogs are pack animals and that domesticated dogs inherit behaviour patterns geared for life in

a pack. A dog's instincts are to feed, sleep and breed in a regular pattern dictated by the sun, moon, weather and food availability. As a young pup it plays and fights with the litter in a manner that simulates adult conditions. When introduced to the pack a wild dog at first has its mother's protection but soon learns that father, uncles and aunts are intolerant brutes. Adult dogs and bitches show displeasure by a sharp snap of the teeth, and the pup learns to submit by lying on its back until the dominant animal walks away.

As it grows up in the pack a pup learns who is its superiors, inferiors and equals. If a male, at one-year-old he will probably challenge the pack leader only to be put in his place. This dominance may have to be reinforced from time to time. If he wins he will become leader and allowed to develop the aggressive tendencies required of a pack leader. Bitches develop the same tendencies, on similar but less positive lines.

These biological facts have a direct bearing on your training problems. As a pack animal your dog learns fast by repetition and example and at some stage will almost certainly challenge for leadership, but will be content once its place in the pack is established. In your case your family represents the pack, and you, and maybe other family members, represent the pack leader. 'Thinking dog' again, you must make your animal feel that its place is below you, and possibly other members of the family provided they earn that position in the dog's eyes. Thus all aspects of early training can be related to enforcing basic pack rules. If you accept this few problems will exist.

This broad view of pack laws has enabled me to train many dogs of

various breeds, while making allowance for variations of temperament. I shall develop this theme later on in this chapter, for it is possible to take different dogs through the same phase in training using entirely different tones or types of command yet achieve the same ultimate response. The rules are fairly basic and simple, but the handler must never forget that once known they may be broken or at least bent by the individual dog and handler. The handler who has a good relationship with a dog keeps the capacity to learn and the humility occasionally to be taught by a dog. There is limited scope for dogma in dog training!

Some basic facts
Let us asssume you have decided to get your dog or bitch from a reputable source and are ready to learn to tackle the problems ahead. You will usually get your puppy at eight-weeks-old. It should look active and fit and be one fat bundle of potential mischief. If in any doubt about its state of health, talk to your nearest veterinarian who may prove reassuring and help you relax. This is important, for even a puppy of those tender weeks can sense a neurotic owner, and the indecisiveness of such owners does more than anything to make puppies difficult and unstable.

A two-month-old puppy spends a lot of time sleeping and much time playing. About four times daily it fills its stomach and twice as often empties it. Bearing in mind this routine, you should provide a comfortable basket, box or make-shift den. This must be kept in a place where your puppy can feel safe and rest in peace. Secondly, allow a play area. Thirdly, supply food at roughly regular intervals. Fourthly, at regular and frequent intervals show it a place where it can defecate and urinate at will.

The den
Besides affording a sleeping place, the den (or basket) provides a secure place where the puppy can chew or inspect a bone, old shoe or retrieved article. Actions like this play an important part in the pup's education. If you have children, dissuade them from interfering with puppies in a box; this can make them fractious.

Incidentally, I am against putting puppies in outdoor kennels, as they fret and whine. They do not learn to socialize and integrate, and it is unnatural in terms of pack law for dogs to be alone.

Play areas
Many a kitchen makes a good play area. Here the puppy learns to manoeuvre around such obstacles as the legs of chairs and a table. It may also meet opposition from the family cat, which it will have to learn to respect. This encounter may be painful, but keep 'thinking dog': your pup will be much more circumspect about the second encounter, if there is one, and will therefore not get injured in the future. It must learn by experience.

If you have another dog, pack law applies, and it will be fascinating to watch the fierce show put on by the older dog and the fawning, submissive behaviour of the new puppy, lying on its back and licking the older dog as a sign of non-aggressive intent. As the pup grows in age and confidence, you can gradually extend its play or living area by letting it into the garden or nearby parks or fields.

Feeding times
Feeding times at this early part of the pup's life are very important. These occasions give you a fine opportunity to begin painless training. The rattle of a food dish is good news to the puppy and should be accompanied by high-

Above: At obedience training classes dogs learn proper comportment, and owners learn that it can be a frustrating experience but one that both dog and owner can profit from.

pitched cries of 'Pup! Pup! Pup!' or the pup's name repeated. The creature will learn to respond to your calls within a couple of days. Much later you will substitute 'Come!' in the tone of a recall command, which should ensure instant obedience if correctly carried out. Incidentally, your early high-pitched cries are the equivalent of the high-pitched whines or squeaks often uttered by a bitch when entering the den with food.

At this quite early stage you can also get the pup used to sitting for its food by saying 'Pup, sit!' or substituting its name, at the same time firmly but gently pressing its buttocks on the ground. It will soon learn to come for its food and sit on command before the food is placed on the ground.

Your puppy's brain is very receptive to simple commands expressed in a consistent and repetitive manner. Remember you will get only a token dropping of the buttocks at this stage, and you should ask for no more. But by making the pup learn reflex responses to the commands 'Sit!' and 'Come!' you will save time and trouble later. You are also getting the pup to associate your voice with the important events of feeding times. In these ways, then, you have already begun asserting your dominance over the pup.

Toilet training
A pup is naturally clean in its habits. It first passes all in the den, and the mother cleans up. At three or four weeks it relieves itself during

excursions out of the den, although accidents happen and again the bitch cleans up. Next the pup begins making efforts to get to its place of relief before emptying itself. This pattern continues through life, intervals between evacuations getting longer as the creature matures.

When you obtain your puppy encourage regular visits to the yard or garden, especially in the five-minutes following feeding. If you live in a flat, put newspapers by the back door. Your pup will learn to use these as occasion demands if encouraged to do so by being picked up and placed on the paper each time you can see an action starting.

It is important not to reprimand at this stage, though it is hard not to if you trek though puddles and tread on stools when you enter the kitchen each morning. Think dog, clear up the mess and accept your pup's welcome.

Soon the dog will be clean, in our sense of the word, although in nature a dog and its bowels often become active at dawn, long before we are awake. I repeat, take no positive action against your puppy about these occurrences. Time and training will solve the problem, reprimand will not be understood. It will only cause nervousness and trouble.

A part of the family
Your pup is now established in the home as a member of the family. It is important that all members of the family handle the pup, make a fuss of it and and cuddle it at times. This helps it to feel secure in its new home as part of the 'pack'.

You can try to put a collar around its neck, so that it gets used to the idea. Most puppies do not object if you start this early enough and for short periods at a time. You can also assist at this stage by calling

the puppy's name in a high tone when entering the room, at the same time stooping and patting your knees. You can also say 'Pup, come!' using the same tone and actions; it invariably works and the puppy enjoys it.

Tone of voice
To achieve different results we use different words of command, like: 'come', 'sit', 'down', 'no', 'stay', 'leave', and 'heel'. But just as important or more so is the way in which tone of voice varies according to the command. I have often seen a handler in a fairly advanced class fail to obtain a response from his dog simply because he used the same tone for every command.

Of the two first commands you teach, 'Come!' should be a slower, more drawn-out command; the 'Sit!' short and sharp. 'Down!' is best spoken with the voice low and hard. A similar command is a sharp hard 'No!', which in dog terms means 'Whatever you are doing or about to do, stop at once or trouble will follow'. It is a command of displeasure. 'Stay!' is nearly as positive but less severe. It means 'Continue with the last command until told otherwise'. 'Heel!' is taught later when the pup is able to walk on the lead naturally. The dog is confined to the left-hand side of the handler and not allowed to put its nose much in front of the handler's knee. Success requires practice and patience, and as lessons progress you can teach the dog to walk to heel without the restriction of a lead.

Teaching to retrieve
Most of us want our dogs to retrieve things for us. Whether this is just for fun or for use as a party trick or in recovering game does not really matter. The degree to which you use this natural attribute is up to you, but it is a great game for most dogs. It seems to be a natural development of their instinct to find food and return with it to their den. A young puppy that finds a bone or old slipper will invariably take it to its box. If out in a field or garden, it will tend to bring its find to you in place of the den. Training should develop along these lines.

You can teach a puppy to retrieve from a very early age by throwing something like a furry toy or ball of suitable size a short distance across the room. The pup will naturally run after it and almost certainly pick it up. Saying 'Come!' while you stoop forward and pat your knees rapidly and repeatedly will encourage the

pup to bring it back. When it does, put a caressing but firm hand under its neck and make a great fuss of it with much praise. This can be followed by the command 'Give!' or 'Drop!' or some other of your own choice, and the object should be gently removed from the pup's mouth — never snatched away. You can then put the object out of reach, saying 'Leave!' and prevent the pup from snatching at it. Repeat the process a few times.

As the pup progresses you can insert 'Sit!' into the proceedings just before the pup gives up the object, and already it is learning a smooth sequence of actions in response to commands.

Be patient and stay calm
From two-months-old until its first birthday, a dog is at its most receptive stage of development. But at eight- to ten-weeks-old it is still very young and can easily get bored and tired. I suggest that even if you have a very bright pup you should not repeat the first few exercises more than three or four times without giving it a rest. Five minutes a day are enough at this stage — the time can be increased as the dog's physical and mental capacity improve towards the age of four or five months.

Quite the worst thing you can do at this stage is make the pup apprehensive. Each early training session should be treated as a time for fun. Praise for all things done correctly is very important: your pup is keen to please you and will respond to praise by repeating the exercise with greater enthusiasm.

It is also important not to use any form of reprimand. Your pup will not understand it properly, if at all, and will become worried about the next performance.

Another important point to remember is that your bearing and manner may reflect the stresses and strains that affect your own life. Your pet can sense this and will react accordingly. If you need companionship or sympathy, it will respond easily; but if you are tense or bad tempered or out of patience, you will be well advised to forget about training until you feel completely better, for all training requires patience and tolerance from the handler, especially in the early stages. Also much harm can be done by short-tempered reactions and sharp criticism.

Fitting a collar and lead
Make sure you buy a leather collar that fits. If you slip it on the dog's neck just before its meal, with any luck the creature accepts it without making a fuss. Whether you leave it on permanently or only fit it occasionally does not matter, provided the puppy gets used to it.

When the pup is around five months of age, you should buy a

Below: One's arm is apt to tire from throwing the stick repeatedly quicker than these Golden Retrievers' legs will tire from chasing it.

Below: A check chain, correctly fitted and employed, allows owners to return their dogs' attention to the task at hand when necessary.

chain collar and attach a lead to one end. Such collars are often called 'chokers', but are more correctly known as 'check chains'. 'Choker' gives an impression of strangulation, whereas 'check chain' implies, as it should, the ability to administer a short sharp check to the dog as a reminder that it can no longer always please itself. For training, I do not recommend the use of nylon or leather slip leads and consider them suitable only for the trained dog.

Dog-training clubs

Once your pup has accepted a collar and you are beginning to come to a mutual understanding, I strongly advise those of you in urban areas to find a dog-training club. This will save the amateur much aggravation and will help him to train his dog under the guidance of experts so that the whole process becomes clear and simple. The company of other dogs also helps to socialize your puppy so that it shows no more than curious interest in other dogs and happenings. Such nuisances as aggressiveness towards others or overexcitement in the form of yapping and hysterical barking can then be checked and controlled in the proper manner.

Walking to heel

Assuming that your puppy sits moderately well for food, retrieves, and can now wear a collar, you must advance your control with some 'Heel!' work. With the dog sitting on your left, the check chain should be looped and applied so that the chain extends from your hand over the dog's neck and back underneath. This allows the chain to hang slack when no pressure is applied to it. The dog must learn that if it jerks forward or back the check chain will pull tight and

Above: A properly trained dog walks at its owner's side and heeds commands as if the two were joined by an invisible bond.

cannot be slipped. In fact you should ensure, by jerking at exactly the right moment, that the chain does serve as a true check.

If you walk along slowly saying 'Heel!' all the time, keeping the dog on your left and with the lead in your right hand, you are likely to make a jerky progression, but this will get smoother as the dog begins to understand and obey your command. The chain collar pulls tight only if the dog does not think or tries to escape by pulling forward or backward.

This is an important advance as the animal now has to think about what is required in response to your

wishes. This stage should be carried out as gently as possible, but with firm insistence. Teach for short periods each day until the lesson is firmly learnt.

Once a dog can walk easily on a check chain, you must develop the habit of stopping with the command 'Sit!' and using a jerk of the chain (with as little force as necessary) to ensure that this is done promptly. Then walk on again, giving the 'Heel!' command and repeat it frequently.

Do not allow your dog to urinate on lampposts or excrete on the path. This can be done by moving the dog into the gutter so that it does not foul the pavement and inconvenience human pedestrians.

Teaching 'Sit' and 'Stay'

Your young dog should now be intelligently looking forward each day to its game of 'fetch' with some favourite object. Now introduce a slight variation. Stoop down by it, put a restraining hand under its neck and give a 'Sit!' command. Still restraining it, throw the object but check the puppy, saying 'Stay!' in a low tone. Hold the dog for a few seconds before continuing the 'Fetch' routine as before. Also put your hand in front of its face at the same time as you say 'Stay!'.

As soon as your puppy learns to stay, take your hand a short distance away from its face each time until it learns to stay still on both the command and the hand signal. Make sure that it cannot escape past you if it decides not to listen. If it should move, grab it firmly and positively, replace it on the original spot and start again. If your reactions are not quick enough to stop it, use the check chain attached to your wrist and let the dog come up against the check with a bang — then replace the dog firmly without showing any of

the sympathy you may feel!

Avoid this exercise if you are jaded. Short-tempered action may replace what should be simple persistence. Do not carry on for too long at a time.

Once the lesson is adequately learnt you can begin teaching the animal to sit and stay as you gradually increase your distance from it. If the dog breaks away start again, but nearer to it.

Teaching the 'Down' command

The 'Down!' command is quickly taught as an extension of 'Sit!' You can teach it at an early stage with an apt pupil, but I find it easier with a more mature puppy.

Give 'Sit!' and 'Stay!' commands as previously described. Repeat the 'Stay!' then return to your dog, press the shoulders down with one hand and slide the legs forward to the 'down' position. You should now be saying 'Down!' in a low tone. If the dog tries to get up, repeat the command and add 'Stay!' until the message gets across. I am not in favour of too much pushing with the hands: it is much better to dominate by voice.

Once 'Down!' is understood, extend the exercise to garden or open space and use the sit-stay-down-stay sequence until obedience is second nature. Then move away from the animal and walk around it at varying distances repeating 'Down!' 'Stay!' as necessary. This exercise can be learnt in one day and perfected in three or four days by repetition.

Jumping over obstacles

It is also simple to teach a jumping command such as 'Up!' or 'Over!' Suit yourself which you use, but stick to the same one. Sit your dog in front of a wall, plank or artificial obstruction, give a 'Stay!' command, then walk to the other

Teaching Sit/Stay

1 *Teaching your dog to sit and stay is a good basic exercise that may prevent a roadside accident or be the first step to more advanced routines. With your dog sitting, hold a hand in front of its face.*

2 *Still holding your hand up, give a 'Stay!' command and move round in front of the dog. Keep a firm hold on the check chain and be ready to jerk it should the dog break away. If it does, start again.*

3 *When you feel the dog understands your wishes, release the lead and move away slowly. Remember to keep your hand up high where the dog can see it clearly and repeat the 'Stay!'*

command as often as needed. As your dog gets used to this routine, you can increase the distance you move back each time. Try this for short periods only to avoid stress to you and your dog.

side of the obstruction repeating 'Stay!' as necessary. Start with something low and not too ambitious — say 12in (30cm) high as an average. Pat the top of the wall with your hand and say 'Come — up!' It may work easily, in which case just say 'Up!' and extend the exercise by making the dog also jump from the same side as you.

If it should try to run around the obstruction, put on a check chain and lead and, using the same method, gently pull the dog over, with the usual great praise at the end of a successful exercise.

Turning right and left
Heel work should now be extended. You should be able to walk your dog at left heel using 'Sit!' 'Down!' and 'Stay!' at will. In fact your dog should automatically sit every time you stop and it is often unnecessary to give the command.

Now go back to using the check lead and teach right turn. All you do is pat your left side repeatedly to get the dog's attention, say 'Heel!' repeatedly, turn right and walk off. Once the exercise is repeated your dog will learn that the 'Heel!' command means a change of

direction, and it will be with you or even slightly anticipating you.

Having firmly fixed this idea in your dog's mind, do the left turn in the same manner, being careful not to tread on the dog as you turn towards it. You can do it in slow motion at first. This exercise can be extended easily to about turns in both directions.

Using hand signals
Your dog should now be watchful and fairly obedient. The 'Stay!' command can be reinforced with your hand held immediately in front of you, palm towards the dog. Ultimately, you can use just the hand signal.

Next, take the dog to open ground, give a 'Sit — stay!' (or 'Down — stay!') command and walk away 100ft (30m) or so. Call 'Come!', and when the dog is half way towards you, 'Down!' Repeat the command as necessary, and get the dog to drop as soon after the command as possible. Reinforce your voice with one hand held high in the air, and, if necessary, put a foot forward and stamp hard on the ground. Your whole attitude should be slightly

threatening and noisy until the dog learns instant obedience to 'Down!' commanded by voice, tone, hand and foot.

I consider it vital to secure instant obedience to this command as in emergencies a swift response can prevent a dog fighting or even a road accident. (But however well trained a dog may be, you should always keep it on a lead in traffic.)

It is also useful to teach your dog to sit at heel when you are stopping. Do this by a tap of the foot. Your dog will be quick to pick up the vibrations through the ground and foot tapping is a useful alternative command.

Commands by whistle
Commands may be given by a whistle instead of by the methods already outlined. I have seen people use various complex techniques involving different whistles, but I prefer a single whistle, preferably a so-called silent whistle too high-pitched for people to hear but well within the dog's hearing range.

I use three basic commands. One long continuous blast is substituted for the voice command and hand signal for 'Down!' Repeated short blasts are used for 'Come!' And I give two short blasts to attract the dog's attention and then signal a direction command with arm and body. If I want the dog to move left I put out my left hand and lean my body that way. To make the animal move right I put out the right arm and lean accordingly. If necessary, I walk in the direction that I want the dog to take to make my intention clear.

Below: A high-pitched whistle and hand signals can be used in place of voice commands. Here a trainer signals a dog to move left.

If you notice your dog getting worried or confused by these advanced exercises do remember that the 'Down!' command is absolute and puts the dog in a comfortable position. While the dog rests you may want to rethink the exercise, or decide to leave it until you have worked it out yourself for another day.

Dos and don'ts
If you meet problems, try to solve them in the dog's terms, always remembering pack law. For instance, when you answer the door make your dog walk with you at heel and sit while you open the door. If all is well your dog will welcome your guest. If you are frightened the dog will sense your fear and be there to support you.

Don't let your dog hurl itself at the door in a frenzied manner when the bell goes. This may be amusing in a pup but it may also lead to biting when the dog is an adult.

Don't let your pet be a nuisance in cars. At an early stage in training command 'Down!' and 'Stay!' so that it rests on the floor.

Don't let your dog jump up at people. Teach it to accept praise by patting it at its own level. If it jumps up, bring your knee up smartly into the dog's chest and say nothing. You will not have to do it more than two or three times.

Do take your dog around with you as much as possible when it is young. It will get bored and mischievous if left alone indoors for long periods.

Don't let your dog run away after a reprimand. Make sure it stays until you release it.

Do a little training every day.

Do enjoy your training and don't take it too seriously. It is supposed to give both of you simple pleasure, and make you and your dog acceptable in the community.

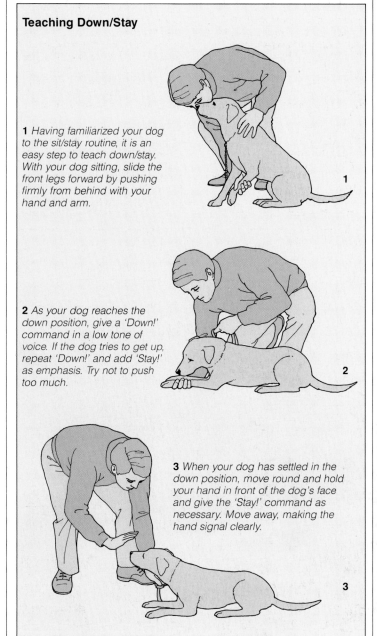

Teaching Down/Stay

1 Having familiarized your dog to the sit/stay routine, it is an easy step to teach down/stay. With your dog sitting, slide the front legs forward by pushing firmly from behind with your hand and arm.

2 As your dog reaches the down position, give a 'Down!' command in a low tone of voice. If the dog tries to get up, repeat 'Down!' and add 'Stay!' as emphasis. Try not to push too much.

3 When your dog has settled in the down position, move round and hold your hand in front of the dog's face and give the 'Stay!' command as necessary. Move away, making the hand signal clearly.

GROOMING AND HEALTH CARE

Grooming is an essential part of the daily routine, undertaken by responsible owners from the day they acquire their dog or puppy. It is important not only to groom enthusiastically but to use the right brushing and combing technique; to know what equipment is required; and to be reasonably well informed about toilet preparations such as shampoos.

In addition to improving the appearance, daily grooming removes dead hair and so reduces the amount of loose hair falling on carpets and other furnishings. Frequent grooming also prevents matting or felting in long-coated breeds and simplifies the work of the dog-clipper or groomer in breeds that require to be formally clipped or stripped at intervals. Properly performed brushing and combing also removes dirt and parasitic insects from fur, and by stimulating the blood supply to the skin produces a healthier and more supple coat. Grooming is even alleged to improve muscle tone in the back and limbs in the same way as massage benefits humans.

Furthermore, regular grooming helps the owner to detect skin ailments and other conditions. This makes possible early veterinary diagnosis. It is amazing how many dogs are presented at surgery in an advanced state of matted fur or with overgrown nails, purely because routine grooming has been neglected.

Grooming equipment
Buy dog-grooming equipment designed for that purpose rather than using combs or hair brushes made for human hair. Selection of tools will depend on the hair type of the dog. Advice can be obtained freely from pet shops and dog shows, where a vast range of

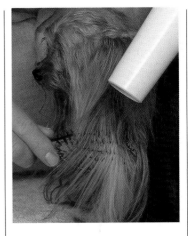

Above: Using a hair-drier is the quickest and most efficient method of drying a long-coated dog after it has had a bath.

Left: If your dog will allow you to clean its teeth, do so at least once a year; if not, have your veterinarian do the job.

suitable equipment can be seen. Also, the breeder from whom you obtain your puppy may tell you of his or her own preferences.

Generally speaking, short-coated dogs should be brushed regularly with a firm brush. This should be used in long, sweeping strokes following the lie of the fur, and it is easiest if the owner always follows the same sequence, for example: back, belly, chest, limbs and tail. Care must be exercised when grooming the head or around other sensitive areas such as the sheath or vulva.

With the long-coated dogs, brushing alone does not suffice because only the top-coat will benefit, while the under-coat — usually responsible for matting or

felting — remains untouched. For these dogs, then, you need not only a bristle brush but a wire brush or a metal comb that will penetrate through to the skin. But it is unwise for an inexperienced owner to use a de-matting comb designed to remove already-formed mats. If used incorrectly, combs of this type may cause severe skin lacerations. Veterinary surgeries and grooming parlours use de-matting combs only as a last resort, in cases of severe neglect, and often with the animals sedated or under an anaesthetic.

As with short-coated dogs, long-haired dogs should be groomed systematically. Use the comb for the soft fur behind the ears, on the feathers down the back of the limbs, the tail, the armpits and any other sites where the fur tends to tangle and knot.

Cleaning your dog
Few people seem to know how often to bath their pets. Regular bathing, using a shampoo or detergent, undoubtedly removes the oils in the coat. But there are times when you must bath a dog because it gets in a mess. In such cases, the dog may be bathed with impunity.

Many dogs of the short-coated varieties may go through their lives without a bath, particularly if grooming is adequate. Breeds such as Poodles, which are clipped at six- to eight-week intervals, are invariably bathed during this process to assist the clipper, and therefore rarely require supplementary baths.

Long-coated dogs, especially those being shown, will probably benefit from baths at intervals of not less than one month to stop them smelling 'doggy'. But bathing a long-coated dog with incipient matting may make the matting

much worse. Frequency of bathing will also depend on the size and co-operation of the dog, and the bathing and drying facilities that you have available.

The dog should be groomed continuously while it is drying, preferably section by section under a hair-drier. Most of the domestic hair-driers are simply not powerful enough for this purpose, and you may need one built for commercial use.

Regarding the choice of shampoo, a medicated or insecticidal shampoo is needed where external parasites such as fleas are present or in summer when the risk of infestation is high. The selection of such a shampoo is often best entrusted to the local veterinarian, whose staff will advise. (Alternatively, aerosol sprays or dusting powder can be substituted satisfactorily for a bath where parasites are seen.) For general cleansing purposes a wide range of dog shampoos are available on the market, though many authorities believe it is best to use a mild, good-quality human shampoo — for example, baby shampoo — and this is often considerably cheaper than proprietary dog preparations.

Above: A non-slip rubber mat placed in the bath or sink will provide your dog with secure footing during its bath.

Your veterinarian may prescribe other types of shampoo for various skin conditions, and these should be used exactly according to instructions and destroyed when the treatment is complete. As with other medications, it is dangerous to store and subsequently use left-over shampoos.

Regular inspections

Many conscientious owners allot a small amount of time at, say, weekly intervals, to attend to various other parts of their dogs. For instance, they check whether the anal glands (scent glands) need to be emptied, as some dogs require this to be done frequently. Owners can be shown how to do this straightforward and simple task, but because it is rather unpleasant many prefer to have it done by a veterinarian or groomer.

Weekly checks on the length of the nails will ensure that these do not grow either so long that they risk snapping off or so curved that

---

A Simple First-Aid Kit

1 Bland eye ointment. If in doubt, seek advice from your veterinarian.
2 Suitable cream or balm for grazes and scalds.
3 Sedative tablets (these should be supplied by a veterinarian, with details of dosage).
4 Aspirin tablets, preferably the soluble variety — one tablet treats a 20lb (9kg) dog.
5 Surgical or methylated spirit for cleansing and sterilizing.
6 Adhesive plaster roll.
7 Crepe bandages for sprains and injured limbs.
8 Suitable antiseptic solution, safe for use with dogs — e.g. antiseptics designed for use with babies.
9 Stomach mixture, e.g. kaolin or bismuth for sickness and diarrhoea.
10 Wound powder. Antiseptic powder for cuts and grazes or after operations. Easy to apply from plastic puffer.
11 White open-wove cotton bandages for dressing cuts and wounds.
12 Lint or sterile dressings for cuts and grazes.
13 Nail clippers.
14 Blunt-ended tweezers, such as eyebrow tweezers, to remove glass, thorns, ticks, etc., from the dog's skin.
15 Cotton wool for dressings and bandages.
16 Curved, blunt-ended scissors (Mayo scissors) useful for trimming fur and removing foreign materials from between pads.
17 Cotton buds for cleansing purposes.

Above: Be sure that you have collected and placed close at hand all the numerous implements you will need for bathing your dog.

they resemble rams' horns. Pay particular attentiion to the dew-claws that many dogs have on the inside of their hind or front legs a few inches above the ground. Because these claws never come into contact with the ground they are not worn down like the main nails of an active dog exercised on a hard surface.

The teeth should also be checked, and small amounts of tartar can be removed carefully by a cotton bud moistened and dipped in a tooth powder. Teeth with severe tartar deposits, however, require veterinary attention, usually under anaesthetic.

The ears should be checked at least once a week, but the owner should not be tempted to probe around any parts of the ear that cannot be seen clearly. Similarly, it is unwise to use ear drops except as prescribed by a veterinarian. A drop of almond oil or olive oil may be safely instilled in each ear the day before the ears are to be cleaned out: this will help to soften and loosen any wax.

Eyes usually require no attention, except in certain breeds such as the Pekingese where there may be an overflow of tears that result in streaks down the cheeks. You can cleanse these tear streaks once or twice daily, using a pad of cotton wool moistened with a human eyewash.

HEALTH CARE

Before you acquire a dog you should ask a reputable breeder or veterinarian about possible inherited risks. It is also a wise safeguard to have your new puppy checked for signs of such ailments within days of purchase, and, if necessary, to make such a purchase conditional on the animal's being found free from congenital disorders. Congenital ailments are those with which puppies are born and may or may not be inheritable when breeding.

Many puppy problems can be

discovered quickly and remedied. But some serious conditions believed to be inherited cannot be diagnosed with certainty in very young animals. For example, a dog must be at least six-months-old before it can be examined for signs of progressive retinal atrophy or hip dysplasia. However, one can minimize the likelihood of acquiring dogs with these conditions by buying from breeding stock already certified as clear.

Vaccinations

Where possible, prevention is better than cure. A number of reliable vaccines free from side-effects have been in use for many years to protect against specific illnesses, notably distemper (hard pad) and canine infectious hepatitis (a liver inflammation, which used to be called Rubarth's disease). Two forms of a serious disease affecting the kidneys and liver are also preventable by vaccination. These are leptospirosis canicola and leptospirosis icterohaemorrhagia (Weil's disease).

In most countries rabies is present and vaccination against it is essential for the sake of the dog and family. At the time of writing, rabies does not occur in certain parts of the world, notably Australasia and the United Kingdom. Here vaccination is not required, and vaccine is not widely available. If you are in doubt, the safest plan is to discuss this subject with your veterinarian, who will advise according to the regulations in effect where you live.

As a rule, vaccination against distemper, hepatitis and leptospirosis (DHL) is commonest at about nine to ten weeks of age; normally two injections, with an interval of two to three weeks, are required to give full protection. Since the immunity given by the initial vaccination can wane, boosters should be given at intervals suggested by your veterinarian. That usually means a yearly trip to the clinic, but anyway this is a good chance for your veterinarian to give the dog a general check and for you to ask any questions that have been at the back of your mind. Most authorities consider that booster vaccinations should be given throughout a dog's life, since there is no reliable evidence to show that age makes dogs less susceptible to the above diseases. Vaccinations are usually free from side-effects, and it is rare for these to be bad enough to preclude giving boosters.

Worms

Deworming is an extremely important and underrated aspect of health care. Dogs can suffer from various types of worms. The common dog roundworm (Toxocara canis) is a great problem in some communities, for the sticky eggs voided by infected dogs may be swallowed by people — especially children. When the eggs hatch and the larvae travel through the human body the results are a variety of unpleasant and serious symptoms.

Inexpensive deworming preparations against roundworms are easily available from veterinarians. Regular dosing of dogs in contact with children is advocated, with common sense hygiene such as removing faeces, washing children's hands and giving the dog its own feeding and drinking receptacles. The dose of such tablets is proportional to the animal's weight, and the dog must be weighed so that the proper dose can be calculated.

Tapeworms are generally regarded as less of a problem, except for the beef and sheep tapeworm (Echinococcus granulosus). This is a particular problem in dogs fed on raw condemned offal, especially where sheep farming is intensive, as in much of New Zealand. Again, the remedy is simple: excluding all such undesirable parts of the diet and regular deworming (say every six months, or annually) with a drug effective for tapeworms. A more common tapeworm in dogs is Dipylidium caninum, acquired by swallowing fleas while self-grooming. This tapeworm is thought to produce few, if any, ill-effects. It, too, is cleared by using a drug toxic to tapeworms. There are now drugs that are effective against both tapeworms and roundworms.

In the United Kingdom hookworms seem of little significance, except in certain kennels where the problem is endemic. Thus you are likely to encounter them only if buying a puppy from such an establishment. In some areas of the world hookworms cause a much greater problem. They will respond to roundworm medications.

Whipworms are basically a parasite of foxes but are occasionally encountered in dogs. Fortunately they are easily treated.

Regular health checks

Like cars, dogs need regular checks. Grooming time is a convenient point, especially for long-coated dogs, which should be groomed frequently and fastidiously. Paws should be checked for length of nails and for flint, glass or thorns sticking in the pads; any grass seeds found in the

Trimming Nails

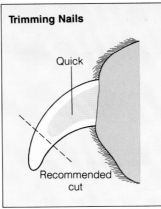

Quick

Recommended cut

web or between the toes should be removed; and foreign material such as chewing gum or plasticine should be clipped carefully from between the pads. If you suspect that your dog has stood in an irritant substance such as paraffin or wet road tar, smother the feet in an emulsifying agent such as oil or butter to soothe and to soften the irritant and then wash thoroughly in washing-up liquid.

Regularly check the eyes for opacity in the cornea and for inflammation. Severe inflammation will cause the eye to be kept half-closed and to water profusely. Dogs so affected will often rub the inflamed eye.

When checking the ears, watch for signs of squelching when rubbing around them, and examine under each flap for signs of excessive wax production. If you find this, have the ears checked by your veterinarian to establish the cause; similarly if the ear canals smell unpleasant. If the animal seems unduly irritated by either ear seek help without delay.

If you find a small, marble-sized mat in your dog's coat, do not try to rake it out. Grasp the mat in both hands, holding the right half between the thumb and forefinger of your right hand and the left half between the thumb and forefinger of your left hand. Pull slowly in opposite directions, being careful to pull parallel with your dog's skin. The mat should separate into two smaller mats that should be small enough to be tugged out gently with the comb.

Above: When clipping nails, have the dog's paw securely in your hand before you do; clip no more than $^1/_{16}$-$^1/_8$in (1.5-3mm), depending on breed size, to avoid cutting the quick; have styptic powder on hand.

Signs to note

There are various general points to bear in mind when inspecting your dog — points that in sickness may greatly help your veterinarian to reach a diagnosis. Does the dog suddenly seem to have gained or lost weight? Weigh your dog at regular intervals, say weekly. This is easily accomplished in all but the largest breeds by lifting the dog and stepping onto the bathroom scales; then, still standing on the scales, put the dog down. The difference in the two readings gives a fairly accurate indication of the dog's weight. For very small dogs and puppies, kitchen scales may be easier; and for very large dogs, a public weighbridge should be used.

Appetite and thirst should also be noted, with any preference changes — for example, eating biscuit meal and refusing meat, or vice versa. If in doubt about fluid consumption, measure out water or milk daily and keep a record of the quantity consumed. Letting your dog also drink puddle or pond water would distort the overall intake (and, in any case, this is a possible source of infection that should be avoided).

Signs of vomiting and diarrhoea should be carefully noted, as these can be a valuable guide. All animals, including humans, have the occasional stomach upset, but if this is persistent or combined with undue lassitude and a refusal to eat, veterinary attention is needed.

Intolerance to exercise or downright unwillingness to walk is important as this may be the first indication of heart disease, especially if it is combined with a persistent soft, dry cough.

It goes without saying that any departure from normal behaviour should be carefully watched. If in doubt, telephone your veterinarian and describe the signs that are worrying you. He or she will either put your mind at rest, or — if in doubt — ask to examine the animal.

Ailments of different body systems

Skin. The commonest problems encountered with skin are probably the direct result of parasites, of which fleas are by far the commonest. Usually found along the back of a dog, fleas leave their droppings (but not their eggs) in the coat, and therefore can be detected easily by little coal-like particles in the fur. Fleas themselves are readily visible to the naked eye; they are brownish and flattened from side to side, and scatter speedily through the hair. If you see fleas give prompt insecticidal treatment in the form of a special shampoo, dusting powder or aerosol. Repeat at suitable intervals if the dog becomes infested again.

If left untreated, dogs may become allergic to flea bites and may scratch persistently or bite at themselves until a patch of self-inflicted wet eczema appears. This patch can vary from $^2/_5$-$^4/_5$in (1-2cm) in diameter to almost a quarter of the body if left untreated, and, as the name suggests, has a shiny, moist-looking surface. Although requiring veterinary attention, wet eczema can sometimes be minimized by applying a soothing cream and administering a sedative or aspirin tablet, which helps to curb scratching and biting.

Lice are greyish-blue creatures usually found on the ear flaps. They hardly move and they cement their eggs (nits) to the fur. Insecticidal treatment is essential, for many lice on one dog can cause anaemia by sucking large quantities of blood.

Ticks embedded in the skin are unsightly and may in certain areas of the world cause problems by transmitting disease. If there are many ticks, insecticidal treatment will clear them; if just one or two, they can be smothered in spirit and a few minutes later removed, using tweezers. Ticks usually let go and leave the dog once they have had sufficient food (i.e. by sucking blood).

Grazes cause little problem and should be cleaned with an antiseptic, followed by the application of a suitable soothing ointment. If the dog persists in licking, seek treatment. Cuts vary greatly in depth, length and position. If you can apply a firm bandage this will usually control bleeding, but stitching is required for any cuts longer than $^4/_5$in (2cm). Bathe cuts with disinfectant, but you should not apply any ointment.

Ears. Ear troubles generally require expert diagnosis and treatment; home treatment does not work satisfactorily. One rather dramatic condition is aural haematoma, a blood blister of the ear flap. This must be drained surgically and the flap secured to prevent recurrence while the flap heals. Aural haematomas are usually caused by an animal excessively shaking or scratching an ear flap.

Eyes. Although it is safe to bathe the dog's eyes in lukewarm water or with an ordinary proprietary eyewash, it is extremely unwise to delay seeking professional advice; such a delay could result in permanent loss of vision. A bland ointment may help, however, until such time as professional assistance can be sought.

Nails. These will need to be cut occasionally, especially the dew-claws which do not come into contact with the ground and therefore do not get worn down. All nails contain a blood vessel and nerve, and cutting should be left to experienced people unless you are quite sure what you are doing. Broken nails usually need to be removed by a veterinarian to save the animal distress and pain.

Digestive system. It is a good plan to watch animals regularly while they are eating, because signs of mouth pain usually show in the way the animals tackle their food. Apart from a suitable temporary analgesic such as aspirin, little can be done to help except seeking professional attention.

Uncomplicated vomiting is common in dogs. The vomit is usually fluid and often described as a froth, which may be white or yellowish. If solid food is returned, this may indicate inflammation of the stomach (gastritis) or mild food-poisoning caused by eating food that is 'off'. But if vomiting is persistent, especially in a young dog with a tendency to swallow stones, there is the possibility of an obstruction and you should seek veterinary attention as soon as possible. In cases of gastritis it is usually effective, or at least helpful, to withhold food for a period of 24 hours, allowing only small, frequent drinks of boiled water.

Liver failure is encountered quite often in dogs and usually requires veterinary treatment and advice. It is undoubtedly aggravated by foods rich in fat; therefore special diets may be needed to minimize the symptoms.

Failure of the pancreatic gland to work efficiently may well result in a dog that eats voraciously yet loses weight and condition. Again, avoid fats; also seek veterinary help to remedy the enzyme deficiency that is the usual cause of the symptoms.

Diarrhoea is probably one of the commonest signs of illness seen at a veterinary surgery. There are many possible causes: an unsuitable diet or a low-grade bowel infection are the commonest; and withholding food for 24 hours followed by a light diet of white meat, such as chicken, veal or fish, will cure mild cases. If the condition persists or recurs, however, qualified treatment by a veterinarian is strongly indicated.

Heart and circulation. These give rise to few problems in young animals, except for rare cases of inherited heart disease. However, dogs of some breeds tend to develop heart murmurs and other signs, usually exercise intolerance, a dry cough of increasing frequency and severity, and progressive lassitude. Veterinary treatment is, of

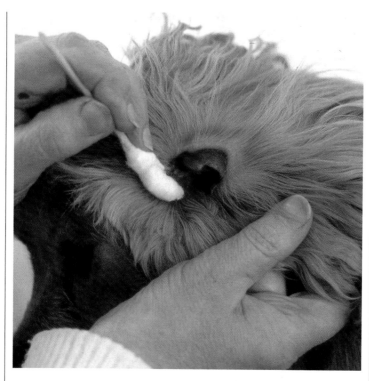

course, necessary, but owners can help by exercising affected dogs at the coolest times of the day during hot weather, providing adequate ventilation indoors, and preventing their pets becoming overweight.

Respiratory system. Fortunately, most dogs have a robust respiratory system. There are few cases of bronchitis and even fewer of pneumonia except when associated with the distemper virus. A troublesome condition against which vaccines are available in some parts of the world is kennel cough, an inflammation of the windpipe (tracheitis). Usually this is not serious except in very young, ill or old animals; and the owner can complement veterinary treatment by giving cough preparations — even the old-fashioned honey and lemon seems to help.

Musculo-skeletal system. One of the commonest conditions is pain in a limb, leading to limping. There

Above: Never insert a cleaning implement further into a dog's ear than your eye can see. And even at close range, work gently.

are many possible causes. The owner should inspect the pads for signs of an embedded piece of glass or a thorn. Until help is obtained, the owner should rest the animal, possibly giving some support to the affected limb in the form of a crepe bandage.

Dogs, like humans, can tear muscles, ligaments and tendons by tripping or jumping awkwardly; and in an older animal, joint disease such as arthritis or muscular rheumatism may well cause limping. In such cases the degree of lameness is often linked with

Below: All dogs' faces need cleaning occasionally. Use soft cotton moistened with lukewarm water or human eyewash.

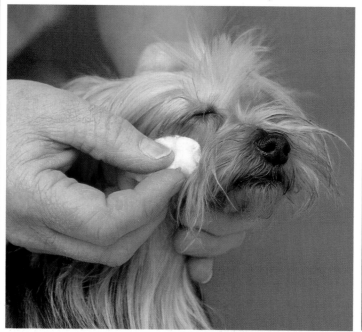

climatic conditions, damp cold weather being the worst. Drugs will help, and in the early stages many veterinarians simply prescribe aspirin, which seems to work well.

Broken limbs are fortunately uncommon and are usually the result of a major trauma such as a road accident. Until professional help is obtained, the golden rules are:

1. Give nothing by mouth.
2. Move the animal as little as possible.
3. Try to immobilize the broken limb or limbs by a splint.

A stretcher of any description helps to reduce pain while the animal is taken to a surgery or hospital. A jacket or coat can be used as an emergency stretcher. The limb will be set, using stainless steel pins or an external plaster of Paris cast, depending on the site of the fracture and the preference of the surgeon.

A common injury to a back leg is tearing a small but important ligament in the knee. Rest may help, but usually the ligament must be repaired, using nylon or a skin graft to strengthen the knee.

Hip dysplasia (abnormal hip development) is widespread among dogs, especially the large breeds. The abnormality seldom shows up while dogs are young. As they age, however, sufferers become stiffer, probably as a result of a superimposed arthritis in the joint, and have difficulty in rising, jumping or walking any distance. In most cases it is possible to remove the malformed hip joint, but various techniques are used to relieve the pain of hip dysplasia and these depend on the surgeon's preference.

Another bone condition is spondylitis, a progressive disease affecting the spinal cord and producing progressive paralysis of the hindquarters, sometimes linked with incontinence. Regrettably, this is incurable.

Urinary system. The main problem here is often the state of the kidneys, for without their effective working the whole body system collapses. Fortunately, as leptospirosis vaccination has become more widespread, kidney disease has apparently grown rarer. But, through wear and tear, the nephron units of the kidneys become damaged anyway and renal disease develops in many dogs as they age. There is no cure, but veterinary help may ensure years of useful, happy and pain-free life. Symptoms are usually a marked increase in water intake, progressive loss in weight, decreasing appetite and a tendency to vomit — especially water after copious drinking. Diagnosis is usually by urine and blood tests; veterinary treatment and dietary advice are helpful.

Cystitis, or inflammation of the bladder, is a more acute condition and must be tackled promptly to save discomfort. It can originate in a simple infection or in combination with bladder tumours, polyps or stones (calculi). Diagnosis and treatment must be left to the professionals. Signs include increased frequency of urination in dogs of either sex. Difficulty and pain on urinating are usual. Veterinarians can sometimes feel causative calculi in bitches, and those in male dogs are often detected when a catheter is inserted in the clinic. If stones are present, they must be removed to secure long-term relief. Blood passed in urine is also a significant sign. Total inability to pass urine — especially in a male dog — merits the fastest possible veterinary treatment.

Reproductive system. This system gives little trouble in male dogs but can cause serious problems in bitches. The only organ likely to worry a male dog is the prostate. As in older men, this enlarges, giving rise to difficulty in passing urine or faeces. Fortunately this problem responds readily to drug treatment.

Not so, necessarily, an inflammation of the female womb — a condition often referred to as metritis. The result may be sterility, and a severe attack can even hazard the animal's life. Though this condition may respond to antibiotics, it is often safest to opt for an entire ovaro-hysterectomy. Danger signs include a progressive vulvar discharge coupled with increasing thirst, decreasing appetite, and a tendency to vomit.

One of the commonest and most annoying conditions encountered in bitches is false pregnancy. About two months after season, the bitch behaves as if she had been mated and will nest, lactate, and foster mock pups such as socks, cushions and toys. In severe cases treatment is required, but it is helpful to remove all make-believe pups and to prevent self-licking of milk glands (which in itself stimulates milk production). You can do this by painting the nipples with distasteful materials such as vinegar and bitter aloes.

Nervous system. Infection of the brain by distemper virus may result in fits that are sometimes controllable by medication. Epilepsy also occurs, and again this is usually treated with a human anti-convulsant drug. Spinal disc injuries are common, especially in long-backed dogs such as Dachshunds. They may be treated by drugs or surgery. It is important to discourage sufferers from jumping on and off chairs, or climbing and descending stairs.

Tumours. Most lumps are benign; for instance, fatty lumps (lipomas), warts (fibromas), and cysts. These do not spread from the site of origin and many can be removed without trouble if this seems desirable. That is particularly true of skin masses and bitches' tumours of the mammary glands. However, as in humans, some benign growths are inoperable because of their position: it is impossible to detach them from surrounding vital tissues.

Cancerous tumours may present a similar problem, and anyway these may not be worth removing if some of their cells have spread through the body to other tissues, or organs such as the lungs. It would be pointless to remove the primary growth only to find inoperable secondary growths elsewhere. A surgeon may use X-rays and laboratory tests to determine the type of tumour and the chance of surgical success. He or she may also take a small sample (biopsy) to get an expert pathologist's assessment. This is also often done after removal to confirm the nature of the mass.

Shock. Dogs may suffer shock after a road accident, following surgery, or in any condition involving extensive internal or external bleeding. Treatment is prompt, skilled veterinary care. In mild cases a small dose of a stimulant such as brandy may be a help, though this can be risky, especially if the dog has to undergo surgery or anaesthesia. Never, of course, give anything by mouth to an unconscious dog: it may choke and die if you do.

Poisoning. Many substances toxic to dogs may be swallowed accidentally or given deliberately. Probably the greatest risk is from rodenticides and garden chemicals — especially slug bait and weedkillers. When using one of these, always observe the container's instructions about safety. If you know that a dog has been poisoned, cause it to vomit by making it swallow a crystal of washing soda like a tablet, a strong salt solution or mustard in water. This works only if done minutes after the dog took the poison. If possible take the poison container to the veterinarian when you seek treatment; it may help him or her to choose the right remedy quickly.

Giving medicines
At some time most owners have to give their pets medicines under the direction of a veterinary surgeon. With all but the most vicious animals this should be accomplished easily. But medicines given by mouth should not be mixed with food: the dog may be too ill to eat all its rations or may detect that its food has been 'doctored' and leave it; or, if fed with other animals, may swap bowls. It is much better to give it a direct dose of the specified quantity to ensure that this is swallowed and therefore effective.

Few medicines come in powder form except those that are palatable and designed to be mixed with the food. When giving powders do not be tempted to pour these into the mouth neat — the dog is sure to cough them up again. Instead, mix them with water, milk, butter, jam or honey, and smear the resulting palatable paste on the tongue or lips.

Tablets, pips or capsules should be given, singly or in multiples, by pushing them to the back of the throat and holding the mouth closed until you see the dog gulp them down. If the dog protests, get an assistant to hold the patient securely during dosage. Lubricating the medicines by dipping in oil or butter may make them easier for the dog to swallow.

Liquid medicines usually should not exceed one teaspoonful (5ml) per dose. Sit the dog and hold the jaws closed with the head tilted well back. Pull out the flap of the lip on one side to form a natural funnel, and pour in the liquid. Do not release the head or jaws until the

---

Below: After placing a pill as far back on a dog's tongue as possible, hold the mouth shut until the dog has swallowed.

dog is seen to swallow.

As with all medicines, ointments, creams and lotions must be applied to the affected areas at prescribed frequencies. It is essential to rub such preparations well into the skin unless otherwise directed. The natural tendency for animals immediately to lick off such applications is reduced if little remains on the skin surface. A good time to apply these medicines is just before taking the dog out for a walk: your pet's attention will be distracted while the drug does its work. If you have to rub the stuff on at, say, bedtime, when you cannot prevent the dog licking, it is a good idea to apply a protective bandage or sock.

Ear drops should be instilled down the largest visible opening to the vertical canal. Being liquid, they will work their way around the ear's nooks and crannies to reach the trouble spot. A little gentle external massage to the ear will assist, and thereafter even frantic head-shaking will not dislodge the drops. Ear powders clog, and a veterinarian will have to remove them by syringeing or other cleansing, so unless these are specially prescribed never be tempted to pour or puff powder inside a dog's ears.

Eye drops or ointments need special handling which owners often find difficult. Always steady the dog in a sitting position with its head slightly raised, if necessary getting someone to help. Eyes are very delicate and will not withstand accidental rough treatment. Hold the head firmly with one hand, using the thumb and index finger to keep the lids open; with the dropper bottle or tube in the other hand, drip the required number of drops onto the open eye. Squeeze ointment from a tube as you would pipe cream onto a cake, but make sure that the tube nozzle does not touch the eye — especially the clear structure (cornea). The natural blinking that follows treatment will spread the preparation over the front of the eye; do not allow the dog to rub with its front paws for a few minutes after application.

Never administer drugs not specifically made for animal use without the guidance and blessing of your veterinarian. Such amateur doctoring may cause undue suffering to your dog. For this reason proprietary medicines bought from the chemists or pet stores are rarely to be commended. Also always store canine medicines somewhere safe from snooping children, who might use them to experiment on themselves; and safely dispose of drugs left over when treatment is completed, otherwise they may become useless or even dangerous. Of course your veterinarian may dispense some drugs that you can safely keep inside your canine medicine chest for future use against specified conditions. If you have medicines like this, clearly mark the container with dose amount and frequency and the particular condition for which the drugs are to be used.

5

SHOWING YOUR DOG

What is the dog showing game? Exactly that: a game — one with an element of chance. We take a gamble by pitting one dog's beauty and conformation against another's with the rules and regulations laid down by kennel clubs.

The 'game' itself involves qualities of leadership, skills of organization and the hard preparatory work of those participating. It has its own language. It evokes feelings of joy, sorrow, bewilderment and anger. It can be likened to an addictive drug. The writer can say so with authority having tried to kick the habit, experienced merciless withdrawal symptoms, gave in and is happily unashamed of the failure.

The breed standard

Showing is an opportunity for people interested in specific breeds to get together socially; but above all, through the element of competition, it is the means by which breeds are kept true to type — to their respective standards.

Breed standards or points are blueprints of the breed that act as a guideline for breeders and judges. Drawn up by the specialist breed clubs, they are approved by the Kennel Club of Great Britain (Kennel Club or KC) and describe desirable features such as conformation, movement, eye shape and colour, and type and colour of coat.

The determination of previous generations to keep breeds true to type so that they could continue to fulfil their original functions largely explains why we are not now left with a product mediocre in height, weight, colour and temperament, and just describable as 'a dog'. This does not decry the worth of the many much-loved, mixed-race Fidos. Rather it explains the choice we have available between say, the

Above: While the handler checks her dog's stance, a judge examines its bite at the 1988 Richmond Show, United Kingdom.

Left: This American Cocker Spaniel reflects good diet, exercise and grooming. The correct show pose or 'stack' is not achieved in a day.

benign and dignified Newfoundland and the extrovert and cocky Yorkshire Terrier.

Interpreting the breed standard is a fascinating task, for sometimes the wording is vague or ambiguous. Weights and heights can be defined precisely thanks to scales and measures, but each breeder and judge may interpret terms such as 'small, dark brown eye' in a slightly different way. Meeting in frequent competition helps to remove this ambiguity, for competitors can see if 'small' gets too small or if 'dark' is growing paler, thus altering the characteristic expression of the breed.

Types of dog show

There are seven distinct types of dog show in the United Kingdom:

1. **Exemption** The only show exempt from most Kennel Club show rules and regulations. Usually held as fund-raisers with pedigree and non-pedigree classes.

2. **Primary** Entries on the day and confined to the showing society's members. Maximum of eight classes with none higher than maiden. No first prize or challenge certificate winners may enter, puppy wins excepted.

3. **Match** A knock-out with dogs having to be Kennel Club registered. Maximum of 64 dogs.

4. **Sanction** Barred to challenge certificate winners. Specialty breed shows can have ten classes, while all-breed shows can have up to 25.

5. **Limited** Like the sanction shows and matches entry is limited to members of the show-holding society only, although exceptions exist for exhibitors living in given areas. Winners of challenge certificates or certain specified prizes are not eligible. Rules require at least 12 classes for specialty breed shows; 16 classes for all-breed shows.

6. **Open** Open to all with no membership qualification. A first prize in breed class for dogs aged 12-18 months brings one point towards a junior warrant. Open shows are often held with an agricultural or county show.

7. **Championship** Can be for either one breed only or all breeds and are the only shows where challenge certificates can be awarded. Open to all, with the exception of Crufts where a qualification is required. The judges are authorized by the Kennel Club.

A glossary of showing terms

To the uninitiated, the terminology of the showing world can be confusing. Here are some basic terms in Kennel Club usage.

Sire and **dam**. A puppy's father and mother.

Affixes. The **prefix** is the first part of a dog's Kennel Club registered name, identifying and exclusive to the breeding kennel. For example, a bitch's pet name may be 'Nana' but her registration would read something like 'Caladh Bahr Gossamer of Gerahmeen' — Caladh being the breeding kennel, and the **suffix** Gerahmeen the owning kennel.

Class is an undefined number of dogs in a competition, which may or may not have sex, age or award limitations. A breed class allows for the entry of one specific breed. A group class embraces several breeds with, say, a common original function, for instance hounds or terriers. A variety class has completely different breeds.

An **exhibit** is a dog or a bitch competing at a show. They need no longer be **entire**: neutered dogs and spayed bitches may enter and be judged normally, the only 'penalty' being that their wins are not entered in the stud book.

The **owner, handler** or **exhibitor** need not be the same person. A dog or bitch may be registered at the Kennel Club in the ownership of more than one person. It may be exhibited or handled by one member of that partnership. Any

exhibit may be handled — i.e. controlled in the ring — by a friend or professional handler, so long as there is a verbal understanding or written agreement.

The **ring** is the area designated for a particular class or breed competition. **Ring numbers** are allocated to individual dogs. Its ring number is a dog's only identification for the judge and is used for class checking and benching.

Benching is a dog's kennel for the day. It may be a small, closed cage or an open-fronted structure on trestles. Both types are provided by commercial agencies. Some shows bear benching costs; at others a small fee is paid by the exhibitor. A Kennel Club rule states that a dog must be on its bench unless being prepared for, or required in, the ring, or unless there is a veterinarian or show committee decision to remove it from the bench. No dog is allowed off the bench for more than 15 minutes at a time for exercise and other activities.

Stewards come in both sexes and their title may be either judge steward or ring steward. They are responsible for the checking of class lists, distribution of ring numbers, calling in of exhibits for judging and announcement of the winners. (The exhibitors are responsible both for attending their classes once the judging has commenced and for any 'mistakes' their dog makes in the ring.) Stewards also assist the judge

with paperwork and help generally in the smooth running of events. The efficiency of any show depends upon the stewards and their worth is recognized.

Judges come in both sexes and two types: 'specialist' and 'all-rounder'. A specialist judge is usually a devotee of one breed, having bred many champions or been involved with that breed in various ways for many years. The 'all-rounder' judge will be knowledgeable about many breeds, and you will meet him or her in variety classes. Probably both types of judge will have gained experience by, perhaps, first stewarding, then judging small shows before the Kennel Club allows them to award challenge certificates. Five years' experience is the minimum prerequisite for this in the United Kingdom.

The judge's task is to determine how close each exhibit comes to his or her mental image of the breed standard compared with other exhibits in the class. The judge closely examines each individual, then its handler moves the animal away from and back to the judge at a gait suitable for the breed. The line taken may be straight, triangular or circular, perhaps all three. Each judge has a preference. Except in cases of fraud, misrepresentation, breach of rules or genuine mistake, the judge's decision is final.

A **Challenge Certificate** (CC) is a championship show award

Above: At benched shows dogs must remain on their benches all day, unless they are in the ring or one of several 15-minute breaks.

given to the best dog and best bitch in each breed.

In the United Kingdom the number of challenge certificates allocated to a breed by the Kennel Club depends on the number of entries in breed classes at all championship shows for the previous three years, i.e. if entries are low, the breed may forfeit a CC; if high, it may gain one.

In order to win the title 'Champion' an exhibit must gain three challenge certificates from three different judges, including one certificate awarded after the age of 12 months.

An **International Champion** is an exhibit that has won four C.A.C.I.B.s in three countries under different judges.

A **Junior Warrant** (JW) is an award granted (on application) by the Kennel club to an exhibit gaining 25 points when between 12- and 15-months old. One point comes from each first prize won in a breed class at an open show and three points are gained from every first prize won in a breed class at a championship show.

The magical **Best in Show** is determined by the type of show. Smaller shows will have all unbeaten dogs competing in the ring, so here the best in show and reserve best in show will be chosen from a miscellany of shapes, sizes and colours. Open and championship shows may warrant the 'group' system. In the breed classes the best dog and the best bitch compete for 'Best of Breed'. The 'Best of Breed' competes in its respective group. Then the group winners compete against each other, and at last one stands alone to receive the ultimate accolade of the day.

The **group** system used for showing dogs is based on their original roles. The six groups used for judging in the United Kingdom are as follows:

Terriers	Gundogs
Toys	Working dogs
Hounds	Utility dogs

The **stud book** is a register compiled by the Kennel Club of awards given to winning dogs at United Kingdom championship shows. Dogs and bitches thus entered — and there are five qualifying bands — are given a number which is considered to be a sign of the dog's worth and is quoted on the pedigree.

A **pedigree** is a record of the dog's ancestry, showing any number of generations. Any champions in the family will be written or underlined in red.

The **schedule** is a contract created between the show society and exhibitors when the exhibitor pays the entry fee and the show society accepts it. The schedule should contain all the information required: details of prize money (or the lack of it); instructions for travelling by rail or in a coach party; list of judges; number and types of classes available to the breeds; catering and parking arrangements; perhaps a tenting plan. The schedule also states the latest time when the exhibitor may arrive at the show and the earliest for leaving.

Catalogues are on sale at shows. These list all the exhibits and the owners' names and addresses. They may also have information on trade stands and other amenities plus private and commercial 'doggy' advertising.

The American system

The same 'show fever' that grips the enthusiast can be found in any country where dogs are shown. The euphoria of the win, the frustration of the loss, the new-found friends, the gala pageantry and the frazzled nerves all add up to one word: fun! It may be difficult for the beginner to understand at first; but it usually takes only one match or show for the 'bug' to enter the life of the dog enthusiast. From that point on, the enthusiast finds that he or she has entered into a new life-style that includes weekends away from home at a dog show or match.

To understand the American system, one must understand the difference between a dog *show* and a dog *match*. Although each is conducted in the same manner, no points towards championship or obedience degrees are awarded as the result of a win at a match. A match is a training ground for both dog and owner. Winners usually receive trophies and/or ribbons for their effort, but it's all in fun. In fact, matches are generally referred to as fun matches.

At a match, some dogs will compete in obedience trials at various levels, and others will compete in the conformation rings. That is, some dogs are judged for their ability to perform various obedience exercises, and others are judged for their conformity to the breed standard as set forth by the American Kennel Club.

Matches are fun, and it is certainly recommended that the beginner enrol in as many matches as possible before ever entering a dog show. A show, though still fun, is also serious business. A dog can earn points towards obedience degrees or the title of 'Champion'.

As in the United Kingdom, there are two types of show: specialty and all-breed. In a specialty show, only dogs of a designated breed can be entered. An example of this would be a specialty show sponsored by the German Shepherd Club; entrants are restricted to German Shepherd Dogs only. An all-breed show is open to all purebred dogs registered with the American Kennel Club.

Animals competing in conformation must earn 15 points to receive the title of 'Champion'. Points earned at each show are based upon the number of dogs in the competition; the more dogs, obviously, the more points the winner earns. An animal may win from one to five points at a show. The 15 points required must be won under at least three different judges. Only one male and one female of each breed can win points at a show. There is no inter-sex competition: males compete against males, females against females.

Animals competing for obedience degrees must score 170 points or more in three separate shows, under three different judges. Obedience trials are divided into four levels of competition. These are Companion Dog (CD), Companion Dog Excellent (CDX), Utility Dog (UD), and Utiity Dog, Tracking (UDT). Each level is more difficult and more complicated than the level below. An owner and dog will enter shows and compete until the first degree is completed (CD), then continue in quest of the higher levels.

In addition to conformation and obedience trials, field trials are held for certain breeds. These are working tests for owner and dog as a team. Field trials test the ability of a breed to perform the function for which that breed was created.

The Continental system

It is rather difficult to generalize about the rules governing dog shows in Europe because they vary

---

Below: This handler has selected an outfit whose colours coordinate nicely with the handsome colour of her Irish Setter.

slightly from one country to another. But they are all very similar in most respects because, instead of each country having its own rules, all are governed by the regulations laid down by the Fédération Cynologique Internationale (FCI). Each country has its own national equivalent of the Kennel Club, but for shows each must stick to the rules laid down by the FCI.

Speaking generally, shows are either of championship status or are much smaller shows — usually held by the breed clubs — more in the nature of fun shows or matches.

At a championship show, the judge has to write a critique on every exhibit, and also give it a grade: excellent, very good, good or sufficient. Any dog that tries to bite is disqualified. Generally, the critique has to be written on the spot, and it is then handed to the exhibitor by the judge. In the Netherlands there is slightly less pressure on the judge because the local rules lay down that such critiques must be sent to the Dutch Kennel Club within 14 days of the show. This kind of judging obviously takes a long time, so it is as well that the classes in European shows are neither as numerous nor as well filled as they are in the UK and the USA. Usually there are only youth, open and championship classes, although additional classes are permitted. Occasionally there are brace or team classes. But it is very

rare to find a European show that has any of the featured variety classes that are staged in the United Kingdom and United States. Whether this is a good thing or not depends upon your point of view; but it certainly takes away some of the appeal of the show.

Only a dog that has received the

grading 'Excellent' may be taken into account for the title 'Best of Sex'. Many countries do not permit the award of an excellent grade to a dog in the youth class, but some do allow this. The youth class is governed by age limits, and this is usually from nine to 24 months.

It is rare for a European show to

Above: The Poodle's face is a study in resignation while the groomer's face is a study in precision. The lead, naturally, matches the dog.

Below: Few of life's moments are as grand as being titled 'Best in Show' at Crufts, the most distinguished show in the United Kingdom.

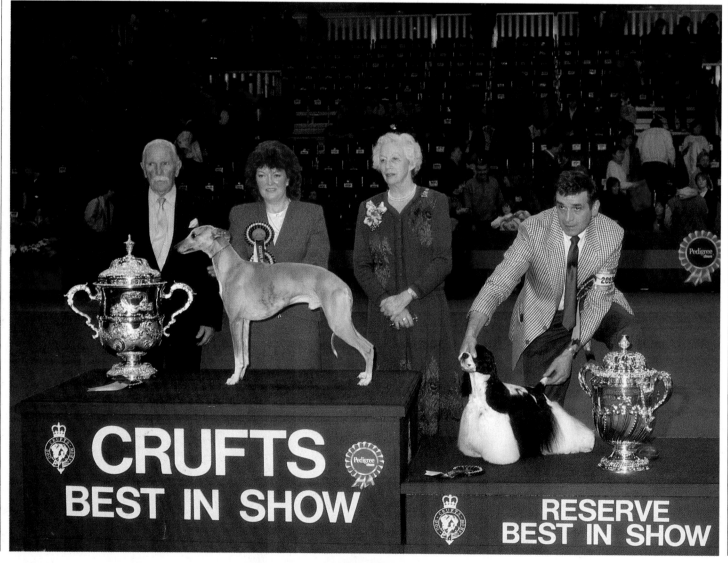

CRUFTS
BEST IN SHOW

RESERVE
BEST IN SHOW

have an award for the best of breed, though this occasionally happens. Without the award there cannot be any group or best in show judging, which is a great pity as there is then no final climax to the show.

After all the dogs at a Championship show have been graded for quality awards may be made of the Certificat d'Aptitude au Championat (CAC). At international championship shows awards of the Certificat d'Aptitude au Championat International de Beauté (CACIB) may be made too. A certificate may be awarded to the winner of the grading 'Excellent', but not necessarily so, because a judge may not consider such a dog, even though excellent, to be of such outstanding merit as to warrant the award of a certificate. Because a dog in the youth class may not receive such a grading, it may well happen that, in one of the few countries that allow an award for best of breed, the judge may put the youth class winner above the winner of a certificate.

To obtain the title of 'Champion', a dog must obtain three certificates, either CACIB or CAC, under two different judges; and the first and last certificates must be won with an interval of 12 months between them. They can be won in any country that is affiliated to the FCI, and since movement of dogs is not restricted between most continental European countries by regulations regarding rabies, there is a fairly large area from which an exhibitor can choose a show.

Most UK and USA shows are thought to be fairly 'cut-throat' in their outlook, but European exhibitors seem to have a different attitude to their shows, and there is a feeling that they are even more 'out for blood'. There are fewer dogs competing, yet the owners appear to take a much more serious view of what happens to them and there is little chatter until all the judgments have been declared.

Shows in Europe are also rather more rigorous in their attitude to permitting removal of exhibits; you will never find a show that says participants may go home at 3.00 p.m., even when there is no real need to stay longer. Perhaps, as there are far fewer shows than in the United Kingdom and United States, the organizers want the dogs to remain so that they can be seen by the late-comers.

But wherever they take place, dog shows are always interesting and usually fun too, and it is from this point of view that a wise owner should regard them.

The Scandinavian system
The Scandinavian showing system is a mixture of the Continental and British systems. There are three main classes: junior (for exhibits from eight- to 15-months-old), open (for exhibits over 15-months-old), and champion classes (for exhibits that have already obtained the title of Swedish, Finnish, Norwegian, Danish or International champion).

In the junior and open classes exhibits are graded on their own merits; they are not in competition against each other. The gradings are: 1st prize (a very good specimen of the breed), 2nd prize (a moderately good specimen), 3rd prize (an exhibit lacking in construction), and 4th prize (a very untypical exhibit).

All those that gain a 1st grading in junior then compete against each other and are placed in order of 1st to 4th. The 1st prize winners in the open classes enter a winner's class and are also placed 1st to 4th.

Some breeds with a well-defined original function have to be highly placed at trials to test that function before they can enter winner's classes, e.g. Field Trials for Retrievers.

The international championship shows in Scandinavia approved by the FCI award the CACIB and the Certificat d'Aptitude au Championat International de Travail (CACIT). An international champion has to gain four CACIBs from three different judges and in three different countries. Between the first and last CACIB there must be an interval of 12 months.

The Australian System
In Australia there is a tremendous enthusiasm among dog owners for basic training, and there is huge membership of training and breed clubs. Obedience training is on a par with everyday sit/stay/heel UK training, with Companion Dog (CD) status awarded on a points system at trials.

Most breeds have specialist breed clubs, which use the Kennel Club breed standards.

The Australian states have individual kennel control organizations overseen by an advisory Australian Kennel Control Council. The availability of dog shows, field trials and obedience tests varies from state to state and is determined by the number of pedigree dogs in the area.

The Royal Agricultural societies of Australia all have dog show sections. The Melbourne Show, for example, runs over 11 days, with only a few breeds judged each day. These shows also cater for breed club obedience displays. Show stewards are professional people and have to pass stringent examinations before taking up their duties.

At these larger shows, the classes

Below: The challenge for anyone in handling a racy breed such as the Afghan is to move about the ring as gracefully as it does.

usually offered are: baby puppy (pups may be shown from three months of age), minor puppy, puppy, junior, intermediate, novice, graduate, limit, state-bred, Australian-bred, and open. These are self-explanatory or similar to the UK classification. The group classification is: Toys, Terriers, Gundogs, Hounds, Working, Utility, and Non-sporting.

Australian champions have to gain 100 points from at least four different shows and from at least four different judges. The method by which a champion gains its crown is complicated but ensures that a superb specimen of a numerically small breed stands an almost equal chance with a superb specimen of a popular breed.

After all the breed classes have been judged, the 1st prize winners in each sex over six-months-old compete for the challenge certificate (CC). The winner gains five points plus one point for each competing exhibit of the same sex over six-months-old, to a maximum of 25 points. (A winning bitch would gain five points for the CC on her own merit, and if the total entry of bitches over six-months-old is ten this would result in 15 points towards the championship of that particular bitch.) The dog CC and bitch CC then compete for the title 'Best of Breed'.

At multi-breed shows the best of breed then enters the group judging. The winner of each group receives five points plus one point for every exhibit in the group, to a maximum of 25 points. The six group winners then compete for best in show, from which the winner gains five points plus one point for every other exhibit entered in ordinary classes, to a maximum of 25 points. No exhibit may receive more than 25 points in one show.

Once 100 points have been gained, the record of the animal's

wins is checked by its respective state control, the appropriate fee is paid, and an Australian champion certificate is issued.

Buying a show dog

The first step is to find an animal with show potential. There are several ways of doing this. The local press may report the success of a nearby kennel. Write to it asking if it has any show-type puppies for sale. Remember to enclose a stamped self-addressed envelope. Courtesy is the key to immediate and future assistance. Do not telephone — the owner might be up to the elbows in feeding bowls, a litter of new puppies, or a veterinary visit. To owners, downing tools to answer verbal queries is not a popular pastime.

A second avenue is through the show secretary of your local canine society, whose advertisements will include the secretary's name and address. Write enquiring about successful kennels in the area. Do not telephone — if the secretary does not have a kennel full of dogs, he or she may well be working on the schedule for a forthcoming event or helping the treasurer balance the books.

A third approach is through the national kennel club, who will help you to track down the secretary of the breed club. This person will probably be gnashing his or her teeth over club affairs while holding pen in one hand and paper in the other with the 'phone firmly off the hook! An inquiry here may well result in your discovering a successfully showing and breeding club member within half a day's journey from your home.

Alternatively there are useful publications. The weekly British magazines *Dog World* and *Our Dogs* carry advertisements for forthcoming shows, activities of various clubs, show results and

breeders' advertisements. In your local library's reference or non-fiction section you may discover an edition of *The Dog Directory*. This is a canine reference work with many aspects, and the search for an experienced exhibitor and successful breeder of your chosen breed may well end here.

Once you have found a likely breeder, make a mutually convenient appointment rather than using a family excursion as the excuse for just arriving at the door. And prepare to answer some disconcertingly searching questions. Show the kennel proprietor you can accept advice and encouragement in yet unknown techniques. You will need no prompting to gaze admiringly at the wall of rosettes and green-edged challenge certificates, the complexities of the pedigrees and the beauty of the dogs themselves.

Caring for your show dog

The initial introduction of a pup to its new home is dealt with elsewhere in this book and is no different be it the result of a street-corner mating or the progeny of generations of champions. It will be lost, terrified and wanting its mother. The breeder will have furnished you with the pedigree and the kennel club registration certificate and helped you to fill in the kennel club application for transfer of ownership certificate. If the owner has been using a commercial brand of puppy food, he or she will probably sell or give you enough to last a few days until you find your own supplier. Do not make drastic changes in the pup's diet — it will only suffer from a tummy upset, giving you extra work with mop and bucket.

Feeding a young pup is basically the same whether or not it is intended for showing. Regular meals of good-quality food with well-balanced vitamins and minerals,

Above: Handlers work to set their dogs to best advantage before the judge moves down the line to inspect the entries.

including trace elements, and plentiful helpings of fresh water lay sound foundations for the future. How much you feed depends on the size of your chosen breed. What you feed is a matter of personal choice and convenience. There are several brands of tinned and dried dog foods used with success by many exhibitors.

If you have chosen a breed that needs extensive clipping or stripping, ignoring experienced advice on coat preparation is the quickest way of making friends with your fellow exhibitors. The breeder will probably do the job for you or recommend a professional or competent amateur. If you are determined to do it yourself, be prepared for a non-showable result — and non-showable for at least six months.

Short-coated breeds need grooming, of course, and a bath two or three days before the show will freshen the coat and enable the natural oils to shine.

The Kennel Club has rules about the use of artificial colouring in altering a dog's appearance to meet the breed standard. It allows chalks and powders to be used in cleaning light-coloured coats, provided the substances are removed before the dogs enter the ring. The same applies to any oil or spray. Finally, I should like to discourage the increasingly popular cult of cutting off muzzle whiskers. Their absence makes little difference to the dog's expression or the judge's decision.

Training for the show ring

Apart from helping to make your dog good to look at, you should be

Above: A handler gaits her Pug while the officiating judge (hands on hips) and a trainee judge watch the animal closely.

aiming to make it confident and happy in show conditions. The breeder or your local canine society can advise if there are ring-craft classes nearby. These classes are invaluable to the novice dog and owner. They accustom dogs to accept each other's presence, and help handlers in the techniques of showing and generally getting the best from their charges.

If you have to go it alone, borrow or buy a book about your breed. Visit one or two shows to see how the exhibitors move and stand their dogs. All toy breeds and some terriers stand for judging on a table so, if you aim to show one of these dogs, use the daily grooming routine to help your dog get used to heights — working on the dog at table height will also be kind to your back muscles. Gently run your hands down its back and lift its lip with a finger; as it gains confidence, increase the pressure of your hands, and fully examine its front teeth. Ask a friend to do the same to get your dog experienced with strangers.

The larger breeds stand on the floor, and this is where grooming is useful. Top, sides and chest can be brushed to your crooning 'Stand! Show!' Tummy and tail can be done

later. This may prevent a sudden 'roll-over' in the ring when the judge runs his hands down the exhibit's legs.

Your dog knows right from wrong only by your reactions and voice. If it pleases you, let it know; if it doesn't, growl — its dam (mother) would do just the same.

Lead training is easier said than done. The task is certainly made much less frustrating to you and your dog if you start in your own home and garden. If your garden is not big enough, try to find quiet streets or use a neighbourhood park when the children are occupied at school. Remember, it would be dangerous to expose your pup to the health risks of lampposts, trees and other dogs before it has been fully immunized. The walking show dog usually keeps to its handler's left side, as in obedience training. To keep its attention happily concentrated on you use patience and encouragement, but if necessary resort to bribery or even coercion. Practise in circles, triangles and straight lines. The pup will learn fastest if one person does all this initial training. When the pup is walking well with proud head carriage, other members of the family, such as the children, can become involved.

Benching is a hurdle to be overcome before the show itself. Your dog will accept this restriction in its first show all the better if it is already used to being tethered for short periods. Start at home by tying one end of the lead to the leg of a chair or table as you cook or write letters; graduate to a park or railway station bench. You can either watch the world go by or read a book. Reassure your dog, at intervals, that you still enjoy its company; content with this knowledge, it will probably snooze.

Make haste slowly. Taking a pup straight from places it has learnt to accept and understand into the alien world of showing without adequate preparation may result in aggressiveness to humans and other dogs or to a condition known as 'being ring shy'. Such an animal loves shops, travel, walks — anything but the show ring. You *may* cure the condition, but probably you won't.

Helpful hints for show day

What you need in show equipment largely depends on your choice of breed. Be sure to bring only what is absolutely necessary. You will take

this advice to heart after your first long trail from the car park to your bench, dog in one hand, show clutter growing ever heavier in the other and admission ticket in your teeth.

A dog show is not the best place to wear your latest Dior creation. Comfortable clothes that allow for a change in weather will make for a happier time.

Some shows make provision for eating out, but it is often simpler and less expensive to take your own snacks and drinks. A small folding chair may save hours of standing by the crowded benches. A small bottle of disinfectant, a pair of scissors and some strips of sticking plaster may prove useful. Two plastic bags — one containing damp cotton wool, the other dry tissue — wil help you cope with any show dustiness or slight accident (human or canine). Shows usually have a veterinarian on call and the services of first-aiders if more help is necessary.

Your dog will need water and food bowls. If you forget them, politely decline any kindly intended offers made by other exhibitors. Go and buy some of your own. Virus infections have no respect for even the most cherished dog. Water and food brought from home may prevent a slight tummy upset, although dog foods are on sale at most shows. If you are tempted to give a new tasty dish just before entering the ring, do not be surprised if your dog offers it to the judge's shoes.

You should use a new collar and lead when you enter the ring. Commercially produced leads come in various strengths, colours and designs, and personal taste determines what you buy.

You will need your usual grooming kit. If you are efficient, you will always keep a spare set with other show paraphernalia in a special bag ready for the next event; but even the most experienced exhibitor will confess to last-minute hunting for a vital piece of equipment.

It is moderately easy to acquire a good dog, and experience and determination may take it to the top. But experience can only be gained

Below: Most handlers, like the first two in from the right here, use some form of 'bait' or food treat to get their dogs' attention and thus hold them in a suitable pose.

by attending shows where you must learn to listen and observe intelligently. Standing in the ring for the first time is an ordeal. You will feel convinced that every eye is on you, and it is no consolation to know that people are really concentrating on your dog. Your feelings will go right down the lead; you need not tell your dog about your nerves — it will sense and share them.

Dos and don'ts

Finally, here are some important dos and don'ts of showing.

Don't take your dog to any show if there is the slightest suspicion of illness; if there is a highly infectious 'bug' in your neighbourhood; or if your exhibit is a bitch in season. It is expressly forbidden for the mating of bitches to take place within show precincts. You might not intend to have your bitch mated, but virile, experienced stud dogs will have other aims.

Do arrive at the show on the right day with the right dog. This reminder may seem superfluous; but exhibitors have been known to arrive on gundog or terrier day with a Toy Poodle, or to have entered a bitch in a bitch class and turn up with a dog.

Do allow plenty of travelling time.

Don't in any way attempt to influence a judge to make show decisions in your favour.

Don't criticize other exhibits out loud — their owners feel about them as you feel about yours.

Don't be upset by unwarranted criticism of your dog by other exhibitors — they may be ignorant, jealous or incubating influenza.

Do give yourself and other exhibitors room to show the dogs.

Do allow your dog to relax when other exhibits are being judged, but keep a watchful eye on the judge in case he looks at you.

Do what is asked by the steward.

Do go to the ringside promptly when you are requested to do so.

Don't charge around the ring shouting commands at your dog. It is not deaf, and the judge is not interested in its name. Such demonstrations only give the other exhibitors amusement.

Do answer the judge's questions on age etc, but offer no other information.

Do accept your dog's placing in a sportsmanlike way: congratulate owners whose dogs gained higher awards than yours and commiserate with owners of pets that come off worse. If you don't get a place, there is always another show with another judge.

If you wish to talk to the judge about your exhibit or its placing, do so when his task is ended. You may be surprised to find him a little weary. He may have had more than 90 dogs to examine. If he gave each dog four minutes, he could have been bending, stretching, peering and feeling non-stop for six hours. Then, too, he may have travelled many miles to reach the show and now be wilting at the prospect of the return journey and the subsequent exercising, feeding and bedding of his own dogs.

6
BREEDING YOUR DOG

Wild dogs owe their survival at least partly to their fertility. The ability to produce young quickly and in quantity has carried over to the domesticated dog, although it seems to be waning in some of the purebred breeds. After her nine-week pregnancy, a bitch produces a litter ranging from two or three in smaller breeds to ten or as many as 14 in Labradors and Irish Setters; the really giant breeds are less fecund. The mother can give birth again six to eight months later, so without contraceptive control imposed by dog owners the world would, in theory, soon be overrun by dogs if their offspring survived.

The breeding cycle
In the wild a bitch would breed only once a year, probably in spring; but good feeding, warmth and the easy life of domestication have shortened the intervals at which she accepts a dog. Oestrus periods ('heats' or 'season') at intervals of six, seven, eight or ten months are normal in the domesticated bitch, although the six-month interval is less frequent than many would claim. The Basenji from central Africa, one of the breeds most recently derived from the wild, still comes into season only once a year, in autumn in the Northern Hemisphere, but in April to June in the Antipodes. Experts believe that a lack of animal protein in the diet, possibly caused by feeding vegetable-based dry diets, may delay the breeding season in the domestic bitch of most breeds.

The breeding cycle in mammals is controlled by the hypothalamus, a part of the brain sensitive to both environmental and internal stimuli. Length of available daylight has a part to play; the kennelled bitch kept in darkness for 12 hours daily may have a different cycle from the

Above: Crates are invaluable for housetraining puppies and for providing them with a sense of security and a quite place to rest.

Left: A Poodle and her four puppies to which she has contributed, in theory at least, one-half of their genetic make-up.

bitch kept in a house. A complex interplay between the hypothalamus and the anterior pituitary gland produces hormones triggering the changes that take place in the vagina of the bitch before mating and the production of follicles that will mature, rupture and produce eggs to be fertilized by the male. Hormones also maintain pregnancy and in due course give the signal for whelping to begin and for the mammary glands to start secreting milk for the puppies.

Female puppies come into season for the first time at six- to ten-months-old. If a bitch has passed her first birthday without being in season, you should consult a veterinarian to see if there is some hormonal imbalance that can be

adjusted. It is possible for a bitch to be mated and conceive at her first season, but she is likely to be too immature to rear a litter successfully without endangering her own health and growth potential. Most professional breeders will consider mating a bitch at her second or third season.

The mental state of the bitch is an important factor: some bitches remain juvenile in outlook and may lack a maternal instinct for settling with their puppies and rearing them properly. The bitch that is very owner-orientated, possibly conditioned by over-association to believe that she is more human than dog, may also prove to be a poor mother or may even refuse to be mated.

While it is possible for a bitch to have her first litter when she is quite old, this is an obvious risk to her health and to the production of healthy puppies; seek veterinary advice before mating a bitch for the first time if she is four or over.

Between any two heat periods a bitch has a long period of sexual inactivity culminating in the beginning of pro-oestrus, when the vulva will begin to enlarge and the bitch may show an alteration in temperament, ranging from overexcitement to irritability. She may lick the vulva, so masking the onset of the bloodstained discharge that marks the beginning of her season. If the bitch is to be mated, you should note the date when bloodstained discharge starts, as mating day is calculated from this time. Incidentally, the flow of bloodstained discharge cannot be compared with the human menstrual pattern. In the bitch, the surface of the very long vagina changes when the bitch is on heat and tiny blood vessels become enlarged and finally rupture.

Bleeding from the vulva increases during pro-oestrus, while the lips of the vulva enlarge and soften. During this time, which will last some nine to ten days, the bitch will be increasingly attractive to males, but she will repulse their advances. The plight of a bitch running loose at this time, pursued by a pack of eager males, is pitiful indeed. An unwilling and unready bitch can be mated only by sheer force and with considerable pain.

However, the domestic bitch prepares for the time when she will be ready for copulation by altering her pattern of urination. By frequently passing small amounts of urine she informs males that something interesting is about to occur. At this time the smell of her body and urine are strong enough to be recognized by some humans and all male dogs, including those castrated as adults. So marked are the cell changes within the vulva of a bitch in season that their study may provide a basis for starting a pregnancy where this has hitherto proved impossible. A veterinarian takes a succession of vaginal smears that are examined under a microscope. This reveals the onset of cell changes providing the right climate for mating.

The right time for mating

The optimum day for mating and maximum fertility at conception will be just before the bitch ovulates (produces from the ovary eggs ready for fertilization by the male). The pattern of sexual readiness in the bitch is capable of infinite variation among individuals: some show no bloodstained discharge and they progress by way of enlargement of the vulva straight to accepting the dog. But normally the right time for mating is when the bloodstained discharge has ceased or paled to straw colour, the vulva is grossly enlarged and tumescent, and the bitch turns her tail aside and otherwise plainly invites copulation.

It is not easy to pinpoint the right day for mating. Physically the bitch may be ready, but trauma due to travelling, even nervous tension transmitted by the owner, may occlude a natural response. A bitch is usually willing to accept a dog over a period of four or five days or even more. The standard time for mating is often put at the tenth, 11th, 12th or 13th day after the bloodstained discharge started, but it would be wiser to ignore such formal timetables and judge each bitch as an individual. Beware the common fault of trying to have bitches mated too early in their cycles.

Incidentally where several bitches are kept together, one coming into oestrus will often trigger oestrus in others. They will play simulated mating games, allowing mounting by other bitches much sooner than they would by a male. Unless the bitches become irritable with each other, such behaviour should not be curbed; by human standards it may seem unacceptable, but it represents a natural expression of a sexual urge geared to blood

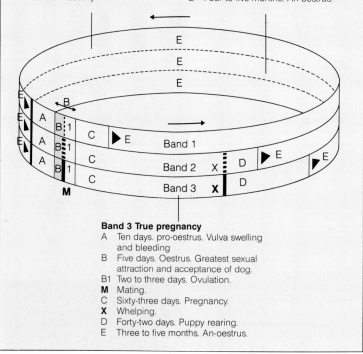

The Oestrus Cycle of the Bitch

Band 1
Normal cycle throughout life
A   Ten days. Pro-oestrus. Vulva swelling and bleeding.
B   Five days. Oestrus. Greatest sexual attraction and acceptance of dog.
B1 Two to three days. Ovulation at beginning of oestrus.
C   Fifteen days. Sex attraction wanes.
E   Five to seven months. An-oestrus. Sexual inactivity

Band 2
Phantom pregnancy
A   Ten days. Pro-oestrus. Vulva swelling and bleeding.
B   Five days. Oestrus. Greatest sexual attraction and acceptance of dog.
B1 Two to three days. Ovulation.
C   Sixty-three days. 'Pregnancy'.
X   Imaginary whelping.
D   Ten days. Imaginary puppy rearing.
E   Four to five months. An-oestrus.

Band 3 True pregnancy
A   Ten days. pro-oestrus. Vulva swelling and bleeding.
B   Five days. Oestrus. Greatest sexual attraction and acceptance of dog.
B1 Two to three days. Ovulation.
M   Mating.
C   Sixty-three days. Pregnancy.
X   Whelping.
D   Forty-two days. Puppy rearing.
E   Three to five months. An-oestrus.

Above: The duration of the oestrus cycle may vary among bitches. The different intervals in that cycle, noted above, are useful averages.

Below: This yellow Labrador bitch does not look as if she has too much longer to wait before she whelps her puppies.

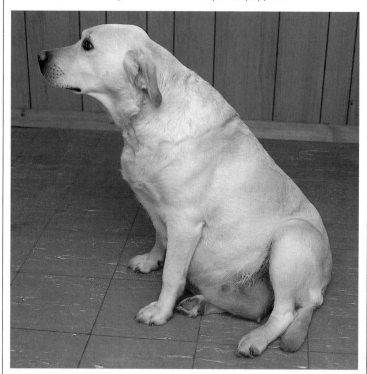

engorgement of the bitches' genital organs.

The male dog

Male puppies just a few weeks old frequently practise mating behaviour as part of generalized play within the litter. When they are put into individual homes, this phase is forgotten and may never again be important.

There is no need for an adolescent or adult male to have sexual experience; indeed this is best avoided for a dog kept just for companionship. A companion dog

used at stud on only one occasion may be disorientated by the experience and tend to wander, show aggression towards other males and increase marking behaviour in the home and garden. If dogs are not going to be used for breeding, they should be neutered or spayed between seven and ten months of age.

The external genitals of the male dog consist of a penis covered in a hairy sheath and two testicles that retain the sperm at the correct temperature for fertility. A proportion of dogs, more in some breeds than others, have only one visible testicle, the other being retained within the body; such a dog is termed a unilateral cryptorchid.

Normally both testicles are inside the body of the male puppy at birth but descend through the inguinal canal to the outside of the body at eight to 16 weeks of age. Where only one appears by that time the undescended testicle may still appear around the age of nine months. Incidentally, in the young puppy there is a tendency for a testicle to retract at times of tension. A veterinarian can tell whether an apparently missing testicle is present and likely to descend, and the buyer of an expensive pedigree male puppy is likely to demand a certificate to this effect, particularly if the dog is intended for show or stud work.

The unilateral cryptorchid dog can be fertile and sire puppies but, as the condition is thought to be hereditary, it is not desirable to use such a dog at stud. Rarely, neither testile descends, in which case the dog is infertile. Unilateral cryptorchid dogs may be exhibited under the rules of the Kennel Club, but the American Kennel Club rules forbid this. Not only is it undesirable to perpetuate dogs with a major anatomical fault, but the retained testicle is prone to tumour formation and will have to be removed surgically.

The mating

During copulation the dog's penis emerges from the hair-covered sheath and increases in size, becoming very flexible. The genitals of the family Canidae are unique in having the bulbus glandis. This structure swells to balloon-like size after ejaculation and, aided by the vaginal muscles of the bitch, enables the mating pair to be locked together or 'tied' for anything up to an hour after copulation; 20 minutes is the average time. The reason for this unique mating scheme has never been satisfactorily explained.

If the bitch is ready for mating and time is allowed for pre-mating play, she will eventually allow herself to be caught by the dog, and will then stand quietly, tail turned to one side, allowing the dog the facility for penetration. The male will mount the bitch, clasping her behind the ribs with his forepaws. With penis inserted into the wide open vagina, the dog will make several thrusting movements and may retract several times and remount but will finally, with shuddering movements,

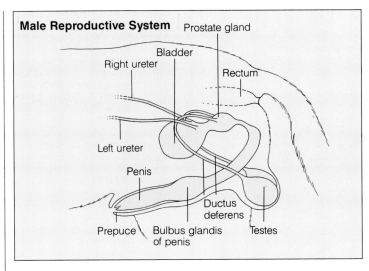

Male Reproductive System

Prostate gland
Bladder
Right ureter
Rectum
Left ureter
Penis
Ductus deferens
Prepuce
Bulbus glandis of penis
Testes

Female Reproductive System

Horns of Uterus
Body of uterus
Right ureter
Vagina
Cervix
Ovaries
Left ureter
Bladder
Vulva

ejaculate sperm high into the vagina, near the cervix.

Dog ejaculate is in three fractions with a momentary pause between each; the first being a lubricating medium, the second containing several thousand sperm, and the final serving to flush the sperm onwards towards the target area of the fallopian tubes.

After this phase is over, the dog will want to ease his position during the long tie. He will dismount and lift a hindleg across the back of the bitch or be assisted to do so by handlers, so that he stands with four feet on the ground, locked together with the bitch but back to back; the dog's penis being bent at 180deg within the bitch. Later, they will break away naturally, and the dog will lick his genitals until the penis returns within the sheath.

It is possible to have a fertile mating without the tie if the dog has remained within the bitch long enough for the sperm-bearing factor of the ejaculate to be deposited. Eagerness to perform a mating and the ability to do so in apparently copybook fashion is no proof that the dog is fertile. He may have too little ejaculate, or the sperm may be abnormally shaped or show bent or double tails so that propulsion is lost.

The health history of the dog is also significant, as a virus infection giving a high body temperature may render a dog infertile for as long as six months although he is apparently fully recovered. It would be rare to find that over-use of a stud dog caused infertility; a dog should be capable of several matings a week over a short period of time. When a dog has mated several bitches without puppies resulting, it is reasonable to suggest that a sperm count and testicular biopsy should be performed.

Some dogs are psychologically inhibited from mating bitches because of past reprimands for anti-social behaviour. Then, too, to some extent we select *away* from the most virile dogs when we choose as companions or for exhibition tractable males easily controlled in the show ring.

Every normal bitch puppy is born with some half-million potential eggs in the ovaries. The breeder's problems lie in getting a handful of eggs fertilized at the right time by

normal active sperm and then implanted in the uterus where the resulting foetuses can be carried to term by the bitch so that she will bear viable puppies. At each oestrus period the bitch releases from four to 20 immature eggs that will take hours or even one or two days to 'ripen' sufficiently for sperm to penetrate them. Fortunately, active sperm can remain alive for up to two days after mating, so there is time for sperm and eggs to meet productively.

Allowing two or even three matings gives sperm and ova the best possible chance to reach each other in peak condition. All the ova are shed at the same time, so there is no chance that whelping will be unduly prolonged even if dog and bitch run together and mate at will over six days; nor will natural matings of this type produce an abnormally high number of pups.

Possible problems with mating

Since the mid-1960s conditions of dog ownership and lack of kennel help have encouraged too much human interference with dog matings. After travelling hundreds of miles to bring his bitch to a carefully selected dog, many an owner frustrates his own designs by demanding instant mating. There is often neither time nor space for the two animals to become acquainted or to perform their stylized mating play. Sometimes the bitch is shackled and held down by two or more helpers, and the dog is lifted on to her back and manipulated until he performs the mating act. Some breeders have been known to say that dogs could not mate without human assistance, yet there is wide concern about the number of unproductive matings from apparently fertile animals.

Many veterinary experts in this

field believe that more fruitful matings would follow a return to the natural running together of dog and bitch, over some days if need be, with just enough human interference to steady the bitch at the time of penetration.

However, by no means all failed matings are the owner's fault. Some bitches seem physically ready for mating yet refuse a dog's advances. Some suffer a hormonal imbalance that makes them too masculine. Others have some abnormality of vulva or vagina causing pain or preventing penetration. Toy bitches that have been over-protected may not allow any dog to come near them,

Below: Puppies develop a preference for an individual nipple when quite young. They retain that preference through puppyhood.

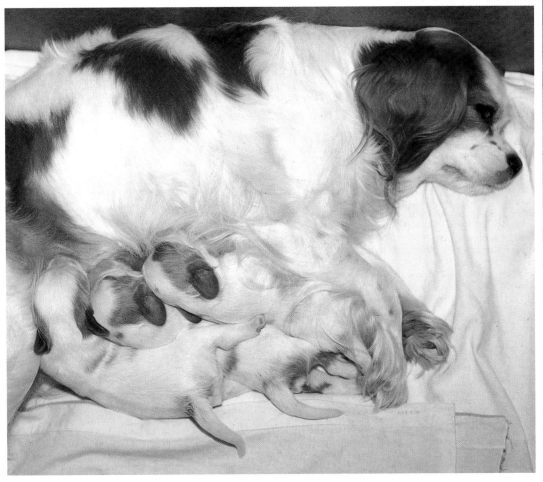

although some behave more naturally if apart from doting and fearful owners.

Using a stud dog

Choosing a stud dog is a process demanding considerable fore-thought. Owners should make inquiries about any hereditary diseases prevalent in the breed, and the owners of both bitch and dog should be prepared to provide copies of certificates of freedom from disease if such documents are issued by their country's breed club or kennel club. It is also important to check that the bitch's current owner has correctly registered her at the national kennel club, otherwise registration of the puppies may be impeded.

A stud fee is payable immediately after mating. A receipt and a copy of the dog's pedigree bearing kennel club numbers should be provided in return for the fee, and if the stud dog owner has to sign an official kennel club form to say that the mating has taken place, this is best done at the same time in the presence of both the dog-owning parties involved.

There may be some temptation to make some other arrangement, perhaps for the stud owner to take a puppy or two puppies in lieu of a fee, or to buy a certain number of the puppies when they are reared. It cannot be emphasized too strongly that such agreements are full of pitfalls. For one thing the bitch owner is committed in advance to dispose of puppies about which they may feel very differently once they are born and reared. Then, too, the litter may not contain the sexes and colours needed to meet the agreement. Almost always someone ends up feeling aggrieved. It is much better to pay the stud fee outright than be bound by another's interest.

Before the mating is even accomplished it is wise to find out how and where tails will be docked and dew-claws removed if these practices are customary in the breed. Veterinary opinion is hardening against such multilations for purely cosmetic purposes. In the United Kingdom a lay person may perform this operation before the puppies' eyes are open, but ear cropping — even by veterinarians — is not permitted, although in some countries in Europe and in the United States ear cropping is accepted in some breeds.

The brood bitch should be chosen from a line with full fertility on both her dam's and sire's side. Avoid lines with a history of birth by Caesarean section and low litter numbers.

Phantom pregnancy

Whether or not a mating was fertile or even occurred, the hormonal changes of pregancy or closely similar changes may ensue in the bitch. So great is the hormonal influence that an unmated bitch may give every impression of being pregnant, even 'thinking' herself into labour pains, producing milk and nursing some toy or household object as her make-believe litter.

It is important not to pander to such a bitch, as humouring her only prolongs the condition and she may become irritable and bad tempered in trying to protect invisible puppies. She is best distracted with increased exercise and play, and her chosen objects and whelping bed should be taken away. Extreme cases may need hormone treatment.

Pregnancy

The bitch who is genuinely pregnant shows little sign for at least a month. She requires no extra food until she is about half the way through pregnancy, which is calculated at roughly 63 days, but allowing for delay in fertilization and breed idiosyncrasy may last a week longer or several days fewer. At the fifth week of pregnancy there should be some thickening of the bitch's shape behind her ribs, and her mammary glands should begin to develop; there may be a little morning sickness and her appetitie may vary from day to day. From the sixth week of her pregnancy you should offer meals three times, or even more frequently, during the day to allow for the displacement of the stomach by the swelling ulterus.

Each embryo puppy floats in fluid enclosed in a double foetal sac attached to the walls of the horn-shaped uterus by a placenta. Growth in the last three weeks of pregnancy is so rapid that the uterus may have to fold back upon itself, making a dramatic change in the outline of the bitch, and seeming to cause her a little discomfort, for bitches often seem to stop eating for a day at this time. Only towards the very end of pregnancy is bone laid down in puppy skeletons, which then show up on X-ray; and towards the end of pregnancy you can see definite movements of the puppies when the bitch is resting.

A milk-like substance may be present already in the mammary glands or may not arrive until after whelping. Owners sometimes worry because the bitch has an uneven number of teats or because there are fewer of these than puppies born, but puppies are resourceful and neither fear is justified.

The whelping (birth)

The beginning of whelping is usually marked by a refusal of food, restlessness and a very deep, nervous painting that seems to use up a great deal of the bitch's energy. This is the most distressing stage of whelping, for the actual labour pains seem to worry her far less than the initial apprehension. Left to her own devices she would seek out a secluded, dark place in which to have her puppies, and, if allowed to, will dig a burrow that will be suitable for the purpose.

A bitch with a newborn litter feels by instinct extremely vulnerable to interference, so her whelping quarters should be arranged to give her the maximum physical and psychological protection. Her whelping box should have high sides and a lid, removable if she needs help and for cleaning; she should be in a room away from household bustle and where she will not feel threatened by the sight or sound of other dogs, and no audience should be invited to witness her whelping.

The veterinarian attending should be warned when the bitch goes into first-stage labour, as veterinary services may be needed at any time, but as the average bitch's labour is so long it is not possible to have a veterinarian in attendance all the time.

The initial stage of panting and

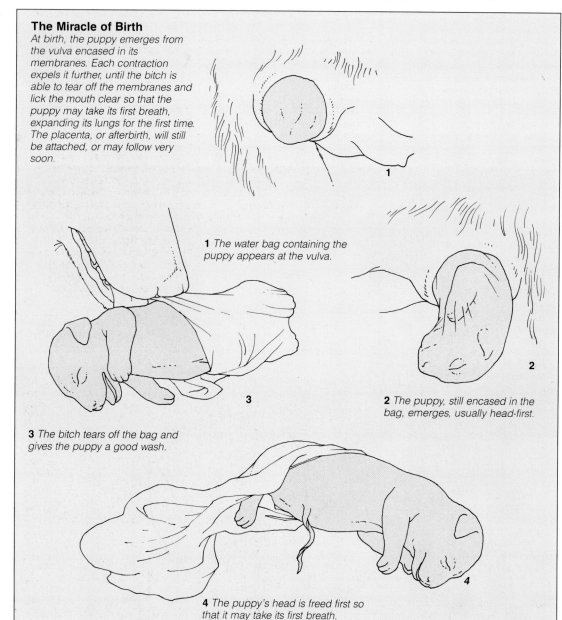

The Miracle of Birth

At birth, the puppy emerges from the vulva encased in its membranes. Each contraction expels it further, until the bitch is able to tear off the membranes and lick the mouth clear so that the puppy may take its first breath, expanding its lungs for the first time. The placenta, or afterbirth, will still be attached, or may follow very soon.

1 The water bag containing the puppy appears at the vulva.

2 The puppy, still encased in the bag, emerges, usually head-first.

3 The bitch tears off the bag and gives the puppy a good wash.

4 The puppy's head is freed first so that it may take its first breath.

Bottle-feeding the Correct Way

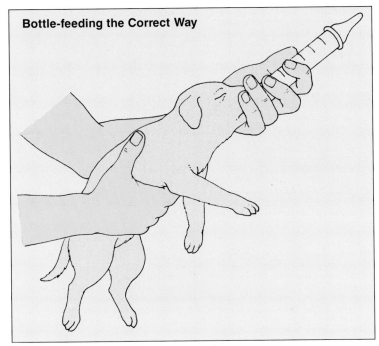

Above: Holding the puppy at a 45 deg angle to your lap, slide the nipple end of the bottle (at top here) gently between it's lips.

apprehension can last for 12 hours or longer and become extremely enervating; the actual expelling pains are quite short and do not seem to distress the bitch very much. Once hormonal action has induced a placenta to separate from the wall of the uterus, the puppy in its sac surrounded by another sac, filled with fluid, rotates and starts its journey through cervix and vagina and on into the outside world. Ideally it arrives head first, although many puppies are born feet first, which seldom seems to matter.

If everything is going well, one or two deep, expelling pains will bring the water bag filled with dark fluid to the vulva, and the subsequent strain will push out the puppy, still in its foetal membranes. These must now be removed as quickly as possible to prevent the puppy inhaling fluid into the lungs. The bitch may instinctively bite open and eat the membranes, bite off the umbilical cord and start to dry the puppy.

If she is still so swollen with puppies that she cannot easily reach her vulva, or if she lacks the instinct to attend to her young, then the attendant owner must open the bags and dry the puppy, cutting the umbilical cord a long way from the puppy, after smoothing any blood remaining in the cord towards the pup. There is no need to tie the umbilical cord in any way.

The placenta; or afterbirth, should arrive with the puppy or very soon after. The bitch will instinctively want to eat the placenta, which looks like a piece of liver, abounds in nourishment and would thus provide a valuable meal for a bitch in the wild at a time when she could not hunt. If the litter is large, the bitch may eat so many placentas that she suffers diarrhoea. Because she will be unwilling to leave her puppies until the last minute, this condition can be extremely inconvenient, so the owner should try to take away at least half the placentas: it is easier to get the early ones, before the bitch realizes what she is losing. As her distended body is eased and the bitch realizes what is happening, she herself will usually attend to later arrivals in the litter.

Puppies should be born into a warm draught-free atmosphere and must be dried quickly as they are unable to adjust their body heat to the lowered temperature of the outside world. More puppies die from chilling than from any other single cause; the most critical period is the first few hours after birth, when the dam is preoccupied with expelling other puppies and the whelping box is continually being drenched with fluids from them. But you should not remove the first-born puppies from the bitch as this distresses her, and their presence and attempts to suckle are said to induce hormonal change that speeds up subsequent births.

It is pleasant indeed if puppies follow each other at 40-minute to hourly intervals until the bitch is obviously empty and at rest. Unfortunately, hold-ups occur if a bitch becomes tired and loses the will to expel the puppies. Then the attendant must judge whether the interval between puppies has been unduly long (say over 90 minutes). If there are indeed still puppies to be born, continuing delay could mean they are dead, but an injection of oxytocin by a veterinarian will usually restart contractions.

Birth trouble can arise if a puppy is grossly over-sized or fails to present at the cervix in a direct manner. Where the bitch is straining but making no progress with birth, delay is dangerous and a veterinarian must be consulted with a view to delivery by Caesarean section, a reasonably safe operation provided it is carried out before the bitch is exhausted.

The early life of the puppies

Puppies will instinctively find their way to a teat and should be encouraged to do so. In the first few hours after birth they receive the all-important colostrum which carries antibodies for diseases that the dam has encountered or been vaccinated against. For some weeks after whelping the bitch will have a discharge from the vulva. This emission is dark at first but later pales to bright, blood red, derived from the attachment sites of the placentas. Thus there is proportionately more discharge for a large litter. Any continuation of a dark or foul-smelling discharge indicates urgent need for veterinary help, as a puppy or a placenta may have been retained, potentially with extremely grave consequences.

The bitch requires a great deal of food and water while feeding her puppies, reaching peak demand three weeks after birth. Later, in imitation of her wild ancestors, she may vomit her own partly digested food for the young puppies to eat.

Puppies are born without sight or hearing, eyes and ears being poorly developed at birth. Eyes open at around ten days and puppies can hear at three weeks, by when they should be moving around, if a little unsteadily. The bitch licks her newborn puppies constantly to clean them and to stimulate urination and defecation, consuming all their body wastes until weaning begins.

If the bitch has plenty of milk, weaning need not start until five or six weeks or until the puppies start to investigate the bitch's own food, showing they are ready for more than milk. If late weaning is contemplated, the bitch should not be shut up with her puppies, unable to escape their ceaseless worrying.

Puppies have much to learn from the dam even after she has stopped feeding them. Although some breeders will want to remove the dam quickly so that she may regain her figure and show condition, in many ways this is a pity, for bitch and puppies enjoy each other's company so much. Ideally, the bitch should have some contact with her puppies until they leave for new homes at eight to 12 weeks of age, the time depending on breed and size.

Contraception

If a bitch is not required for breeding puroses, she and her owner are spared a great deal of trouble if she has her reproductive organs removed once she is adult and fully developed. The veterinarian calls this operation an ovario-hysterectomy; the popular phrase is having her spayed.

It is of no physical or mental advantage to the bitch to allow her to have one litter. This folk legend has meant that a lot of surplus puppies have been bred by people with little knowledge of the subject, inadequate premises and inability to find permanent homes for them.

After being spayed, the bitch need not put on weight or become lethargic: the outcome depends on owner management. Spayed bitches may be exhibited in the United Kingdom provided they have had a litter registered at the Kennel Club; the same ruling applies to castrated dogs but they are seldom in top-class competition. The American Kennel Club permits exhibition of neither spayed bitches nor castrated dogs.

An alternative method of contraception, and one that leaves breeding options open, is giving the bitch a branded form of progesterone. This hormone inhibits ovulation in a similar fashion to the human contraceptive pill. Several versions of this drug have been marketed, to be given orally or by injection, and the much improved latest editions are perfectly safe and allow manipulation of the oestrus period so that the bitch can be brought into season and readiness for breeding at the owner's convenience.

Vasectomy (cutting the excretory duct of the testicles) is possible for the male dog. This operation should make him infertile but will not prevent active mating behaviour and urine marking of territory, so it is of little value to the pet dog owner, although a vasectomized dog might be a valuable addition to a kennel to indicate when bitches are ready for mating, especially if they are to be taken to a distant stud dog.

Below: When a puppy is first weaned, it often has to be introduced gently to its new food by its owner.

GLOSSARY

Words in *italics* refer to separate entries within the glossary

A

Action The way a dog moves.

AKC American Kennel Club.

Albino Animal with pigmentation deficiency.

All-rounder A judge qualified to adjudicate all recognized breeds.

Almond eyes Oval-shaped like an almond, slanted at corners.

Amble A relaxed, easy *gait* in which the legs on either side move almost, but not quite, as a pair. Often seen as the transitional movement between the *walk* and the faster *gaits*.

Angulation The angles formed by a meeting of the bones: mainly, the shoulder, upper arm, *stifle* and *hock*.

Ankylosis The abnormal adhesion of bones, especially those forming a joint; stiffening of a joint.

Anorchid A male dog without testicles.

Anticipating In obedience training, acting before receiving a command.

Apophysis An outgrowth or projection, especially one from a bone.

Apple-headed Having a skull rounded on top. Not desirable in most breeds.

Apron The long hair on the throat and below the neck on long-coated dogs.

B

B (or b) Abbreviation for bitch.

Babbler A hound that barks when not on the *trail*.

Back Variable in meaning depending upon standard. In some standards defined as the vertebrae between the *withers* and the *loin*.

Bad mouth Teeth crooked or misaligned; *overshot* or *undershot* bite.

Balanced A consistent whole; symmetrical, typically proportioned as a whole, or as regards its separate parts: e.g. balance of head, of body, or balance of head and body.

Bandy legs Legs bent outwards.

Barrel Rounded rib section.

Barrel hocks *Hocks* that turn out, causing the toes to turn in (also called spread hocks, or divergent hocks).

Basewide Having a wide footfall, resulting from a *paddling* movement, and causing body to rock from side to side.

Bat ears large, stiff open ears pointing outwards (like a French Bulldog's).

Bay The long-drawn-out sound made by a hound in pursuit.

Beard The very profuse, bushy *whiskers* of the Griffon Bruxellois, as opposed to terrier whiskers.

Beauty spot A distinct spot, usually round, of coloured hair, surrounded by the white of the *blaze*, on the top of the skull between the ears (e.g. Boston Terrier).

Beefy Over-heavy development of the *hindquarters*.

Belton The lemon- or blue-flecked colour of certain English Setters, notably the Laverack strain. Also orange or liver belton.

Bench show A dog show at which the dogs competing for prizes are 'benched' (leashed on benches).

Best In Show The animal judged to be the best of all the breeds in a show.

Bevy A flock of birds.

Bilateral cryptorchid See *cryptorchid*.

Bird dog A sporting dog trained to hunt birds.

Bitch a female dog.

Bite The position of the teeth when the mouth is shut.

Blanket The colour of coat on the back and upper part of the sides, between the neck and the tail.

Blaze A white stripe running up the middle of the face, generally between the eyes.

Blenheim A variety of spaniel with white and reddish markings.

Blinker A dog that points a bird and then leaves it, or, upon finding a bird, avoids making a definite *point*.

Blocky Having a square or cube-like formation of the head.

Blooded Of good breeding; pedigreed.

Bloom The glossiness of a *coat* in the very best condition.

Blue merle Blue and grey mixed with black. Marbled.

Bluies Coloured portions of the coat with a distinct bluish or smoky cast. This colouring is associated with extremely light or blue eyes, and liver or grey eye rims, nose and lip pigment (e.g. Pembroke Welsh Corgi).

Board To kennel and care for a dog in its owner's absence, for a fee.

BOB Abbreviation for Best of Breed.

Bobtail (1) A naturally tailless dog, or a dog with a tail *docked* very short. (2) Common name for the Old English Sheepdog.

Bodied up Mature, well developed.

Bolt To drive or 'start' an animal out of its earth or burrow.

Bone A well-boned dog is one with limbs that give an appearance and feel of strength and spring without *coarseness*.

Bossy With overdevelopment of the shoulder muscles.

Braccoid Belonging to the *hound* family of dogs.

Brace A pair of dogs of the same type.

Breastbone Bone running down the middle of the chest, to which all but the *floating ribs* are attached; *sternum*.

Breeching The tan hairs on the inside and back of the thighs, seen in Manchester Terriers.

Breed A variety of *purebred* dog; a dog or bitch with a *pedigree*.

Breeder Someone who breeds dogs.

Breeding particulars *Sire*, *dam*, date of birth, sex, colour, kennel club registration details, etc.

Brindle A mixture of light and dark hairs, usually darker streaks on a grey, tawny of brown background.

Brisket The part of the lower chest that includes the breastbone.

Brock A badger.

Broken colour *Self colour* relieved by white or another colour.

Broken-haired A roughed-up wire coat.

Broken-up face A receding nose, together with a deep *stop*, *wrinkle*, and *undershot* jaw (e.g. Bulldog, Pekingese).

Brood bitch A *bitch* kept for breeding.

Brush A bushy tail; a tail heavy with hair (e.g. Alaskan Malamute).

Brushing A *gaiting* fault, when parallel *pasterns* are so close that the legs brush in passing.

Bull baiting A cruel sport of bygone days in which a dog or dogs baited a bull.

Bull neck A heavy neck, well muscled.

Burr The irregular inner part of the pinna of the ear.

Butterfly nose A nose of two colours, usually dark brown or black spotted with flesh colour.

Buttocks The rump or hips.

Button ear Ear that folds over in front, with tip drooping forward, as in the Fox Terrier.

Bye At *field trials*, an odd dog remaining after the dogs entered in a *stake* have been paired in *braces* by *drawing*.

C

Camel back Arched back, like that of a one-hump camel.

Canine Applies to dogs, foxes, wolves and jackals.

Canines The two upper and two lower sharp-pointed teeth next to the *incisors*; fangs.

Canter A *gait* with three beats to each stride, two legs moving separately and two as a diagonal pair. Slower than the *gallop* and not as tiring.

Carinated Keel-shaped; having a prominent central line like the bottom of a ship.

Carpals Bones of the *pastern* joints.

Carp back Arched back.

Castrate To remove the testicles of a male dog; to geld.

Catch dog A dog used to catch and hold a hunted animal, so that the huntsman can take it alive.

Cat feet Short, compact and round feet common to terriers, as opposed to *splay feet*.

CD (Companion Dog) A suffix used with the name of a dog that has been recorded a Companion Dog by the *AKC* as a result of having won certain minimum scores at three obedience trials under three different judges.

CDX (Companion Dog Excellent) A suffix used with the name of a dog that has been recorded a Companion Dog Excellent by the *AKC* as a result of having won certain minimum scores in three *open classes* at obedience trials.

Cephalic index The ratio, multiplied by 100, of the greatest breadth of the dog's head from side to side, to the length from above the root of the nose to the occiput.

Challenge Certificate (CC) Award given, at *judge's* discretion, to best of sex of *breed* at UK championship shows.

Champion A dog that has won three *challenge certificates* under three different *judges* at championship shows in the UK. In the USA the title is awarded on points won at major shows.

Character Expression, individuality, and general appearance and deportment as considered typical of a *breed*.

Cheeky With cheeks prominently rounded, thick, or protruding.

Chest The part of the body or trunk enclosed by the ribs.

Chicken-breasted With a short, protruding *breastbone*.

China eye A clear blue eye.

Chippendale front Named after the Chippendale chair: forelegs out at *elbows*, *pasterns* close, and feet turned out. See also *fiddle front*.

Chiselled Clean-cut in the head, particularly beneath the eyes.

Choke chain/collar A chain or leather collar fitted to the dog's neck in such a way that the amount of pressure exerted by hand tightens or loosens it. Also referred to as a check chain.

Chops The thick upper lips that hang below the lower jaw (e.g. in the Bloodhound).

Chorea A nervous jerking caused by involuntary contraction of the muscles, usually affecting the face or legs.

Clip A type of *trim*, as used on the Poodle.

Clipping The back foot striking the front foot during the *gait*.

Cloddy Low, thick-set, rather heavy.

Close-coupled Having a short back or a short body.

Coarse Without refinement.

Coat The dog's hair covering.

Cobby Short-bodied, compact.

Collar (1) A marking around the neck, usually white. (2) A circle of leather or chain used to direct and control the dog when the leash (lead) is attached.

Condition Health, shown by coat, weight, general appearance and deportment.

Conformation Form and structure, make-up and shape: arrangement of the parts in conformance with breed *standard* requirements.

Corky Active, lively, alert.

Couple A pair of hounds.

Couplings The length of the body between the last rib and the pelvis.

Coursing The sport of chasing the hare by Greyhounds.

Covering ground The ratio of the distance between the ground and the *brisket* and the distance between the front and rear legs.

Cow-hocked With *hocks* turned towards one another.

Crabbing Moving with the body at an angle to the line of travel. Also referred to as side-winding, side-wheeling or yawing.

Crank tail A tail carried down with the tip held outwards in the shape of a crank.

Crest The upper, arched portion of the neck (e.g. Chinese Crested).

Crop To cut off the tops of the ears so that they stand erect. Illegal in some countries.

Cross-bred The progeny of *purebred* parents of different *breeds*.

Crossing over Unsound *gaiting action* that starts with twisting elbows and ends with criss-crossing and toeing out. Known also as weaving and purling.

Croup The rear part of the back, above the hind legs.

Crown The highest part of the head: the top of the skull.

Cry The *baying* of the hounds.

Cryptorchid An adult dog whose testicles have not descended into the scrotum. Bilateral cryptorchids are affected on both sides: unilateral cryptorchids on one side only.

Cull A pup that is a very inferior specimen of its *breed*.

Culotte The feathery hair on the backs or the legs.

Cur A mongrel.

Cushion Fullness or thickness of the upper lip.

Cynology The study of *canines*.

D

Dam The mother of a *litter* of puppies.

Dappled A mottled colour — generally patches of silver and tan, black, or black and tan.

Dead grass Tan or dull straw colour.

Depigmentation Partial or complete loss of coloration.

Derby *Field trial* competition for young, novice sporting dogs, usually between one and two years of age.

Dew-claw A claw on the inside of the leg, which is usually removed in early puppyhood but retained by some breeds.

Dewlap Loose hanging skin under the throat and chin (as in the Bloodhound).

Diagonals Right front and left rear legs constitute the right diagonal: left front and right rear legs constitute the left diagonal. In the *trot*, the diagonals move together.

Diehard Nickname for the Scottish Terrier (or Aberdeen Terrier).

Dish-faced Having the nasal bone higher at the nose than at the *stop*.

Disqualification A decision made by a *judge* or show committee, ruling that a dog has a condition making it ineligible for further competition under the *dog show* rules or under the *standard* for its breed.

Distemper teeth Teeth marked, pitted, ringed and often stained, due to distemper or other severe infection.

Divergent hocks See *barrel hocks*.

Dock To shorten the tail by cutting, usually done in early puppyhood if breed *standards* demand.

Dog (1) Any member of the species *Canis familiaris*. (2) A male of that species (see *bitch*).

Dog show An exhibition at which dogs are judged in accordance with an established *standard* of perfection for each breed.

Dolichocephalic Having a disproportionately long head, the skull and *muzzle* both being long and the *bite* even: a skull with a *cephalic index* below 75.

Dome The rounded part of the skull, as in spaniels.

Double coat An *under-coat* of soft, thick hair to warm the body, and an outer coat of coarse, strong hair to keep out dampness and cold.

Down-faced The *muzzle* inclining downwards from the skull to the tip of the nose.

Down in pastern Weak or faulty *pastern* set at a pronounced angle from the vertical.

Drag A trail prepared by dragging along the ground a scent impregnated bag.

Drawing Selection by lot of dogs to be run, and in which pairs, in a *field trial stake*.

Drive A solid thrusting of the *hindquarters*, denoting sound locomotion.

Drop-eared When the ears are pendent, and hanging close and flat to the side of the cheeks.

Dropper A *bird dog* cross.

Dry neck The skin taut: neither loose nor wrinkled.

Dual champion Dog that has won championships in both *dog shows* and *field trials*.

Dudley nose Flesh-coloured nose.

E

Elbow The joint between the upper arm and the forearm.

Elbows out Elbows pointing away from the body.

Entropion A condition in which the eyelid turns inward and the lashes irritate the eyeball.

Even bite Meeting of front teeth at edges with no overlap of upper or lower teeth.

Ewe neck Concave curvature of the top neckline.

Expression The general appearance of all features of the head as viewed from the front and as typical of the *breed*.

Eye-teeth The upper *canines*.

F

Faking Changing the appearance of a dog by artificial means, with the objective of deceiving the onlooker as to its real merit.

Fall Long hair overhanging the face.

Fallow Pale yellow colour.

Fancier Someone active in the sport of breeding, showing and judging *purebred* dogs.

Fangs See *canines*.

Fawn A rich light golden tan.

FCI Fédération Cynologique Internationale.

Feathering Long, fine fringe of hair seen on the ears, legs, tail and body of breeds such as spaniels.

Feet east and west With the toes turned out.

Femoral-tibial joint The joining of the thigh and shin bone.

Fetch (1) The retrieval of *game* by a dog. (2) The command to do so.

Fiddle face An elongated, pinched-in *foreface*.

Fiddle front The front of a dog with bandy or croooked forelegs; French front.

Field trial A competition for certain *hound* or sporting breeds in which dogs are judged on their ability and style in finding or retrieving *game* or following a game trail.

Field Trial Champion (Field Ch.) A prefix used with the name of a dog that has been recorded a Field Trial Champion by the *AKC* as a result of beating strong competition in specified competitions at AKC licensed *field trials*.

Flag The fringe or *feathering* found under the tails of setters and some retrievers, long at the base and shorter at the tip.

Flank The side of the body between the last rib and the hip.

Flare A *blaze* that widens as it approaches the top of the skull.

Flat bone The leg bone whose girth is elliptical rather than round.

Flat-sided (Ribs) insufficiently rounded as they approach the *breastbone*.

Flat withers An unattractive fault that is the result of short upright shoulder blades that join the *withers* abruptly.

Flecked Lightly *ticked* with other colours, as in the English Setter, and neither *roan* nor spotted.

Flesh nose Pink or tan nose.

Flews Hanging upper lips, like those of a Bulldog; usually refers to the lateral parts of the lips.

Flexor-cubital muscle A muscle the action of which is to flex the joint at the *elbow*.

Flicking pasterns Extremely loose movement of the lower forelegs.

Floating rib The last, or 13th rib, which is unattached to other ribs.

Fluffies A coat of extreme length with exaggerated *feathering* on ears, chest, feet and legs, underparts and *hindquarters*.

Flush To drive birds from cover, to force them to take flight: to spring.

Fly-eared Ears that should be erect fall or tilt at the tips; usually a blemish.

Flying lips Unsettled lips, not assuming the correct position.

Flying trot A fast *gait* in which all four feet are off the ground for a brief second during each half stride. Because of the long reach, the oncoming hindfeet step beyond the imprint left by the front. Also called suspension trot.

Forearm The bone of the foreleg between the *elbow* and the *pastern*.

Foreface The front part of the head before the eyes: the *muzzle*.

Foster mother A *bitch* used to nurse another animal's *whelps*.

Foul colour An uncharacteristic colour or marking.

Foxy Having a pointed nose and short *foreface*.

French front See *fiddle front*.

Frill Long hair under the neck and on the forechest.

Fringes The *featherings* of long-coated breeds.

Frog-face Extending nose accompanied by a receding jaw, usually *overshot*.

Front The whole front part of the body.

Frontal bone The skull bone over the eyes.

Furnishings The long hair on the *foreface* of certain breeds.

Furrow A groove running down the centre of the skull, as in the Bulldog: also called median line.

Futurity stake A class at *dog shows* or *field trials* for young dogs that have been nominated at, or before, birth.

G

Gait A style of movement, e.g. running or trotting.

Gallop Fastest of the dog *gaits* or *paces*; a four-beat rhythm and often an extra period of suspension during which the body is propelled through the air with all four feet off the ground.

Game Birds or other animals that are hunted.

Gay tail A tail carried straight up.

Gazehound A hound that hunts by sight.

Geld See *castrate*.

Genealogy Recorded family descent.

Giving tongue *Baying* on the trail of *game*.

Goose rump A sharply sloping rump.

Graioid Belonging to the Greyhound family.

Grizzle Bluish-grey colour.

Groom To brush, comb, trim and otherwise prepare a dog's coat for show or pleasure.

Groups The breeds are grouped to facilitate judging.

Guard hairs The longer, smoother, stiffer hairs that grow through the *under-coat* and normally conceal it.

Gundog Dog trained to assist the hunter in the field (e.g. retrievers, setters, spaniels and pointers).

Guns Those who shoot at *field trials*.

Gun-shy Frightened by the sound of a gun being fired.

H

Hackles Hair on the neck and back raised involuntarily in fright or anger.

Hackney gait A vigorous, proud, high-stepping *gait*.

Ham Well-developed hindleg muscles just above the knee.

Handler A person who handles (shows) a dog at *dog shows, field trials*, or obedience tests.

Hard-mouthed Given to biting down hard on *retrieved game*: a serious fault.

Hare feet Long, narrow, close-toed feet, as in the hare.

Harlequin A combination of colours in patches on a solid ground as in the coat of a Great Dane: usually blue on white.

Harness A leather strap shaped around the shoulders and chest, with a ring at its top over the *withers*.

Haunches Back part of the thighs, on which the dog sits.

Haw A third eyelid or nictitating membrane in the inside corner of the eye.

Heat Seasonal period of the female, normally every six months.

Heel Command by *handler* to keep the dog close to his heel.

Heel free Command whereby the dog must walk to heel without a *lead*.

Height Dog's height measured from the ground to the top of the shoulder.

Heterometropia A condition in which the degree of refraction is different in the two eyes.

Hie on A command to urge the dog on: used in hunting or *field trials*.

High-standing Tall and upstanding, with plenty of leg.

Hindquarters Rear assemby of dog (pelvis, thighs, *hocks* and paws).

Hip dysplasia Malformation of the ball of the hip joint: usually hereditary.

Hocking out Having *barrel hocks*.

Hocks Those joints in the hind limbs below the true knees, or *stifle* joints.

Hocks well let down *Hock* joints close to the ground.

Holt The lair of a fox or other animal in a bank, drain or other hideout.

Honourable scars Scars from injuries suffered as a result of work.

Hound A dog commonly used for hunting by scent or sight.

Hound colours White tan, and black, in order of predominant colour.

Hound jog The usual *pace* of the *hound*.

Hound-marked Fox Terriers are described as hound-marked if their body patches conform to the pattern of hound markings.

Hucklebones The top of the hip bones.

I

Inbreeding *Mating* within the same family: a *bitch* to her sons, or a *dog* to his daughters.

Incisors The upper and lower front teeth, between the *canines*.

In season In *heat*; ready for the act of *mating*.

In-shoulder Shoulders point in, not parallel with the backbone — a fault found in dogs with shoulder blades too far forward on the chest.

Interbreeding The breeding together of different varieties.

Isabella Fawn or light bay colour.

Ischium Hip bone.

J

Jabot A white stripe down the chest, like a shirtfront.

Jowls Flesh of lips and jaws.

Judge The adjudicator of dogs in *dog shows*, obedience tests and *field trials*.

K

KC Kennel Club (United Kingdom).

Kennel Structure where dogs are kept for shelter.

Kink tail A tail that is sharply bent.

Kiss marks Tan spots on the cheeks and over the eyes.

Knee joint *Stifle* joint.

Knuckling over Condition in which the front legs bend forward at the wrist (carpus).

Kyphosis An abnormal curvature of the spine, with convexity backward.

L

Lack of type Deficiency in traits that define the fundamental make-up of a *breed*.

Landseer A Newfoundland that is not all black, but white with black (as depicted by the famous artist Sir Edward Landseer).

Layback The angle or the shoulder blade as compared with the vertical.

Lead A strap, cord or chain attached to the *collar* or *harness*, for the purpose of restraining or leading the dog; a leash.

Leather The flap of the ear.

Leggy Having legs too long for the body.

Level back One that makes a straight line from *withers* to tail, but is not necessarily parallel to the ground.

Level bite When the front teeth (*incisors*) of the upper and lower jaws meet extactly edge to edge; pincer bite.

Level gait Dog moves without a rise or fall of the *withers*.

Liam A *lead*.

Licence Formal permission granted by the *AKC* to a non-member club to hold a *dog show*, or obedience test or *field trial*. In the UK all shows in which *purebred* dogs are exhibited are held under Kennel Club licence.

Light eyes Yellowish eyes.

Line breeding The mating of related dogs of the same breed, within the line, or family, to a common ancestor. e.g. a dog to his grand-dam.

Lion colour Tawny.

Lippy Having thick, hanging lips.

Litter The pups from one *whelping*.

Liver A dark reddish-brown colour.

Loaded shoulders Shoulders that are much too thick and heavy.

Loin The part of the body between the last rib and the back legs.

Lordosis Hollow back: *saddle back*; curvature of the spine.

Lower thigh See *second thigh*.

Lumber Extra flesh.

Lumbering Awkward (*gait*).

Lupoid Belonging to the wolf family.

Lurcher A *cross-bred hound*.

Lymer A *hound* of ancient times led on a *lead* (liam).

M

Mad dog A dog with rabies.

Mane Long and profuse hair on the top and sides of the neck.

Mantle Dark-shaded portion of the coat on the shoulders, back and sides.

Manubrium The portion of the malleus (hammer bone in the ear) that represents the handle.

Mask Dark shading on the *foreface*.
Masseter A powerful masticatory muscle passing from the zygomatic arch to the lower jaw.
Match show Usually an informal *dog show* at which no championship points are awarded.
Mate To breed a *dog* and *bitch*.
Mealy Covered or flecked with spots.
Median line See *furrow*.
Merle A blue-grey mixture streaked or ticked with black, a coat colour seen in some Shetland Sheepdogs and collies.
Milk teeth First teeth. (Puppies lose these at four to six months.)
Miscellaneous class A competitive class at *dog shows* for dogs of certain specified breeds for which no regular dog show classification is provided. In the UK this is usually called AV (Any Variety) not classified.
Mismarks Self colours with any area of white on the back between withers and tail, on the sides between elbows and back of hindquarters, or on the ears. Black with white markings and no tan present.
Molars Dogs have two molars on each side of the upper jaw, and three on each side of the lower jaw. Upper molars have three roots, lower have two roots.
Molera Incomplete, imperfect or abnormal ossification of the skull.
Molossoid Belonging to the Mastiff family of dogs.
Mongrel A dog whose parents are both of mixed breeding.
Monorchid A male dog, one of whose testicles has not descended into the scrotal sac; also called a unilateral *cryptorchid*.
Mort A flourish on the hunting-horn at the death of *game*.
Moving close When the *hocks* turn in and the *pasterns* drop straight to the ground and move parallel to one another, the dog is 'moving close' in the rear. Action places severe strain on ligaments and muscles.
Moving straight Term descriptive of balanced *gaiting* in which angle of inclination begins at the shoulder or hip joint, and the limbs remain relatively straight from these points to the pads of the feet, even as the legs flex or extend in reaching or thrusting.
Music The *baying* of the hounds.
Mute To run mute, to be silent on the trail, i.e. to trail without *baying* or barking.
Muzzle (1) The part of the head containing the mouth and nose. (2) A device to prevent biting.
Muzzle band White marking around the *muzzle*.

N

Neck well set on Good neckline, merging gradually with strong *withers*, forming a pleasing transition into *topline*.
Nick A breeding that produces desirable puppies.
Nictitating membrane See *haw*.
Non-slip retriever The dog that walks at heel, marks the fall, and *retrieves game* on command: not expected to find or *flush*.
Nose The ability to scent, most acute in breeds such as the Bloodhound.

O

Oblique shoulders Shoulders well laid back. The ideal shoulder should slant at 45 deg to the ground, forming an approximate right angle with the humerus at the shoulder joint.
Occipital protuberance A prominently raised *occiput*, characteristic of some *gundog* breeds.
Occiput Upper, back point of the skull of the dog.
Open class For all dogs of the *breeds* or varieties for which a class is provided and eligible for entry at the show.
Otter tail Thick at the root, round and tapering, with the hair parted or divided on the underside.
Out at elbows *Elbows* turning out from the body, as opposed to being held close.
Out at shoulder With shoulder blades loosely attached to the body, leaving the shoulders jutting out in relief and increasing the breadth of the front.
Out at walk To lease or lend a puppy to someone for raising.
Out-crossing The mating of unrelated individuals of the same breed.
Oval chest Chest deeper than it is wide.
Overhang A heavy or pronounced brow.
Over nose wrinkle A fold of loose skin dropping forward from the skull onto the bridge of the nose: seen in Pugs, Pekingese and some other short-nosed breeds.
Over-reaching Fault in the *trot* caused by more angulation and drive from behind than in front, so that the rear feet are forced to step to one side of the forefeet to avoid interfering or *clipping*.
Overshot When the upper teeth project beyond the lower: also called pig jaw.

P

Pace A *gait* that tends to promote a rolling motion of the body. The left foreleg and left hindleg advance together, then the right foreleg and right hindleg.
Pack Several *hounds* kept together in one *kennel*. A mixed pack is composed of dogs and bitches.
Paddling A *gaiting* fault, so named because it resembles the swing and dip of a canoeist's paddle. Pinching in at the elbows and shoulder joints causes the front legs to swing forward on a stiff outward arc. Also referred to as being tied at the elbows.
Pads The tough, cushioned soles of the feet.
Paper foot A flat foot with thin *pads*.
Parti-colour A term used for a dog of two colours in equal proportion, usually red and white or black and white.
Pastern Commonly recognized as the region of the foreleg between the carpus (wrist) and the digits.
Patellar luxation The knee cap or *stifle* slips or dislocates. An abnormality said to be hereditary, and found in several small breeds.
Peak An unusually prominent *occiput*.
Pedigree Written record of the names of a dog's ancestors going back at least three generations.
Pencilling The dark lines on the surface of the toes in some breeds, notably the English Toy Terrier [Manchester Terrier (Toy)].
Pepper and salt Coat colour consisting of an even mixture of grey and black hair, as in the Schnauzer.
Pied When two colours occur in irregular patches, one more than the other, a dog is said to be pied.
Pigeon-breast A chest with a short protruding *breastbone*.
Pigeon-toed With toes pointing in.
Pig jaw See *overshot*.
Pile Dense *under-coat* of soft hair.
Pily A coat that contains both soft and coarse hair.
Pincer bite See *level bite*.
Pitching Severe rocking of the *haunches* as the rear legs swing forward in a wide arc, rather than flexing normally at the *stifle* and *hock*.
Plumes Whereas the *brush* is not always soft, the term plumes refers to the soft hair on the tail of the Pekingese and Pomeranian.
Poach When hunting, to trespass on private property.
Point The immovable *stance* of the hunting dog taken to indicate the presence and position of *game*.
Points Colour on face, ears, legs and tail when correlated — usually white, black or tan.
Poke To carry the neck stretched forward in an abnormally low, ungainly position, usually when moving.
Police dog A dog trained for police work (often the German Shepherd Dog).
Pompon Ballof hair left on the end of a Poodle's tail after it has been clipped.
Pounding *Gaiting* fault resulting when a dog's stride is shorter in front than in the rear: forefeet strike the ground hard before the rear stride is expended.
Prick ear Carried erect, and usually pointed at the tip.
Professional handler A person who shows dogs for a fee.
Progressive Retinal Atrophy (PRA) Sometimes incorrectly called 'night blindness': a hereditary defect of the eyes, found in several breeds, and causing early loss of sight.
Pump handle Long tail, carried high.
Puppy A dog under one-year-old.
Purebred A dog whose *sire* and *dam* belong to the same *breed*, and are themselves of unmixed descent since the recognition of the breed.
Purling See *crossing over*.
Put down (1) To prepare a dog for the *show ring*. (2) Unplaced in competition. (3) Humanely destroy an old or terminally sick animal.

Q

Quality Refinement, fineness.

R

Racy Lean, long-legged, slightly built.
Ragged Muscles appear ragged rather than smooth (as in the English Foxhound).
Ram's nose See *roman nose*.
Rangy Long-bodied, usually lacking depth in chest.
Rat tail Long pointed tail, with short thin hair.
Reach of front Length of forward stride taken by forelegs without wasted or excessive motion.
Register To record details of a dog's breeding with the respective kennel club.
Retrieve To bring back shot *game* for the huntsman.
Ribbed up With long ribs that angle back from the spinal column (45 deg is ideal): the last rib is long.
Ringer A substitute for another dog: a dog closely resembling another.
Ring tail Carried up and around almost in a circle.
Roached A dog's back is roached when it arches convexly, as in the Dandie Dinmont, Italian Greyhound and Whippet.
Roan Mixture of white with another colour, usually blue or red, in equal proportions, as in the Cocker Spaniel.
Rocking horse Stance with both front and rear legs extended out from the body as in an old-fashioned toy rocking horse.
Rolling gait Swaying, ambling *action* of the *hindquarters* when moving.
Roman nose A nose whose bridge is so comparatively high as to form a slightly convex line from forehead to nose tip: also called ram's nose.
Rose-eared When the ear, neither *pricked* nor *dropped*, folds or twists over, showing the inside, as in the Bulldog.
Rounding To cut or trim the end of the ear *leather* (English Foxhounds).
Rubber hocks See *twisting hocks*.
Rudder The tail.
Ruff Thick, longer hair growth around the neck.

S

Sable The colour of a light coat shaded with black, as in the Collie.
Sabre tail Carried in a semi-circle.
Saddle A black marking over the back, like a horse's saddle.
Saddle back Over-long back, with a dip behind the *withers*.
Scapula The shoulder blade.
Scent The odour left by an animal on the *trail* (ground scent), or wafted through the air (air-borne scent).
Scissor bite A *bite* in which the upper front teeth slightly overlap the lower front teeth.
Screw tail A short, twisted tail tapering to a point.
Second thigh That part of the *hindquarter* from the *stifle* to the *hock*, corresponding to the human shin and calf; also called lower thigh.
Seeing eye dog A guide dog for the blind (in USA).
Self colour One colour, or whole colour, except for lighter shadings.
Self marked A dog is so-called when it is a whole colour, with white or pale markings on the chest, feet and tail-tip.
Semi-prick ears Ears carried erect with just the tips leaning forward.
Septum Very thin dividing wall between the nostrils.
Set on Insertion or attachment of tail or ears.
Set up Posed so as to make the most or the dog's appearance for the show ring.
Shelly Having a long and narrow body, like that of the Borzoi.
Shoulder height Height of dog's body as measured from the *withers* to the ground.
Sickle-hocked Unable to straighten the *hock* joint on the back reach of the hind leg.
Sickle-tail Carried out and up in a semi-circle.
Side-wheeling See *crabbing*.
Side-winding See *crabbing*.
Sighthound A hound that hunts by sight rather than scent, also called a gazehound.
Single tracking All footprints on a single line of travel. When a dog breaks into a trot, its body is supported by only two legs at a time, which move as alternating diagonal pairs. To achieve balance, the legs angle inwards towards a centre line beneath the body, and the greater the speed, the closer they come to tracking on a single line.
Sire The father of a *litter* of puppies.
Skully Thick, coarse-looking skull.
Slab sided Having flat ribs with too little spring from spinal column.
Sled dogs Dogs used in teams to pull sleds.
Slew feet Feet turned out.
Slipping stifle See *patellar luxation*.
Sloping shoulders Shoulders laid well back on the body.
Smooth coat Short sleek hair lying close to the skin.
Snatching hocks A *gaiting* fault indicated by a quick outward snatching of the *hock* as it passes the supporting leg and twists the rear pastern far in beneath the body. The action causes noticeable rocking in the hindquarters.
Snipy Narrow, weak (in the *muzzle*).
Soft-mouthed Able to carry retrieved *game* in the mouth without damaging it.
Soundness The state of mental and physical health when all organs and faculties are complete and functioning normally, each in its rightful relation to the others.

Spay To perform a surgical operation (hysterectomy) on the bitch's reproductive organs to stop conception.

Speak To bark.

Spectacles Shadings or dark markings over or around the eyes or from eyes to ears.

Spike tail Straight short tail that tapers rapidly along its length.

Spitz A *breed* of dog with a tapering *muzzle*.

Splashed Irregularly patched, colour on white or white on colour.

Splay feet Feet with toes spread wide.

Spread Width between the forelegs when accentuated (Bulldog).

Spread hocks See *barrel hocks*.

Spring See *flush*.

Spring of ribs Curvature of ribs for heart and lung capacity.

Squirrel tail Tail carried up and curving more or less forward.

Stake A competition held at a *field trial*.

Stance Manner of standing.

Standard The standard of perfection for each *breed*.

Stand-off coat Rough, coarse hair that stands away from the body.

Staring coat Coarse hard hair, curling at the end.

Station Height of a dog from the ground.

Stern Tail of a sporting dog or *hound*.

Sternum See *breastbone*.

Stifle That joint in the hindleg of a dog approximating to the knee in man, particularly relating to the inner side.

Stilted Having a stiff, awkward way of walking.

Stop The depression between and in front of the eyes, corresponding roughly to the bridge of the nose.

Strabismus Cross-eyed.

Straight hocks *Hocks* that are absolutely straight vertically.

Straight in pastern With little or no bend between joint and foot.

Straight shoulders Shoulder blades running almost straight up and down without any *angulation*.

Stud Male used for breeding.

Stud book A record of the breeding particulars of dogs of recognized breeds.

Superciliary arch The ridge, projection or prominence of the frontal bone of the skull over the eye: the brow.

Suspension trot See *flying trot*.

Sway back A sagging back.

Symmetry Pleasing balance between all parts of the dog.

T

Tail set How the base of the tail sets on the rump.

Terrier A group of dogs used originally for hunting vermin.

Terrier front Straight front, as found on the Fox Terrier.

Thigh The *hindquarter* from hip to *stifle*.

Throaty Having far too much skin around the throat.

Thumb marks Circular black marks around the ankles.

Ticked With small, isolated areas of black or coloured hairs on a white ground.

Timber Bone, especially of the legs.

Tongue Noise made by *hounds* when on the *trail* of *game*.

Topknot The longer, finer hair on the top of the head, rather like a powder-puff, as in the Dandie Dinmont.

Topline The dog's outline from just behind the *withers* to the tail set.

Toy dog One of a group of dogs characterized by very small size.

Trace A dark line of hair running down the back, as seen in the Pug.

Trail To hunt by following ground scent.

Triangular eye An eye set in surrounding tissue of triangular shape: a three-cornered eye.

Tricolour A term used when dogs have three colours more or less proportionate, usually black, tan and white, as in *hounds*.

Trim To groom by plucking or clipping.

Trot A rhythmic two-beat diagonal *gait* in which the feet at diagonally opposite ends of the body strike the ground together, i.e. right hind with left front and left hind with right front.

Trousers The hair on the *hindquarters*.

Trumpet The slight depression or hollow on either side of the skull just behind the orbit or eye socket, the region comparable with the temple.

Truncated Cut off. (The Old English Sheepdog standard calls for a jaw that is square and truncated.)

Tucked-up When the *loins* are lifted up but the chest is deep, giving a *racy* appearance, as in Borzois, Greyhounds, Whippets and a few other breeds.

Tulip ears Ears carried stiff and straight, slightly open and leaning forward.

Turn-up An up-tilted *foreface*.

Twisting hocks A *gaiting* fault in which the *hock* joints twist both ways as they flex or bear weight. Also called rubber hocks.

Type The characteristic qualities distinguishing a *breed*: the embodiment of a *standard's* essentials.

U

Under-coat The soft, furry wool beneath the outer hair of some breeds, giving protection against cold and wet.

Undershot Having the lower jaw projecting: the opposite of *overshot*.

Underslung Low to the ground, with short legs. Examples are breeds such as the Pug and Bulldog.

Unilateral cryptorchid See *cryptorchid*.

Up-face A *foreface* slanting upward, as in the Bulldog.

Upper arm The humerus or bone of the foreleg, between the shoulder blade and the *forearm*.

V

Varminty Having a bright, searching, very alert expression: usually seen in terriers.

Vent Both the anal opening and the small area of light hair directly beneath the tail.

W

Walk *Gaiting* pattern in which three legs are in support of the body at all times, each foot lifting from the ground one at a time in regular sequence.

Wall eyes Eyes *parti-coloured* white and blue, seen in *merle*-coloured collies and sheepdogs; often keenly valued.

Weaving See *crossing over*.

Weedy Having a light, rather scrawny build.

Well boned See *bone*.

Well let down Having short *hocks*.

Well-sprung ribs Roundness or curvature of the rib cage.

Wet neck Loose or superfluous skin, with *dewlap*.

Wheaten Pale yellow colour.

Wheel back Another term for the *roached* back: a back that is arched or convex.

Whelping Giving birth to puppies.

Whelps Newly born puppies.

Whip tail A tail that is stiff and straight, as in the Pointer when the dog is *pointing*.

Whiskers The *beard* of a dog, as in the Miniature Schnauzer.

Whitelies Colour type that is white with red or dark markings (Pembroke Welsh Corgi).

Wind To catch the *scent* of *game*.

Winging A *gaiting* fault where one or both front feet twist outwards as the limbs swing forward.

Winners Awards give at *dog shows* to the 'Best Dog' (winner's dog) and 'Best Bitch' (winner's bitch) competing in regular classes.

Wire-haired Having a tough, dense, harsh coat.

Withers The highest point of the shoulders, just behind the neck.

Wolf colour Black, brown and grey distributed in equal amounts.

Wrinkle The loose folds of skin puckered up on the brows and sides of the face in Bloodhounds. St Bernards, Basenjis, Pugs, etc.

Wry mouth Mouth in which the lower jaw does not line up with the upper.

X

Xiphoid Sword-shaped.

Y

Yawing See *crabbing*.

FURTHER READING

Allcock, J. *A Dog of Your Own*, Sheldon Press, London 1979

American Kennel Club Official Publication, *The Complete Dog Book*, Howell Book House Inc., New York 1979

American Kennel Club Staff, *American Kennel Club Dog Care & Training*, Howell Book House Inc., New York 1992

Bengtson, B. and Wintzell, A. *The Dogs of the World*, David & Charles Ltd., Newton Abbot, UK 1979

Carricato, A.M. *Veterinary Notes for Dog Breeders*, Howell Book House Inc., New York 1992

Cruft, C. *Charles Cruft's Dog Book: Popular Breeds & Their Care*, Trans-Atlantic, Philadelphia 1983

Fiorone, F. *The Encyclopedia of Dogs*, Hart-Davis MacGibbon Ltd., St Albans, UK 1977

Fisher, C. *The Pan Book of Dogs*, Pan Books Ltd., London 1977

Fogel, B. and Caras, R. *RSPCA Complete Dog Care Manual*, Dorling Kindersley, London 1993

Fox, Dr. M.W. *Understanding Your Dog*, Blond & Briggs, London 1974

Fuller, C. *A Beginner's Guide to Dog Care*, TFH Publications, New Jersey

Gerstenfeld, S.L. *Taking Care of Your Dog*, Addison-Wesley, London 1979

Glover, H. *A Standard Guide to Pure-bred Dogs,* Macmillan, London 1977

Hawcroft, T. *The Howell Book of Dog Care*, Howell Book House Inc., New York 1992

McGinnis, T. *The Well Dog Book: The Classic, Comprehensive Handbook of Dog Care*, Random House, New York 1991

Manolson, F. *D. is for Dog*, Pan Books Ltd., London 1978

Miller, H. *Common Sense Book of Puppy & Dog Care*, Bantam, New York 1987

Palmer, J. *Training and Caring for Your Dog*, Ward Lock Ltd., London 1980

Piers, H. *Taking Care of Your Dog*, Barron, Hauppauge, USA 1992

Sutton, C.G. *The Observer's Book of Dogs*, Frederick Warne & Co. Ltd., London 1978

The Monks of New Skete Staff. *Art of Raising a Puppy*, Little Brown, New York 1991

Turner, T. (Ed). *Veterinary Notes for Dog Owners*, London 1991

Vanacore, C. *Dog Showing: An Owner's Guide*, Howell Book House Inc., New York 1990

White, K. *Dogs: Their Mating, Whelping and Weaning*, K & R Books Ltd., Leicester, UK 1977

Whitney, L.F. and Whitney, G.D. *Complete Book of Dog Care*, Doubleday and Company, New York 1985

Woodhouse, B. (Foreword) *Dogs*, Orbis Publishing Ltd., London 1980

GENERAL INDEX

Page references to illustrations are in *italics*.

INDEX OF BREEDS

Page references to illustrations are in *italics*. Main entries are in **bold** type.

PICTURE CREDITS

Illustration
All linework and colour artwork is the copyright of Salamander Books Ltd. John Francis and John Green were the individual artists responsible for the dog profiles on the following pages:
John Francis: 8, 14, (top) 25, 27, (centre and bottom) 57, 59, 63, 65, 67, 71, 72, 73, 75, (top) 77, 79, 81, 87, 89, 91, 93, 95, 97, 99, 102, 105, 107, 111, 113, 115, 117, 119, 123, 125, 127, 129, 131, (top) 133, 135, 137, 141, 143, 145.
John Green: 11, 13, 15, 17, 19, 21, 23, (bottom) 25, 29, 31, 33, 35, 37, 39, 41, 43, 45, 47, 49, 51, 53, 55, (top left) 57, 61, 69, (bottom) 77, 83, 85, 101, 103, 109, 121, (bottom) 133, 139.

Photographs
The publishers would like to thank the photographers listed below who have supplied photographs for the book; by page, the sources are:

Endpapers: Salukis by Marc Henrie (MH); **page 1:** MH; **2/3:** MH; **4/5:** MH; **6/7:** MH; **10:** MH; **11:** (left) Animals Unlimited (AU), (right) Animal Photography Ltd (APL); **16:** Anne Cumbers (AC); **20:** AC; **22:** (top right) APL, (bottom right) AC, (bottom left) APL; **24:** (top right) AU, (bottom left) APL; **26:** (centre) AC, (bottom right) AU; **28:** (top right) AU, (bottom left) AC; **30:** (top right) AC, (bottom right) APL, (bottom left) AC; **32:** (top right) AC, (bottom right) APL; **34:** (top right) APL, (bottom right) AU; **42:** APL; **44:** all APL; **50:** both AC; **56:** APL; **58:** AC; **60:** (top) AC, (bottom left) AU; **62:** MH; **63:** AC; **64:** Anne Roslin-Williams (ARW); **66:** APL; **70:** both ARW; **74:** MH; **76:** (top right) MH, (bottom left) AU; **78:** AU; **80:** APL; **84:** both APL; **86:** MH; **87:** AC; **90:** both AC; **92:** AC; **96:** both AC; **100:** Animal Graphics (AG); **108:** both AC; **110:** APL; **114:** (top

right) APL, (bottom left) AU; **118:** AU; **120:** (top right) AG, (bottom left) AU; **122:** AU; **124:** APL; **126:** APL; **128:** both APL; **130:** (top right) APL, (bottom left) AU; **132:** MH; **136:** both APL; **142:** APL; **144:** (top right) APL, (bottom left) AU; **146/147:** Cyril Laubscher (CL); **148:** AU; **149:** AU; **150:** both MH; **151:** both MH; **152/153:** MH; **153:** MH; **154:** MH; **155:** both MH; **156:** both MH; **157:** both MH; **158/159:** CL; **159:** CL; **160:** MH; **161:** all MH; **162:** Phil Maggitti (PM); **163:** MH; **164/165:** MH; **165:** MH; **166:** both MH; **167:** MH; **168:** (top) MH, (bottom) CL; **169:** CL; **170/171:** MH; **171:** MH; **172:** MH; **173:** MH; **174:** both MH; **175:** MH; **176:** MH; **177:** both PM; **178/179:** MH; **179:** MH; **180:** MH; **181:** MH; **183:** MH.

Publisher's Acknowledgment
The original edition of this book was written by Joan Palmer and her work remains the backbone of this revised edition. She was helped in her task by the British Kennel Club, the National Dog Owners' Association, Pedigree Petfoods Education Centre, and a host of breed club secretaries and other individuals too numerous to mention. Joan Palmer received contributory chapters to the original work from a number of specialists in their field: Michael A. Findlay B.V.M.S., M.R.C.V.S on grooming and health care; John R. Holmes M.R.C.V.S. on training; Muriel Shearwood on showing; and Kay White on feeding and exercise, and breeding.
Also to be thanked for their original contributions are Elizabeth Pegg of the Royal Veterinary College, London, for advice on dog parasites; Margaret Osborne, Liz Cartledge and Jackie Ransom for information on various international showing systems.